D1605711

LOOKING FOR BOOTSTRAPS

Economic Development in the Maritimes

DONALD J. SAVOIE

Nimbus Publishing Limited
3731 Mackintosh St, Halifax, NS, B3K 5A5
(902) 455-4286 nimbus.ca

Printed and bound in Canada

NB1289

Design: John van der Woude, JVDW Designs

Library and Archives Canada Cataloguing in Publication
Savoie, Donald J., 1947-, author
Looking for bootstraps : economic development in the Maritimes / Donald J. Savoie.

Includes bibliographical references and index.
Issued in print and electronic formats.
ISBN 978-1-77108-481-9 (hardcover).—ISBN 978-1-77108-482-6 (HTML)

1. Economic development—Maritime Provinces. 2. Maritime Provinces—Economic conditions. I. Title.

HC117.M35S38 2017 338.9715 C2016-908037-4
C2016-908038-2

Nimbus Publishing acknowledges the financial support for its publishing activities from the Government of Canada, the Canada Council for the Arts, and from the Province of Nova Scotia. We are pleased to work in partnership with the Province of Nova Scotia to develop and promote our creative industries for the benefit of all Nova Scotians.

To K. C. Irving, one of the world's leading entrepreneurs of the last century, a visionary, a builder, and a deeply committed Maritimer.

CONTENTS

PREFACE

I am a Maritimer, to the core. I love my region, all of it, from northern New Brunswick to the eastern tip of Cape Breton, and everything in between. I am a Monctonian, but I take great pride in seeing Halifax prosper. I have spent the bulk of my academic career at the Université de Moncton, but I applaud the success of Dalhousie University and its ranking as one of Canada's leading universities.

I have, on several occasions, left my region to study, to undertake research at other universities, and to pursue economic opportunities. I have always returned. I have, on a number of occasions, declined employment opportunities that carried more remuneration and prestige than did my long association with the Université de Moncton. No matter, I wanted to remain a Maritimer, and I have remained one. I am one of the lucky ones. I know far too many Maritimers who were forced to leave the region, never to return. For many, their preference was to come back, but for a lack of opportunities, they never did.

I am also an Acadian *pure laine*. Acadians, as is well-known, have a deep attachment to their roots. *Le grand dérangement,* or the 1755 expulsion of the Acadian population from the Maritime provinces, may well explain our strong attachment to our communities. Some of my Acadian ancestors were able to escape the expulsion, and others were able to make their way back to the region. We cling to our community and to one another because of our roots, our culture, and our history. It has been and remains a question of survival.

I have long held that history matters in all things, and economic development is certainly no exception. Economic activities do not surface in a vacuum. People, their culture, their religion, and their history also account for an important part of a community's economic success or decline. I hold that the people factor and the ability of government to establish the circumstances for economic success matter a great deal more in explaining a region's economic standing than is generally believed.

We Maritimers are a collage of people who came together under trying circumstances. We all have a past that did not suggest a promising economic future. Acadians refused to pick sides in a conflict that involved the two superpowers of the day. We paid a heavy price. The Loyalists, who came to Saint John and Halifax after the American Revolution, picked the wrong side in the war and had to leave. The Highlands Scots came to Pictou County in Nova Scotia dispirited after losing the Battle of Culloden and the process of land commercialization in Scotland. The Irish came to eastern New Brunswick in the aftermath of Ireland's potato famine. The Mi'kmaq and Maliseet did pick a side but hardly the one that was in their interest. Slaves of African descent rode the Underground Railroad to what they hoped would be their freedom in Saint John, Shelburne, and Halifax. They soon realized that what was promised and what they encountered were two vastly different things. It was not a promising beginning for our region and its peoples.

In 2006 I published a book on regional development, *Visiting Grandchildren: Economic Development in the Maritimes*, and wrote that my plans were "to exit the field with this book." As you may guess from the book you now hold in your hands, I have had a change of heart. I have become increasingly concerned about the future of my region, its ties to Canada's national political institutions, how our provincial governments are planning for economic development, and how we Maritimers view our economic future. I owe it to my region to speak truth, as I see it, to both fellow Maritimers and to Canadians. I simply cannot stand by and say nothing while my region confronts new and far-reaching economic challenges. My purpose would be served if this book helps Maritimers understand the reasons for our region's lack of economic development and if it stimulates a debate about the future of the Maritime provinces among all interested parties.

This book draws heavily on my past involvement in regional development and on my earlier work. I served as senior policy advisor to the then minister of the Department of Regional Economic Expansion (DREE) while on loan from the department, which eventually disbanded, and I played a role in its demise. A few years later, the prime minister asked me to consult a cross-section of Atlantic Canadians and write a report on the establishment of the Atlantic Canada Opportunities Agency (ACOA). The time has come to report on my involvement in these important machinery of government changes that continue to have a profound impact on my region. They also hold important lessons for both my region and the regional development field.

I have published extensively in the field of regional development and, on occasion, I borrow directly from this work; however, this book differs from my earlier work. For one thing, my focus here is exclusively on the three Maritime provinces. For another, I wish to bring a fresh perspective to an age-old problem: why has my region not developed as well as the other Canadian regions, and what can we do about it? For yet another, the region is confronting daunting economic challenges it has not faced before, notably a fast-aging population, adjustments to federal transfer payments, and a highly competitive global economy that reaches into every community, however small.

How best can Maritimers meet our challenges? We cannot look only to governments for solutions—that much is certain. As the following pages attest, governments have not always been a positive force in shaping the economy of the Maritime provinces. In any event, the appetite for governments to intervene in my region is not nearly as strong as it once was. I offer some prescriptions in this book in the hope that they will motivate Maritimers to offer new solutions, to debate them, and to get involved.

I decided to dedicate this book to K. C. Irving. He was a business genius who built a business empire in my home province by pulling against gravity in tenaciously pursuing one remarkable success story after another in virtually every economic sector, and this in a have-less province. He built an oil refinery that is nothing short of an engineering marvel. It is the largest refinery in Canada and employs 1,400 people who did not have to go down the road to secure a well-paying job. He decided to build the refinery in Saint John, New Brunswick, when business logic might have suggested otherwise. He first struck a tentative agreement to build the refinery with oil giant BP, but BP asked him to build it somewhere else. He resisted. When BP pushed him to explain why Saint John, he replied, "Because I live there." In the end, Irving turned to another partner to help build the refinery.

I often wonder what K. C. Irving would have accomplished had he decided to build his business empire in Southern Ontario, where economic gravity and national policies would have lent him more than a helping hand. One can only begin to imagine what he would have built, given that he would have lived next door to Ottawa at a time when the federal government decided to pour all its resources into building the country's 1940s war effort in Central Canada.

Capitalism is not without its critics, and capitalists are often criticized. K. C. Irving was our capitalist; his and now his sons' commitment to our region remains deep. They and their head offices have remained in the region. They decided not to follow the lead of other large Maritime businesses and move their head offices to Toronto or the Boston area. When universities, hospitals, and community groups from the region decide to launch fundraising campaigns, often the first door they knock on is one of the Irving doors. This is one of many advantages that head offices bring to a region. I do not often see the thousands of head offices in Toronto extending a helping hand to institutions in my region.

I met K. C. Irving only once. He and I hail from small Acadian communities in Kent County, New Brunswick. K. C. Irving remains very well regarded there. His family has continued to endow the community with first-class facilities and infrastructure. But K. C. Irving did something even more important: he hired many Acadians to work for him, something that anglophones did not often do in the 1930s and 1940s. This enabled them to stay in the region rather than move to New England or Central Canada, as so many of their contemporaries did.

Dedicating the book to K. C. Irving is both a tribute to a business giant from my home province and a precursor of what comes next in the book. I suggest here that there are rough waters ahead for the region, and that we have to look to the private sector to lead the way in wealth and job creation. The private sector, albeit in partnership with others, can fuel economic development in the highly competitive global economy. More to the point, the local homegrown private sector is our region's best bet.

I ask the reader to look around the region at who has always remained committed to the Maritimes. Refineries such as Imperial Oil in Dartmouth have left town, and so have many pulp and paper mills. One only has to look to Bathurst and Dalhousie in New Brunswick to see evidence of this. The Irvings, John Bragg, Joe Shannon, and Normand Caissie, among others, have stayed the course in our region. They are not going anywhere else, because they live here. I hope their contributions will inspire other Maritimers.

I have many people to thank. Richard Saillant was always willing to share his thoughts on economic development and to push me to justify my own views. Valery Martial Tankou Kamela helped me navigate the various data streams from Statistics Canada with competence and tenacity. I once again want to thank two outstanding women who have always been there for me: my wife, Linda, for her patience, support, and continued willingness to put up with my insatiable appetite for work, and Ginette Benoit for her unfailing competence, good cheer, and uncanny ability to read my handwriting. Céline Basque, with her keen eye, has caught more errors than I care to admit, and Paula Sarson made many of my sentences read better.

As always, I take responsibility for any defects in this book, and I am fully responsible, answerable, and accountable for all of them.

—Donald J. Savoie
Canada Research Chair in
Public Administration and Governance

Chapter 1

INTRODUCTION

John K. Galbraith, the well-known Harvard economist, put the following questions to Maritimers in 1986: "The Maritime provinces are in the middle of two of the world's leading economic hot spots—Western Europe and the eastern seaboard of the United States. Why has economic development skipped over your region to the eastern seaboard of the United States, the edges of Western Europe and central Canada?" Why, he wondered, "could the region not take advantage of its strategic geographical location?"[1] The two questions have stayed with me ever since. To be sure, there are no easy answers, which likely explains why no one has sought them over the past thirty years.

Galbraith was not the only one to point to the region's location as a strong economic asset. The government of Canada made a presentation to the Organisation for Economic Co-operation and Development (OECD) in April 2015 and pointed to the region's "strategic location connecting North America with global markets."[2] The presentation, however, did not explain why the region has never been able—thus far at least—to take advantage of its strategic location.

One thing is clear: economic development in the three Maritime provinces continues to lag behind the rest of Canada. It was not supposed to be like this. Every important new innovation, the region was told, would herald major economic opportunities or, in modern parlance, be a game changer. For example, the region was informed that Canadian confederation and the construction of the national railway would open new markets. It was believed in some quarters that the Maritime provinces would become the centre of Canada's manufacturing sector.[3] Confederation and the railways did open new markets, but not for the Maritime provinces. In fact, the National Policy shut down some traditional markets in the region and inhibited it from pursuing new ones.

The region was also assured the arrival of the Internet would finally deal effectively with its two liabilities: size and geography.[4] Distance, at least in terms of generating new economic activities, was now dead; the Internet was lowering the cost of communications to such an extent that geography and location were no longer relevant. The world was flat and economic opportunities, capital, and jobs were now freer to move to low-cost regions.[5] Of course, it has not worked out that way; on the contrary, it seems that both Confederation and new means of communication have only made matters worse. History has shown that Confederation has certainly not been a positive force for the Maritime provinces, and much more is said about this later. We also know that, even more so than traditional industries, the new economy has an "inherent tendency toward geographical agglomeration."[6] As Philip McCann points out, the Internet and globalization have made both space and place more, rather than less, important, notwithstanding early predictions.[7]

Many new economic development ideas were also viewed by policy-makers as "the solution" for the Maritime provinces. Among numerous others, François Perroux's growth pole theory and Richard Florida's creative class would, the argument went, bring new economic opportunities to the Maritime provinces, if properly applied. New economic development ideas continue to arrive in regions before the court of economic development specialists as blushing debutantes, beautifully gowned, soon to be embraced in marriage and, not long afterwards, divorced.[8] None, whether it was their design or their implementation, have lived up to expectations—at least in the three Maritime provinces.

After all these years, I decided to try to answer Galbraith's two questions. On the face of it, one might argue that Galbraith was asking the wrong questions. Why, for example, ask the questions about the Maritime region and not the state of Maine or any number of other regions located adjacent to economic hot spots where economic development has bypassed them? Why worry about a region in decline when the requirements of the global economy place a premium on self-sustaining economic engines, usually found in large urban areas and high-growth regions, to fuel national economies? These questions, however, remain vitally important for the Maritime provinces because they go to the heart of the region's economic history, its relations with the federal government, and its self-image. These are also important questions for other peripheral regions and for national economies.

Underdeveloped regions are very often a drain, or at least regarded as such, on national economies and on national budgets. However, national governments—and the Canadian government is certainly no exception—will not always stand idly by and let the unfettered market call the adjustment tune. They will intervene and attempt, as best they can, to promote economic development, to prop up slow-growth regions with transfers, subsidies, and other measures to attenuate the sting of economic misfortune.[9] The three Maritime provinces have long qualified for such transfers and federal regional development measures.

Certainly, the economic underdevelopment of the three Maritime provinces has puzzled policy-makers for well over a century. It has been the subject of heated political debates, several Royal Commissions, and a plethora of government programs designed to promote economic development.[10] None of the programs have lived up to expectations.[11] Regional disparity has grown in recent years, and Canada is now home to the third-widest regional disparities across all the countries in the OECD.[12] Yet, both the federal government and the OECD maintain that Canada has the best regional economic development model.[13] So what gives?

We know that regional economic development efforts designed by national governments to alleviate regional economic disparities have fallen out of favour of late. This is the case in Canada, where the national government has created a regional development agency for every region, so that even Bay Street—the heart of Canada's financial district—now has access to a federal government regional economic development agency. The point could not be made clearer: alleviating regional economic disparities is no longer on the National Policy agenda. In any event, the government of Canada now readily admits it is no longer in the business of alleviating regional disparities.[14] The view, widely held in Canada and elsewhere, is there are only a limited number of regions in a national setting that can drive growth, and both capital and labour are, or should be, increasingly drawn to them.[15] Few, however, bother to ask how strong economic regions became strong or why weak ones became weak.

The view that government-backed economic development measures should be directly tied to the private sector is now sacrosanct. The thinking, particularly in high-growth regions, is that for countries to compete in the global economy, governments need to stop efforts designed to alleviate regional economic disparities; cut public spending and taxes; reduce red tape and government regulations; and then let the private sector do what it does best—innovate, create jobs, and manage economic activities. A consensus has emerged (particularly in anglo-American countries in recent years) that the private sector should lead the way and be left free to locate activities wherever it decides, and government should get out of the way with its *dirigiste* approach to economic development.

We live in neoconservative times and in a highly competitive global economy. Neoconservatives have a theory to promote more even economic development between regions. As is well-known, mainstream economic theory maintains that both labour and capital will move to where it makes economic sense for both without the help of government. Labour will move from communities and regions to areas of labour shortage or from slow-growth regions to high-growth regions in search of employment and higher wages. Conversely, capital will move in the opposite direction to take advantage of surplus labour and lower wages. The process will continue until there is balanced or relatively even growth between regions, so the theory goes. Proponents of this theory will not examine why certain regions became strong, at least in the Canadian context, or if government played a historical role in helping the hidden hand of the market in locating economic activities.

The theory also does not explain why economic development skipped over the Maritime provinces. The region has, at various points in Canadian history, witnessed both periods of interventionist government policies and laissez-faire economics; yet, it has consistently remained a have-less region for over 125 years. To some Maritimers, interventionist government policies tend to create an economic dependency while laissez-faire economics tend to promote out-migration and stagnant economic growth. To them, theories explain very little about the state of their region's economic structure or prospects. They insist that government officials should be very cautious about drawing policy implications from economic development theories.

One can, however, consult the economic development literature for guidance. I simplify the term *economic development* to mean economic growth as measured by earned per capita income, business creation, employment, and a high degree of independence from government transfer payments. To be sure, the literature offers important insights into the pace and location of economic activities, and more about this follows. The insights, however, do not provide the answers we are looking for. Economic theories explain a great deal about the behaviour of individuals and organizations; however, they are of limited benefit in understanding the workings of regional economies. As we will see, to the private sector executive or to the economic development practitioner in the field, regional economic development theories are too high a level of theoretical abstraction to have much practical value. They are also all too often ignored.[16]

Some sixty years ago, well-known Canadian economic historian Harold Innis rejected any thinking that economic theories held universal applicability. He argued that any theory could be formulated only on the basis of a thorough analysis of a specific situation. He went on to make the case that theories formulated in Europe, for example, could not easily apply in Canada because of the country's distinct political institutions and history, and vice versa.[17]

One of Canada's leading economists of his day, Richard Lipsey, observed that "for all the concern about regional area development and regional problems in Canada, we don't really have an underlying theory. We don't know what we would have to do, what are the conditions under which we would have regional equality, however we define equality."[18] In uncharacteristic fashion, the Economic Council of Canada summed up the situation this way: "Doctors used to try to cure syphilis with mercury and emetics. We now know that mercury works but emetics do not and, moreover, that penicillin is best of all. We suspect that the regional disparity disease is presently being treated with both mercury- and emetic-type remedies, but we do not know which is which. Perhaps one day an economic penicillin will be found."[19] The Economic Council did not discover such an economic penicillin, nor has one been discovered to date. Indeed, economists in economic departments in Ottawa—notably in finance and industry—continue to have little interest in discovering an economic penicillin for slow-growth regions. Their concern is the health of the national economy, a view reinforced at the political level, given that the more heavily populated provinces decide who holds power in Ottawa.

Others, however, particularly politicians representing slow-growth regions, continue to lead the search for an economic penicillin to strengthen slow-growth regions, albeit recently with fewer resources and less clear goals. We have, over the years, tried a variety of measures from tax incentives, cash grants, special regional development agreements between the two senior levels of government, and the list goes on. But, after all these years and numerous measures to promote development in the region, we still do not know why economic development skipped over the Maritime provinces or how best to promote economic growth in the region or if we will ever find an economic penicillin.

That said, we now have a wealth of experience to draw from to try to answer Galbraith's questions. We have a growing body of literature on economic development, some sixty years of government measures to promote regional economic development, and a new understanding of economic forces flowing out of a more integrated global economy. Few now believe that government can successfully alleviate economic disparities. Thus, the focus has shifted away from economic disparities to promoting regional economic development in all regions, including high-growth ones. What does this shift mean for the three Maritime provinces?

We look to past economic development efforts in the Maritime region, to history, to the literature, to the role of government, and to other forces to gain a better understanding of why economic development skipped over the Maritime provinces in comparison to other regions. Economists have all too often failed to pay sufficient attention to history and space in their analysis, since these do not fit neatly in their economic models. Mainstream economists have always had a problem with geography and how to deal with the regional dimension in economic development. But their analysis and public policies are rarely geographically neutral—unwittingly or not, they have a bias, with some regions benefitting more than others.

ANSWERING GALBRAITH

This book answers Galbraith's questions by focusing on public policy, on the role of government, and how the private sector has responded to both. This book is about economic development in an economic space, the Maritimes. The three provinces have strong historical, economic, and cultural ties. What divides them are political boundaries that have generated distinct political units with separate identities, political processes, and expectations. It will be recalled—at least by a handful of historians—that the three provinces constituted a single territorial entity prior to partition in 1769.[20]

Political boundaries and political institutions serve to reinforce regionalism by providing a geographical focus for loyalty, identity, political debates, and political power.[21] They enable political leaders to articulate a vision, a strategy to develop the physical space they are asked to lead. Provincial premiers are solely concerned with the economic health of their respective province—one of the main reasons why they are elected. Former Nova Scotia premier John Savage summed it up well with his remark, "When I go to Toronto to meet with chief executive officers to promote Nova Scotia as a place to invest, I very often discover that Frank McKenna [former premier of New Brunswick] has already been there."[22] Savage explained that McKenna constituted an important stumbling block to promoting economic development in his province. Both McKenna and Savage focused their efforts to promote economic development in a territory defined by political boundaries with little concern for the broader Maritime region; McKenna saw Savage and Nova Scotia as the competition, and vice versa. The goal for any politician is to get elected or re-elected, and there are no votes to be had for a premier seen helping another province, even a neighbouring province.

Some students of economics and public policy maintain that, in the economic development field, the region may not be a valid concept for analysis. They argue our attention should be directed to "people prosperity" as opposed to "place prosperity." A change of economic activity from one area to another is relevant only in the context of its consequences for individuals. They maintain space, or regional, concerns ought not to be the primary issue. After all, the argument goes, potential opportunities cannot be limited to particular places in which individuals find themselves. Consequently, the appropriate objective is to maximize potential opportunities and economic well-being for individual citizens, not for individual regions.

This view certainly has merit from the perspective of economic efficiency. However, equally strong arguments can be made for governments to be concerned with place prosperity. In a federation, it is unlikely that all provincial governments will subscribe fully to the view of people prosperity rather than place prosperity. Nova Scotia's government, for example, may well be primarily concerned with people prosperity or the well-being of all residents within its jurisdiction; the same can be said for Ontario or any other province. Viewed from the perspective of the country as a whole, however, this constitutes an emphasis on place prosperity. Province-building (provincial governments stimulating growth within their jurisdiction) has become a fact of life in Canada. It certainly remains a fact of life in a small region like the Maritimes, where three provincial governments continue to compete intensely for economic activities and jobs.

The government of Canada may well insist that it is concerned primarily with the economic well-being of Canadians. Viewed from a global perspective, however, it is concerned with place prosperity, or the development of Canada's space. Within this space, the case can be made that its policies continue to favour some regions over others.

The reader may well ask why I did not include Newfoundland and Labrador and write about the Atlantic region. People from outside Atlantic Canada are much more comfortable with the term *Atlantic Canada* than are people from the region. The political, economic, and cultural ties between the four Atlantic provinces are weak. Attempts at promoting economic co-operation between the four provinces have always missed the mark, by a wide margin. As Jim Bickerton argues, "Atlantic Canada" is more of a convenient construct for Ottawa-based officials than it is a region.[23] I consider myself a Maritimer, not an Atlantic Canadian.

Former Newfoundland premier Joey Smallwood summed up things well when he pointed out that his province had no interest in joining the three Maritime provinces to study either political or economic union.[24] He said that Newfoundland would be more open to joining Cape Breton and Prince Edward Island than the three Maritime provinces, because the three islands had something in common. Alex Campbell, former premier of Prince Edward Island, was even more to the point: "We sit here under the banner of an Atlantic regional caucus when in fact there is no such thing. The only people who consider Atlantic Canada as a region are those who live outside of Atlantic Canada, the planners and the bureaucrats in Ottawa, the newscasters in Toronto and the airline executives in Montreal."[25] Former New Brunswick premier Louis Robichaud, who launched an initiative to unite the three Maritime provinces, captured the heart of the issue when he said, "Newfoundland is quite a distance from the rest of the country, and they have their own ways of life that are completely different from those of people from Prince Edward Island, Nova Scotia and New Brunswick."[26] I leave the last word to historian James Hiller: "There is a strong sense that while the Maritimes may indeed constitute an historical region, Newfoundland does not fit."[27]

I recognize that the word *region* means different things to different people at different times. What constitutes a region does vary. Cape Breton, Labrador, Moncton, and Southeast New Brunswick are all regions. The three Maritime provinces constitute a region in the eyes of many, including mine, because of history, shared economic geography and circumstances, and because it is made up of three provinces with defined political boundaries. These boundaries gave them a voice and political legitimacy. Political and administrative institutions in these three jurisdictions, together with regional and national institutions, play an important role in shaping economic activities.

As noted, I argue that history, the people factor, government, and public policy continue to play a more important role in shaping the pace and location of economic activities than is generally believed. This remains true, notwithstanding the call for government to get out of the way and let private sector firms compete in a highly competitive global economy. I argue that government continues to be good at establishing the circumstances for economic success. Government has not been up to the task when it attempts to manage political success through economic development measures. This, in turn, holds wide implications for the three Maritime provinces. I argue that the federal government has not been as successful in establishing the circumstances for economic success in the Maritime region as it has been in other regions. Rather, the federal government has sought to manage political and economic activities in the Maritime region, which has inhibited economic development. I hasten to add, however, that the federal government has not been the only actor trying to manage political and economic activities in the region—the three provincial governments have also attached a great deal of importance to managing political success through economic development efforts.

I recognize that many reasons explain why high-growth regions outperform other regions, for instance proximity to markets, natural resources endowment, the right urban-rural structure, and the quality of human resources. The role of government, however, also looms large, and Canada is no exception. This is not to suggest that the federal government has been unwilling to promote economic development in the Maritime provinces. We have seen, especially since the early 1960s, a plethora of federal government measures designed to promote economic development in my region. I review these later.

It is worth repeating that partisan political considerations explain in large part the nature of the measures introduced, and in the Maritime region, the federal government has been preoccupied with managing political success rather than establishing circumstances for economic success, for fear of disturbing its ability to establish such circumstances where it truly matters politically. We see evidence of this both over time and in virtually all areas of government activities. The goal of federal regional development efforts in the Maritime region continues to be enabling politicians' claim, "We are doing something about promoting economic development in your region."

I answer Galbraith's question by making the case that there is not one factor at play to explain the region's relative underdevelopment. Indeed, there are four important factors all reinforcing one another: geography, history, National Policy, and Maritimers themselves. It is a mug's game trying to pin down the influence of one factor over another, and to do so requires a leap of faith. It also requires an ability to answer a series of questions tied to "what it might have been like" had the region or the country taken a different course.

Geography is a critically important factor, and when it comes to regional economic development, it may well explain "two-thirds of everything."[28] The end of "sea and sails" and the arrival of the national railway alone changed the pace and location of economic activities in the Maritime provinces. The work of national political institutions, however, makes a difficult situation even more difficult to this day. A combination of the geography and national political institutions has sapped the confidence of Maritimers in their ability to conceive and pursue new activities. There is an old dictum in economic development: "success breeds success and failure breeds failure," and it applies very well to the Maritimes.

Geography of the mind also matters. Politicians and senior public servants view public policy from the prism of where they come from, where they studied, and where they currently sit. Geography of the mind speaks to politicians and the regions they represent and to public servants and the departments where they work.

The National Capital Region (NCR) also speaks to geography of the mind. Decisions struck over the past thirty years to concentrate more and more public servants in the NCR have important implications for Canada's regions. Ottawa is located smack in the middle of the two most populous provinces that effectively decide who holds political power in Canada. This power is unencumbered by an effective upper house able to speak to the interest of the smaller provinces—something not tolerated in other federations.

The "Ottawa system" has its own biases, its own economic interests to protect, and is influenced by regional stereotypes. The Maritime stereotype does not hold much economic promise. The young, the ambitious, and the upwardly mobile public servants, including those with Maritime roots, quickly learn to behave according to the expectations of Ottawa or, in the words of a former public servant, run the risk of being "relegated to the photocopying machine."[29] The role of the federal government in shaping the national economy and in giving life to economic activities is far more influential than generally believed, as the following chapters illustrate. Canada's institutional organization of political power and bureaucratic influence tied to the workings of individual interests operating within them continue to hold a bias that plays against the economic interest of the Maritime provinces. Indeed, the bias plays to the interest of the more populous provinces.

Maritimers have had to make do with a bad hand dealt by economic geography and Confederation. Many have moved away, or in Maritime parlance "gone down the road," in pursuit of economic opportunities. Many others have stayed in the hope that things will finally turn around. Globalization and modern means of communications should have, to some extent, attenuated the obstacles posed by geography. As noted, the impact, thus far, has been modest. It is in this context that I answer Galbraith and offer some prescriptions for the region's economic future.

Some readers, particularly non-Maritimers, may well want to stop reading halfway through the book. They will likely think that I am blaming Confederation, the national government, and Ottawa for all the region's economic woes. I urge readers to read to the end. They will see that there is enough blame to go around, and Maritimers need to share some of it.

While I wish for Maritimers to gain an appreciation of their place in the Canadian federation and an understanding of their economic history, I also would like for many other Canadians to appreciate how national policies have favoured their own regions and the impact of the good fortune of large ground deposits of oil and gas to create a strong entrepreneurial culture in some regions. That said, my hope is that Maritimers can bring closure to the blame game, because there is no market for it in a highly competitive global economy.

The Maritime region cannot rewrite history. And the more populous provinces are not about to acknowledge that their political clout, the lack of an effective upper house to speak to the interest of the smaller provinces, and national policies account for some of their economic successes. The have provinces see important economic challenges in their own backyards brought about by globalization and will press the federal government to implement measures to help them deal with these challenges. As for the Maritime provinces, Ottawa and the more populous provinces will continue to tell Maritimers, Pull yourselves up by your own bootstraps.

THE OUTLINE

The book is divided into five parts. The first part sets the stage for answering Galbraith's questions. I review in detail the people factor and its relation to the Maritime provinces; I look to history, to how the region was populated and by whom, to establish the region's people factor.

I also review lessons learned from the literature and economic development theories. There is no shortage of theories to explain the location and pace of a country's or a region's economic development. Discussion includes the more important ones, as they apply to the Maritime region. We have also seen significant new contributions to literature in recent years, contributions that focus mostly on *what* can be done to promote economic development rather than on *why* a region has lagged behind. Still, we need to understand the *why* so we can better appreciate *what* can be done.

Maritimers have long pointed to national political institutions and national policies to explain their region's underdevelopment in relation to other regions. There is more than a shred of truth to their argument, and part 2 explores this contention. We need to fully explore the question, if only because many Maritimers are convinced it explains, in large measure, their region's underdevelopment. I argue that at critical moments in Canada's development the federal government effectively suspended market forces to direct where economic activities should be located. Ottawa's war efforts and the work of its Department of Reconstruction are cases in point; the three Maritime provinces were left out in the cold on both occasions. A focus on the past not only provides an understanding of our economic history but also offers hope that it is less likely to reoccur. I hope that it will also provide Canadians with a better understanding of why the Maritime provinces have had to pull against gravity in their efforts to promote economic development.

It is no less important to revisit the federal government's efforts in the regional economic development field. Though less than is widely assumed outside the region, the Maritime provinces have benefitted from these efforts. I have been an active participant in developing some of these measures, and I draw from this experience in part 3. The time has come to report in detail on the forces that led Ottawa to overhaul its approach to promoting regional economic development and my involvement in some of these developments. I also draw from my extensive published work in the field.

But that can scarcely provide the complete answer to Galbraith's questions. Maritimers also need to look in the mirror and question their own roles and that of their provincial governments in developing the region. Resistance to change remains strong in our region. Frank McKenna argued that the Maritime region has a particularly strong "fear of the unknown." He remarked, "We ran into a big controversy in the effort to build a bridge between New Brunswick and Prince Edward Island where a referendum was held with the island split almost in two. Today, the results would be closer to 100% in the favour of the bridge."[30] As is well-known, public sector employment constitutes a larger share of total employment in the Maritime provinces than any other region, perhaps because public-sector unions are better equipped to embrace the status quo than their private sector counterparts. The region is also aging at a faster rate than other Canadian regions, with wide implications for productivity and the delivery of public services. An aging population also favours the status quo. Part 4 explores these considerations.

The global economy has put Canada's economy on a different footing, and the impact is being felt in all regions. We have also witnessed, in recent years, a shift favouring the attributes of individuals over those of the community. There is much less appetite today than forty years ago for federal regional development programs or transfer payments to have-less provinces. As noted, Maritimers are now being told to pull themselves up by their bootstraps. But this leads to two questions: what bootstraps are available to Maritimers, and how can they pull themselves up?

In part 5, I offer a prescriptive perspective for the region. It is one thing to understand how economic development skipped over the Maritime provinces, but it is quite another to offer suggestions for the way ahead. Answering Galbraith's questions also offers important lessons about what works in the regional economic development field. Given the limits to applying regional economic development theories for reasons outlined in following chapters, the best we can do is devise an economic development agenda for the region.

I propose such an agenda in the concluding chapters, which applies to all economic actors in the region. To be sure, not every Maritimer will agree with the proposed agenda. But nothing will be lost if the book serves to encourage a debate, both at the regional and national levels, on what can be done to promote economic development in the region.

NOTES

1 John K. Galbraith made these observations with the local media after his Josiah Wood Lecture at Mount Allison University, fall 1986. Galbraith once asked me the same questions. I met Galbraith on several occasions. Ben Higgins, a former colleague and a good friend of Galbraith, first introduced me to him in 1988.

2 *Canada: A Longstanding Commitment to the RDA Model* (Ottawa: The Regional Agencies, April 29, 2015), 4.

3 Leonard Tilley, a Father of Confederation from New Brunswick, declared that "with their coal, iron and water-power the Maritimes will be manufacturing centres for this vast Dominion." Quoted in Richard Starr, *Equal as Citizens: The Tumultuous and Troubled History of a Great Canadian Idea* (Halifax: Formac Publishing, 2014), 31.

4 See, among others, Donald J. Savoie, *Regional Economic Development: Canada's Search for Solutions* (Toronto: Toronto University Press, 1992).

5 See, among others, Thomas L. Friedman, *The World is Flat: A Brief History of the Twenty-first Century* (New York: Farrar, Straus and Giroux, 2005).

6 See ibid.; and Enrico Moretti, *The New Geography of Jobs* (Boston: Mariner Books, 2012), 5.

7 Philip McCann, "Globalization and Economic Geography: The World is Curved, Not Flat," *Cambridge Journal of Regions, Economy and Society* 1, no. 3 (2008): 351–70.
8 Benjamin Higgins, "The Task Ahead: The Search for a New Local and Regional Development Strategy in the 1980s," United Nations Centre for Regional Development, Nagoya, Japan, November 11–16, 1981, 1.
9 OECD, *Promoting Growth in All Regions* (Paris: OECD, 2012), 15.
10 See, among others, Andrew R. Duncan, W. B. Wallace, and Cyrus Macmillan, *Report of the Royal Commission on Maritime Claims* (Ottawa, 1926).
11 See, among others, Donald J. Savoie, *Visiting Grandchildren: Economic Development in the Maritimes* (Toronto: University of Toronto Press, 2006).
12 OECD, *Regional Outlook 2014—Regions and Cities—Where Policies and People Meet* (Paris: OECD, 2014).
13 OECD, *Regional Development Policies in OECD Countries* (Paris: OECD, 2010).
14 *Canada: A Longstanding Commitment to the RDA Model*, 3.
15 See, among others, Benjamin Higgins and Donald J. Savoie, *Regional Development Theories and Their Application* (New Brunswick, NJ: Translation Publishers, 1995).
16 See Savoie, *Visiting Grandchildren*, 17.
17 Harold A. Innis, *Fur Trade in Canada: An Introduction to Canadian Economic History* (Toronto: University of Toronto Press, 1956), 358.
18 Quoted in André Raynauld, ed., *Seminar on Regional Development in Canada: Transcript of the Proceedings* (Montreal: Centre de recherche en développement économique de l'Université de Montréal, 1980), 105.
19 *Living Together* (Ottawa: Economic Council of Canada, 1977).
20 Luke Flanagan, "The Political Union Debate in Canada's Maritime Provinces, 1960–1980: Why Did a Union Not Happen?" (PhD dissertation, University of Edinburgh, 2012), 45.
21 Richard Simeon, "Regionalism and Canadian Political Institutions," *Queen's Quarterly* 82, no. 4 (Winter 1975): 499.
22 Savoie, *Visiting Grandchildren*, 230.
23 James P. Bickerton, *Nova Scotia, Ottawa and the Politics of Regional Development* (Toronto: University of Toronto Press, 1990), 66.
24 See Flanagan, "The Political Union Debate in Canada's Maritime Provinces," 201.
25 Quoted in H. Wade MacLauchlan, *Alex B. Campbell: The Prince Edward Island Premier who Rocked the Cradle* (Charlottetown, Prince Edward Island Museum, 2014), 234.
26 Louis J. Robichaud, quoted in ibid., 158.
27 James Hiller, "The Origins of the Pulp and Paper Industry in Newfoundland," *Acadiensis* 11, no. 2 (Spring 1982): 43.
28 I borrow this phrase from David Foot with Daniel Stoffman, *Boom, Bust & Echo: How to Profit from the Coming Demographic Shift* (Toronto: Macfarlane Walter and Ross, 1996), 4.

29 Consultations with a former senior public servant, Moncton, January 6, 2015.

30 Frank McKenna, "An Address to the 12th Atlantic Canada Energy Summit," Saint John, New Brunswick, October 24, 2014, 8.

Part 1

THE SETTING

Chapter 2

THE PEOPLE FACTOR

There are now libraries of material on regional economic development produced by students of public policy, geography, political science, and economics, as well as by think tanks, government departments and agencies, and local practitioners in the economic development field. And yet, it remains a relatively new field of study, barely more than sixty years old. It has, however, made up for lost time by borrowing from several disciplines. The drawback is that core disciplines will dismiss the field, insisting it lacks its own central theories and is thus easily challenged.

Some view regional science and the study of regional economic development as a poor cousin to other disciplines, notably economics and political science. The field has also lost standing in academic circles in recent years, much like it has in government.[1] The rise of neoconservatism, the global economy, past failures widely reported in the media, and the tight fiscal situation confronting governments in much of the Western world have contributed to putting proponents of regional development on the defensive.

Ever since Adam Smith published his *Wealth of Nations* in 1776, economists have sought to explain the wealth or poverty of nations by looking to climate, soil, and abundance or scarcity of natural resources. Many who took their cue from Smith have sought to explain why nations and regions have had more economic success than others by looking mainly to natural resources. These attempts, however, have always fallen short of the mark, as Switzerland and Japan have so clearly demonstrated over the years, given that neither is hardly rich in natural resources.

If natural resources endowment does not always explain the wealth of nations or regions, then what does? Many have stressed the importance of entrepreneurship and the differences in managerial, scientific, engineering, technical, and labour skills to explain uneven regional development.[2] But why are entrepreneurs better able to flourish in one region over another? Why are people in some regions more productive than in others? Why are they more innovative? Why are they more dynamic, more ambitious? To be sure, culture and the people factor have something to do with the discrepancies, as I argue in this book. But why are some cultures more open to economic development than others? Why can individuals flourish in one culture but not in another?[3]

In the next chapter, I review the most promising theories to explain the location of economic activities. But first, in this chapter, I stress the importance of the "people factor." Again, I hold that the people factor, culture, and history matter in economic development to a much greater extent than is generally believed by economists and by government officials. To address the people factor in one brief chapter, I must turn to a level of generalization that will leave the specialists *sur leur faim*.

I am hardly the first to point to the people factor as one of the key determinants in economic development. Nobel laureate Gary Becker made the case: "The primary determinant of a country's standard of living is how well it succeeds in developing and utilizing the skills, knowledge, health and habits of its population."[4] Notwithstanding Becker's assertion, many economists continue to overlook the people factor in explaining the location of economic activities, at least in part because the people factor does not fit neatly in their economic models.

IT'S ABOUT HISTORY, CULTURE, AND PEOPLE

Canada has a rich history, with a wide range of founding peoples and cultural diversity. Events—some positive, some negative—have shaped the capacity of the country's people and communities to promote economic development. Events shape attitudes, and attitudes have an impact on the ability of individuals to conceive and pursue opportunities. Some of the economic development literature links attitudes to entrepreneurial ability, entrepreneurial human capacity, regional innovation capacity, and the success of regional clusters.[5]

We know that in French Canada, some of the richer and better educated settlers retreated back to France after the conquest, depriving it of much of its economic and political elite and its innovative capacity. France itself showed little concern for the fate of its former colonists once the colony itself was lost. Far from helping to rebuild its economy after a damaging and costly war, France even renounced its debts to the colony. The impact of defeat was profound.

No longer in control of their own land and finding themselves, for one reason or another, at a disadvantage in competition with the British conquerors, the French withdrew to a large extent from economic competition. They looked to their traditions and cultivated a local nationalism, consoling themselves for their failure to participate fully in the economic life of their province with assurances that they did not wish to do so anyway. They preferred the gentility and humanity of their own life, their own Roman Catholic faith, values, and culture to the vulgar materialism of the victors. As time went by, these attitudes became formalized and ritualized.

The hugely popular Radio-Canada radio and television series *Les belles histoires des pays d'en haut,* which ran between 1956 and 1970 throughout French Canada, spoke to the moral values of the time. The interactions of the French Canadian community in the Laurentides depicted a miser and evil man that dominated the economic life of the village. He was pitted against the parish priest and the good people, the habitants happily eking out a living on the farm or in the woods. There were no entrepreneurs or business leaders in the series, only the good people, the priest (also portrayed as good), and the villain, Séraphin Poudrier. The series was an adaptation of Claude-Henri Grignon's 1933 novel, *Un homme et son péché,* set in the 1880s. I recall listening to Séraphin, which was by far the most popular radio and television series in my village. No one in French Canada ever wanted to be or become a Séraphin.

So persuasive was this ideal of a serene, agrarian society led by the Roman Catholic Church and a cultivated elite indifferent to wealth that many French Canadians began to think French Canada really was like that. Thus, in 1898 Sir John Bourinot, Clerk of the House of Commons in Ottawa and Secretary of the Royal Society of Canada, wrote:

> As a rule, the *habitant* lives contentedly on very little. Give him a pipe of native tobacco, a chance of discussing politics, a gossip with his fellows at the church door after service, a visit now and then to the county town, and he will be happy. It does not take much to amuse him, while he is quite satisfied that his spiritual safety is secured as long as he is within sound of the church bells, goes regularly to confession, and observes all the *fêtes d'obligation*. If he or one of his family can only get a little office in the municipality, or in the "government," then his happiness is nearly perfect.[6]

J. P. Beaulieu of Quebec's Department of Industry wrote in a similar vein as recently as 1952, although he showed more appreciation for industrialization, which was then taking place: "Quebec, barely half a century ago, a picturesque region in a vast country, over most of its extent farm lands alternated with forest, rivers, villages and freshly cleared colonization centres. This was Quebec little changed from pioneer days with the old ways kept alive from one generation to the other by the rural population."[7] I stress that both Bourinot and Beaulieu were French Canadians writing about their community.

The conclusion seems to be that until the 1960s, French Canadians lagged behind the rest of the country because they preferred it that way, in order to preserve their religious and cultural traditions. French Canada did not provide proper support to its own entrepreneurs; entrepreneurship—and to a considerable degree, capital as well—came from outside. In short, for a long time in French Canada, the people factor valued neither business activities nor entrepreneurship and looked to the Church for guidance in all things.

Frontier theory would also explain this lack of entrepreneurship, by pointing out that Quebec was originally settled by *grands seigneurs* and peasants, not by commercial farmers. The physical environment lent itself to create one major city, on the border of Ontario, and was economically dominated by English Canadians and Montreal's St. James Street. There were few "log-cabin-to-riches" stories among French Canadians. The thinking was that this gap could be closed only when conditions allowed for a change in French Canadian attitudes, so that a larger share of the entrepreneurial function in Quebec was carried out by French Canadians themselves. This transformation, of course, is precisely what has taken place over the past fifty years or so. But fifty years is not a long time in economic development, at least when compared with other cultural groups that have held a pro-business bias for centuries.

The foregoing account also describes the evolution of the Acadian population in the three Maritime provinces and its relationship to economic development. The differences are that Acadia was not settled by *grands seigneurs*, and it was located on the periphery of a continental economy. In addition, ties between Acadians and France were lost for two centuries. The impact of *le grand dérangement* was deep; it is still felt to this day. As is well-known, Acadians were forcibly uprooted from their homes, their houses were burned, their land confiscated, and families torn apart and sent off to distant lands. Some Acadians escaped, and many returned to the Maritimes. For two centuries, Acadians in all three Maritime provinces fished and farmed in small and relatively isolated rural villages. They kept to their own because they had little choice if they wanted to retain their language, culture, and religion. They also had to deal with a hostile colonial power that saw them as an "awkward people" dominated by the Roman Catholic Church.[8] They asked for nothing more than to be left alone, and they withdrew to their communities and their church.

Although things are changing, Acadian communities remain small and isolated, with many still looking to the sea to survive. It is hardly possible to overstate the point that, until the late 1960s, Acadians looked to the Church and the local parish priest for guidance, both spiritually and economically, and to natural resources to eke out a living. Neighbours helped neighbours to the extent that they could, and extended families looked after family members. The parish would help the poor with food and shelter whenever possible. For a long time, nuns provided health care. They ran things on a shoestring, taking care of the sick even if they could not afford it. The Church or the community was there to give a helping hand. The economic goal was simply one of survival.

I recall well growing up in a small Acadian hamlet nearly fifty kilometres north of Moncton. Good Roman Catholics, we attended Mass every Sunday, never ate meat on Fridays, and we made sacrifices throughout the four-week Advent period before Christmas and again during the six weeks of Lent before Easter. The business community was largely foreign to us. Entrepreneurs were few. Women stayed at home to raise large families (I am from a family of seven, a typical Acadian family in my day). Men fished, farmed, cut trees, or worked for businesses owned by foreigners and non-Acadians.

Religion provided a strong bond between economic classes to the extent that they existed in Acadian communities. Heaven and hell were the great equalizers. I recall the priest in his Sunday sermons telling us, "It is easier for a camel to go through the eye of a needle than for a rich man to enter into the Kingdom of Heaven."[9] I actually felt sorry for the few highly successful businessmen. For the most part, they were anglophone and Protestant, led astray by a misguided religion, so we thought. How could one possibly want to sacrifice eternity for a few years of economic success on earth? The community believed that in the end everything would equal out, with the poor having a much greater chance of seeing heaven than the wealthy. There was no need to be cynical or even envious of the well-to-do, because we believed they would pay the ultimate price. To be sure, we saw little merit in trying to emulate them. The cost was too high. All to say, entrepreneurship was not for us; rather, it was for the anglophones and Protestants. *Le grand dérangement* had taught us to become self-reliant and to rely on one another, to embrace the Church as a security blanket, and to keep our heads well below the parapet. Our rewards were in the next life.

As in Quebec, Acadian communities would turn to *les caisses populaires* for their saving and borrowing. The collective nature of *les caisses populaires* held—and still holds, though now to a lesser extent—a strong appeal to Acadians. The local parish priest was one of *les caisses populaires'* biggest supporters, the best marketing strategy one could have at the time.

Home-grown entrepreneurs were few, and they operated in the natural resources sector—the fishery, farming, or the construction industry. They did not enjoy the kind of infrastructure support available to others; they only had access to a one-person accounting and law firm, often in a nearby community, with very limited knowledge of the business world. Young Acadians who went to college were encouraged to enter the priesthood or to become physicians and lawyers. In short, there were precious few accountants or other role models to encourage young Acadians to enter the business world.

I recall that E. P. Melanson operated a lobster processing plant in Cocagne in the 1950s, a fishing community not far from my own. We all knew he was an Acadian businessman who employed other Acadians, which was rare in my community and in neighbouring communities. Still, he was regarded in my community as a "Séraphin," not a role model to be emulated. Word got out in the late 1950s that he had run into serious financial problems. A well-known anglophone local businessman called to offer a word of encouragement and urged him to battle back, as best he could. Melanson explained the problem: "I have these guys from Ottawa calling me about income tax. What the Christ is that?"[10]

When the Roman Catholic Church began to lose its grip on French Canada, French-speaking Quebecers could turn to their provincial government for economic support. Thus, Quebec Inc. was born and gave rise to a number of new successful businesses and economic activities. It also gave rise to role models in the business sector and new and expanded programs in business schools. Quebec's francophone business community has thrived since the days of the province's Quiet Revolution. Acadians had no government of their own to turn to. New Brunswickers, however, elected Louis Robichaud to power in 1960. He provided the tools, the institutions, and the confidence for Acadians to look to career possibilities other than the clergy, medicine, and law. Robichaud led the way to a more secular life and toward an interest in government and business.

What Acadian communities lacked until the 1960s was indigenous entrepreneurship. Entrepreneurship and financial success were, until recently, not valued among Acadians. Consequently, Acadian communities were insignificant in entrepreneurial activities associated with industries in their own province. Industrialization was conducted throughout French Canada by "foreign" entrepreneurs, such as English Canadians, Americans, and others who were a "sub-dominant" elite in French Canadian society.

Why was entrepreneurial activity taken over by so-called foreigners? The school of historians at the University of Montreal once explained the whole matter in terms of conquest. The economic inferiority of the French Canadian community, they said, is the fatal consequence of being placed in servitude as a vanquished nation, conquered and occupied, reduced to the status of minority. As is so often the case in economic development, a vicious circle was then created. Debarred by defeat from full participation in the economic life of the country, French Canadians retreated into their traditions and nurtured French Canadian "nationalism."

They found solace in the superiority of their values and their civilization to those of the rest of Canada. As Monsignor Paquet wrote in 1902, "Our mission is less to manage capital than to preserve ideals; it consists less of lighting the fires of factories than of maintaining and spreading the luminous fires of religion and thought."[11] The message also resonated in all Acadian communities until the 1960s. In one of its manifestations, this set of attitudes took the form of a "return to the land" movement. As late as 1895, Paquet, the leading bishop in Quebec, stated that agriculture is the normal estate of man here below, that it is on the farms that man is in most direct relationship with God, and that only through agriculture could French Canadians "accomplish the grand destinies indubitably reserved for them by Providence."[12]

This view permeated French Canada until fairly recently. Justin Trudeau wrote that his father explained the "political and religious elites were concerned about protecting the province's French Catholic character within largely Protestant North America. Simply put, the emphasis was therefore on maintaining a society of farmers and lumberjacks, with a small cadre of lawyers, priests, doctors, and politicians to oversee it. Money and business were left to *les Anglais*."[13]

The Acadian community shared this belief. There is an economic price to pay for not embracing entrepreneurial and financial success, but when a community does finally embrace it, it takes time to generate self-sustaining economic activities and to create a successful business to pass on to the next generation. In terms of economic development, it takes time for success to grow an entrepreneurial culture.

THE PEOPLE FACTOR AND THE MARITIMES

"Culture" was invoked by at least one keen student of regional development to explain the underdevelopment of the Maritimes. James Bickerton explained, "The by-now-accepted explanation for Maritime underdevelopment based on geography, technological change, and lack of resources was supplemented and reinforced by claims of a regional parochialism and conservatism that led to such deficiencies as lack of entrepreneurship and initiative and an irrational resistance to change."[14] Culture has thus been recruited in an effort to explain the historic failure of Maritime firms to diversify, invest in new technologies, embrace entrepreneurship, and take the necessary risks in establishing or expanding manufacturing ventures. One variation of this type of explanation points to a lack of adequate entrepreneurship, or the people factor, as a residual influence in accounting for Maritime underdevelopment.

To this day, the Maritime provinces' population remains relatively homogeneous. The region has been populated largely by First Nations peoples, people of African descent, and Western Europeans. In recent years, the Maritime provinces have been unable to attract and retain a sufficient number of new Canadians to the same degree as other regions; hence, the region's population is mostly old stock.

Aboriginal communities were thrown to the wind when Western Europeans arrived. The land of the Mi'kmaq, at the time, extended to Cape Breton, all of mainland Nova Scotia, Prince Edward Island, and northern New Brunswick. The Maliseet inhabited the western side of the St. John River and its tributaries.

We know the Europeans posed extremely daunting challenges for the Aboriginal communities. For one thing, European diseases wiped out a large percentage of the population. Aboriginal peoples also had an ingrained egalitarianism in their cultures, which began to give way when some were able to acquire European goods. For those who did, it provided more prestige and more authority than they had in pre-contact bands of hunter-gatherers.[15]

Aboriginal peoples have never been able to fully integrate with the broader Maritime community—more accurately, the broader community has not encouraged integration. As recently as 1936 and 1959 respectively, the Nova Scotia government declared that the province was settled by five races: the French, the English, the Irish, the Hanoverians, and the Scottish.[16] Nothing was said about Aboriginal peoples or Nova Scotians of African descent. Until recently, they were never considered true Nova Scotians, let alone Maritimers. Ian McKay and Robin Bates summed up regard for certain ethnic groups well: "Judging from official statements and publications no natives, blacks or Asians were really settlers of Nova Scotia. Nor, for that matter, were the province's numerous Eastern Europeans, Jews or Lebanese."[17] The government of Nova Scotia has only recently come to acknowledge in its publications that "the Mi'kmaq are the founding people of Nova Scotia."[18] However, for the most part, Aboriginal peoples in Nova Scotia remain in small reserves, remote from urban centres.

Things were not much different for Aboriginal peoples in New Brunswick. W. S. MacNutt's *New Brunswick: A History, 1784–1867* pays little attention to the province's Aboriginal communities. But when he does, it is both revealing and insightful. MacNutt remarked, "The experiment (i.e., education) dragged on for many years at Sussex, where the natives were bribed to release their children to the instruction of the school. Mixed motives prevailed. Neighbouring farmers were eager to purchase the services of Indian boys as apprentices. The women were debauched.... The school at Sussex was finally closed in 1826, after being roundly condemned by the company which had financed the experiments."[19] MacNutt goes on to report that the white population played fast and loose with land allocating. He observes that "of the total of 62,000 acres reserved, white men had acquired dubious titles to 15,000 by purchase, generally offering a lug or two of rum, or a few pounds of gunpowder. Some of these lands, illegally acquired, had been sold and resold, so that there was a large vested interest in denying the Indian title."[20] As more and more European settlers arrived, they kept pushing Aboriginal residents off their land and further "into poverty, dependence and hopelessness."[21]

Andrew Parnaby notes that the colonial government "viewed the Mi'kmaq not as an ally or even an enemy, but as a problem."[22] It is difficult to see how a "problem" can be turned into a positive force for economic development. Reading Parnaby, one is struck by how well Aboriginal inhabitants managed, notwithstanding the nearly impossible position they were forced into. If, as I believe, the people factor is a key determinant of economic development, then Maritimers need to ask how best to help Aboriginal communities develop their economic potential. Aboriginal history points to a very difficult relationship with neighbours, not at all conducive to promoting economic development and an entrepreneurial culture. I can not do better than to quote Chief Roland Willson: "We were gathered and put on reserves, placed off to the side, and we were told that we would be taken care of. For one reason or another, our membership, our people, our elders believed in that. They sat by and allowed things to happen."[23] It is easy to recognize the negative impact on the people factor in Aboriginal communities and on the capacity to develop and promote economic activities.

The people factor in Aboriginal communities is also complicated by how some Aboriginal representatives actually see economic development. Many are not prepared to compromise their identity, heritage, and culture in the name of economic development. Representatives of Aboriginal communities recently told the Standing Senate Committee on Aboriginal Peoples, for example, that they were not willing "to give up who we are in order to gain from economic development. We do not want to lose our traditions, culture, language or religion."[24]

Aboriginal communities also have a different relationship with government than other Canadians. Though changes are evolving, provincial governments have long hesitated to deal with Aboriginal communities. They look to the constitution and regard responsibility for Aboriginal populations to fall under federal jurisdiction. Provincial governments in the Maritime provinces, like other provincial governments, fear "federal off-loading" of Aboriginal issues. This despite the fact that provincial governments are, by definition, closer to the people and have a much greater capacity to deliver programs and services, notably in key sectors such as education and social services.

At least since the Charter of Rights and Freedoms was incorporated in our constitution, Aboriginal communities have turned to the courts rather than to governments to get things done.[25] Courts interpret the law and treaties, and they do not hesitate to declare winners and losers. Aboriginal communities have secured a number of favourable court decisions relating to land use, the fishery, forestry, and the right to be consulted in a number of sectors. They would not have been able to secure these benefits had they relied solely on government. Aboriginal leaders in the Maritime provinces have made it clear to governments that, henceforth, difficult decisions about their future and their ability to participate in various economic sectors will be made by the courts, not governments.[26]

Dealing with the courts holds important advantages for Aboriginal communities. It takes politics out of the equation and provides for clearer decisions. Although discussion further on reveals that government policies, programs, and operations are important factors influencing the pace and location of economic activities, when it comes to the people factor, Aboriginal citizens have not had the support and encouragement of the broader community, notably governments, to help them conceive and pursue new economic activities. Passive government policies over the years have served to disempower Aboriginal communities and created both a welfare economy and an economic dependency.[27]

The Royal Commission on Aboriginal Peoples summed up the issue well by insisting that "most Aboriginal nations and communities are highly dependent on funds from other governments." It pointed to the "ghosts of history" as the root cause of the problem. The terms of Confederation were negotiated without reference to "Aboriginal nations." Sir John A. Macdonald declared in the early days of Confederation that the goal was to "do away with the tribal system and assimilate the Indian people in all respects with the inhabitants of the Dominion." It did not work out as envisaged, and in 1885, the government decided that "no outsider could come onto a reserve to do business with an Aboriginal resident without permission from the Indian agent."[28] This is by no means the way to promote economic development or an entrepreneurial culture.

Largely through the courts, Aboriginal communities have made progress on the socioeconomic front in recent years. But progress has been slow and spotty, with some becoming as self-sufficient as any other non-Aboriginal community while most remain highly dependent on passive government policies. The formidable challenges confronting aspiring entrepreneurs in Aboriginal communities include the Indian Act, remoteness of location, and access to financing, in addition to history and low "university completion rates."[29]

BLACK LOYALISTS

Maritimers of African descent have not fared any better. Many Black Loyalists opted for Nova Scotia (Shelburne and Halifax) and New Brunswick (Saint John), after fighting for the British side during the American Revolution, even though the Maritime region was home to slaves—many arriving as "property" of American Loyalists after the American Revolution. Slavery died out in the region by the 1820s.[30] Black Loyalists were promised their freedom and land if they fought for Britain. Some 30,000 escaped to British lines with more than 3,500 coming to Nova Scotia. Before the American Revolution, people of African descent never counted more than 300 in the region. But the American Revolution would change this. At one point, Nova Scotian Black Loyalists constituted the largest settlement of free blacks outside of Africa. Another wave of Black Loyalists—having received the same promises and having been renamed Black Refugees—came to the Maritime region after the War of 1812.[31]

Black Loyalists and Black Refugees soon realized, however, that promises of land were rarely kept, and those that were delivered land plots much smaller than offered and were located in areas poorly fit for agricultural purposes. For example, the *Regulus*, carrying 377 escaped and liberated slaves from the War of 1812, arrived in Saint John in 1815. The promised land grants were finally given in 1836, an inauspicious beginning for any chance of an entrepreneurial culture. Black Refugees were the last major influx of black settlers into New Brunswick before Confederation.[32]

The harsh winters only worsened matters for a people unaccustomed to a northern climate. MacNutt, in his history of New Brunswick, claims that Black Loyalists and Black Refugees "showed no disposition to farming";[33] however, he never addressed whether the land granted was arable. Other historians have, and report that Black Loyalists and Black Refugees were allocated only small rectangular, rocky plots after a long wait. The allotted acreage was too small for multi-plot farming or to divide into smaller pieces.[34] In brief, the land was never suitable for farming or for much else. A British company decided to offer Black Loyalists relocation to Sierra Leone, in West Africa, and about half accepted the offer, including seventy families from the Saint John area and over one thousand from Nova Scotia.[35]

Barry Cahill asserted that Black Loyalists in the region were more myth than reality. He explained, "Neither the Black Loyalist hypothesis nor the myth to which it gave rise allows for the fact that it was racism *tout court* which prevented the fugitive-slave refugees from being, or being seen to be, Loyalists."[36] No matter how one may wish to classify people of African descent in the Maritime provinces, they encountered—and still encounter—deep-seated prejudice and discrimination.[37] Thus, the people factor for Maritimers of African descent remains unconducive to producing new economic activities or to growing an entrepreneurial culture.

THE CHOSEN LOYALISTS

In contrast, the arrival of White Loyalists had a profound and lasting impact on both the political and economic life of what are now the Maritime provinces. The great majority of these Loyalists were of British origin, though some were German, Dutch, or Irish. Their arrival doubled the region's population overnight, created a new province, transformed the region from a New England outpost into growing and relatively sophisticated communities in Halifax and Saint John, and lessened considerably the presence and position of the Mi'kmaq and Acadians in the region.[38] It is no exaggeration to suggest the arrival of the Loyalists pushed everybody and everything aside.

When the United States declared its independence from Britain, some 100,000 settlers decided to remain loyal to the Crown and leave. Nearly 44,000 went north to the British colonies, with the bulk of them, 35,600 or about 80 per cent, coming to what was then Nova Scotia. As noted, the region's population doubled over a short period, with 21,000 of the settlers going to what is now Nova Scotia, 14,000 to New Brunswick, 500 to Prince Edward Island, and 100 to Cape Breton. The settlers were drawn to the region because of its economic potential and an ability to remain loyal to the British Crown and British-inspired institutions, notably its common law system.[39] Outside of the eastern seaboard of the United States, the Maritime region held, at the time, the most promising economic future. Still, it is important to stress that the migration of the Loyalists was not voluntary, and starting anew in a foreign land in the eighteenth century was a daunting challenge.[40] The Loyalists did pick a side in the American Revolution, but their side lost; they came to the region as a defeated people. Some, accused of treason, had to escape or face certain death. Some were rich, but the great majority arrived destitute. The first few years were particularly difficult for the Loyalists as they searched for shelter and food, seeking to establish a new beginning.

Though they picked the losing side, the White Loyalists were, in time, handsomely rewarded for their loyalty. They mostly settled near the ports where they first arrived: Halifax, Saint John, Sydney, Shelburne, and Charlottetown. They then spread throughout the Maritime region to create new economic activities. They were granted the best agricultural land with heads of families receiving 100 acres, which was later increased to 200 acres. They were also given assistance—food, tools, and building materials—to help ease their settlement. Because they believed they had sacrificed everything for their loyalty to the British Crown, they insisted Britain owed them land, financial support, and government jobs, even if the incumbents had to be let go. Their deep sense of entitlement would "poison relations between them and the rest of the population for decades."[41]

The sudden influx of people, combined with the rudimentary forms of transportation and communications, forced the partition of Nova Scotia and the founding of New Brunswick. Britain also split Cape Breton from Nova Scotia in 1784, which was later merged (1820) once again. A leading historian summed up succinctly why Britain decided to partition Nova Scotia: "Geography made it seem reasonable. History made it inevitable."[42]

The Loyalists joined other settlers in developing the Maritime region. Britain had encouraged foreign Protestants, mostly Germans, to populate Nova Scotia to counterbalance the presence of Acadians. British agents turned to the then friendly southwest regions of Germany and to Swiss and French Protestants to populate the Lunenburg region of Nova Scotia. Some 2,400 farmers and tradesmen came to the south shore of Nova Scotia between 1750 and 1753 to pursue opportunities offered by British agents and to practice their religion. They were different Maritime settlers in that they came neither as a defeated people nor to escape from a revolution or famine, but to pursue opportunities and enjoy the freedom to practice a religion that was not tied to the Roman Catholic Church.

The Scots came to Nova Scotia at different times and for different reasons. Some came following defeat at the Battle of Culloden in 1746, to escape an untenable political situation at home, where the Loyalists to the English Crown outmatched and outmanoeuvred the Jacobites and proved extremely brutal in victory. They sought to integrate the Scottish Highlands in Great Britain by putting in place measures to weaken Gaelic culture; wearing the tartan and speaking the Gaelic language were banned, and even playing the bagpipes was forbidden. Wounded Highlanders were put to death, many were persecuted for high treason and then transported or banished to British colonies.[43]

Other Scots came as part of the Planters wave from New England in the 1760s, invited to cultivate the fertile land that Acadians had forcibly abandoned, and after the Napoleonic Wars.[44] Still other Highlands Scots arrived in the 1830s and 1840s, also destitute, and the first few years in the region were particularly difficult for them.[45] It is wrong, however, to assume that all Scots came as a defeated people; many came to the region to pursue a more promising economic future, much like they did when they migrated to other North American regions.

The Maritime region also welcomed a steady stream of Irish immigrants, with many arriving before the Great Famine. They too tended to stick to their ports of arrival, notably Saint John, Halifax, and the Miramichi, in search of employment rather than to establish farms. The steady stream turned into a wave by the late 1850s, when some 500,000 Irish had arrived in British North America to escape the potato famine.

Saint John and Chatham became home to large numbers of Irish immigrants, as did Prince Edward Island and Halifax. The Maritime region was a popular destination, in part because of the Irish population already in these communities, but also because passage to the region was cheap, the distance to travel was shorter than to Upper or Lower Canada and the United States, and fares were also cheap on returning empty ships to load timber. At the time, the region held a great deal of economic potential, at least compared to the land they were leaving behind, and appealed to people looking for a fresh start after facing starvation. Those that arrived after the Great Famine were no less hungry and destitute than some of the Scots that arrived before them. They had little choice but to turn to the Roman Catholic Church for a helping hand. For many, the goal was to avoid starvation and simply survive. Saint John and Halifax in particular "received a significant number of the Irish forced out by the Famine."[46]

A GOLDEN PERIOD

Between 1815 and 1865, well over a million migrants crossed the Atlantic Ocean to settle in British North American colonies. The Maritime region received a sizable portion of the migrants. Phillip Buckner remarked that "for the first and last time in its history it was, in fact, central to the process of European colonization in North America rather than an unimportant peripheral region."[47] It truly was the Maritime region's golden period. The high point of immigration to the region from Western Europe occurrred in the 1840s, and the region's demographic has changed little ever since.

Because of inadequate records, we do not know precisely the number of Europeans who came to the region. We do know, however, that the region's population was about 80,000 in 1800 but grew to 700,000 by the early 1860s.[48] Urban centres in the Maritimes were starting to take shape by that time, land suited for agriculture had been granted to settlers, and forestry was making an important contribution to the region's economy. The region was building the necessary infrastructure—primarily roads, telegraph lines, and railways—to attract economic activities and migrants. Businesses in the region were establishing contacts abroad and successfully exploring new markets.

By the 1860s the region was a collection of different allegiances still evident today, notably Aboriginal peoples, Acadians, Loyalists, Black Loyalists, Irish, Scots, and some Yankee Americans who decided to migrate north. The pre-Confederation Maritime region was able to attract its share of migrants. But as Confederation neared, European migrants looked increasingly to other regions.[49] By this period, the Canadas were able to attract more and more European migrants because they had more land suited for farming, the key economic growth sector in the nineteenth century. Given its location, the region was well poised to take advantage of economic benefits flowing from Confederation.[50]

One thing is certain: the number of migrants to Central Canada has grown since Confederation, but not so in the case of the Maritime provinces. It is important to stress that immigration is a critical element in the people factor in economic development. Migrants continue to come to Canada for a fresh start and bring vitality to their host communities. The economic impact of immigration has been well documented. The *Economist* magazine reported that "fully 18% of the Fortune 500 list as of 2010 were founded by immigrants, (among them, AT&T, DuPont, eBay, Google, Kraft, Heinz and Procter & Gamble)." The same article pointed out that if one includes the children of immigrants the figure is 40%. It went on to note that immigrants founded a quarter of successful Fortune 500 high-tech and engineering companies between 1995 and 2005, and that they "obtain patents at twice the rate of American-born people with the same educational credentials."[51]

New Canadians are an important component to the people factor, because in their pursuit of a fresh start and economic opportunities, they bring energy and a deep desire to improve their economic standing. The Economic Council of Canada had this to say about immigration: "It would be hard not to recommend an increase when immigrants can gain so much and Canadians not only do not lose but actually make slight economic gains."[52] Relying on old stock tends to favour the status quo in both the political and economic spheres.

THE MARITIME REGION DOES NOT MEASURE UP

Canada has one of the highest per capita immigration rates in the world.[53] New Canadians come not only for economic opportunities but also for Canada's political stability and respect for human rights. Canada has vast wide open spaces, abundant natural resources, and a labour shortage in some sectors.

If, as I believe, migrants are a key contributor to the people factor, then the Maritime provinces have not measured up since Confederation. During the past ten years, the Maritime provinces have been home to less than 1 per cent of new Canadians. Ontario and Quebec accounted for 40 and 20 per cent of new Canadians, respectively, with Western Canada also seeing sharp increases in recent years.[54] Migrants classified as "business class" have turned mostly to Ontario, Quebec, British Columbia, and Alberta as their destination. The flow of business-class migrants to the Maritimes has been so low that the data does not even register.[55]

The three Maritime provincial governments are well aware of the challenge. They remain the most culturally homogeneous provinces in Canada, leaving aside Newfoundland and Labrador. A recently published high school history textbook in Prince Edward Island reports, "the Island is only recently getting interesting in terms of ethnic diversity. Our gene pool is mostly British (110,000) and Acadian (15,000).... There are also about 500 Mi'kmaq."[56] This from a population base of 146,000.[57]

All three Maritime governments have launched programs to attract new Canadians. As is the case for other things in the region, attracting new Canadians to the Maritime provinces is much like pulling against gravity. New Canadians tend to go where other new Canadians are and where economic and employment opportunities exist. Much more is said about immigration later in the book. Suffice to note here that immigration has not been able to enrich the economy of the Maritime region anywhere near the extent to which it has in other Canadian regions.

LOOKING BACK

This chapter highlights the importance of the people factor in economic development. The people factor encompasses historical processes, attitudes, education, and all the other forces that affect the capacity of a people to contribute to their community's economic development and its own well-being. The people factor also speaks to the skills, energy, and self-confidence that are essential for a people and individuals to conceive, launch, and manage new economic activities. It partly explains why some countries lacking in natural resources have been able to achieve economic prosperity. Too many economists pay scant attention to the people factor in developing economic models, although there are exceptions, as the next chapter makes clear. Richard Florida's work on the creative class, for example, speaks directly to the population factor.

The population base of the Maritime provinces harks back to pre-Confederation. As noted, we remain a homogeneous population—British, Irish, Scots, French, and Aboriginal descent. As also noted, new immigrants bring energy, enthusiasm, and new approaches to those established in the region; whereas, lack of immigration encourages the status quo and conservatism.[58] In short, the Maritime region has had to rely for its people factor on its old stock populations that lived through very trying circumstances in establishing communities in the region.

Recently, Aboriginal communities have had little choice but to turn to the courts rather than representative democratic institutions to participate more fully in the region's economic life. Representative democracy has all too often shut the door on them. Steve Gignish was speaking of the people factor when he said, "The image of Aboriginals in New Brunswick is that we are just a bunch of lazy and drunken Indians living off the government."[59] Widely respected former Mi'kmaw chief Albert Levi observed, his "people [are] a broken people."[60] Gignish added, "At the first sign of adversity Aboriginals will all too often give up."[61] Successful entrepreneurs are known for their tenacity, and it takes a strong-willed Aboriginal citizen to put aside history, years of discrimination, and perhaps a culturally-derived poor self-image to conceive and pursue new economic opportunities.[62] Economic models fall short in accounting for Gignish's observation. Promoting economic development among broken communities is a far different challenge than in well-established and vibrant communities.

Acadians were also a broken people as recently as fifty years ago. They looked to one another and to the Roman Catholic Church for guidance and, until fairly recently, had limited interest or success in launching new businesses. Since the Charter of Rights and Freedoms was incorporated in our constitution, Acadians have also been looking to the courts to secure linguistic rights rather than to representative democratic institutions.

Until the 1960s, the very few businesses Acadians owned were, by and large, geared to the local market and included convenience stores and small one- to three-person firms in the construction sector. Men and women worked in primary resource extraction or processing industries. They relied on traditional means to find work and economic sufficiency. Entrepreneurship was not part of the Acadian culture, and they had few role models to emulate in the business world. In addition, educational standards were very poor, and those few who pursued post-secondary education were encouraged on specific paths. Acadian political and administrative institutions were extremely weak. Indeed, a few local county councils in Acadian areas actually went bankrupt in the late 1950s and early 1960s. School boards in Acadian regions simply did not have the resources or the expertise to maintain first-rate teaching programs or even to hire qualified teachers in many instances.

Though Acadians still live under the shadow of their history, things are very different today. The Acadians' people factor has been vastly improved. Louis J. Robichaud, the first Acadian elected premier of New Brunswick, set in motion a series of events and measures that would transform the province's Acadian society. It is perhaps ironic that when reflecting on his accomplishments some thirty years after being elected to office, he observed, "It was like a Native being elected Premier of New Brunswick today."[63] What he meant, of course, was that in 1960, an Acadian was not expected to be elected premier of the province. Acadian society was too weak and lacking in confidence, and it had only limited influence in key political and economic circles in New Brunswick society to see one of its own elected to lead the province.

Entrepreneurship has now taken root in Acadian regions. For example, the level of new business start-ups in one Acadian region in the mid-1990s, in per capita terms, was the highest in the Maritime provinces. Acadians have become important business leaders in several economic sectors, exporting their products internationally. Institutions have arisen and now enjoy the full support of the Acadian community—Université de Moncton is but one example—and few, if any, are at risk of going bankrupt. These developments make the case once more that the people factor is a key ingredient in economic development.

Many—but not all—of the Loyalists, Black Loyalists, the Irish, and the Scots came to the region to escape a bad situation and not simply to pursue new economic opportunities. Loyalists came to the Maritimes because they were not prepared to let go of the status quo, many Scots and Irish to escape a very difficult situation at their respective homes. The White Loyalists had to strike a new beginning while leaving most of their assets in New England and New York. Though they were given a helping hand in carving out a new start, the transition involved many challenges, as historians have documented.[64] Their sense of entitlement born out of loyalty to the British Crown did not encourage an entrepreneurial culture. Since Confederation, however, new Canadians continue to look to other Canadian regions rather than to the Maritimes in pursuit of a new beginning. The Maritime provinces have not been able to benefit from the energy and ambitions new Canadians bring to their communities to the same degree as other regions.

Moreover, many dynamic elements of the region's old stock have left to pursue opportunities elsewhere. The Maritimes have produced more than their share of visionary leaders for Canada's business community. Claude Taylor left Salisbury, New Brunswick, to develop Air Canada. Purdy Crawford left Five Islands, Nova Scotia, to make a substantial contribution to both corporate law and securities regulations. Max Aitken, as in Lord Beaverbrook, left the region to pursue endeavours in politics, finance, and newspapers. Izaak Walton Killam left Yarmouth, Nova Scotia, for St. James Street, Montreal, to develop, among other sectors, Canada's financial industry. James Dunn left Bathurst, New Brunswick, to develop Ontario's steel and shipping industry. Because of the substantial funds generated from duties on succession by the Killam and Dunn estates, the government of Canada was able to establish and endow the Canada Council for the Arts.[65] There are still other visionary pioneers who left the region to make their mark, for instance, in banking (Cedric Ritchie and Rowland Frazee) and in the food industry (Richard Currie and Ron Joyce). Maritimers have long lamented the loss of our best in the people factor to other regions. The remaining chapters seek to answer why this occurs. Not only did the Killams, Dunns, Taylors, and Crawfords leave the region to make their respective marks and substantial economic contributions elsewhere, but also one is hard-pressed to identify individuals from other regions who came to do likewise in the Maritime provinces. For Maritimers, going down the road has been a one-way street.

NOTES

1 See, among others, Niles Hansen, Benjamin Higgins, and Donald J. Savoie, *Regional Policy in a Changing World* (New York: Plenum Press, 1990).

2 Higgins and Savoie, *Regional Development Theories and Their Application*, 19.

3 Ibid.

4 G. Becker, "Human Capital and Poverty Alleviation" (Washington, DC: World Bank, Human Resources Development and Operations Policy, working paper, 1995), 1.
5 See, among others, Yannis Georgellis and Howard J. Wall, "What Makes a Region Entrepreneurial? Evidence from Britain," *Annals of Regional Science* 34, no. 3 (September 2000): 385–403; and David Audretsch and Erik Monsen, *Entrepreneurship Capital: A Regional Organizational Team and Individual Phenomenon* (Jena, Germany: Max Planck Institute of Economics, Entrepreneurship, Growth and Public Policy Group, n.d.).
6 Sir John Bourinet, *Canada* (New York: G. P. Putnam and Sons, 1898), 438–9.
7 J. P. Beaulieu, *Province of Quebec Industrial Expansion Publication* (Quebec: Office provincial de publicité pour le ministère de Commerce et Industrie, 1952).
8 Ian McKay and Robin Bates, *In the Province of History: The Making of the Public Past in Twentieth-Century Nova Scotia* (Montreal and Kingston: McGill-Queen's University Press, 2010), 21.
9 Mark 10:25.
10 The caller was K. C. Irving and this story was told to me by his son Arthur Irving.
11 Louis-Adolphe Paquet, "*La terre canadienne,*" Études et appréciations 2 (Quebec: Imprimerie Franciscaine Missionnaire, 1918), 3–12; and "*La vocation de la race française en Amérique,*" *Discours et Allocutions* 1 (Quebec: Imprimerie Franciscaine Missionnaire, 1915), 187.
12 Paquet, "*La terre canadienne,*" 3–12.
13 Justin Trudeau, *Common Ground* (Toronto: HarperCollins Publishers, 2014), 92.
14 Bickerton, *Nova Scotia, Ottawa and the Politics of Regional Development*, 14.
15 See, for example, McKay and Bates, *In the Province of History*, 23.
16 Ibid., 254.
17 Ibid., 256.
18 Government of Nova Scotia, *Aboriginal People in Nova Scotia* (Halifax: Office of Aboriginal Affairs), n.d., http://novascotia.ca/abor/aboriginal-people/.
19 W. S. MacNutt, *New Brunswick: A History, 1784–1867* (Toronto: Macmillan, 1963), 78–79.
20 Ibid., 300.
21 Ed Whitcomb, *A Short History of Nova Scotia* (Ottawa: From Sea to Sea Enterprises, 2009), 13.
22 Andrew Parnaby, "The Cultural Economy of Survival: The Mi'kmaq of Cape Breton in the Mid-19th Century," *Labour/Le Travail* 61 (Spring 2008): 69–98.
23 Chief Willson of the West Moberly First Nations quoted in Gerry St. Germain and Nick Sibbeston, *Sharing Canada's Prosperity—A Hand Up, Not A Handout* (Ottawa: Standing Senate Committee on Aboriginal Peoples), March 2007, 3, http://www.parl.gc.ca/content/sen/committee/391/abor/rep/rep06-e.pdf.
24 Quoted in ibid., 5.

25 See, among others, William C. Wicken, *The Colonization of Mi'kmaw Memory and History, 1794–1928: The King v. Gabriel Sylliboy* (Toronto: University of Toronto Press, 2012).

26 See, among many others, "N.B. Natives Dismiss Report as Inadequate," *Globe and Mail* (Toronto), March 26, 1999, A6.

27 Mathew Tomm, "Public Reason and the Disempowerment of Aboriginal People in Canada," *Canadian Journal of Law and Society* 28, no. 3 (December 2013): 293–314.

28 Canada, *People to People, Nation to Nation: Highlights from the Report of the Royal Commission on Aboriginal Peoples* (Ottawa: Minister of Supply and Services Canada, 1996), www.aadnc-aandc.gc.ca/eng/1100100014597/1100100014637#archived.

29 National Aboriginal Economic Development Board, *The Aboriginal Economic Progress Report 2015* (Gatineau, QC: NAEDB, 2015), 30.

30 William Renwick Riddell, "Slavery in the Maritime Provinces," *The Journal of Negro History* 5, no. 3 (July 1920): 359–75; and Harvey A. Whitfield, "The Struggle over Slavery in the Maritime Colonies," *Acadiensis* 41, no. 2 (Summer/Autumn, 2012): 17–44.

31 "Black History Canada," *Historica Canada*, n.d., http://www.blackhistorycanada.ca/.

32 W. A. Spray, *The Blacks in New Brunswick* (Fredericton, NB: Brunswick Press, 1972).

33 MacNutt, *New Brunswick*, 83.

34 Harvey A. Whitfield, "The Development of Black Refugee Identity in Nova Scotia," *Left History* 10, no. 2 (Fall 2005): 16.

35 MacNutt, *New Brunswick*, 84.

36 Barry Cahill, "The Black Loyalist Myth in Atlantic Canada," *Acadiensis* 29, no. 1 (Autumn 1999): 82.

37 See, among others, George Elliott Clarke, "White Niggers, Black Slaves: Slavery, Race and Class in T. C. Haliburton's *The Clockmaker*," *Nova Scotia Historical Review* 14, no. 1 (June 1994): 13–40.

38 See, among others, Stephen A. Davis, *Mi'kmaq* (Halifax: Nimbus Publishing, 1997).

39 See, among others, MacNutt, *New Brunswick*, chapters 2 and 3.

40 Phillip Buckner, "The Transformation of the Maritimes: 1815–1860," *The London Journal of Canadian Studies* 9 (1993): 13–30.

41 Whitcomb, *A Short History of Nova Scotia*, 13.

42 Ibid., 42.

43 J. M. Bumsted, "Scottish Emigration to the Maritimes 1770–1815: A New Look at an Old Theme," *Acadiensis* 10, no. 2 (Spring 1981): 65–85.

44 McKay and Bates, *In the Province of History*, 33.

45 Buckner, "The Transformation of the Maritimes: 1815–1860," 9.

46 Ibid., 21.

47 Ibid., 18.

48 See Alan A. Brookes, "Out-migration from the Maritime Provinces 1860–1900: Some Preliminary Considerations," *Acadiensis* 5, no. 2 (Spring 1976): 26–55.

49 Buckner, "The Transformation of the Maritimes: 1815–1860," 23.

50 Douglas McCalla, "The Wheat Staple and Upper Canadian Development," *The Historical Papers* 13, no. 1 (1978): 43.

51 "Schumpeter: Fixing the Capitalist Machine," *Economist*, September 29, 2012, 22.

52 Canada, *Economic and Social Impacts of Immigration* (Ottawa: Economic Council of Canada and Supply and Services Canada, 1991).

53 See, for example, Canada, *A Fast and Flexible Economic Immigration System: Jobs, Growth and Long-Term Prosperity. Economic Action Plan 2012* (Ottawa: Citizenship and Immigration Canada, 2012).

54 Canada, "Immigration Overview: Permanent Residents," *Facts and Figures 2013* (Ottawa: Citizenship and Immigration, 2014).

55 See, for example, British Columbia Table 1—Immigration to Canada by Province of Destination, www.welcomebc.ca/welcome-bc/media (site discontinued).

56 Rob MacDonald, "History of Prince Edward Island" (course notes, Colonel Gray Senior High School, Charlottetown, PE, 2011), 4.

57 Government of Prince Edward Island, "Overview," *Prince Edward Island Population Report 2014* (Prince Edward Island: Statistics, 2014).

58 The Maritime provinces recognize this. See, for example, Government of New Brunswick, *Be…Where Opportunities Await* (Fredericton: Population Growth Secretariat, n.d.).

59 Steve Gignish quoted in Donald J. Savoie, *Aboriginal Economic Development in New Brunswick* (Moncton: Canadian Institute for Research on Regional Development, 2000), 117.

60 Quoted in ibid., 119.

61 Quoted in ibid., 117.

62 See, for example, Donald J. Savoie, *Harrison McCain: Single-Minded Purpose* (Montreal and Kingston: McGill-Queen's University Press, 2013).

63 Louis J. Robichaud, quoted in ibid., 71.

64 See, among many others, Elwood Jones, "The Loyalists and Canadian History," *Journal of Canadian Studies* 20 (Fall 1985): 156.

65 See, among others, Douglas How, *A Very Private Person: The Story of Izaak Walton Killam and His Wife Dorothy* (Halifax: Trustees of the Estate of the late Dorothy Killam, 1976).

Chapter 3

A THEORY FOR EVERY SEASON

There is still a "missing element"[1] in defining a theory that explains why and where economic development takes place, as Allen Scott and Michael Storper point out. This chapter takes stock of the regional economic development literature and reviews the long and tangled history of previous efforts to identify this missing element that continues to perplex both students and practitioners of regional economic development.

A cursory look at the world map reveals that many of the world's great cities have ports, countries close to the equator have slower economic growth than countries in the northern hemisphere, and, with some exceptions, countries that have embraced Western-inspired political institutions continue to outperform those that have not.[2] Harbours, ports, railways, and roads are, of course, important to economic development. But they are not enough. China today and its capacity to generate new economic activities is far different from the China of the 1970s. The new infrastructures alone hardly explain the transformation; Chinese political leaders unleashed a new political and economic culture that continues to generate foreign investments and a new class of entrepreneurs that has transformed the country. There are a host of factors that influence the pace and location of new economic activities; ports, highways, and airports can never constitute the full story.

This complexity accounts for why there are numerous theories, at times conflicting ones, to explain the location of economic activities and why some regions outperform others. [3] I limit my review to the theories that have inspired regional development measures in the Maritime provinces and those that square with the region's economic circumstances.

FROM THEORY TO EFFORTS ON THE GROUND

Many theories exist but, apart from having a missing element, they are all too often lacking, misunderstood, or misapplied by policy-makers or, much more often, ignored. The main difficulty is that many of the theories, and a good chunk of the literature, exude an aura of other-worldliness to policy-makers. The result, with a few notable exceptions, is that the theories have had limited immediate influence outside the halls of academe. The influence, to the extent that it has been felt in government, has been indirect as graduates in public policy and regional studies joined government departments, bringing a regional perspective to government. They have not, however, been successful in challenging mainstream economists operating in central agencies or in academia.

Politicians, meanwhile, have a four-year planning horizon. While senior public servants are too often preoccupied with the details of the day, politicians try, as best they can, to respond to the wishes of their constituents. Recent studies reveal that senior public servants in Canada, and in many other Western countries, no longer climb up the ranks of a single-line department and remain in the department for most of their careers. We also know that on average deputy ministers in the federal government—the permanent head of a government department—now stay less than three years in thier post.[4] The result is that senior government officials do not stay in a department long enough to master the finer points of their departmental policies, let alone appreciate fully how the literature about their sector could assist them. Their focus is to manage as best they can in a highly volatile political environment and help their political masters make an impact in a relatively short time.

In my career I have dealt with many public servants, served in government at both the federal and provincial levels, and interviewed hundreds of public servants in Ottawa, Washington, Paris, and London. The great majority of senior public servants have only a passing knowledge of the academic literature, and regional economic development is certainly no exception. I recognize that many do not have the time, or even the inclination, to debate the merits of economic development theories and how they may apply to their departments. Both politicians and senior public servants lead very busy lives, and they will focus on things that bring career rewards or deal with the problems at hand. Economic development theories have little to offer on this front.

That said, ideas and policy solutions do not surface in a vacuum. Lord Keynes put it well when he wrote, "practical men who believe themselves to be quite exempt from any intellectual influence, are usually the slaves of some defunct economists."[5] Again, regional economic development is no exception. Though regional economic or location theories are no match for political considerations and bureaucratic survival, they do explain a great deal more about the pace and location of economic activities than "practical" men and women are prepared to accept.

All public policies, programs, and many government decisions are the product of numerous rivulets of thought, and it is not always possible to pinpoint why and how an economic development policy or program was born. As noted, senior government officials were once students of economics, political science, public policy, and law—among other disciplines—and they bring knowledge gained in their studies to bear on their work. In this sense, theories and the literature have an influence on government policies, however indirect. In addition, should an academic contribution grab the attention of the media, then government officials will take note, and policy analysts down the line will be asked to prepare briefing notes for pertinent senior departmental officials and the minister.

CANADA'S CONTRIBUTION

Canadian scholars led the way in regional economic development theory. Harold Innis and W. A. Mackintosh made the case in the 1920s that Canada's economy was regional in character and argued that the ability to export natural resources to more advanced economies defined Canada's economy. All Canadian regions continue to have different staples to export, such as fur, timber, grain, and oil—hence the staples theory. Each staple left its stamp on a region (for instance, cod and Newfoundland or timber and New Brunswick), and the shift to new staples produced periods of crisis in which adjustments were painful.[6]

The staples theory seemed to fit the Canadian setting well. Indeed, the premise of this theory is that Canada's poorer regions were at one time prosperous, which, in fact, explains why they were populated in the first place. The staple that gave rise to this prosperity began to decline in importance, because of overexploitation, because of changes in world demand, or because of competition from lower-cost producers elsewhere. This decline, in turn, led to a decline in the region's fortunes. This theory has a strong appeal, if only because it appears to be a succinct explanation of Canada's economic history. New Brunswick's forest industry, for example, accounted for that province's prosperity at the turn of the twentieth century. With the decline of the forest sector, New Brunswick's economic prosperity took a downward turn.

In short then, the economic fortunes of a region, according to the staples theory, depend on the availability and marketability of its natural resources. On the face of it, the theory seems to explain the changing economic fate of the Maritime provinces. James Bickerton observed, "The application of the staples model to the case of the Maritimes led to the widely accepted thesis that the economic stagnation of the region within Confederation was the outcome of inexorable technological changes that left its resource endowment marginal to the pattern of growth in twentieth century North America."[7]

By the 1960s, the staples theory was challenged, and its sweeping historical generalizations were subjected to empirical scrutiny. The Economic Council of Canada, for instance, argued that "the absence of resources in Switzerland does not prevent economic success, and their presence in Argentina does not guarantee it."[8] The theory itself was undermined by new approaches and methodologies in the social sciences, including behavioural and systems approaches. E. R. Forbes made the case that the staples theory has, if anything, contributed to the misunderstanding of the Maritimes: "The view of Canada's history as the story of the development of a series of staples for export...contributed only slightly more to understanding of the Maritimes. Accounts of the fur trade touched on the Maritimes only in the earliest period; those on the timber trade largely petered out with confederation. Harold Innis' *Cod Fisheries* devoted but two of fifteen chapters to the Atlantic fishery after 1867, and studies of the wheat economy ignored the Maritimes entirely."[9]

URBAN AND REGIONAL SCIENCE

The study of urban and regional economics began to develop as a separate field in the late 1950s and early 1960s and grew "with astonishing rapidity" throughout the 1960s and 1970s.[10] If there is one name that made the study of regional economics fashionable on university campuses during this period, it is Walter Isard.

Isard founded the Regional Science Association, was the first chair of the Department of Regional Science at the University of Pennsylvania, and published extensively on location theory. He led the way, and soon departments of regional and urban studies sprang up in universities in many jurisdictions, and new graduate programs were launched in these fields. The *Journal of Regional Science* was established in 1958 and was followed by the *International Regional Science Review, Regional Science and Urban Economics,* the *Canadian Journal of Regional Science,* and similar specialized journals in the same or closely related fields. Regional economics and regional economic development would also soon have a home and programs on university campuses.

The regional science approach underlines the importance of space in economic analysis. It seeks to understand why a firm decides on one location over another and looks to transportation, labour, and material costs for answers. It also stresses the importance of a region's industrial structure, more so than conventional economic analysis, and its export capacity. Regional science draws upon a variety of economic theories; it has not been able to define its own core theory. The Economic Council of Canada echoed Scott and Storper when it concluded, "although the regional science approach is rich and complex, some important elements are missing."[11] This may well explain why regional science began to lose currency in the 1980s, and the number of regional science programs on university campuses has declined substantially from the heyday in the 1960s and 1970s.[12]

Still, the establishment or expansion of government departments and agencies designed to promote regional development grew in tandem with increasing university-based interests in regional science, urban studies, and regional development. The regional science approach led the search for theories in universities and some government agencies to explain the location of economic activities and what could be done to transform slow-growth regions into dynamic ones. The regional science literature has made some progress in developing a new perspective on regional economic development; however, the literature has not produced a comprehensive theory of regional development, as the Economic Council of Canada pointed out. It argued that the regional science approach "draws upon many economic theories, it is not itself a theory."[13]

LOOKING TO ENTREPRENEURSHIP

One school of thought that has always been in fashion in regional economic development theory centres on entrepreneurship. The argument goes that lack of entrepreneurship in some regions and its concentration in others explains why regional disparities exist. Though some economists may not readily see the link between the people factor and entrepreneurship, cultural differences among regions and the environment in which people grow up can have profound impacts on entrepreneurship. Expecting the son or daughter of a Bay Street lawyer to launch a business is quite a different matter from expecting the same of the son or daughter of an Aboriginal resident living in a small, isolated, poverty-stricken community in northern New Brunswick. There are, of course, also more economic opportunities to pursue in the Toronto area than in an Aboriginal community in the Maritime provinces. But opportunities need entrepreneurs to pursue them and entrepreneurs need opportunities in order to flourish.

One can trace the study of entrepreneurship to Adam Smith, Max Weber, and Benjamin Franklin. It is not possible to give a full account of the voluminous literature on entrepreneurship in a few short pages. Rather, I will highlight the work of arguably the most important contributor to the field: Joseph Schumpeter. Schumpeter ranks among the giants in the history of economic thought, and his main interest was economic development. Schumpeter built his theory around entrepreneurship in innovative and institutional settings. The entrepreneur, for Schumpeter, sees opportunities for introducing innovation, a new commodity, or an improved organization. He insisted that the supply of entrepreneurship was the ultimate determining factor of a region's economic growth.[14]

Schumpeter underlined the importance of innovation to entrepreneurship and economic development. He argued that the entrepreneur is not the inventor, but rather the individual who sees the opportunity for introducing an innovation, a new technique, or an improved organization.

He drew a clear distinction between invention and innovation. Invention is the art of creating something new, but in economic development what really matters is innovation, or the act of bringing the invention to market. For instance, Ray Kroc was not the inventor of fast food, but rather the innovator. The role of the entrepreneur is to raise the funds to launch the new business, to give economic life to innovation, and get the organization going.[15]

What about the age-old question: are entrepreneurs born or made? In other words, is there an "entrepreneur gene" at play that dictates who will become an entrepreneur?[16] Schumpeter believed that entrepreneurs depend on the social climate, a complex structure reflecting the whole social, political, and psychological atmosphere within which entrepreneurs must operate. This, in turn, includes social values of a country or region, the class structure, the educational system, and the society's attitude toward business success. A critical factor is the entrepreneur's understanding of the rules of the games, or the conditions under which the entrepreneur must operate. For Schumpeter, only the innovators who were able to conceive and organize new enterprises were the true entrepreneurs and deserving of high rewards.

Schumpeter also stressed the importance of a society's structure for entrepreneurs and aspiring entrepreneurs, but he did not tell us how to create entrepreneurs where they do not exist. This question has puzzled policy-makers and regional economic development specialists for generations. Harvard psychologist David McClelland and his colleague David Winter maintain that it is possible to create entrepreneurs. What is required is appropriate training for carefully selected individuals. They also recognize, however, the importance of economic opportunities for entrepreneurs to prosper.[17]

There still remains a wide range of views among social scientists regarding entrepreneurship and development. At one extreme are those who argue that entrepreneurship is needed for development, and that it is a rare, delicate hothouse plant, requiring careful nourishment with juicy monopolies. At the other end of the spectrum are those who argue that it is only necessary to get something going—a major resource discovery, a new road, a factory—and entrepreneurs will spring up under every tree, or even in the desert. Between these extremes is the majority who say, "It depends." But on what?

Governments have been pursuing an answer to the "on what" question ever since regional development came into fashion in the 1960s. The pursuit has only intensified in recent years, as governments have been adopting the "pull yourself up by your own bootstraps" strategy. This has been particularly evident in the Maritime provinces, as we will see. It was a fundamental building block of Atlantic Canada Opportunities Agency programs. The strategy also enables governments to tell communities and regions to "heal thyself," suggesting their economic development problems are their own doing and what is needed is more entrepreneurs. ACOA borrowed a page from McClelland and Winter and sponsored a variety of education and training programs to support entrepreneurship.

Certainly, the government of Canada sees considerable merit in promoting entrepreneurship. It is highly visible on several of its departmental websites. Provincial governments have been singing from the same hymn book for the past forty years. Schumpeter had it right when he stressed the importance of entrepreneurship and innovation to economic growth. The problem is that governments still do not know how to translate Schumpeter's thinking into policies and programs. It remains a missing element in the regional development tool kit, and this has been very evident in the Maritime region.

COMPARATIVE ADVANTAGE

What has really interested classical economists from Adam Smith to Paul Samuelson is international trade, the engine of economic growth. Classical economists believe that the volume and pattern of trade between two countries or two regions depend on the amount of labour required to produce various commodities in each region. To take David Ricardo's famous example, suppose that a certain amount of labour will produce twenty bolts of cloth or ten tuns of wine in the United Kingdom, and ten bolts of cloth or twenty tuns of wine in Portugal. If there are no restrictions on trade, and transport costs are not exorbitant, the United Kingdom will specialize in textiles and Portugal in wine. Trade will take place at a rate of exchange of one bolt of cloth for one tun of wine, since the amounts of labour entailed in the producing country are the same, and transport costs are the same in both directions. In effect, Portugal and the United Kingdom are exchanging one person-day of British labour for one person-day of Portuguese labour. In this example, and in any other case where trade takes place, both countries or regions are better off than they would be if each tried to produce both commodities.

The point is that capital-rich regions should focus on goods that employ high levels of technology while regions with less costly labour should focus on labour-intensive goods. The notion of international trade and comparative advantage still holds considerable appeal for government officials operating in economic development departments, and policy-makers continue to turn to some semblance of the comparative advantage theory to plan regional development measures.

One of the most forthright efforts to construct a general theory of regional development on the foundation of the base-industry-export-multiplier principle was made by noted economic historian Douglass North.[18] He began his well-known book *The Economic Growth of the United States 1790–1860* with this statement: "The gist of the argument is that the timing and pace of a country or a region's economic development has been determined by: 1) the success of its export sector, and 2) the characteristics of the export industry and the disposition of the income received from the export sector." He continued, "Why does one area remain tied to a single export staple while another diversifies its production and becomes an urbanized, industrialized economy? Regions or nations which remain tied to a single export commodity almost inevitably fail to achieve sustained expansion."[19] North published his book in 1961; his conclusions resonate to this day and hold importance for all Canadian regions, notably the Maritime provinces.

North argues whether or not a regional economy achieves sustained development depends on three factors: the natural endowments of the region, the character of the export industry, and changes in technology and transfer costs. Borrowing a page from the staples theory, he maintains the first of these factors determines how growth begins in any region. If the endowment factor results in a clear-cut comparative advantage in one industry, production will be concentrated in that industry at the outset. If, on the other hand, there are a good many commodities for which comparative advantage is not much less than in the leading sector, development of the region is likely to lead to diversification. The Maritime region continues to see a concentration of activities in the natural resources sector, notably the fishery and forestry, suggesting it is difficult for the region to promote sustained development.

The Maritimes is rich in some natural resources, but so are other Canadian regions, many of which are endowed with a greater variety of them. Other Canadian regions have more diversified economic activities and a broader character of their export industry. As we will see later, the Maritime provinces also lag behind other regions when it comes to technology and transfer costs.

GROWTH POLES

Of all the concepts utilized since World War Two in the formulation of regional policy and preparation of regional development plans, none generated so rapid a rise in popularity, nor so early and so complete a disillusionment, as growth poles. During the late 1960s and early 1970s, there was scarcely a developed or a developing country that did not make use of the concept in formulating its regional economic development policy. In the form in which it was usually applied, the notion of growth poles made regional development seem simple. All that is necessary is to push or pull some industries into an urban centre in a retarded or disadvantaged region through construction of infrastructure and incentives or regulations for private investment, and then sit back and watch the "spread effects" of this investment eliminate the gap between that region and the more prosperous and dynamic ones in the same country.

To employ an old Maritime expression, the government of Canada bought the concept hook, line, and sinker, which anchored the government's approach to regional development when the policy was at its zenith, that is, when Ottawa had more financial resources than it could spend and when many politicians believed regional economic disparities could be eliminated or substantially reduced. Canada was not alone in tying its regional development efforts to the growth pole concept.

The concept is closely associated with the work of French economist François Perroux. Perroux's own theory was imperfectly understood and still more imperfectly applied. But applied it certainly was, and Canada was no exception. Many more governments have stated officially that they were pursuing a growth pole strategy, at least in the urban and regional aspects of their development policy, than have claimed to be guided by any other philosophy, apart from laissez-faire. It became the guiding principle for regional planning in France, Belgium, and Italy as early as 1960, in

Canada in the late 1960s, and in the 1970s it spread to Spain, the United States, Japan, Latin America, Africa, and Asia.

However, as Perroux initially presented it, the theory was too complex, too abstract, and too non-operational to use as a basis for planning. Indeed to apply Perroux's pure theory would require global planning, if we take into account his insistence on planning transmission lines and receptors as well as generators of growth. Perroux's economic space, in which spread effects are felt, is global. He argued that Latin America's true growth poles still lie in Europe and, to some degree, in the United States. Such a concept is useless for regional planning, which is confined to a single country—albeit now less so. Consequently, economists who found themselves involved in practical regional planning simply discarded the pure theory of Perroux after only a few years trying to implement it.

They converted it into a totally different theory, which treated growth poles as urban centres and spread effects as generated in a particular geographic space, namely the region adjacent to the urban centre itself. Once this happy doctrine was accepted, it was possible to imagine that by pushing and pulling new enterprises (mostly industrial enterprise) into urban centres of retarded regions, it was possible to reduce regional disparities, decentralize urbanization and industrialization, and accelerate national and regional development all at once.[20] The assumptiom was that government could do all of this; it merely had to allocate resources and put in place the required programs in designated slow-growth regions. Once the programs were implemented, economic development was sure to follow throughout the region.

It was, however, a long march from Perroux's own theory to giving a capital grant to Volvo to make Halifax into a development pole or a subsidy to the Royal Bank of Canada to set up a call centre in Moncton, generating propulsive effects in the form of higher employment and incomes through the Maritime provinces. Indeed, Perroux was quite specific that it is "untenable to reduce the theory of development poles to a mere instrument of regional policy." But mere instruments of regional policy continue to be the stock and trade of government officials trying to make regional development measures work. Even Perroux recognized that one could not implant any old kind of productive activity anywhere one wishes in any kind of environment and assume a growth pole would be created and economic development would follow. Perroux explained, "Clearly, the market, full as it is of monopolies and various imperfections, is not up to these two tasks."[21]

To many government officials everywhere, it was never clear how Perroux's theory could contribute to their work. John Friedmann saw the problem with the theory first-hand when he worked in Latin America. He observed that once you designated a growth pole, "it wasn't long before other cities and towns lined up to be awarded this new badge of distinction in hopes that investments would follow."[22] The problem was hardly limited to Latin America. Still, government officials tried for a while to make the theory work, and I return to Perroux's growth poles later. Despite its shortcomings, Perroux's thinking played a central role in defining Ottawa's approach to regional development, particularly in the policy's early years. It was the one time Ottawa tried to tie its approach to regional economic development to a specific regional economic theory.

THE DEPENDENCY DEBATE

There are two diametrically opposed sides to the dependency debate. One is inspired by neo-Marxist thought and the other by neoclassical economic theory. Though the proponents of the dependency theories and the neoclassical approach talk about dependency, they do not share the same perspective.

Proponents of the neo-Marxist perspective attribute dependency to "the systematic draining of capital and resources from one region by other regions."[23] Canadian sociologist Ralph Matthews contended, "dependency theorists can legitimately argue that the eastern regions of Canada would not need today's transfer payments if they had not earlier been drained of their wealth."[24]

In its purest form, the dependency theory argues that continued underdevelopment and poverty in lagging regions is not the result of the failure of international capitalism but of its success in keeping wages and peasant (or small farm) incomes down in order to keep profits up. Rising peasant or small farm incomes would exert upward pressure on industrial wages, since poor peasants and farmers are a "reserve army" of cheap labour on which capitalists can draw for industrial expansion. The theory has been applied both to developing countries as a whole and to relatively poor regions in industrialized countries. On the international scene, dependency is linked to colonialism and neocolonialism, and some writers have attributed lagging regions in economically advanced countries to species of "internal colonialism."[25]

Dependency theorists also argue that governments and international economic forces, notably the multinationals, have made local communities and small entrepreneurs dependent on forces they cannot control. Rather than providing a setting in which local initiatives can be defined and carried out, the system does the opposite. Major economic decisions are taken in Washington, New York, Toronto, London, and Tokyo, and new economic plans and possible initiatives are defined in far-away Ottawa, in provincial capitals, or worse still, in countless federal-provincial committees of officials who are often scarcely visible to those outside government. The result is that regional economic plans are formulated by officials tied to remote political and economic forces, and local communities and small entrepreneurs have no choice but to play by rules established elsewhere and that will make them dependent on policy-makers or economic actors from away. This dependency theory resonates in many parts of the Maritimes, notably in Cape Breton where foreign investors and federal government initiatives for the island have come and gone.

Leon Trotsky wrote about patterns of uneven and combined development. He argued that capitalism promotes a pattern of development where a core area "projected its wealth on a periphery of regional economic dependencies but never transformed them in its own image." It made peripheral regions dependent on the economic health of wealthier regions. Ian McKay and Robin Bates looked to Trotsky to explain behavioural industrial capitalists located in Boston, London, and Montreal, investing in Nova Scotia's coalfields and steel mills.[26] However persuasive the dependency theory may be to some in explaining the location of economic activities, government officials have paid scant attention to it. They may see merit in the theory's logic, but they find it of little use in defining new measures or in bringing policy and program prescriptions to their political masters. More to the point, they regard it as a complete nonstarter in their work and better left to academics to sort out its strengths and contradictions.

A DIFFERENT DEPENDENCY

Thomas Courchene's 1981 article "A Market Perspective on Regional Disparities" shook Canada's regional economic development community to its core and put it on the defensive. It is still trying to recover. The article became required reading in economic departments, central agencies in

Ottawa, and schools of public policy. Department of Finance and other central agency officials pointed to Courchene's article to challenge regional development programs within the federal government. Officials in the Department of Regional Economic Expansion (DREE) sought to dismiss Courchene's argument, insisting that it ignored national unity considerations and overlooked the department's contributions and their impact on slow-growth regions. DREE had, however, little empirical evidence in the form of solid evaluation reports, or other evidence, showing that its efforts had had a clear positive impact.[27]

DREE launched a policy review in the late 1970s and early 1980s, which to a very large extent sought to square with Courchene's thinking. DREE, or at least its senior officials, no longer saw the department with a mandate to alleviate regional disparities. Rather, it increasingly saw itself as an economic development department with a mandate to focus on all regions, including the have regions. The DREE minister and senior departmental officials told the Senate Standing Committee on National Finance that "DREE is not a welfare agency....Our primary objective...is to help each region of Canada nurture and cultivate those areas and prospects with the best potential for development." This could be best accomplished by "intensive analysis...to identify the comparative advantages of each region."[28] Ottawa's fight against regional economic disparities was over, never to make a reappearance. Accepting that, there was a need for regional development programs because, politicians insisted, the shift away from alleviating regional disparities had the full support of central agencies. Senior DREE officials also saw it as a way for the department to survive in the emerging political and economic environment.

Courchene's contribution to the debate, however, went beyond regional economic development programming. He also linked the dependency argument to federal transfer payments. In a nutshell, Courchene argued that a strong reliance on federal government programs and transfer payments will invariably make a region dependent on them to support current levels of consumption and services, which are much higher than could be sustained by the economic output of the region. He insisted that federal transfers were a "disincentive to efficiency" and "should be scrapped."[29] The dependency syndrome, according to Courchene, also served to blunt the required long-term adjustment that would bring production and consumption into line.

The importance of Courchene's work on policy-makers and public policy is significant. I can think of no article other than his that both unnerved a good number of policy-makers in the regional development field in Ottawa or that had such a seminal impact on policy-making. Some politicians from slow-growth regions tried to dismiss him in the media but with little success. On the eve of the 37th Premiers' Conference in Jasper, the Ontario government released a report on social policy that Thomas Courchene had prepared. The report recommended that the federal government withdraw from a number of social programs. The premiers had gathered on the train that would take them from Edmonton to Jasper, and on the train ride, they discussed the Courchene report. Later, Brian Tobin, then premier of Newfoundland and Labrador, was quoted by the press as claiming, "Courchene was thrown from the train."[30]

It is, of course, one thing to provide a catchy quote for the media to pounce on, but quite another matter to dismiss Courchene's ideas. Courchene gave officials in Ottawa central agencies the ammunition to question federal government regional development programming or at least reinforce their own views. His published work armed already predisposed government officials to tell politicians from slow-growth areas and officials operating in regional development departments that their work was misguided. The Maritimes, more than any other region, felt the impact of Courchene's work, given its reliance on federal transfer payments and the perception that it benefitted the most from regional development programs.

RECENT LITERATURE ON REGIONAL DEVELOPMENT THEORY

Notwithstanding the growth in the number of university programs in regional studies and faculty members sitting in universities puzzling over regional development problems since the 1960s, we have not seen a grand theory to rival that of Adam Smith, Lord Keynes, or Joseph Schumpeter. To be sure, we continue to see a wide array of attempts to describe what is happening in individual regional economies and in some cases to explain why. We have made some progress, but we are still searching for Scott and Storper's missing element.

Certainly, we face daunting challenges. The global economy and how regions fit in it is very confusing and difficult to document. This and other factors, including the fact that regional development has to draw from several academic disciplines, may well explain why we are still struggling to define a general theory that can explain why some regions perform better than others.

However, it has not been for a lack of efforts in developing new theories. We now have theories of polarization, polarization reversal, theories of agglomeration, theories of clustering, new endogenous growth theory, Williamson's comparable general equilibrium model, and the list goes on.[31] All explain only a dimension of the problem. The point is that all these theories are valid somewhere or sometimes, but not everywhere and not all the time. Some are partly relevant to the Maritime region, but many are not. Some have relevance to policy-makers, but most do not.

New trends in technological advances have made managerial decision-making a much more sophisticated and flexible affair. As Allen Scott and Michael Storper put it, "The existing literature on the geography of high-technology industry agrees on one point, i.e., that the classical Weberian theory of location with its emphasis on the individual decision maker is unequal to the task of accounting for the emergence and deployment of whole new sectors of production over the economic landscape. Most attempts to explain the spatial pattern of high technology industry have by contrast struggled to gain a systemic view of its concrete development paths in space and time."[32] The literature helps us understand, albeit to some modest extent, the why, but is limited in helping define the what that can be done to turn slow-growth regions into dynamic ones.

More recent authors have grabbed the attention of policy-makers and somewhat influenced policy-making in the regional development field by focusing on both the why and the what. We need to highlight their contributions. Governments, including some in Canada, continue to look to them for prescriptive measures to promote economic development in regional or urban settings.

FROM FLORIDA TO MORETTI

Richard Florida added a new twist to the debate when he coined the term *creative class* to explain why some regions outperform others. Florida's work has been widely debated on university campuses, in government circles, and in the mainstream media. He argues that a creative class has emerged to become the engine of economic growth at the regional and community levels.[33] He defines creative class as made up of those whose function is to create meaningful new forms. This includes scientists, engineers, university professors, poets, artists, entertainers, think tank researchers, and creative professionals employed in the high-tech sector, financial services, the legal and health-care professions, and business management. Florida writes that many businesses understand what is necessary to attract creative class employees—including relaxed dress codes, flexible schedules, and new work rules in the office—but most civic leaders have failed to understand that "what is true for corporations is also true for cities and regions."[34]

Florida asks why some regions become destinations for the creative class while others do not. His answer: as economists speak of the importance of industries having "low entry barriers," it is similarly important for a place or a region to have low entry barriers for creative people, that is, to be a place where newcomers and creative people are accepted quickly into all sorts of social and economic arrangements. He maintains regions "that thrive in today's world tend to be plug-and-play communities where anyone can fit in quickly. These are places where people can find opportunity, build support structures, be themselves, and not get stuck in any one identity. The plug-and-play community is one that somebody can move into and put together a life—or at least a facsimile of a life—in a week."[35] Florida's thinking resonates better in larger urban settings capable of generating a plug-and-play environment than in the economic environment found in the Maritime provinces, which remains rural to a greater extent than other regions.

We have sought to test Florida's work on the four Atlantic provinces. Four variables were developed by Florida and his colleagues to measure the performance of Canadian city-regions and determine their position in the creative class ranking. They are: the Talent Index, which is the percentage of the population (twenty years and over) with a bachelor's degree; the Bohemian Index, which measures employment in artistic and creative occupations; the Mosaic Index, which is the percentage of the population that is foreign-born; and the Tech Pole Index, which reflects a city-region's degree of specialization in technology-intensive activity. Florida then uses correlations in an effort to measure the strength of linear relationship between pairs of variables. In other words, his methodology does not establish causality between variables. To assess Florida's hypothesis, we selected four urban centres in the region—St. John's, Charlottetown,

Halifax, and Moncton—and evaluated their performance against the top ten city-regions in Canada.[36]

The four Atlantic urban centres did well with respect to the Talent and Bohemian indices but poorly in the others (see table 1 below). The Mosaic and Tech indices are particularly important for a region, because they point to a growing high-tech sector found in high-growth urban centres. The Mosaic Index, meanwhile, points to new Canadians arriving with the determination to have a fresh start for themselves and their families. Both indices also point to the "why" and "what" factors, or why a region has not grown as well as other regions and what can be done to promote economic development. And both reveal that the urban centres in the three Maritime provinces are underperforming when compared with urban centres in other regions. Findings in table 1 reveal the only urban centre in the region that offers promise is Halifax.

Table 1. Creative Class Indices Ranking Summary

Rank by Population	Rank by Creative Class Index			
	Talent	Bohemian	Mosaic	Tech Pole
1 Toronto	1 Ottawa-Hull	1 Vancouver	1 Toronto	1 Toronto
2 Montreal	2 Toronto	2 Victoria	2 Vancouver	2 Montreal
3 Vancouver	3 Guelph	3 Toronto	3 Hamilton	3 Ottawa-Hull
4 Ottawa-Hull	4 Calgary	4 Montreal	4 Windsor	4 Vancouver
5 Calgary	5 Halifax	5 Calgary	5 Kitchener	5 Calgary
6 Edmonton	6 Vancouver	6 Ottawa-Hull	6 Abbotsford	6 Edmonton
7 Quebec	7 Victoria	7 Halifax	7 Calgary	7 Quebec
8 Winnipeg	8 Kingston	8 Winnipeg	8 Guelph	8 Winnipeg
9 Hamilton	9 Saskatoon	9 Ch'town	9 Victoria	9 Kitchener
10 London	10 Montreal	10 St. John's	10 London	10 Halifax
13 Halifax	12 Ch'town	33 Moncton	36 Halifax	17 St. John's
19 St. John's	13 St. John's		39 Ch'town	25 Moncton
29 Moncton	23 Moncton		41 St. John's	30 Ch'town
45 Ch'town			42 Moncton	

Source: Nicole Barrieau, in collaboration with Donald J. Savoie, Creative Class and Economic Development: The Case of Atlantic Canada's Urban Centres *(Canadian Institute for Research on Public Policy and Public Administration, October 2006).*

Florida's work has been challenged on several fronts in recent years. Richard Florida himself recognized some of its shortcomings. He conceded, "On close inspection, talent clustering provides little in the way of trickle-down benefits."[37] Though his work generated a debate in government circles in all three levels of government in the Maritime provinces and generated government spending, it has had little lasting impact on the region's economy.

KRUGMAN AND THE CONCENTRATION OF ACTIVITIES

Nobel laureate Paul Krugman writes that there has been a surge of interest recently in "where economic activities take place."[38] The where in economic activities may not matter to all economists, but it does matter to all politicians. Krugman documents some of the factors that affect geographical concentration of activities: market size and labour markets. He explains that industrial concentration supports a strong local labour market, notably for specialized skills, which enables employees to find employers more easily and vice versa.[39] This accounts for the concentration of the financial industry in Toronto, though rental office space is considerably more expensive than, say, Moncton. It is also easier to find a concentration of marketing or human resources experts, for example, in Toronto than Saint John, New Brunswick. Krugman's work speaks to the importance of head offices to a region's economic health.

Politics and government are also critical elements in the concentration of economic activities. As Krugman noted, "The role of political centralization in causing primacy is at one level fairly obvious: it results both from the direct demand and employment created by the government apparatus and the more subtle advantages of access to government officials. When one asks Japanese executives why they are willing to pay the high cost of keeping their headquarters in central Tokyo, access to officials is usually the first thing they mention." Beyond this direct impact, there is also the multiplier effect or, as Krugman argued, "perhaps even a catalytic effect."[40] As we will see later, this matters in the Canadian context and particularly for the Maritime provinces, given the heavy concentration of power in Ottawa and of senior federal government officials in the NCR.

MORETTI'S NEW GEOGRAPHY

Enrico Moretti's *The New Geography of Jobs* documents the growing difference between the economic well-being of both individuals and communities through geographical lenses. His focus is on the United States, but his observations apply no less to Canada and to the Maritime provinces more specifically. He wrote that the economy has shifted from one centred on producing physical goods to one centred on innovation. He focuses on what he labels the innovation sector and its impact on the location of economic activities.[41]

Moretti maintained that the "distance is dead world," where the Internet would make geography irrelevant has not happened. The key for communities and regions is to grow innovation. He asserted, "Once a city attracts some innovative workers and companies, its economy changes in ways that make it even more attractive to other innovative workers and companies. This tends to generate a self-sustaining equilibrium...which is bound to strengthen over time."[42] He tied innovation to Schumpeter's view of entrepreneurship and the "creative destruction" inherent in innovation. "A market economy is never static. Products that are cutting-edge today will soon be commodified and easy to make. Industries that are on the technological frontier will become mainstream, and later, relics of the past. What is a good job today will inevitably become a bad job in the future....By its very nature, the innovation sector is the part of a market economy where creative destruction matters the most."[43]

How can communities or regions create an innovative culture or promote Schumpeter's creative destruction? How can communities move to the top of the innovative class and stay there? According to Moretti, the key is the arrival of extraordinary entrepreneurs. The arrival of William Shockley, the high-tech entrepreneur who invented the transistor, fuelled the growth of an innovation industry in San Francisco. Had he decided to move to Portland, Maine, Silicon Valley may well have been born between Portland and Boston. I recognize, however, that had Shockley moved to a peripheral region away from a major urban area, the business cluster would have developed elsewhere. Geography still explains two-thirds of everything. Moretti made the point that Henry Ford developed the automobile in Detroit. Detroit did not develop Henry Ford. I note, however, that Detroit is located close to the middle of North America.

To be sure, having a high-functioning research and development (R&D) infrastructure, including a top-flight university in the region, is important, but it is not enough. Moretti concluded that, besides the arrival of extraordinary entrepreneurs, "the economy of a successful city is based on an equilibrium between labor supply and demand: innovative companies (the labor demand) want to be there because they know they will find workers with the skills they need, and skilled workers (the labor supply) want to be there because they know they will find the jobs they are looking for."[44]

Moretti's work and his "distance is not dead" argument are particularly relevant to the Maritimes. The region applauded the arrival of the Internet, convinced that it would help turn things around. The region also bought into the innovation agenda as the way ahead for the region, and governments in the Maritimes continue to commit substantial financial resources to innovation. Indeed, there is no sign to suggest that ACOA and the three provincial governments are abandoning the search for an innovation strategy and R&D activities to spur economic development.

Economic development theorists and many senior government officials started to tie innovation to productivity gains by the 1990s. Innovation in manipulating data and communications enabled firms and workers to produce more goods and services and also to produce them more efficiently. The argument goes that innovation can fundamentally reshape markets, products, and national and regional economies.[45]

The Maritime region has been left to compete against larger and better resourced regions, from Silicon Valley to Waterloo, Ontario, to develop and pursue an innovative strategy. Two students of regional development looked at innovation in Atlantic Canada and sought to establish a difference between "being first or being there." They maintained that the "greatest benefit of R&D spending may not be to increase a firm's ability to develop innovation," but rather "to increase its ability to adopt them."[46] The point is that it may well be better for the Maritime region to pursue a strategy of being there rather than being first. More is said about this later.

NEW REGIONALISM

There is a growing body of literature on new regionalism that ties regional economic development to free trade agreements, globalization, and the new knowledge-based economy. Students of economic development have taken note of the explosion of various forms of regional projects, from an expansion of the European community to the North American Free Trade Agreement (NAFTA), and to assess the impact on regions. We have since seen a plethora of regional trade agreements to which Canada has been a signatory.[47]

The twenty- to thirty-year period after World War Two is regarded as the old regionalism, when there was a "shallow" integration of the regions into the global economy.[48] The impetuses for the new regionalism are regional trade agreements. The thinking is that expanded trade constitutes an important component of economic development. However, there is also a political and governance component to new regionalism: assessing the development of postnational forms of governance. We are seeing local and regional governments operating on their own initiatives, at times in direct conflict with those of their national governments.[49] And we are seeing evidence of this in Canada, as we will see further on.

New regionalism theorists focus on trade, financial and investment flows, the economic integration of regional economies, and the role innovation and knowledge play in regional economies. Regional economies that are "outward-looking" and embrace a neoliberal perspective tend to be more successful, so the argument goes.[50] Canadian students of new regionalism have focused, for the most part, on urban areas and regions as the drivers of economic development. Two political scientists have contrasted the new regionalism with the old, arguing that new regionalism looks to governance rather than government, to process rather than structure, to collaboration rather than coordination, and to trust rather than accountability.[51]

Canadian practitioners of economic development have also been looking at positioning their regions to take advantage of economic opportunities flowing out of new regionalism. Not only are all provincial governments pursuing an outward-looking strategy to capture opportunities flowing out of regional trade agreements, but also the federal government's six regional development agencies are putting in place measures to assist their regions in mapping out their assets to innovate and compete better in the global economy. Looking outward means Canadian regions are looking less and less to one another in pursuing new economic opportunities. If economic ties are growing weaker, so are political ones. This has wide implications for Canada's ability to continue to function as a "giant mutual insurance company."[52]

LOOKING BACK

A single chapter cannot possibly cover the growing body of literature on regional development. This chapter focuses on some of the more important contributions to regional development theory and the literature that resonates better with the Maritime provinces. For this reason and in the interest of space, I have not explored the many contributions that do not apply easily to the Canadian context, and more specifically to the Maritime provinces, or hold the interest of policy-makers or practitioners. All the theories surveyed here hold a kernel of truth, but none provide the complete answer. Indeed, many observers can see merits on both sides of the dependency debate, though both start from a vastly different perspective.

Most of the contributions reviewed are from the United States, Britain, France, and Sweden. And most of the contributors are from large urban centres that are high-performing economic areas (Perroux and Paris; Florida and now Toronto; Moretti and Berkeley). By and large, Canadian policy-makers and students of regional development have adopted and sought to apply theories from abroad. With the exception of the staples theory, homegrown theories of regional economic development are very rare.

Canada, unlike the United States or even Australia, has sought to produce an ambitious regional development policy at the national level.[53] The policy has indeed gone through various reincarnations. Leaving aside Perroux's growth pole, which can hardly be called a success, theories have been of limited assistance to policy-makers in gaining a strong understanding of when government intervention makes sense and when it does not.

Though they likely prefer it that way, Canadian policy-makers at the national level have been able to freewheel, to improvise, to shape measures to meet the requirements of the day, and more importantly, political considerations. Canadian policy-makers have not been able to look to the national governments in other federations (e.g., Australia, the United States, Germany) for lessons in the regional development field because both the economic circumstances and prescriptions in these countries have been and continue to be vastly different. They have also been able to dismiss much of the literature, particularly after they saw that Perroux's growth poles could never constitute the answer while creating political problems in his theory's wake. It bears repeating that what Perroux had in mind could scarcely benefit Canadian policy-makers. But, no matter, Canadian policy-makers sought to apply as best they could Perroux's growth pole theory to the country's slow-growth regions. They soon abandoned the approach, convinced that it was fraught with political problems.

A handful of regional development theories have been tried but they never worked out as envisaged. No theory and no prescriptive measure are a match for political considerations. The only principles or economic theory that appear to prevail, at least for politicians and government officials, are "it depends" and "anything goes." Thus, the regional development field in particular will lend itself to politicians wishing to score political points and to manage political success. This explains how and why regional development efforts have been shaped and reshaped over the years in the Maritime provinces with very limited input from economic theories, as the following chapters make clear.

NOTES

1 Allen J. Scott and Michael Storper, "Regions, Globalization, Development," *Regional Studies* 37 (August–September 2003): 580.

2 Daron Acemoglu and James A. Robinson, *Why Nations Fail: The Origins of Power, Prosperity and Poverty* (New York: Crown Business, 2012).

3 See, among others, Higgins and Savoie, *Regional Development Theories and Their Application.*

4 See, among others, Donald J. Savoie, *Whatever Happened to the Music Teacher? How Government Decides and Why* (Montreal and Kingston: McGill-Queen's University Press, 2013).

5 J. M. Keynes, *The General Theory of Employment, Interest and Money* (Cambridge: Cambridge University Press, 1936), 383.

6 Harold A. Innis, *The Fur Trade in Canada: An Introduction to Canadian Economic History* (Toronto: University of Toronto Press, 1956).

7 Bickerton, *Nova Scotia, Ottawa and the Politics of Regional Development,* 12–13. See also John H. Dales, *The Protective Tariff in Canada's Development* (Toronto: University of Toronto Press, 1966).

8 See, for example, David Easton, *A Systems Analysis of Political Life* (New York: Wiley, 1965).

9 Ernest R. Forbes, "In Search of a Post-Confederation Maritime Historiography 1900–1967," in *Eastern and Western Perspectives,* ed. D. J. Bercuson and P. A. Buckner (Toronto: University of Toronto Press, 1981), 48–49.

10 Ibid.

11 *Living Together: A Study of Regional Disparities* (Ottawa: Economic Council of Canada, 1977), 29.
12 David Boyce, "A Short History of the Field of Regional Science," *Papers in Regional Science* 83 (2004): 31–57.
13 *Living Together: A Study of Regional Disparities*, 28.
14 See Joseph Schumpeter, *The Theory of Economic Development: An Inquiry into Profits, Capital, Credit, Interest and the Business Cycle* (Cambridge: Harvard University Press, 1934).
15 Scott A. Shane, *A General Theory of Entrepreneurship: The Individual-Opportunity Nexus* (Cheltenham, UK: Edward Elgar Publishing, 2003). See also Janice L. Reiff, *Chicago Business and Industry: From Free Trade to E-Commerce* (Chicago: University of Chicago Press, 2013).
16 Scott Shane appears to think so in his *Born Entrepreneurs, Born Leaders: How Your Genes Affect Your Work Life* (Oxford: Oxford University Press, 2010).
17 David C. McClelland and David G. Winter, *Motivating Economic Achievement* (New York: Free Press, 1969).
18 Douglass North, *The Economic Growth of the United States 1790–1860* (Englewood Cliffs, NJ: Prentice-Hall, 1961).
19 Ibid.
20 Benjamin Higgins and Donald J. Savoie, eds., *Regional Economic Development: Essays in Honour of François Perroux* (London, UK: Allen & Unwin, 1988); François Perroux, "Economic Space: Theory and Applications," *Quarterly Journal of Economics* 64, no. 1 (1950): 89–104; François Perroux, "Note sur la notion de pôle de croissance," *Économie Appliquée* no. 1 and 2 (1955); and Karen Polenske, "Growth Pole Theory and Strategy Reconsidered: Domination Linkages, and Distribution," in Higgins and Savoie, *Regional Economic Development*, 93.
21 Higgins and Savoie, *Regional Economic Development*, 54 and 56.
22 John Friedmann, "Planning for Sustainable Regional Development" (keynote address at UNCRD Expert Group Meeting on Integrated Regional Development Planning (May 28–30, 2013), 4.
23 Ralph Matthews, *The Creation of Regional Dependency* (Toronto: University of Toronto Press, 1983), 75.
24 Ibid.
25 See, among many others, Stuart Holland, *Capital Versus the Regions* (London: Macmillan, 1976).
26 McKay and Bates, *In the Province of History*, 77.
27 See, among others, Savoie, *Regional Economic Development: Canada's Search for Solutions*.
28 Canada, *Proceedings of the Standing Senate Committee on National Finance*, no. 3, February 21, 1978, A7 and A8.
29 Thomas J. Courchene, *Economic Management and the Division of Powers*, volume 67 of the Background Studies for the Royal Commission on the Economic

Union and Development Prospects for Canada (Toronto: University of Toronto Press, 1986).

30 See, among others, "Premiers Meet and Bicker," *The Canadian Encyclopedia*, an article reproduced from *Maclean's*, September 2, 1996, www.thecanadianencyclopedia.com.

31 See, for example, Ron Martin and Peter Sunley, "Slow Convergence? The New Endogenous Growth Theory and Regional Development," *Economic Geography* 74, no. 3 (July 1998): 201–27.

32 Allen J. Scott and Michael Storper, "High Technology and Regional Development: A Theoretical Critique and Reconstruction," *International Social Science Journal* 112 (May 1987): 220.

33 Richard Florida, *The Rise of the Creative Class: And How It's Transforming Work, Leisure, Community, and Everyday Life* (New York: Basic Books, 2002).

34 Richard Florida, "The Rise of the Creative Class: Why Cities without Gays and Rock Bands Are Losing the Economic Development Race," *Washington Monthly*, May 2002, https://www.creativeclass.com/rfcgdb/articles/national%20journal%20Rise%20of%20the%20Creative%20Class.pdf.

35 Florida, *Rise of the Creative Class*, 7–8.

36 Nicole Barrieau in collaboration with Donald J. Savoie, *Creative Class and Economic Development: The Case of Atlantic Canada's Urban Centres* (Moncton: Canadian Institute for Research on Public Policy and Public Administration, 2006).

37 Quoted in Joel Kotkin, "Richard Florida Concedes the Limits of the Creative Class," *The Daily Beast*, March 20, 2013, http://www.thedailybeast.com/articles/2013/03/20/richard-florida-concedes-the-limits-of-the-creative-class.html.

38 Paul Krugman, "The Role of Geography in Development" (paper presented for the Annual World Bank Conference on Development Economics, Washington, DC, April 20–21, 1998), 1, http://siteresources.worldbank.org/DEC/Resources/84797-1251813753820/6415739-1251813951236/krugman.pdf.

39 Ibid., 3.

40 Ibid., 21.

41 Enrico Moretti, *The New Geography of Jobs* (New York: Mariner Books, 2013), 10.

42 Ibid., 146.

43 Ibid., 148.

44 Ibid., 187–8.

45 See, among many others, OECD, *A New Economy? The Changing Role of Innovation and Information Technology in Growth* (Paris: OECD, 2000); and M. Pohjola, ed., *Information, Technology, Productivity, and Economic Growth* (Oxford: Oxford University Press, 2001).

46 Yves Bourgeois and Samuel LeBlanc, *Innovation in Atlantic Canada* (Moncton: Canadian Institute for Research on Regional Development, 2002), 37 and 39.

47 Stephen Harper could boast that by the time he left office, Canada had free trade agreements with forty-three countries compared to five when he came to office.

48 See, among many others, W. J. Ethier, "The New Regionalism," *The Economic Journal* 108, no. 449 (1998): 1149-61.

49 Shaun Breslin, Christopher W. Hughes, Nicola Phillips, and Ben Rosamond, eds., *New Regionalism in the Global Political Economy: Theories and Cases* (London: Routledge, 2002).

50 I cannot possibly do justice to the emerging body of literature on new regionalism. I would suggest the reader consult, among others, Robert Gilpin, *The Challenge of Global Capitalism: The World Economy in the 21st Century* (Princeton: Princeton University Press, 2000).

51 Edward C. LeSage Jr. and Lorna Stefanick, "New Regionalist Metropolitan Action: The Case of the Alberta Capital Region Alliance" (paper presented to the Canadian Political Science Association meetings, Winnipeg, June 2004, 11.)

52 Premier Allan Blakeney quoted in Richard Simeon, "Thinking about Constitutional Futures: A Framework" (paper prepared for the C. D. Howe Institute, December 1990), 12.

53 See, for example, Hansen, Higgins, and Savoie, *Regional Policy in a Changing World.*

Part 2
THEY ARE TO BLAME

Chapter 4

HOW IT ALL BEGAN

Canada's regional problem is long-standing and, in many ways, it is peculiar to the country. By contrast, in the United States different regions have taken turns at high growth, as if Adam Smith's invisible hand were constantly at play. It is not much of an embellishment to suggest that United States regional development policy consists essentially of the Senate, defence, and infrastructure spending together with some relatively modest measures for slow-growth areas.[1] To the extent that Canadian regions have taken turns at high growth, it has been tied to natural resources, notably oil and gas, rather than national government policies or programs.

In Canada, the call on the federal government to intervene in the name of regional development or regional equality dates back to Confederation. The Confederation deal had basic flaws that have never been properly addressed. Instead, politicians have sought to deal with the matter through special agreements, ad hoc side deals, and some regional development measures. This chapter looks to history to discuss how Canada was born, what political institutions were put in place, and how they were designed to deal with the country's regional circumstances.

AT FIRST IT WAS ABOUT THE MARITIMES

In September 1863, Charles Tupper, the rising star of Nova Scotia politics, visited Saint John, New Brunswick, to show his support for a political and administrative union of the three Maritime provinces. There, he met Samuel Leonard Tilley, who was no less committed to Maritime union. They also enjoyed the support of the Crown's influential representative in New Brunswick, Arthur Hamilton Gordon, who favoured a conference of the three Maritime colonies to explore full political and administrative union.[2] Gordon only saw benefits to full union, convinced that the three colonies operating independently did not have the necessary human resources to manage properly the affairs of three separate jurisdictions. A former member of Parliament and the son of a former British prime minister, Gordon was a close confidant to W. E. Gladstone, the long-serving British prime minister of the nineteenth century. He held a number of colonial governorships and had special standing in London.

The region's political leadership, with the full support of the Colonial Office, began work on a plan for legislative and administrative union of the three Maritime provinces, leaving it to Queen Victoria to decide where to locate the new capital. By the early 1860s, Maritime union was in the air throughout the region, and the idea was fully debated in the newspapers in the three colonies and among the political and economic elites. Nova Scotia was strongly supportive; New Brunswick had some concerns but only over the details; and Prince Edward Island wanted some concessions given that its debt was less than the other two colonies. The Colonial Office in London favoured union, convinced it would not only lessen its financial burden but also lead to better administration. The three colonies passed resolutions in 1864 in their legislatures, calling for a conference to give life to political and administrative union of the three Maritime colonies.[3]

The conference was to be held in Charlottetown between September 1 and 9, 1864. Work on the details of the proposed union continued throughout the summer of 1864, though signs surfaced that there were challenges ahead. Prince Edward Island had a growing list of concerns, but plans for the conference continued. Both Tupper and Tilley remained strongly supportive.[4]

Sir Charles Stanley Monck, the last Governor General of the province of Canada and the first Governor General of Canada, wrote to the Lieutenant Governor of Nova Scotia, asking for permission to send delegates to attend the Charlottetown Conference. The Maritime provinces agreed to invite them as guests only but, in doing so, set in motion the process that would create Canada.

On the face of it, many participants at the Charlottetown Conference saw merit in a wider political union. The devil, at least from the perspective of the three Maritime provinces, was in the details. But the idea of uniting the British North American colonies held wide appeal in London and at least in Upper Canada or Canada West (Ontario). Political deadlock between Canada East and West led them to look for solutions, and bringing in the Maritime colonies offered promise. There were few other solutions available. Some in Canada East saw a broader federal union as a way to ensure that it could retain its French Canadian identity with a provincial capital in Quebec, while Canada West saw a way to break the impasse between the two Canadas and pursue new market opportunities to the east. The capital of the province of Canada relocated six times in its twenty-six-year history, and the province had to deal with a political crisis every year, at times twice a year between 1854 and 1864.[5] Between 1861 and 1864, there were four governments with none able to provide any degree of stability. All to say that Canada had to deal with a debilitating political problem, and the way to solve it was to bring the Maritime colonies into the equation. Unlike Maritimers, the Canadians were trying simultaneously to get out of a political union that did not work, while creating a new one.[6]

Britain also saw a union of the colonies in a highly favourable light, convinced that it would make them more economically and financially independent. But Britain became concerned, as did all the colonies to the north, with the perception that they favoured the confederacy during the American Civil War. In addition, the War of 1812 was little more than fifty years past, and the horrors of the American Civil War convinced the colonies they should remain loyal to Britain and British-inspired political institutions.

The Fenian raids, including one along the Maine-New Brunswick border in 1866 and its impact on security, were important factors for all the British North American colonies. The Fenians hoped that the Irish immigrants and French Catholics would join forces with them and break away from British influence. While this did not happen, the British colonies felt their security was nevertheless threatened, which translated into support for Confederation.[7] The pro-Confederation forces at home and in Britain exaggerated the menace of the Fenian threat, convinced that it would strengthen their hand.

The failed reciprocity trade negotiations with the Americans in 1866 also favoured a union of the colonies. Canada was looking for new markets, and the three Maritime provinces were nearby and part of the broader British family of colonies. All the colonies also shared a common problem, a weak fiscal position, precisely at the moment when money was needed to finance railway and canal construction.[8]

The Maritime colonies also saw merit in a broader union than in a Maritime union. Prince Edward Island could retain provincial status rather than merge into a full political and administrative union with the other two Maritime provinces. After the United States put an end to its reciprocity agreement with the British colonies to the north in 1866, some—but by no means all—business interests in the Maritime colonies saw potential in an expanding market to the west in contrast to a closed marked to the south.[9]

On the first day of the Charlottetown Conference, Tupper presented a proposal for Maritime union. There was limited traction for Tupper's proposal, and Canadian delegates were waiting in the wings to present their proposal for a larger union. W. S. MacNutt provided a summary of the proposal from the Canadians:

> Cartier's promise that the building of a great nation could be reconciled with the retention of provincial rights and identities, Brown's stress upon the Maritime Provinces as one of the three great regions within the nation, Macdonald's depiction of a strong central government that could protect the interests of all British North Americans, and the financial acumen of Galt, whose mastery of figures overshadowed even Tilley's and who showed that within the federation the three provinces would not really lose revenue, accomplished their desired effect. By the second day of the conference it was the broad mechanism of the proposed federation that engrossed the attention of the Maritimers.[10]

The die in favour of Confederation was cast, and participants were left looking at how to structure the deal. MacNutt added, "There seems little doubt, from what emerged from the unrecorded and semi-secret Charlottetown Conference, that the Canadians were the mentors and the Maritimers the pupils."[10] George Brown, a Father of Confederation, was openly dismissive of Maritime delegates and their "administrative ability."[12] The Charlottetown Conference became known for its lavish entertainment and vast quantities of alcohol rather than any attention to the details of how the new political union might work. That was left to the Quebec Conference.

THE TERMS OF UNION SHIFT

The pressure to have a strong central government overshadowed all other issues. As is well known, Sir John A. Macdonald favoured legislative union, a unitary state. He had to abandon his preference in the face of stiff opposition from Maritimers and French Canadians. He reluctantly settled for the next best thing—a strong central government, convinced that the problems with a weak central government were made evident by the American Civil War, which was still raging during the Charlottetown and Quebec conferences. Indeed, one can question whether Macdonald even had a confederation in mind, let alone a federation. If anything, Macdonald saw regionalism as something to be ignored or at least contained. British political institutions made little concessions to regionalism, and for Macdonald, so should Canadian ones.

Macdonald attached a great deal of importance to importing British-inspired institutions to the new country with minimum modifications. His views carried a lot of weight, given the force of his personality and the fact that he drafted fifty of the seventy resolutions that created the Canadian federation. His vision of a strong central government is evident throughout these resolutions. If Macdonald could have had his way, he would have imported British-inspired institutions to Canada lock, stock, and barrel; he came very close to it. The preamble to the British North America Act reads that Canada's constitution is "similar in Principle to that of the United Kingdom."[13]

Macdonald had a vastly different view on government than the Americans. The American Revolution was against the authoritarian rule of the British monarchy, which led American leaders to craft a series of checks and balances in their constitution to make certain the authoritarian power of a branch of government would not resurface. They ensured adequate balance between the executive, the legislative, and the judicial. For Macdonald, this served to weaken government, and he repeatedly pointed to the civil war raging south of the border as evidence. Federalism was a new concept, and few in Britain understood its finer points. Macdonald also had little interest in understanding the finer points of federalism. His purpose was to solve Canada's problems, unite the British colonies, and concentrate all political power in the hands of the new central government.

Macdonald sought to weaken the federation nature of the union to the point that it would become indistinguishable from legislative union. He wrote, "The true principle of Confederation lies in giving to the general government all the principles and powers of sovereignty, and in the provision that the subordinate or individual states should have no powers but those expressly bestowed upon them. We should thus have a powerful central government, a powerful central legislature, and a powerful decentralized system of minor legislatures for local purposes."[14]

THE DEVIL IS IN THE DETAILS

The difficulty the Maritime colonies had with the proposed union was not with Confederation itself but rather with the terms of the union. Delegates from the region sought constitutional protection for the interest of the smaller provinces, albeit with little success. The fear, as Phillip Buckner explained, was that "Confederation would create a monster, an extraordinarily powerful and distant national government, highly centralized federal union in which Maritimers would have limited influence."[15]

Albert Smith, a leading political figure in New Brunswick, urged New Brunswickers to reject Confederation. He fought against Confederation in the 1865 election and won handily. He told New Brunswickers that the deal would invariably place the interest of Canada ahead of their province. He argued that it was put together by the "oily brains of Canadian politicians" because that colony was "suffering from anarchy and disquiet," while New Brunswick was in a strong political and economic position. He made the case that the Canadas were looking to the Maritime colonies to solve their own political problems and that Canadians would only increase their "dominance as their population and appetite grew."[16]

Smith was not the only Maritimer who voiced strong objections to the Quebec Resolutions that created Canada. Indeed, if today's political rules had applied from 1864 to 1867, Canada, as we know it, would not have been born. No referendum was held in any of the three Maritime provinces, and Nova Scotia never accepted the terms of Confederation.

In New Brunswick, Lieutenant Governor Arthur Gordon simply decided that Confederation was in the best interest of the colony, and he set out to do something about it. He precipitated a crisis with the Smith government by accepting a strongly worded pro-Confederation reply to the Speech from the Throne from the Legislative Council, the colony's unelected upper house. It flew in the face of responsible government with Smith insisting it was his right to be consulted and to recommend. Gordon had little time for the "rights of colonials," barely more than ten years after responsible government came to New Brunswick. The Colonial Office was taken aback by Gordon's initiative, because it was creating a precedent to have an appointed council addressing the Queen on a clearly political issue. Smith was forced to call an election.[17]

Smith took to the hustings denouncing both Gordon and the Quebec Resolutions. He told a packed hall in Saint John that Confederation would render the province "utterly powerless. We are under the controlling power of Messrs. Macdonald and George-Etienne Cartier. And, though in time there would be a change of Government, it would be no better for the people of the Maritime provinces. The interests of Ontario were entirely distinct and at variance with all the other provinces."[18] Smith called for a referendum on any act of Confederation, equal representation for provinces in the upper house, a restricted number of MPs, an assurance of a Cabinet minister for each Maritime province, a court to deal with federal-provincial conflicts, and strict control over taxation.[19] The Colonial Office saw no need for a referendum and nothing came of the suggestions.

Smith would lose the election to pro-Confederation candidate Sir Leonard Tilley, who had the strong backing of the Colonial Office—no small advantage in 1866. He received from Sir John A. Macdonald $5,000 to bribe voters and help persuade the undecided. Luck also intervened on Tilley's side. The Fenians launched raids along the Maine–New Brunswick border precisely at the time Smith and Tilley, with Gordon's help, were crossing swords over the merit of Confederation. The raids considerably weakened anti-Confederation forces in the region, making the case that New Brunswick needed outside help to protect its border through a strong central government.

There were other developments. Gordon's term in the New Brunswick colony was coming to an end, and he did not become an issue in the campaign. Smith's alternative to Confederation ran into difficulties. It proved challenging to secure funding to extend the railway into Maine and the United States market. The United States–Canada reciprocity trade agreement was terminated by the Americans, which had a profound impact on New Brunswick. The Confederation debate had also pushed Maritime union off the political agenda.

Charles Tupper had even greater challenges than Tilley in New Brunswick, attempting to convince Nova Scotians to accept the Confederation deal as struck at the Quebec Conference. Few Nova Scotians shared Tupper's enthusiasm for Confederation as defined by the Quebec Resolutions.[20] When the terms of the Quebec Resolutions, or 72 Resolutions, became known, opposition to Confederation became rampant. Some of Tupper's key political allies, like William Annand, broke ranks, insisting that the Quebec Resolutions were patently bad for Nova Scotia. He saw problems on all fronts: unlike the Canadian colony, both Nova Scotia and New Brunswick would lose financial clout in exchanging customs and tariffs to Ottawa for an eighty-cent subsidy; I return to this point further on. Annand argued Ottawa would use Nova Scotia resources to build canals in Central Canada and to open up the west.

Annand could not understand why Tupper would accept representation by population, which would leave Nova Scotia with only 19 MPs out of 194, with the proportion declining as Canada expanded to the west and north (today Nova Scotia has 11 MPs out of 338). With no ability to counterbalance "rep by pop," he saw Central Canada dominating the federation at will. The Nova Scotia business community also saw little advantage in the new arrangement. Merchants opposed the deal, insisting their markets were across the seas, east and south, and not inland in Canada. Joseph Howe, a powerful orator and editorialist, decided to jump in the debate to oppose the Quebec Resolutions.[21]

Tupper knew full well that he did not enjoy the support of Nova Scotians. Much like Tilley, however, he enjoyed the unconditional support of the Colonial Office and the colony's Lieutenant Governor, then Sir William Fenwick Williams. Tupper did not have to call a general election before 1867 and so could play for time. The Confederation project was not even mentioned in the 1866 Speech from the Throne. When thorny issues about the resolutions were raised, Tupper said he would fix them at the London Conference or the next round of negotiations.

Tupper did introduce a motion in 1866 calling for Maritime union and not Confederation. An MLA, presumably in a side deal with Tupper, cleverly countered with a resolution calling for the appointment of a delegation to attend the final round of negotiations in London with the goal of securing a better deal than the Quebec Resolutions offered. In approving the motion, the assembly was, at least as far as Tupper and Williams were concerned, approving Confederation. The vote went thirty-one to nineteen.[22]

Prince Edward Island rejected Confederation, with delegates from the Island insisting that a country built solely on representation by population would always work against the interest of the province. The proposed Confederation deal only allocated five MPs to Prince Edward Island, a number that would decline as the country expanded west. Island delegates argued essentially for a Triple-E Senate: elected, equal, and effective. But Macdonald and other Canadian delegates rejected it.[23] They favoured an appointed Senate that would resemble Britain's House of Lords. Macdonald and the Colonial Office would not give up so easily on Prince Edward Island or, for that matter, the anti-Confederation forces in Nova Scotia and New Brunswick.

AN EFFECTIVE UPPER HOUSE TO COUNTERBALANCE REP BY POP

Maritime delegates became convinced that "true power" would reside with the House of Commons, given that its members would be elected through rep by pop. As is well-known, the Fathers of Confederation spent an inordinate amount of time debating the mandate and composition of the Senate—a full six of the fourteen days during the Quebec Conference. The proposed Senate mattered to Maritime delegates because they saw it as a way to bring regional balance in national political institutions. In the end, senators were to be appointed rather than elected, and representation would be based on regional equity rather than provincial equity. Delegates from Ontario and Quebec rejected the call for an elected Senate. Ontario delegates feared the two houses would be at loggerheads, and Quebec delegates feared the Senate could not protect their cultural and linguistic position if it had the same number of senators as the smaller provinces.[24]

It was decided that the Maritime provinces would consist of one region while Ontario and Quebec would consist of two, and therein lies the problem. The Americans were forced to have equal representation in their Senate in 1787 to "appease" the small states. No state, no region dominated the negotiations. As Buckner explained, "In the end it was the comparative equality of the two regions which compelled the delegates at Philadelphia to agree to the 'Great Compromise.'" There would be no great compromise in shaping Canada's Confederation because Canada and the Maritimes were of such unequal size. [25]

Sir John A. Macdonald and his fellow delegates from Canada West saw little need for an effective upper house that would speak to Canada's regional circumstances. Federalism was in its infancy and he saw no lesson from the United States model. Macdonald quickly dismissed the call from A. J. Smith of New Brunswick to "give small provinces at least the guard which they have in the United States (i.e., an equal and effective Senate), although we ought to have more, because, here, the popular branch (i.e., the executive branch) is all-powerful."[26] History has proven Smith right. While Maritime delegates pushed for a strong Senate to become the watchdog of regional and provincial rights, delegates from Canada saw the Senate as a safeguard against the potential excesses of democracy rather than a voice for the region. It was to their advantage to see it this way. Sir John A. Macdonald labelled the Senate a place of "sober second thought."[27] For Macdonald, a check on full-blown democracy was far more important than a check on power flowing from rep by pop. Macdonald saw Canada taking shape through the prism of the political and economic interest of Canada West.

Macdonald's label has stuck through the ages, and it has taken away from the Senate's "most crucial role according to the constitution—to give the regions of Canada an equal voice in Parliament."[28] The national media, notably the *Globe and Mail*, the *National Post*, the *Ottawa Citizen* and the CBC, often refer to the Senate as the "chamber of sober second thought" rather than to its regional role.[29] Even the Library of Parliament ranks "regional representation" as the second general role of the Senate behind its sober second thought role.[30] The perceived role, combined with the tendency for prime ministers to reward party faithfuls by appointing them to Senate, has rendered the upper house of little relevance when it comes to representing regional interests. Indeed, Maritime delegates at the Quebec Conference, who insisted the Senate would be too weak to defend regional interest, would be proven correct shortly after Confederation. Canadian delegates ensured that effective political power would reside in the House of Commons when they insisted that the Senate be a politically appointed body with the power to appoint placed in the hands of the prime minister.[31]

There was still, at the time, a healthy distrust of the word *democracy*. The French Revolution and all its excesses were only eighty years old. Even the architects of the American system of government concluded that the will of the people needed to be "tempered by an acute awareness of the potentially negative effects of citizen power, particularly citizens who were not of the chosen body." They were concerned that the "masses" would simply "vote themselves free beer and pull down the churches and country houses."[32] James Madison, in the *Federalist Papers*, issued a strong warning against pure democracy: "Such democracies have ever been spectacles of turbulence and contention, have ever been found incompatible with personal security or the right of property and have in general been as short in their lives as they have been violent in their deaths."[33] This, among other forces, including the desire to model our system of government on Westminster, gave rise to an unelected Canadian Senate.

There was no democratic model for an upper house to guide the Fathers of Confederation. The Westminster model was home to the House of Lords, a hereditary body with some newly minted earls as a check against the excesses of democracy. Senators in the United States were, at the time of Confederation, chosen by the state legislators. Sir John A. Macdonald had no interest in delegating this power to the provincial governments.[34]

Rather than embrace an effective upper house to deal with the demands of the Maritime delegates, the Ontario representatives argued persuasively that the Maritime provinces could always count on Quebec if their province ever attempted to dominate Confederation. It would have been very difficult to assume in 1867 that Quebec would ever agree to support Ontario's economic interests, and vice versa, given the tension between the two at the time. For Canada West, that should have constituted enough assurance to the Maritime colonies that Ontario could never dominate the national political agenda.

They also persuasively argued that the Maritime provinces were in the enviable position of playing the honest broker role between Canada East and Canada West. This would give the Maritime region the balance of power in Confederation and plenty of political clout. Time would show that it by no means constituted a lasting arrangement. Quebec premier Philippe Couillard made this clear when he addressed the Ontario legislature in 2015 and said Ontario and Quebec are "natural allies. Central Canada is an economic force. It is a political force."[35] His comment led the *National Post* to argue in an editorial that "the message here is not Canada First. It's central Canada First."[36] It has always been thus. In recent times, Ontario and Quebec allied themselves in 2014 to develop a list of "local" demands on the Energy East Pipeline project. The two central provinces have also agreed to open up their procurement to each other's companies, but not to any other province.[37]

The trend began not long after 1867, when Ontario and Quebec began to look after each other's economic interests. This was true in building canals, managing the railways, and planning the war efforts. Before Alberta and Saskatchewan were created, some Prairie politicians called for "one Prairie province." The Laurier government rejected the proposal "for the simple reason that such an entity would threaten the dominance of Ontario."[38]

In the pre-Confederation discussions, it was agreed that the Maritimes would have one-third of Cabinet posts to compensate for the representation by population in the Commons. Maritime delegates pressed to have this enshrined in the constitution; however, the request was firmly rejected by Canadian delegates, and it remained only an agreement of convenience designed for the time. Macdonald and other representatives from the Canadas wanted no part of it in the constitution, convinced that it could never square with the Westminster-inspired parliamentary system and that it would fly in the interest of their own region.

Key Maritime representatives, notably Tupper and Tilley, stayed the course. Though both had reservations about the details of the deal, they still saw merit in Confederation because it would lead to the completion of the railway, which, they believed, would open new markets to the west, a stronger capacity to remain loyal to Britain, and enhanced security at home. Tilley, in particular, had his mind set on completing the railway through his province and saw Confederation as the one way to get it done. Both Tupper and Tilley also held out hope that they would be able to modify the Quebec Resolutions at the London Conference.

Macdonald, meanwhile, had one goal in mind: to give all substantive power to the central government, relegate provincial governments to a junior status, and then declare that this was "the best, the cheapest, the most vigorous, and the strongest system of government we could adopt."[39] Not only did British-inspired institutions have little to offer to accommodate regional circumstances, Macdonald had lived with the deadlock between the interests of Canada West and Canada East. His main objective was to deal with the Canadian problem. However, his view of Confederation came at a price for the Maritime provinces. As Margaret Conrad observed, "The structure of Confederation created the framework for the Maritime region's marginalization....Small political jurisdictions had little chance of shaping national policy to meet their needs."[40]

Once the terms of Confederation were made known, there was little enthusiasm in the Maritime colonies for union. As noted, Prince Edward Island opposed union when it could not secure a guarantee that it would have six members in the proposed House of Commons and equal representation in the Senate. The 72 Resolutions were never submitted to the legislatures of Nova Scotia and New Brunswick. As noted, the pro-Confederation party was soundly defeated in New Brunswick in 1865. The New Brunswick electorate had a "latent suspicion toward Canada," and the province's business community saw more promise in developing "railway connections with the United States" than with Canada East and Canada West.[41]

The only support Tilley (in New Brunswick) and Tupper (in Nova Scotia) could secure from their legislatures in the form of resolutions was to continue negotiations in London in 1866. As is well-known, Tupper was able to bring Nova Scotia into Confederation without an election, but his party suffered resounding defeats in both the provincial and federal elections held in the fall of 1867 (thirty-six out of thirty-eight anti-confederationists were elected to the provincial legislature and eighteen MPs out of nineteen in Ottawa).[42] The province had spoken, but the Colonial Office and Canada had other plans.

The deliberations in London can hardly be described as negotiations. The London Conference simply reviewed the 72 Resolutions and later essentially outlined them in a bill that would become law. The New Brunswick and Nova Scotia legislatures never approved the Quebec Resolutions, only a mandate to negotiate better terms—something that they were never able to accomplish. Tupper, for one, came with a specific list of demands and had told the anti-Confederation movement in Nova Scotia that he would push hard for amendments. However, the door to negotiations had already been shut before he arrived, and Tupper failed to secure a single amendment. The Canadian delegates, meanwhile, went to London with a mandate from their legislature not to negotiate but rather to proceed with the Quebec plan. They won the day. Macdonald explained, "These resolutions were in the nature of a treaty, and if not adopted in their entirety, the proceedings would have to be commenced *de novo*."[43]

Objections to the Quebec Resolutions from the Maritimes were politely heard but little came of them. MacNutt remarked, "The Canadians went to London as a disciplined team."[44] One New Brunswick delegate recalled no less than forty objections to the Quebec Resolutions debated in the New Brunswick legislature, but again, nothing came of it in London.[45] At one point, Tilley threatened to go home, but Macdonald knew full well that it was too late for Tilley to back away from the deal.[46] Canadian delegates "manipulated the Quebec Conference and outmanoeuvred the divided Maritimers."[47] In the end, Maritimers had a choice: disregard their commitments to negotiate the Quebec Resolutions and sign on or go home empty-handed. They signed on, realizing that Confederation was only possible through the Quebec Resolutions. If anything, the London Conference weakened further the position of the two Maritime provinces: the London Conference decided to give Ottawa full responsibility for the fishery rather than a shared federal-provincial responsibility like agriculture.[48]

The Canadian delegates, for the most part, simply dismissed Maritime concerns, while colonial officials, with little experience with federalism, were in no mood to intervene on behalf of the Maritime delegates. They were highly in favour of the new union with a strong central government inspired by the Westminster model and saw only advantages to imperial government. Canada, named after the Canadian colony, was born in full accordance with the Quebec plan.

Macdonald, Brown, and Cartier knew very well the Maritime colonies had nowhere to go but to join Canada.[49] Maritime union was off the table, and joining the United States held limited appeal. Macdonald and Cartier were in London to see the deal through as it was defined at the Quebec Conference. Macdonald had Ontario's interest top of mind and Cartier had Quebec's. Macdonald and Cartier did what politicians do—looked after the interest of the political space they represented. Tilley and Tupper tried to do the same and failed, if only because the rules of the political game were vastly different in 1864–1867 than they are today.

Maritimers saw early on that they would lose out on key issues. The 72 Resolutions gave all the power to both indirect and direct taxation to the federal government, leaving the provinces access only to direct taxation, which held very limited possibilities in 1867. Moreover, the Maritimes' main source of revenue at the time of Confederation was indirect taxes (notably customs), but much less so than in Ontario and Quebec. In contrast to Ontario and Quebec, the region also had an extremely weak municipal structure, essentially limited to Halifax and Saint John. Municipal governments, as creatures of the provinces, were able to impose direct taxation in the form of property taxes—the only direct taxation acceptable to citizens in 1867. It soon became clear that New Brunswick and Nova Scotia, with a weak municipal structure and the loss of their main revenue source, would not be able to cope under the new arrangement. Thus began federal transfers to the provinces on a per capita basis. As Richard Saillant has noted, Ontario and Quebec, as a result, "got subsidies that were greater than their needs at the time while the fiscal position of New Brunswick and Nova Scotia would soon become intolerable."[50]

In 1866 customs and excise represented 75 per cent and 72 per cent of revenues for the colonies of Nova Scotia and New Brunswick respectively but only 56 per cent for Canada. Revenue from "realty," meanwhile, represented 23 per cent of revenue for Canada but only 7 per cent for Nova Scotia and 9 per cent for New Brunswick. In relinquishing the right to levy customs and excise taxes and transferring it to the federal government, the two Maritime colonies lost a great deal more than Canada.[51]

Canada and the Colonial Office won the day, but anti-Confederation sentiments in the region did not die. Anti-Confederation sentiments were widespread in Nova Scotia in 1867. Many houses and businesses in Halifax and Yarmouth were draped in black in protest. Effigies of Tupper were burned in Halifax.[52]

As noted, Nova Scotia elected eighteen anti-Confederation MPs to Canada's first Parliament out of nineteen, and five out of fifteen MPs from New Brunswick supported their position. (Charles Tupper, the only pro-Confederation MP, won in Amherst.) The goal of the anti-Confederation MPs was to reverse the decision to join Confederation. Thomas Killam, an anti-Confederation MP elected in Yarmouth, Nova Scotia, declared that the election results in Nova Scotia "proved the hostility of the people to Confederation and the manner in which it was forced on them."[53]

Thirty-six of the thirty-eight provincial seats in the 1867 provincial election went to anti-Confederation candidates. Led by Joseph Howe in Nova Scotia and Albert Smith in New Brunswick, many Maritimers insisted the terms of Confederation were detrimental to their region's political and economic interests. Best to leave Confederation early before the damage was done. Britain, however, was quick to serve notice that it would not allow Nova Scotia to secede from Canada. Responsible government, at the time, be damned.

As Confederation took root, more and more Maritimers concluded that Confederation, no matter the deal, was incompatible with the region's economic interest. They argued the region should, as it had in the past, look to the seas and to trade for economic opportunities. Looking inland was neither in their region's tradition nor ultimately in its economic interest, and it could only benefit the two central provinces.[54]

The anti-Confederation movement lived on in the Maritimes for decades. William S. Fielding led his Liberal Party to victory in Nova Scotia in 1886 on a campaign to take Nova Scotia out of Confederation. He successfully secured a resolution from the Legislative Assembly to ask Ottawa to help the province leave Confederation. Fielding went to New Brunswick and Prince Edward Island to seek their support for seceding from Confederation and also to promote Maritime union. The other two Maritime provinces did not respond and Fielding was prepared to proceed alone. However, his own party split on the issue in the 1887 federal election. More importantly, Britain once again made it clear that it would not agree to Nova Scotia's request to secede.

Prince Edward Island decided to join Confederation in 1873. The colony had rejected Confederation when the Legislative Assembly adopted in January 1866 a strongly worded resolution saying it would not send a delegation to the London Conference. The resolution passed twenty-one to seven, despite strong pressure from the Colonial Office. The Colonial Office and Sir John A. Macdonald did not accept the rejection and continued to apply pressure at every turn until the Island became Canada's fifth province. By the early 1870s, the Colonial Office had the helping hand of Canadian authorities, or perhaps Canadian authorities had the helping hand of the Colonial Office, to persuade Prince Edward Island to join. Britain made it clear that it was "the strong and deliberate opinion of Her Majesty's government that Prince Edward Island should unite with Canada."[55]

The colony ran into serious financial difficulties and encountered problems securing loans to finish the railway construction. In 1869 Britain refused to guarantee a loan to the local government to purchase land from absentee owners—the Island had long sought to deal with absentee land owners with little success—and required the colony to pay the salary of its own Lieutenant Governor. The government sent a message to Ottawa that it was open to joining Confederation, provided it secured a better deal than that set out in 1867. Macdonald jumped at the opportunity, concerned with rumours that the Americans had made overtures to the Island to join the United States. Macdonald had no interest in reforming national political institutions, notably the Senate, but was prepared to give the Island six MPs rather than five as was the case in 1867. (The number has since been adjusted down to four.) In addition, Ottawa agreed to take possession of the railway that was on the verge of bringing the colony to bankruptcy and provide a per capita transfer of $45, an $800,000 loan to buy out absentee land owners, and "continuous" transportation and communications with the mainland.[56]

SIR JOHN A. MACDONALD TAKES CHARGE

Governor General Lord Monck informed Prime Minister Macdonald that he was being called upon to form Canada's first ministry. Ontario and Quebec were well represented in Canada's first Cabinet from day one. Macdonald, from Ontario, turned to Quebec politician Alexander Tilloch Galt to lead the powerful Finance department, though Tilley certainly thought himself competent for the post and expected the appointment. Macdonald turned to another Quebec politician, George-Étienne Cartier, to lead the Department of Militia and Defence; to fellow Ontario politician William Pearce Howland to lead the Inland Revenue Department; to Jean-Charles Chapais from Quebec to lead the Agriculture Department; and to Toronto politician William McDougall to head the high-spending patronage-prone Public Works.

Quite apart from the terms drawn up in Quebec, New Brunswick and Nova Scotia also resented the fact that they were greatly underrepresented in the federal public service. The new service consisted of "little more than" the old bureaucracy of the former United Province of Canada.[57] Officials from New Brunswick and Nova Scotia were, for the most part, frozen out of government appointments in Ottawa. Shortly after Confederation, the civil service numbered five hundred and only two came from the Maritimes.[58] Public servants who retired from the old Canadian bureaucracy were given a pension, while those from Nova Scotia and New Brunswick were not.[59] Tupper and Tilley left for Ottawa to enjoy the benefits of their labour. Others were left to pick up the pieces in Nova Scotia and New Brunswick. Some of the anti-confederates from the two provinces also went to Ottawa to fight Confederation from there, but with no success.

It soon became clear that Albert Smith and Joseph Howe had been right all along: the Maritime provinces were the junior partners in Confederation, with limited influence on the country's political and administrative institutions. Macdonald left no doubt that he saw the provinces precisely in that light. For example, when he went to Halifax to deal with calls from the region for "better terms," he ignored the provincial government. Macdonald met with Joseph Howe to deal with the matter but refused to meet with any provincial politicians, even the premier. For Macdonald, MPs in the House of Commons represented the regions and provinces in Ottawa, while provincial governments were best ignored.[60]

The Great Coalition—Sir John A. Macdonald, George-Étienne Cartier, and George Brown—drove the Confederation deal to bring resolution to the political crisis dividing Canada West and East. They had a debilitating political problem to solve and were less concerned about the finer points of federalism. In contrast, the American federation was inspired by James Madison, Alexander Hamilton, and John Jay, who sought to understand how to make federalism work. They recognized the union of the American states extended over a vast territory and thus the need for a two-house legislature elected on contrasting bases of representation. They saw that simply adapting political institutions designed for a unitary state to a new federation was fraught with danger.[61]

Canada was born at a time when a civil war was raging south of the border. Macdonald and other fathers of the Canadian federation became convinced that a weak central government in Washington was the problem. If Canada had been born fifty years earlier or later, we may well have had national political institutions better suited to accommodate the country's political requirements.

THE MARITIME RIGHTS MOVEMENT

By the 1920s, regional grievances in the Maritimes had reached another boiling point. One of the reasons that led to the Maritimes signing on to a larger political union—railway construction and the subsequent promise of new markets—had been turned on its head, at least from the region's perspective. The Canadian National Railway was mandated to play a key role in managing Canada's railway system, and the integration of the Intercolonial into the national railway system spelled bad news for the Maritimes. Freight rates skyrocketed for Maritime producers to ship to Central Canada, and it became all too clear that they could no longer compete in that market. The railway became a *bête noire* for the Maritimes and "probably the single most important source of anti-Ottawa animus."[62] Western farmers were able to obtain a renewal of the Crow's Nest Pass Agreement on freight rates in 1927, but Maritimers were unable to secure assistance to deal with a "40 percent increase in freight rates."[63] Maritimers also blamed Ottawa for the underutilization of their ports.

A Maritime Rights Movement came into being in the 1920s, and there is now a whole body of literature on the movement, its supporters, its demands, its successes, and its failures.[64] One point is worth stressing: it was non-partisan. As Ernest Forbes explains, the movement had no specific founder or leader, and all of the political parties tried to use the protest movement. But, he adds, the movement was essentially a spontaneous expression of the economic and social frustrations of Maritimers. In the process, however, it brought home the point that the region had been turned into a supplicant. This time, there was less talk of secession from Canada and more about the region becoming an equal participant in the country's economic development. The agenda was one of redress, of bringing pressure to bear on Ottawa to see the light and deal with real regional grievances. The movement gained credibility to the point that in the 1921 general election "regional anger had created a force stronger than party loyalty," a rare development to this day. [65]

The movement was in response to the impact of Ottawa's National Policy that was felt in the 1890s and the region's deindustrialization that followed World War One. Initially, the National Policy had a positive impact, but the wind went out of its sails—at least when it came to the

Maritime provinces—by the turn of the twentieth century. This is discussed further in the next chapter.

The movement met with some success: through the efforts of the movement and its political impact, Maritime supplicants were able to secure *some* concessions. For example, in 1922 it saw a 7.5 per cent decrease in freight rates and the re-establishment of Atlantic regional headquarters of the Canadian National Railway in Moncton (the Canadian government established the Canadian National Railway in 1919, and in doing so had closed the head office of the Intercolonial Railway located in Moncton and moved the staff to Toronto). The Conservatives under Arthur Meighen responded to some of its demands, as did the Liberals under Mackenzie King. The region used its political clout to punish Meighen in 1921 (the Liberals won twenty-five of the region's thirty-one seats), and then Mackenzie King in 1925 (the Conservatives won twenty-three of twenty-nine seats). The results of the 1925 election, as is well-known, led to a period of political and even constitutional instability in Ottawa.

THE DUNCAN COMMISSION

These measures were not enough to satisfy the region, and so Mackenzie King finally decided in 1926 to appoint a Royal Commission, the Duncan Commission, to "focus the discussion into a practicable program."[66] The Nova Scotia government, in its presentation to the commission, argued that national policies had forced the region into a condition of "dilapidation and decay."[67] The Duncan Commission did acknowledge the region's economic difficulties and decline since joining Confederation, but it insisted that factors other than Confederation had been at play.[68] However, when it actually came to explaining the region's underdevelopment, it often pointed to decisions taken in Ottawa and had little to say about the other factors.

The contribution of the Duncan Commission was limited by several restrictions placed on its mandate. It was not to deal with tariff and trade issues, for example, because they were "a matter properly to be considered by the Tariff Advisory Board."[69] But the government's tariff and trade policy, though favourable to Central Canada, had a highly negative impact on the Maritime provinces.

On the question of freight rates and transportation, the commission reported it had definitely "come to the conclusion that the rate structure as it has been altered since 1912 had placed upon the trade and commerce of the Maritime provinces a) a burden which, as we have read the pronouncements and obligations undertaken at Confederation, it was never intended it should bear and b) a burden which is, in fact, responsible in very considerable measure for depressing abnormally in the Maritimes today business and enterprise which had originated and developed before 1912 on the basis and faith of the rate structure as it then stood."[70]

The commission also looked at the steel industry in the region. Again, it stressed that it was beyond its mandate to deal with tariff and trade issues. But, it observed, "Independent evidence of an expert character was given to us, that if due regard were paid to the economic unit of production in steel, there was no reason why it should not be produced as efficiently and cheaply in Nova Scotia as anywhere else in Canada." It added, "A calculation was given to us to show that as a result of the operations of the Customs Tariff, if labour employed in the production of iron and steel and its raw products is taken as the unit for measuring protective value, the protection afforded to Nova Scotia labour is only 28 percent, whereas in Canada the protection to labour is between 85 percent and 100 percent."[71] The commission never reconciled these findings with its claim that factors other than Confederation explained the region's economic decline. Ottawa's National Policy was designed to establish the circumstances for Central Canada's economic success, and Ottawa was not about to jeopardize that.

It bears repeating that Ottawa did not allow the Duncan Commission, or anyone else, to deal properly with tariff and trade issues—which in many ways went to the heart of the problem, given that it was increasingly clear many of the Maritime producers could not compete in the national market. This inhibited the commission's ability to come up with a complete set of practical solutions. In addition, as it became all too apparent later, King's objective in establishing the commission was to defuse Maritime agitation and to engage in a policy of delay. He succeeded.

The region would never again embrace the kind of non-partisan approach to pressuring the federal government as it did under the Maritime Rights Movement. Leaving aside the 2015 general election, the region would never vote as strategically as it did in the 1921 and 1925 general elections. Maritimers, even more than voters in other regions, came to embrace established national political parties and remain loyal to them. Regional grievances would eventually give rise to new political parties in the West (Reform) and Quebec (Bloc Québécois), but not in the Maritime provinces.

The Duncan Commission was allowed to find some practical solutions to the Maritimes' difficulties, but not at the expense of Ontario's economic interests. The fact that Duncan was instructed not to deal in any concrete terms with tariffs and trade issues is ample evidence of this. Duncan also completely ignored the impact of the region's declining representation in the House of Commons and its implications for the three Maritime provinces. Clearly, the commission was established to deal with a political problem rather than a constitutional or economic agenda. When things appeared to get out of hand in political terms, as they did in 1921 and 1925, commissions and special inquiries could serve a useful purpose: diversionary tactics. As history now shows, Mackenzie King (of the famed comment, "conscription if necessary, but not necessarily conscription") was a master in the art of delaying dealing with urgent public policy issues. Mackenzie King successfully employed his considerable skills in the case of the Maritime Rights Movement.

New measures that did result from the Duncan report findings were not nearly as ambitious or, in the end, as effective as the Maritime Rights Movement had initially hoped. Follow-up measures from the Duncan Commission included modest adjustments to federal subsidies to the three Maritime provinces, but the commission's findings gradually disappeared from the public policy agenda. Historian David Frank summed up the legacy of the report in this fashion: "The failure of the report and the weakness of subsequent action may simply have increased Maritime cynicism about the prospects for achieving significant changes through the political process.... For many Maritimers it simply confirmed their skeptical appreciation of the weakness of the hinterland within the Canadian state."[72] Regional ministers from the Maritime provinces would still do their best to secure the odd project for their province, but there was little appetite left in Ottawa to take a broad, comprehensive approach to economic development in the region. The Great Depression was soon on Canada's doorstep, and the prime minister was in no mood to make concessions to the Maritimes.

This is not to suggest that Maritime provincial governments gave up on pressing their claims on Ottawa. For example, in 1944 the Nova Scotia government appointed a Royal Commission containing high-profile and credible members from outside the province to review the "province's disabilities in Confederation." The commission decided to focus on tariff issues. Commission staff sought to provide a cost-benefit estimate of tariffs by calculating the amount by which the tariffs raised prices in each province and subtracting any increases deemed beneficial. To the surprise of no one, the three Maritime provinces came out the heavy losers.[73]

But there has never been any market in Ottawa for this line of thinking, and the Nova Scotia Royal Commission had little impact. Federal government payments to the three provinces could be adjusted, but tariffs went to the heart of the Ontario and Quebec economy. They established the circumstances for economic success in these two central provinces but did the opposite in the Maritime provinces. The nation's political power, concentrated in these two provinces, would decide on its own terms if tariffs could be changed and by how much. Tariffs were central to the health of the national economy, and the national interest—not about to be sidetracked by regional concerns—conveniently aligned, at least from a political perspective, with the two more populous provinces, while the regional interest pertained to the three Maritime provinces.

DEFINING THE NATION THROUGH GOVERNMENT INITIATIVES

From the mid-1930s onward, Maritime concerns became subsumed by the nation's broader socioeconomic problems. By then, many in Ottawa started to accept as inevitable the decline of the Maritime economy, given its location on the periphery of a tariff-protected Canadian market. In any event, the nation had bigger issues to address. The Great Depression was one, another was the federal government's apparent inability to respond to the challenges it presented. If the National Policy constituted the first phase in Canadian nation-building, the federal government's spending power would constitute the second.

The Great Depression had harshly revealed Ottawa's inability to use public policy to deal with a disastrous economic downturn. In addition, many leading intellectuals and Canadian nationalists in Ontario became disturbed over the resurgence of assertions of provincial rights. Keynesian economics, which advocated government spending as the way out of economic depressions, came into fashion in Ottawa. But Ottawa could not do this, if only because provincial governments were, on the whole, more concerned with trying to balance their budgets by cutting spending and raising taxes than with introducing new spending measures to stimulate economic activities. Such practices were precisely what Lord Keynes argued would only serve to worsen matters.

In 1937 Mackenzie King established the Rowell-Sirois Commission to carry out "a re-examination of the economic and financial basis of Confederation and of the distribution of legislative powers in light of the economic and social developments of the last seventy years."[74] The problem, according to Ottawa, was straightforward. Canada's constitution, then the British North America Act, had in its day granted the federal government all-important political and economic power, but times had changed, and the Act was ill-suited to respond to current realities. In light of the Depression years and the development of the modern state, Canada required access to public policy levers that the constitution had given to the provinces. The key ones were social welfare and the implementation of macroeconomics policies such as those inspired by Keynesian economics.[75] That said, Ottawa recognized that amending the constitution, as Canadian history has so often revealed, would be difficult, if not impossible.

It came as no surprise, then, that the 1940 Rowell-Sirois Report stressed the need for integrating federal-provincial fiscal policies more effectively and, at the same time, sought to give Ottawa a much stronger hand in managing them. By the time the report was tabled, Ottawa had already begun to carve a role for itself in the social policy field. For example, it had done the impossible and secured a constitutional amendment to allow the federal government to assume full responsibility for unemployment relief, which enabled it to establish an Unemployment Insurance Fund. In addition, as part of managing the wartime economy, the federal government was able to convince the provinces to leave the personal and corporate income tax field for the duration of the war in return for grants calculated on estimates of what the provinces would have collected. When the war ended, Ottawa tried to retain its monopoly on income tax, but the provinces disapproved. It had been only thirty years since the provincial governments had granted "consent" for the federal government to enter the income tax field. They were not about to vacate the field completely to let Ottawa have a free hand in imposing new taxes.

The result was the development of an elaborate system of shared revenues and responsibilities, the remnants of which can still be found today in health, education, and social services spending. It was not Ottawa's preferred option, but it would have to do. It did, however, hand the federal government a great deal of power over the country's fiscal policies. Historian W. L. Morton labelled the 1936–49 period "the Revival of National Power,"[76] and it served Ontario well. As John Ibbitson wrote, "After the Second World War, Queen's Park and Ottawa collaborated to ensure that the rest of the federation served the interests of the economic heartland."[77] Ibbitson could have added that Ontario and Ottawa have always looked after the interests of the economic heartland, starting with the terms of the constitution and the National Policy as defined in 1878.

Why, one may ask, would Maritime premiers agree to an expanding role for the federal government in the postwar period? They would have a first-hand appreciation of the bias that Ottawa, C. D. Howe, and his bureaucrats had for Central Canada. In addition, Oxford-educated New Brunswick premier J. B. McNair understood the finer points of the Canadian constitution—probably better than many of the other provincial premiers—and one can only assume he was well aware New Brunswick no longer had the political clout to influence Ottawa in the event the federal government was able to carve out a greater role for itself. Furthermore, McNair had repeatedly stressed the importance of provincial autonomy.

There were, it appears, two reasons for New Brunswick's support for an expanded role for the federal government. First, when McNair replaced A. Dysart as premier in 1940, New Brunswick was literally on the edge of bankruptcy, and the "province's Montreal bankers were threatening to foreclose."[78] With the bankers at its throat, the province was scarcely in a position of strength to bargain with Ottawa. Indeed, it needed Ottawa's financial help simply to continue to operate. As well, McNair was a partisan Liberal. Partisan politics had come to matter a great deal more in New Brunswick in the 1940s than it had in the 1920s, and McNair took a back seat to no one when it came to partisan politics.

Second, Maritime premiers would have had reasons for a degree of optimism in supporting the findings of the Rowell-Sirois Report. While it is true the report did not look directly at tariff issues, trade patterns, or for that matter, economic development, it did the next best thing, at least from a Maritime perspective. It recommended "that the wealth produced nationally should be taxed nationally and redistributed on a national basis, instead of being taxed in the main by the central provinces for the benefit of the central provinces."[79] In other words, while the commission did not want to change the location of wealth produced in the country or the circumstances it had established for economic success in Central Canada, it argued the resultant benefits should be shared nationally. More to the point, it was now prepared to not only establish circumstances for economic success, but also manage the benefits of economic success. Ontario, and to some extent Quebec, would benefit from the circumstances for economic success established by Ottawa, while the Maritime provinces would benefit from Ottawa's desire to manage economic success.

Janine Brodie nicely summed up the findings of the Rowell-Sirois Commission in her observation: "The grants would simply help to underwrite some of the social costs of uneven development within certain political jurisdictions, for example, New Brunswick, while the economic relationships that promoted uneven development remained unchallenged."[80] Thus, the idea of a form of fiscal equity in Canada was born so that, while the national economy (as defined by Ottawa) should be promoted, dividends flowing from it should be shared with all regions.

When then prime minister Mackenzie King sought to overhaul Canada's taxation and social policy infrastructure and implement the findings of the Rowell-Sirois Report at a federal-provincial conference, he met with firm and highly vocal opposition from both Ontario and Quebec. The notion that Quebec would never side with Ontario—a point Canadians made to convince Maritimers to join Confederation—no longer held. Anyone with any foresight should have known in 1867 that it hardly constituted much of a guarantee over the longer term. The premiers of Ontario and Quebec told Mackenzie King the initiative was a nonstarter, so much so that Ontario premier George Drew hysterically characterized the reform package as Hitlerism. Ontario saw little merit in sharing the wealth produced nationally, and Quebec objected to Ottawa's intrusion in its jurisdiction. But Quebec and Ontario's opposition served another purpose: "The central Canadian premiers' opposition confirmed the Maritime premiers' good opinion of King's plans."[81]

Ontario's opposition to sharing wealth melted by the 1950s. Then Ontario premier Leslie Frost argued in 1956 that the Maritime provinces should receive additional transfer payments because of their greater need.[82] Ernest Forbes explained why: "A Maritimer replacing a refrigerator might expect to borrow the money from a Toronto-based bank, insure the loan through a Toronto-based insurance company, and buy an Ontario-manufactured appliance wholesaled and retailed through a Toronto-based department store. The funds transferred to the Maritimes one month, either through increased equalization payments or through federally-funded social programmes, could be expected to return to the metropolis the next through the purchase of goods and services."[83]

THE GORDON COMMISSION

About fifteen years after the Rowell-Sirois Commission tabled its findings, the St-Laurent government asked Walter Gordon to chair yet another Royal Commission, this one on Canada's economic prospects. The Maritime provinces decided to participate actively in the work of the Gordon Commission. The region prepared twenty-three submissions; virtually all of them "were couched in the now familiar language of regional grievance."[84]

The Gordon Commission is perhaps best known for expressing serious concerns over the impact of foreign ownership in the Canadian economy. It also had important things to say about the deepening patterns of uneven development. It went beyond the issue of fiscal need to suggest ways to improve the performance of regional economies. Still, the commission decided not to address "the causes of uneven development" between the regions.[85] Such inequity was taken as a given that need not be revisited. Instead, the challenge, as the commission saw it, was to find ways to promote economic development in slow-growth regions without hurting the stronger provinces, in particular Ontario.

Hugh John Flemming, then New Brunswick premier, played a lead role on behalf of the Maritime provinces in the work of the Gordon Commission and in making representations to Ottawa in support of the region. He decided to organize a major conference in New Brunswick on the region's economic prospects and invited the other three Atlantic premiers to participate. He felt that having four provinces speaking to a new economic plan would force Ottawa to take the proposed agenda seriously. The other three premiers agreed, and the first ever conference of Atlantic premiers was held in Fredericton on July 9, 1956. Flemming led the charge, arguing the region should press Ottawa for subsidies based on fiscal need, assistance for resource development, a new regional transportation policy, different monetary and fiscal policies to stimulate economic development, and a new tariff policy in line with the region's economic interests. Nova Scotia then premier Henry Hicks recommended they ask Ottawa to place more defence industries and contracts in the region as the United States had done and continues to do. The difference is that in the United States, the Senate was making the call, not the lone voice of a premier operating over a thousand kilometres from the nation's capital.[86] Still, the region was becoming more demanding. The focus was no longer restricted to fiscal needs for provincial governments but on a helping hand to promote economic development.

At the same time, however, there were concerns increasingly heard in Ottawa that the federal government ought not to play regional favourites; that is, Ottawa should not agree to any special concessions for the Maritime provinces in the economic development field, unless it was prepared to make them available to the other regions. The prevailing view in Ontario was that all federal payments to the provinces should be made on an "equal" basis. New Brunswick historian MacNutt rebutted this view: "Where is the equalization in the operation of tariff policy...in the St. Lawrence Seaway, in the pipeline contract? We can say that, since we started on fairly even terms in 1867, equalization as seen from Ottawa has had some curious results."[87] In its last budget, the St-Laurent government announced plans to introduce annual Equalization payments to the have-less provinces. By that time, the Gordon Commission had also submitted an interim report and recommended that "a bold, comprehensive and coordinated approach" be implemented to resolve the underlying problems of the Atlantic region, which, in the commission's opinion, required special measures to improve its economic framework. These recommendations included a federally sponsored capital project commission to provide needed infrastructure facilities to encourage economic growth and measures to increase the rate of capital investment in the region.

In many ways the Gordon Commission was breaking new ground by advocating for the involvement of the private sector in promoting development in slow-growth regions. Perhaps for this reason, the commission expressed concerns about any negative impact on other regions. It argued that "special assistance put into effect to assist these areas might well adversely affect the welfare of industries already functioning in more established areas of Canada."[88] The point was once again clear: the government could assist the Maritime provinces, but not at the expense of other regions, notably Ontario. However, the fact that Ontario benefitted from National Policy and the war efforts at the expense of the Maritimes (as we will see later), did not seem to figure in the equation. No one told Ottawa from 1878 onward that its special assistance to Central Canada should avoid adversely affecting the welfare of industries already established in the Maritimes. National political institutions were designed to give voice to rep by pop and thereby give political power to the more populated regions, leaving the regional voice on the outside with no effective influence, let alone power.

DISCOVERING REGIONAL DEVELOPMENT

In retrospect, it is now clear that the election of John Diefenbaker as prime minister constituted a watershed for the Maritime provinces. Unlike long-serving prime ministers Sir John A. Macdonald, Sir Wilfrid Laurier, William Lyon Mackenzie King, and Louis St-Laurent, Diefenbaker was from neither Ontario nor Quebec. Furthermore, he had strong political ties to the Maritime region. Hugh John Flemming moved Diefenbaker's nomination at the party's national leadership convention, and Robert Stanfield, the newly elected premier of Nova Scotia, delivered the convention's keynote address. Diefenbaker's Conservatives had garnered 112 seats in the June 1957 general election, 61 more than the party had in the previous general election. He went on to form a minority government, having won only 7 seats more than the Liberals. In forming his government, he appointed a twenty-two-member Cabinet, including four ministers from Atlantic Canada. For the first time in Canadian history, there were more ministers from Atlantic Canada and Western Canada than from Central Canada.

Diefenbaker had included an "Atlantic Manifesto" as an important part of his 1957 election platform. The manifesto borrowed heavily from Flemming's Fredericton conference of Atlantic premiers and the Gordon Commission. It urged the federal government to provide assistance in the following areas: electrical power development in the region, further freight-rate adjustments, capital projects, adjustment grants to the provinces, a Canadian coast guard, and a national resource-development program.[89] Though the federal

Department of Finance was quick to recommend a "go-slow" approach to Atlantic Canada, Diefenbaker had, within a year of coming to power, implemented several significant measures for the region, including a loan to help develop the Beechwood Dam in New Brunswick and a $25 million special adjustment grant to Atlantic Canada.[90] In addition, measures to promote economic development on the Prairies would indirectly help the Maritime provinces. The Diefenbaker government introduced a number of regional development measures designed to promote development in slow-growth rural areas with a focus on Western and Atlantic Canada. Thus began the alphabet soup of acronyms for regional development programs—the Agricultural Rural Development Act (ARDA) and the Fund for Rural Economic Development (FRED). This would gave rise to the Department of Regional Economic Expansion (DREE), which I review later.

LOOKING BACK

Most historians agree that the terms for Confederation adopted at the Quebec Conference reflected "Canadian needs and Canadian priorities" and ensured that Central Canada would dominate the country's national political institutions.[91] Canadian delegates and the Colonial Office, which had very little appreciation for the workings of federalism—in particular how to balance representation by population with regional interests—drove the negotiations. From a Maritime perspective, Confederation was a flawed deal, and the flaws remain visible to this day. The institutional setting put in place by Sir John A. Macdonald and others of like mind did not fit with a continental landscape that remains home to distinct regional economies. How national political institutions were formulated made the Maritime provinces the big losers in the Confederation deal, and the impact has been deeply felt through the years.

There was no referendum, and elected representatives from the Maritime provinces had strong reservations about the merits of Confederation. In fact, a majority of Nova Scotians were opposed to the deal, and their opposition to Confederation did not diminish after 1867. Indeed, a secessionist government was once again elected in Nova Scotia in 1886, but Britain continued to emphasize that leaving Confederation was a nonstarter, notwithstanding what electors felt. Apparently, Britain's Colonial Office was in collusion with colonial politicians from all the colonies to ensure

Confederation would see the day with no concern for how best to accommodate regional circumstances in a federal state.

For Sir John A. Macdonald and other delegates from Canada West, regionalism was something to be contained rather than accommodated. For evidence, they only had to look to the civil war raging in a federal state to the south and to the political instability in the Canadas, where, as the Earl of Durham wrote, "Two nations [were] warring in the bosom of a single state."[92] Macdonald wanted to solve the Canada problem, and the Maritime provinces represented a convenient means of doing so. Macdonald also saw the need to reconcile the conflicting interests of two linguistic communities to address the fear of the westward expansion of the United States and to build or improve a railway that cut through several colonies. He and his colleagues from Canada West also saw the need for a strong central government to pursue these goals and to implement in Ottawa Westminster-styled political and administrative institutions.

Though concerned about giving substantial power to the central government, George-Étienne Cartier's goal was to ensure the English and French languages would enjoy equal states in Parliament and in the legislature and courts of the province of Lower Canada. Cartier got what he wanted out of his negotiations. The key architects of Confederation—Macdonald, Brown, Galt, and Cartier—also got what they wanted: a treaty to create a country out of *deux nations*, with the Maritime colonies little more than convenient pawns. Brown got "representation by population" to establish political power and an ineffective Senate. Cartier got some protection for the French language in the new Parliament and the courts. Galt got financial terms that favoured Central Canada. And Macdonald got a highly centralized federation with British-inspired institutions to guide it. Tupper and Tilley got a commitment to build a national railway that would in time serve the economic interests of Central Canada, given the country's geography and the National Policy, which favoured east-west trade. A number of politicians and journalists from Central Canada often dismiss this as "regional envy" and "Maritime grievances." It is an easy and convenient way to deal with the issue. They make little effort to understand the root cause of "regional envy."[93]

Other than the commitment to build a national railway, Tupper and Tilley did not get what they wanted, and Prince Edward Island simply walked away from the negotiations. The three Maritime colonies wanted a capacity at the centre to accommodate regional interests and not, in the words of Albert Smith, to be "utterly powerless, under the controlling power of Messrs. McDonald and Cartier."[94] Unlike Canadian delegates, Maritime delegates were never able to negotiate from a position of economic and political strength between 1864 and 1867. No one knew this better than Sir John A. Macdonald and the Colonial Office. Nothing has changed on this front since 1867. If anything, the political and economic strength of the Maritime provinces has weakened substantially over the past 150 years.

Leaving aside the Charter of Rights and Freedoms, Canada has not been able to change its constitutional arrangements and the workings of its national political institutions to accommodate fast-changing socioeconomic circumstances. Canada, and the requirements of the modern economy, look vastly different today than they did in 1867; however, our constitution and our national political institutions, notably the Senate, look fundamentally the same. The Senate is today a largely discredited institution unable to articulate, let alone promote, Canada's regional interests. Time will tell if Justin Trudeau's modest reform package will have much of a positive impact for the smaller provinces. Other federations have a legitimate upper house as a central feature of their national political institutions designed to give voice to regional perspectives. Our Senate has a confused mandate, oscillating between occasionally speaking for the regions and acting as a chamber of sober second thought, all the while lacking political legitimacy. A weak Parliament combined with a powerful executive that draws its power from the most populous provinces has enabled the big dogs to eat first. This, among other developments outlined in following chapters, explains why many Maritimers view the Canada to which they owe their loyalty as the Canada we have failed to create.[95]

Politicians have been left to accommodate regional concerns on the fly. They have tried to patch and to spot-weld here and there with Royal Commissions, special fiscal arrangements, and regional development measures. These, however, have only played at the margin and have never addressed the fundamental regional problem in Canada. The following chapters review the efforts at spot-welding the Maritime economy and at promoting regional economic development.

NOTES

1 See Higgins, Hansen, and Savoie, *Regional Policy in a Changing World*, 195.

2 MacNutt, *New Brunswick: A History*, 415.
3 Ibid., 418.
4 Ibid., 418–9.
5 See, for example, J. M. S. Careless, *The Union of the Canadas: The Growth of Canadian Institutions 1841–1857* (Toronto: McClelland and Stewart, 1967).
6 Phillip A. Buckner, "CHR Dialogue: The Maritimes and Confederation: A Reassessment," *The Canadian Historical Review* 71, no. 1 (March 1990): 25.
7 Greg Marquis, *In Armageddon's Shadow: The Civil War and Canada's Maritime Provinces* (Montreal and Kingston: McGill-Queen's University Press, 1998).
8 Savoie, *Visiting Grandchildren*, 23.
9 See Marilyn Gerriets and Julian Gwyn, "Tariffs, Trade and Reciprocity: Nova Scotia, 1830–1866," *Acadiensis* 22, no. 2 (Spring 1996): 22–39.
10 MacNutt, *New Brunswick: A History*, 420.
11 Ibid., 421.
12 See, among others, Richard Gwyn, *John A: The Man Who Made Us* vol. 1 (Toronto: Vintage Canada, 2008), 365.
13 "British North America Act 1867 Document," *The Canadian Encyclopedia*, last edited December 16, 2013, www.thecanadianencyclopedia.ca/en/article/british-north-america-act-1867-document/.
14 Quoted in Ed Whitcomb, *The Canadian Government and Federalism* (Ottawa: From Sea to Sea Enterprises, forthcoming), 94.
15 Phillip A. Buckner, "The Maritimes and Confederation: A Reassessment," *Canadian Historical Review* 71, no. 1 (March 1990): 117.
16 C. M. Wallace, "Smith, Sir Albert James," in *Dictionary of Canadian Biography*, vol. 11, University of Toronto/Université Laval, 2003, www.biographi.ca/en/bio/smith_albert_james_11E.html.
17 Ibid.
18 Albert Smith quoted in ibid.
19 Wallace, "Smith, Sir Albert James."
20 Whitcomb, *A Short History of Nova Scotia*, 29.
21 Ibid., 30.
22 Ibid.
23 Ibid.
24 See, among others, Jack Stilborn, *Senate Reform: Issues and Recent Developments* (Ottawa: Library of Parliament, 2008).
25 Buckner, "CHR Dialogue: The Maritimes and Confederation," 7.
26 Quoted in ibid., 49.
27 See, among others, the Honourable Noël A. Kinsella, *Forewords: The Senate Report on Activities, 2010*, n.d., http://sen.parl.gc.ca/portal/AnnualReports/2009-2010/forewordhnk-e.htm.
28 Richard Foot, "Senate," *The Canadian Encyclopedia*, last edited May 13, 2016, www.thecanadianencyclopedia.ca.

29 See, among many others, "A Senate Still Searching for Sober Second Thought," *Globe and Mail*, February 13, 2013.

30 Stilborn, *Senate Reform: Issues and Recent Developments*, 2.

31 Buckner, "CHR Dialogue: The Maritimes and Confederation," 28.

32 Cheryl Simrell King and Camilla Stivers, "Citizens and Administrators: Roles and Responsibilities," in *Public Administration and Society: Critical Issues in American Governance*, ed. Richard C. Box (London: M. E. Sharpe, 2004), 272.

33 James Madison, "The Federalist Papers, No. 10: The Utility of the Union as a Safeguard against Domestic Faction and Insurrection," *Daily Advertiser* (New York), November 22, 1787, http://www.constitution.org/fed/federa10.htm.

34 See, among others, Gwyn, *John A: The Man Who Made Us*; and Richard Gwyn, *Nation Maker: Sir John A. Macdonald: His Life, Our Times*, vol. 2 (Toronto: Random House Canada, 2011).

35 "Quebec Premier Couillard Addresses Ontario Legislature, First Premier to Do So in over 50 Years," *National Post*, May 11, 2015.

36 "This Is Not Federalism," *National Post*, May 13, 2015, A8.

37 Ibid. See also "Premiers Wynne and Couillard Set Seven Criteria for Energy East," *Globe and Mail*, November 21, 2014.

38 David E. Smith, Federalism and the Constitution of Canada (Toronto: University of Toronto Press, 2010), 24.

39 Quoted in Peter Waite, *The Life and Times of Confederation, 1864–1867* (Toronto: University of Toronto Press, 1963), 40.

40 Margaret Conrad, "When Ottawa Sends Money to Atlantic Canada, It's Called a Handout," n.d., available at www.uni.ca/lb_conrad_e.html (site discontinued).

41 Hugh Thorburn, *Politics in New Brunswick* (Toronto: University of Toronto Press, 1961), 12.

42 G. A. Rawlyk and Doug Brown, "The Historical Framework of the Maritimes and Confederation," in *The Atlantic Provinces and the Problems of Confederation*, ed. G. A. Rawlyk (St John's: Breakwater, 1979), 10.

43 Quoted in George F. G. Stanley, "Act or Pact Another Look at Confederation," Presidential address, Canadian Historical Association, 1956, mimeo, 12.

44 MacNutt, *New Brunswick: A History*, 456.

45 Ibid., 457.

46 Donald Creighton, *The Road to Confederation: The Emergence of Canada, 1863–67* (Toronto: Macmillan, 1964), 444.

47 Buckner, "CHR Dialogue: The Maritimes and Confederation," 3.

48 Whitcomb, *A Short History of Nova Scotia*, 31.

49 Gwyn, *John A: The Man Who Made Us*, 364.

50 Canada, *Report of the Royal Commission on Dominion-Provincial Relations*, 1 (Ottawa:King's Printer, 1940). Also known as the Rowell-Sirois Report.

51 Claude Bélanger, *The Maritime Provinces, the Maritime Rights' Movements and Canadian Federalism*, mimeo, n.d., 3 and 4.

52 "Provinces and Territories" Library and Archives Canada, last modified October 10, 2014, www.bac-lac.gc.ca/eng/discover/politics-government/canadian-confederation/Pages/nova-scotia-1867.aspx.

53 Quoted in How, *A Very Private Person: The Story of Izaak Walton Killam and His Wife Dorothy*.

54 Ibid.

55 Ibid.

56 Francis Bolger, *Canada's Smallest Province: A History of Prince Edward Island* (Halifax: Nimbus, 1973); and Frank MacKinnon, *The Government of Prince Edward Island* (Toronto: University of Toronto Press, 1951).

57 Janine Brodie, *The Political Economy of Canadian Regionalism* (Toronto: Harcourt Brace Jovanovich, 1990), 145.

58 See Starr, *Equal As Citizens*, 30.

59 Whitcomb, *A Short History of Nova Scotia*, 33.

60 Ibid., 33–34.

61 John Dunn, *Setting the People Free: The Story of Democracy* (London: Atlantic Books, 2005).

62 Rawlyk and Brown, "Historical Framework of the Maritimes and Confederation," 26.

63 David Frank, "The 1920s: Class and Region, Resistance and Accommodation," in *The Atlantic Provinces in Confederation*, ed. E. R. Forbes and D. A. Muise (Toronto: University of Toronto Press, 1993), 253.

64 For an excellent history of the movement, see Ernest R. Forbes, *The Maritime Rights Movement, 1919–1927: A Study in Canadian Regionalism* (Montreal and Kingston: McGill-Queen's University Press, 1979).

65 Ibid., 29.

66 Ibid., 158.

67 Frank, "The 1920s: Class and Region, Resistance and Accommodation," 258.

68 Quoted in David G. Alexander, *Atlantic Canada and Confederation: Essays in Canadian Political Economy* (Toronto: University of Toronto Press, 1983), 36.

69 D. A. Muise, "The 1860s: Forging the Bonds of Union," in *The Atlantic Provinces in Confederation*, ed. E. R. Forbes and D. A. Muise (Toronto: University of Toronto Press, 1993), 36.

70 See ibid., 21.

71 Sir Andrew Duncan, *Report of the Royal Commission on Maritime Claims* (Ottawa: F.A. Acland, 1926), 21.

72 Frank, "The 1920s: Class and Region, Resistance and Accommodation," 261.

73 Ibid., 229.

74 Donald Smiley, ed., *The Rowell-Sirois Report*, Book 1 (Toronto: McClelland and Stewart, 1963), 2.

75 Janine Brodie added, "measures to reconstruct a peacetime economy." See Brodie, *The Political Economy of Canadian Regionalism*, 149.

76 W. L. Morton, *The Kingdom of Canada* (Toronto: McClelland and Stewart, 1963), 465.
77 John Ibbitson, *Loyal No More: Ontario's Struggle for a Separate Destiny* (Toronto: HarperCollins, 2001), 5.
78 Carman Miller, "The 1940s: War and Rehabilitation," in *The Atlantic Provinces in Confederation*, ed. E. R. Forbes and D. A. Muise (Toronto: University of Toronto Press, 1993), 326.
79 Ibid., 479.
80 See, among others, Brodie, *The Political Economy of Canadian Regionalism*, 145.
81 Miller, "The 1940s: War and Rehabilitation," 328.
82 J. L. Kenny, "Politics and Persistence: New Brunswick's Hugh John Flemming and the Atlantic Revolution 1952–1960" (master's thesis, University of New Brunswick, 1988), 68–88.
83 Ernest R. Forbes, ed., *Challenging the Regional Stereotype: Essays on the 20th Century Maritimes*, (Fredericton: Acadiensis Press, 1989), 210.
84 Margaret Conrad, "The 1950s: The Decade of Development," in *The Atlantic Provinces in Confederation*, ed. E. R. Forbes and D. A. Muise (Toronto: University of Toronto Press, 1993), 407.
85 See, among others, H. Lithwick, "Federal Government Regional Economic Development Policies: An Evaluative Survey," in *Disparities and Interregional Adjustment*, ed. K. Norrie (Toronto: University of Toronto Press, 1986), 116.
86 See, among others, "The Fredericton Conference of Atlantic Premiers," *Atlantic Advocate*, September 1956, 28. See also Conrad, "The 1950s: The Decade of Development," 408.
87 W. S. MacNutt, "The Fredericton Conference: A Look Backward and a Look Forward," *Atlantic Advocate*, September 1956, 13.
88 Canada, *Report of the Royal Commission on Canada's Economic Prospects* (Ottawa: Queen's Printer, 1957), 494.
89 See *Atlantic Advocate*, July 1957, 11.
90 See Conrad, "The 1950s: The Decade of Development," 413.
91 See, among others, Buckner, "CHR Dialogue: The Maritimes and Confederation."
92 Sir Reginald Coupland, *The Durham Report, an Abridged Version with an Introduction and Notes* (Oxford, 1945), 15. For an unabridged edition see that published by Methuen & Co. Limited, London, 1992; or Sir Charles Lucas, *Lord Durham's Report on the Affairs of British North America*, vol. 2 (Oxford, 1912).
93 See, among others, Jeffrey Simpson, "State of the Nation: Canada a Country that Has Stood the Test of Time, July 1, 2016, http://www.theglobeandmail.com/news/politics/globe-politics-insider/jeffrey-simpson-state-of-the-nation/article30716505/.
94 Quoted in Wallace, "Smith, Sir Albert James," 6.
95 Northrop Frye, *The Modern Century: The Whidden Lectures* (Toronto: Oxford University Press, 1967), 122–23.

Chapter 5

NATIONAL POLICY

John Ibbitson, a *Globe and Mail* journalist, wrote a book in 2001 titled *Loyal No More,* making the point that Ontario's loyalty to Canada is no longer certain.[1] Ibbitson misdiagnosed the case. Ontario has always been loyal to Ontario first and remains so to this day. Its loyalty to Canada has always been tied to its own economic interest, going back to the day the country was born. Canada has served well the economic interest of Ontario; however, that province is no different than others in wishing to pursue its economic interest with federal government policies and programs. The difference is Ontario has more political clout than other provinces to do so.

A more globally integrated economy and free trade agreements have changed the dynamics for Ontario, as they have for all provinces. But Ontario is about Ontario, like Newfoundland and Labrador is about Newfoundland and Labrador, and so on it goes. The fact is that Ontario has had more reasons to be loyal to Canada, because national political and administrative institutions and national policies have served the province better than they have other provinces.

Ontario's insistence on rep by pop before Confederation and during the Confederation debate suited its own interest at the time and to this day. It is worth pointing out, however, that until Ontario's population overtook Quebec's population around 1850, it was a strong proponent of equality of the provinces or the colonies: a classic case of *deux poids, deux mesures.*[2] Ontario continues to oppose Senate reform, notably the Triple-E version, because it is in its political and economic interest to do so, rather to see the House of Commons decide who holds effective political power. Ontario holds 121 seats in a 338-seat House of Commons. Combined, the three Maritime provinces hold 25 seats. As we have seen, at the time of Confederation, political leaders from the Maritime provinces were told not to worry about rep by pop since the region would then constitute one-third of the Cabinet, and there was little chance that Ontario and Quebec would ever team up to promote their economic interest. Though it may have made sense to some at the time, it was not long before both assurances were tossed overboard.

I believe it is vitally important for Maritimers to come to terms with what Confederation brought to the region. Does Confederation answer fully Galbraith's question posed in the introduction? I think not, but it does explain a great deal about the region's relative underdevelopment, a great deal more than people outside of the region likely assume or are willing to admit, but also less than many Maritimers likely believe.

This chapter looks at how national political institutions operate, the impact of national policies, the image outsiders and Maritimers have of the region and the region's people factor. The chapter also explores how the national media portrays the Maritime region and how regions have been able to influence National Policy. These factors may not always show in economic models, but they matter.

THE IMAGE AND THE NATIONAL MEDIA

The national media—concentrated in Toronto, Ottawa and Montreal—not only tend to define national issues from an Ontario-Quebec perspective, they also have a deep influence in shaping a region's political and economic image at the national level. Ottawa-based officials read the *Globe and Mail*, the *Toronto Star*, and the *Ottawa Citizen*, and, if they should happen to be bilingual, perhaps *Le Devoir* or *La Presse*. They do not read the *Cape Breton Post*, the *Saint John Telegraph-Journal*, *L'Acadie Nouvelle*, or the *Winnipeg Free Press*. The media regarded Trudeau, Mulroney, Chrétien, and Martin as national politicians while Diefenbaker, Harper, and Manning were often described as regional politicians. As Stephen Tomblin noted, "Regional stereotypes have drawn national attention to peripheral regions, rather than to Central Canada."[3] Regional stereotypes include Maritimers, Newfoundlanders, and western Canadians, never central Canadians.

When the national media refer to the Senate, they more often than not speak to its "sober second thought," rather than to its regional role. It is, of course, a great deal easier to belittle an unelected house in modern democracy when it is tied to a "sober second thought" role than to regional interests. In a *Globe and Mail* column, Lysiane Gagnon wrote, "The Canadian Senate never lived up to its promise as a chamber of sober second thought." She simply dismissed out of hand a possible regional role, arguing, "Why have a chamber representative of the regions when we already have 10 strong provinces and three territories?"[4] More is said about this further on, but suffice to note here that other federations do not rely on states or provinces to speak to regional interests in their national institutions, because they are not equipped to do so. In any event, in Canada not all provinces are strong. How can provinces help shape national policies when some premiers live and work thousands of kilometres from the national capital with no, or very little, access to the process that gives rise to national policies or programs? Recall that some prime ministers, including Stephen Harper, decided to govern without calling formal federal-provincial First Ministers' Conferences. There is mounting evidence that prime ministers govern from the centre with Cabinet relegated to playing a focus group role. If ministers are often frozen out of the process, one can only imagine what it is like for the provincial premiers, particularly those representing the smaller provinces.

One would also be hard-pressed to find a positive stereotype in the national media in recent years about the Maritime provinces. Harry Bruce's *Down Home* documented the "cultural imperialism" of CBC Toronto and the "insistence" that stories from the Maritimes deal with "Anne of Green Gables, Highland games, national parks, and fishermen in rubber boots."[5] Jeffrey Simpson, one of Canada's most widely read columnists, wrote, "Atlantic Canada has a bit of an image problem. It's been down, economically speaking, for so long that people in the rest of Canada think of the region as nothing more than four provinces full of friendly people looking for handouts. You know the image. Unemployment insurance, seasonal workers, make-work projects, regional development agencies, pork-barrel politics, equalization."[6] Simpson neglected to add that Canada's unemployment program applies to Ontario, that Ontario alone has twice as many federal regional development agencies as all of Atlantic Canada, and that in dollar terms, in 2013–14, Ontario and Quebec received more than three times the amount of federal transfers under Ottawa's Equalization program, designed for have-less provinces, than the three Maritime provinces combined.[7]

Though "national journalists" readily tie patronage to Maritime provinces, they have little evidence to back up the claim. They simply keep repeating it, turning the claim into a self-fulfilling prophecy. Jeffrey Simpson was at it again in the immediate aftermath of the 2015 election, when he remarked, "Atlantic Canadian Liberals practised the politics of patronage and the pork barrel for decades."[8] Simpson is by no means the only Ottawa-based journalist to make this claim.[9]

Many Maritimers are puzzled by these claims, and so am I. I worked in Ottawa as a senior public servant and as a visiting fellow at the Treasury Board Secretariat. If one is looking for patronage both at the political and bureaucratic levels, one does not have to leave town; if one wants to see pork barrel politics, one does not have to leave Ontario and Quebec. Industry Canada has provided $22 billion in subsidies over the years, including over $3 billion to Pratt and Whitney Canada, well over $1 billion to Bombardier (and more may well be on the way), $1 billion to de Havilland, billions to General Motors, Ford, and Chrysler, $500 million to Bell Helicopter, and the list goes on to include Honeywell, Litton Systems, Spar Aerospace, and others.[10]

In spending $50 million when Canada hosted the G8 meeting in 2010, Tony Clement, the Treasury Board president in the Harper government, could show Maritimers a thing or two about how to dole out patronage. The $50 million was designed to strengthen border infrastructure. A good part of the money made its way into several communities in Clement's constituency, far from where the G8 meeting took place and from the United States border.[11] I could list other similar examples. The patronage stereotype, however, somehow never sticks to Ontario.

Edith Robb, a veteran Maritime journalist, was asked to survey the national media during the 2004 election campaign for Moncton's daily newspaper, the *Times & Transcript*. It is worth quoting her at length:

> Hardly anybody had anything at all to say about us. And if they did, it was in reference to us as a poor, rather backward, Ottawa-dependent province full of people working in the fishery or on the

> farm and collecting pogey most of the year. Here are some examples: CTV came to New Brunswick to report on the election and ended up writing about our "horrible" roads. The *Toronto Star* focused on "fishing families" of the east coast, along with potholes and gas prices. They described eastern voters as "wearing overalls and jeans," noting picturesquely "the hands [the candidate] shakes spend a lot of time in warm red dirt or cold ocean water." The *Star* also described our region as a place where Employment Insurance is used as an industrial subsidy. The *National Post* had us all as cagey strategists who liked to be "on the winning side," presumably to protect our pogey. The Canadian Broadcasting Corporation described us as a region where "the Liberals remain popular where a benevolent Ottawa is a matter of the region's very survival." The Canadian Press described us as "an area with chronically high unemployment and major reliance on economic props."[12]

Media stereotypes are like codes that give the reader a ready understanding of a region or a group of people. Stereotypes can also become realities in the eyes of the region itself and of policy-makers. As Edith Robb explained, "Stereotyping can also impact on a region's self-image. We start to think that if this is the way others see us, then perhaps that is the way we are. The confidence to trust yourself when others doubt you is not in great supply."[13] Research shows that the media are a highly important influence on the daily work of both elected and unelected government officials.[14]

One of Frank McKenna's most important contributions to economic development in New Brunswick during his term as premier was to instill in New Brunswickers a sense of pride and a can-do attitude. McKenna asked an outside firm to assess New Brunswickers' views of themselves and of their province and to get a sense of the perceptions other Canadians had of New Brunswick. The report card was not positive. It revealed that New Brunswickers' pride focused on their local community, their cultural heritage, and on being Canadian; pride in their province trailed behind almost everything else. Perceptions of New Brunswick in the rest of Canada were dominated by the have-not image. Except for those who had a personal connection with the province, the rest of Canada, the wealthier provinces in particular, viewed New Brunswick as a place they had to subsidize.[15]

Policy-makers and advisors are not indifferent to how the national media portrays a region. As it is often said in Ottawa, in politics perception is reality. Many rivulets of thought go into shaping policy and decision-making in government, and media reports are an important ingredient. The image that outsiders and Maritimers themselves have of the Maritime region was not born in a vacuum; there are reasons why the image persists, many of them historical, and we need to review them.

IT'S NOT ABOUT THE MARITIMES

As noted, Ontario, formerly Canada West, was Confederation's biggest promoter and became its biggest beneficiary.[16] A long-serving deputy minister in Ottawa, Nick Mulder, put it very well when he observed that Canada has produced over the years the most successful regional development policy anywhere: "Look at Ontario and its history of economic development. Ottawa has done a pretty good job at regional development."[17]

Thomas Courchene, one of Canada's leading economists, has, as already noted, challenged Canada's regional development policy and federal transfer payments to slow-growth regions. I recall participating in a roundtable session in Ottawa at a time when Canada was debating the proposed Canada–United States Free Trade Agreement. Courchene supported the agreement but warned there was risk of a "maritimization" of the Ontario economy. His point: economically stronger United States regions would, in time, come to dominate the North American economy much like Ontario came to dominate the Canadian economy. Somehow, it does not hurt the national interest, however defined, to see the "maritimization" of the Maritimes, but it becomes a different story when Ontario may suffer the same fate. Space, it seems, matters when it is cast at the national level, but less so at the regional level.

The Canadian federation has a fundamental flaw that has never been fixed and that has long favoured the more populous provinces, while it has been deeply detrimental to the Maritime region. John Reid, noted historian, provided an insightful summary of Canada's constitutional flaw for which the Maritime region continues to pay a very heavy price: "There is a built-in illogic in a federation where 'rep by pop' is the key to the control of fiscal and other policies by the residents of the most populous provinces, which also tend to be the most prosperous."[18] The ones that may have the necessary clout to fix the fundamental flaw—the more populous provinces—have no interest in doing so. Informed politicians and observers know, or should know, that there is a fundamental flaw in Canada's constitutional arrangement and where it lies.

Former prime minister Paul Martin, among many other politicians, recognized the problem, but nothing ever came of it. Martin lamented the fact that "when a regional issue arises in central Canada it very quickly becomes a national issue," but that this is not the case for other regions. He added, "We cannot allow national issues in British Columbia to be relegated to the sidelines as regional issues."[19] He explained, "What I am talking about is the absolute necessity of reducing the distance between the nation's capital and the regions of the country, a distance which is not measured in kilometres, but a distance which is often measured in attitude."[20] Stephen Harper, for his part, continuously stressed the need for "a greater voice for regions outside Quebec and Ontario."[21]

Liberal member of Parliament David McGuinty spoke directly to the problem when he observed that Alberta politicians in Ottawa are being too "provincial" when they focus on the energy sector: "They are national legislators with a national responsibility, but they come across as very, very small-p provincial individuals who are jealously guarding one industrial sector, picking the fossil-fuel business and the oil-sands business specifically."[22]

The one industrial sector, fossil fuel, matters a great deal to British Columbia, Alberta, Saskatchewan, Nova Scotia, and Newfoundland and Labrador. No matter, in the eyes of McGuinty it is a regional sector, and politicians who focus on it are parochial. However, McGuinty, other MPs from Ontario, and the national media view the automobile sector as national. Yet, for nine of Canada's ten provinces, the automobile industry is a regional sector, far more than the fossil fuel sector, which for half of the provinces is a critical element for their economic growth.

The Canada–United States Automotive Products Agreement (also known as Auto Pact) is not a product of the market or Adam Smith's hidden hand. It stems from government. Ontario's bootstraps are tied to a historical event initiated in Canada by the federal government. The Auto Pact allowed firms to bring parts and autos into Canada without any tariff, provided the firms created jobs and generated investments in Canada. The Auto Pact was signed in January 1965 by then prime minister Lester Pearson and president Lyndon Johnson after months of Ottawa-Washington negotiations.

The agreement benefitted large American automakers and, essentially, Southern Ontario. In exchange for tariff-free access to the Canadian market, the Big Three United States automakers agreed that automobile production in Canada would not fall below 1964 levels and that for every five new cars sold in Canada, three new ones would be built here. The Auto Pact had an immediate effect: In 1964 only 7 per cent of the automobiles built in Canada were sold in the United States; the proportion jumped to 60 per cent by 1968. By 1999 Canada had become the fourth largest automaker in the world. This sector was the largest component of Canada–United States trade; it went from just $715 million in 1964 to about $92.7 billion in 2000 (but dropped to $65.3 billion in 2012).[23] There were 146,495 Canadians working in the auto, vehicle, and auto parts manufacturing industries in 2001, but that number dropped to 115,000 by 2012.[24] Ontario was home to 130,000 of these jobs, that is, about 90 per cent of all jobs in the industry in Canada.[25] The 2008 recession hit Canada's auto industry hard, losing some 43,500 jobs between 2007 and 2009. The sector has since witnessed only modest job growth. It remains largely concentrated in Ontario where it still employs 97,000 people.[26]

As Jim Stanford explained, all of this development did not "happen by accident: the main instrument for their developments was the 1965 Canada-US Auto Pact."[27] The Auto Pact was a free trade agreement in one sector in the interest of one region or one province whose economic interests and political influence—from an Ottawa point of view at least—flowed quite nicely into a national perspective. It explains why both politicians and senior career officials in Ottawa worked to ensure its signing and implementation.

In recent years, the industry has also been able to secure federal funding to modernize its operations.[28] When the auto sector confronted serious financial difficulties in 2008–09, the federal government rushed in to save GM and Chrysler from bankruptcy with financial support amounting to $9.1 billion. I note that other countries, including the United States, also bailed out their auto sector at the same time. The minister of Industry claimed the move "saved more than 50,000 jobs." However, the Auditor General would later report that the government came to the rescue with "limited analysis showing how the restructuring actions would improve the financial situations of GM and Chrysler's Canadian subsidiaries, what concessions had been made by stakeholders and how the companies would repay their loans."[29] Ottawa sold all its GM shares in April 2015 at a loss of $3.5 billion.[30] It takes the Atlantic Canada Opportunities Agency about ten years to spend that amount of money, with a good chunk of it in repayable loans.

THE DEMISE OF REGIONAL MINISTERS

There was a time when powerful regional ministers could generate a "breakaway" for their province, bringing home the bacon so to speak, and here, the Maritimes were no exception. This is less so today. As noted earlier, governing from the centre is how things now work in Ottawa. The federal government's policy-making machinery works as follows: the prime minister and a handful of advisors run the policy process and shape the government's policy agenda to the extent they wish or that their crowded agenda will allow. We know the role of the national media is vitally important to the prime minister and immediate advisors; they monitor it and are deeply influenced by it. Public opinion surveys and focus groups also serve to shape the agenda. But all important, and even many less important, decisions now flow into the hands of the prime minister and his courtiers.

I have documented elsewhere the several reasons why regional ministers have lost influence over the past forty years or so.[31] First, nothing belongs to a single department anymore: all policy and many program issues cut across several departments, making it more difficult for a minister to exert influence. Issues are controlled from the centre to ensure that all relevant parties are consulted. The twenty-four-hour news cycle, social media, the rise of spin specialists, and permanent election campaigns have had a profound impact on government. The blame-generating and blame-avoiding game has strengthened the hand of the prime minister and his courtiers. They need to control not only the policy-making levers, but also the message from the centre in order to position the government in a positive light in the twenty-four-hour news cycle.[32]

In addition, the prime minister and close advisors no longer need to look to the more powerful regional ministers to gain an appreciation of how well the government and its party are faring in different regions or what needs to be done to gain support. Public opinion surveys are regarded as more accurate than regional ministers in assessing a region's political mood. Indeed, a public opinion survey can enable the prime minister and his close advisors to challenge the view of ministers. Pollsters and their public opinion surveys are also less demanding on the prime minister and his courtiers than are regional ministers. Justin Trudeau decided not to appoint regional ministers when he came to power, without explaining why. Few voices were heard, even in the smaller provinces, asking that they be re-instituted, which speaks to their growing irrelevance.

There are other factors that strengthen the hand of the prime minister. Suffice to note that all decisions of any importance flow to that office. With regard to permanent election campaigns, the prime minister will focus on poll numbers and where to find the potential seats to win the next election. The Maritime provinces factor less and less in this equation. All politicians are familiar with the old Canadian saying, "You win power in Ontario and a majority government in Quebec." Things have changed somewhat in recent years. A party still wins power in Ontario, but it can now look to either Quebec or Western Canada to win a majority government.

The 2015 election speaks to this point. Throughout the campaign, the national media stressed the importance of Ontario and Quebec, as they should, in a representation by population world. The Liberal Party won 184 seats, a majority of 14 seats. Within days following the election, the national media pointed to Toronto and Quebec as the big winners. The *Globe and Mail* ran the headline "Toronto Poised to be Powerhouse in the Trudeau Cabinet" because the Liberals won 49 of 54 seats in the Greater Toronto area.[33] Meanwhile, CBC reported that Trudeau won his majority mandate in Quebec, where he won 40 seats.[34] The Liberal Party won all the seats in the Maritime provinces—the first time in history a political party has ever won every seat in the region. I could argue the region gave Trudeau the 14-seat majority and 11 more to spare.

Other federations, notably the United States, Germany, and even Australia (which, like Canada, has a Westminster-styled parliamentary system) have an elected and effective upper house to balance the rep by pop lower houses. I have long argued for a Triple-E Senate for Canada. I am not alone, though many, particularly from Western Canada, have jumped off the wagon in recent years. Canada covers the largest territory, has the biggest gap between the most and least populous provinces, has the most regionally diverse economy, but—unlike the other federations—does not have an effective upper house to counterbalance the power of a "rep by pop" lower house.

Donald Smiley, one of Canada's most eminent scholars of federalism, wrote about "interstate" and "intrastate" federalism. He explained: "Interstate federalism involves the constitutional distribution of powers between the central and regional governments," while "intrastate federalism channels the central government itself." He pointed out that interstate capacity in the operations of the Canadian government is extremely weak, weaker than in other federations. The Senate is the central cause. Smiley went on to argue that the West German Bundesrat and the Australian Senate have been more effective in giving life to intrastate influences within their national governments.[35] Ronald L. Watts, another well-known student of federalism, wrote, "Experience would suggest that there is much to be said for bicameral institutions and that provision in some form or another for representation on a regional basis may be an important way to strengthen the commitment and loyalty of regional groups to the national institutions."[36]

Sir John A. Macdonald and others from Canada West saw no reason to deal with intrastate federalism issues. Not only were they dealing with fixing the political instability between Canada West and East, but also Canada was the first political community to combine the Westminster model of parliamentary government with federalism.[37] The inability to integrate intrastate federalism influences in the national government remains the fundamental flaw in the Canadian federation for which the Maritime provinces, in particular, have paid a hefty price.

Until recently, Western Canada was the country's most vocal supporter of Senate reform, the Triple-E variety. Roger Gibbins, a well-known Calgary political scientist, once argued that, in the case of the United States, "effective territorial representation within national political institutions has promoted national integration, strengthened the national government, broadened its reach and reduced the power of state governments to a degree unimagined in the founding years of the American republic." He added, "Strengthening regional representation at the centre would provide a mechanism for the further nationalization of Canadian policies."[38] One could also add that, coincidentally or not, American regional economic development policy has been quite different from the Canadian experience; in the United States, different regions have taken turns at high growth far more often than in Canada.[39]

There are powerful forces resisting Senate reform in Canada. Otherwise it would have occurred a long time ago. The Ontario government wanted to abolish the Senate, and Quebec threatened to take the federal government to court should it proceed with Senate reform without the consent of the provinces. It is highly unlikely that these two provinces will agree on Senate reform. I have received a number of emails and telephone calls from Ontario- and Quebec-based politicians over the years, insisting that I hold misguided views on Senate reform. They argue that a Triple-E Senate does not square with a Westminster-styled parliamentary system (while saying nothing about how Australia, with its Westminster-styled system, has been able to make a reformed upper house work); that it would only lead to deadlock in policy- and decision-making; or that under no circumstances could Ontario and Prince Edward Island have the same number of senators in an effective Senate (conveniently leaving aside the example of California and Wyoming in the United States Senate).

Matthew Mendelsohn, the former head of Ontario's Mowat Centre and deputy secretary to the Cabinet in the Privy Council Office (PCO) in Justin Trudeau's government, dismissed out of hand the prospect of a democratically elected Senate because, he insisted, the required provincial government consent is simply not in the cards. He made a revealing observation: "Today, the Senate does not really matter for decision-making....So the fact that New Brunswick has ten seat[s] in the Senate and British Columbia has only six is an oddity but not a big concern. It doesn't really matter because the Senate doesn't really matter."[40] That of course serves the interest of the two most populous provinces: Ontario and Quebec.

Stéphane Dion argued, "So why not simply elect the future senators instead of letting the prime minister appoint them? There is a basic problem in that logic, one that derives from the unequal distribution of senators per province. To elect senators with the current distribution of seats would be unfair for the underrepresented provinces, Alberta and British Columbia, who have only six senators each, whereas New Brunswick and Nova Scotia, with about one quarter of their population have ten."[41] The whole point of having an effective Senate in a federation is to bring regional balance to National Policy–making or, as Gibbins argued, to bring "effective territorial representation within national political institutions." The whole point of having a federal system rather than a unitary one is that political structures have to be established to better accommodate regional interests. To ensure this, there is a need for smaller provinces or states to be overrepresented in the upper house. Dion basically said the United States, Australia, and Russia have it all wrong with an equal number of senators for every state, no matter their population. I hear very few Americans and Australians making the same point.

Dion and others of like mind also offer no solution to counter rep by pop in a federation as large and as diverse as Canada, suggesting they may not recognize the problem. One can only conclude they believe that smaller provinces and regions in a federation such as Canada should simply rely on rep by pop if they want to be heard and have influence in a national setting. As Canadian history has so clearly demonstrated, this does not work. One thing is clear, the status quo—or abolition—brings comfort to Ontario. Both play to its advantage.

Western Canada appears to be losing interest in a Triple-E Senate. The election of the Stephen Harper government and the shift of economic and political power to Western Canada have changed its agenda. A Triple-E Senate was not a problem for Gibbins in the 1990s, but now it is. Roger Gibbins, a long-time supporter of Senate reform and former head of the Canada West Foundation, has had a change of heart. He argued in 2012: "If we have a Senate that's elected and effective to some degree—but the seat distribution doesn't change—then we're into a situation where an elected Senate may be detrimental to the interests of the West."[42] He believed that "another reality is sinking in that westerners must drop their demand for a Triple-E Senate." He explained: "To the extent that the Senate becomes a more influential body...it would shift power into Atlantic Canada and away from the West."[43] Though it may come as a surprise to Gibbins, Ontario and Quebec would agree with him. Others in Western Canada, including Saskatchewan premier Brad Wall, have echoed Gibbins's view on Senate reform with Wall calling for abolition.[44]

Preston Manning has been more forthcoming. He once asked how "will western interests be effectively represented in a one-house Parliament where Quebec and Ontario have an absolute majority of seats?" Today, things are different, even for Manning. He commented: "With the rapid growth of population in the western provinces and the shift in the country's political centre of gravity from the old Laurentian region (Quebec and Ontario together) to the new alignment between Ontario and the West, Senate reform is not as high on the western agenda, as it once was."[45]

One can only conclude that the West's push for Senate reform was motivated not by the national interest or by bringing balance to the Canadian federation, but rather solely by the interests of the West. That is how Canada is governed, and where big dogs compete to eat first. Once Western Canada felt that it had the needed political and economic clout to influence Ottawa, it lost interest in its old cry, "the West wants in." Ontario and Quebec, as noted, are hostile to Senate reform because it is in their economic interest to oppose reform, thus far at least. The 2015 election results have shifted some political power away from Western Canada to Ontario and Quebec. Time will tell if Western Canada will have another change of mind on Senate reform.

Where does that leave the Maritime provinces? Over the years, Maritime premiers have sent mixed messages on Senate reform, and only one Maritime premier, David Alward, in recent history has made it a priority.[46] These premiers have hesitated joining the Triple-E Senate reform movement coming out of Western Canada in the 1980s and 1990s for partisan reasons (their federal Liberal or Progressive Conservative cousins never embraced the Triple-E movement, because they need Ontario and/or Quebec to win power) and they feared losing some of their status as regional spokespersons for their province.

WHY IT MATTERS

Maritimers, starting with the Fathers of Confederation from the region, had every right to express strong reservations about the terms of Confederation. Historian Phillip Buckner went to the heart of the matter when he remarked, "Opposition of the Maritimes to the plan of union evolved at the Quebec Conference in 1864 has been interpreted as opposition to the idea of Confederation rather than for what it really was: opposition to the Quebec Resolutions and the kind of union that they envisaged."[47]

One of New Brunswick's Fathers of Confederation, Albert Smith, insisted on a United States–styled Senate to speak to regional concerns in shaping National Policy and to act as a check on the power of rep by pop generated by the House of Commons. Prince Edward Island, as discussed in an earlier chapter, initially rejected the terms of Confederation because it would "have an insignificant voice in a centralized legislature, and as a result they feared that their local needs would be disregarded."[48] The legislature declared that a union with Canada "would prove politically, commercially and financially disastrous to the right and best interests of its people."[49]

One-off deals, special compensation arrangements, and federal-provincial agreements have been struck to keep Canadian federalism rolling on. This, more than any other factor, explains why regional development policy in Canada has been cast in terms of provinces in contrast to regional development policy in the United States, which has been cast more in terms of regions.[50] In return, Canadian institutional arrangements that have been giving the more populous provinces the upper hand have been left intact. Special fiscal arrangements with the smaller provinces were a small price to pay to have "national" political institutions define and pursue "National Policy" that squared with the interest of the two or three provinces that decide who would have political power. Canada's institutional arrangement encourages a strong focus on place prosperity, more specifically on the place that holds the largest number of constituencies.

NATIONAL POLICY

Much has been written about the National Policy (introduced in the late 1870s) to promote a strong manufacturing sector and an east-west trade pattern. The policy consisted of high tariffs on most imported manufactured goods. Sir John A. Macdonald's National Policy was highly popular in Ontario and Quebec. Macdonald also had close ties to business interests in both Toronto and Montreal that were able to draw important economic interests from the policy. Initially at least, the policy was well received by the business community in the Maritimes. However, over time, things began to change both in Western Canada and the Maritime provinces.

In western Canada, the policy was never well received, and it eventually gave rise to the Progressive Party in the 1920s. The western provinces tried through legislation to attenuate the impact of the National Policy; however, the federal government was able through its power of disallowance to kill anti-National Policy legislation from Western Canada. Sections 55, 56, and 57 of the British North America Act 1867 gave the federal government the power to refuse bills from provincial governments. Between 1867 and 1920, ninety-six provincial laws were disallowed, with the bulk of them from Western Canada, and the single most important reason was to support Ottawa's National Policy. There is now a constitutional convention that the federal government will not use its disallowance again, and it has in fact not been used since 1943.[51]

In the Maritime provinces, the policy has been held up time and again to explain the region's economic woes. Some—but not all—of the criticism is valid. The Maritime region did not have a strong regional metropolis like Quebec (Montreal) and Ontario (Toronto). The Maritimes had Moncton, Saint John, Amherst, Halifax, Truro, New Glasgow, and as T. W. Acheson explained, a rather "curious distribution of growth centres" based on "human and historical" factors rather than geography.[52] The region lacked the financial structure to support large industrial entities.[53]

But the implementation of Ottawa's National Policy also has a lot to answer for. The policy, combined with geography and Canada's transportation policy, put the region at serious economic disadvantage over time. Tariffs tied to the National Policy, though they initially favoured the region, would in time inhibit economic development in the Maritimes. T. W. Acheson put it succinctly: "In many respects the National Policy simply represented to the entrepreneur a transfer from a British to a Canadian commercial empire. Inherent in most of his activities was the colonial assumption that he could not really control his own destiny, that, of necessity, he would be manipulated by forces beyond his control."[54]

The National Policy would in the end serve to promote Canada's manufacturing sector and, in doing so, strongly favour the Windsor-Quebec City corridor. Tariffs were a matter of government revenues, of protection, and a tool for economic development. Canadian manufacturers looked to domestic markets for growth because there were few alternatives available. Manufacturers argued that the domestic market should be reserved for them, given the failure to achieve lasting reciprocal trade relations with the United States. Ottawa agreed, since it had "become apparent that a more rapid rate of industrialization was essential if progress was to be made with plans for a better balanced, more diversified and more tightly integrated economic development. Without a strong industrial base, there could be little hope of lessening Canada's dependence on external conditions for prosperity."[55]

The National Policy emphasized an east-west continental economy, and by ricochet, it protected emerging central Canadian producers. It meant that Maritimers would have to import their manufactured goods from Montreal and Southern Ontario or pay duties of 50 per cent in some instances to import goods from traditional sources such as England or the New England states. Maritimers concluded that under the National Policy they were compelled to buy what they consumed in a substantially protected home market but had to sell their products in a virtually unprotected one.

Over time, economic protectionism and the National Policy forced producers in the Maritimes to ship their goods on expensive rail routes to Central Canada rather than on ships to their traditional export markets in the New England states, the Caribbean Islands, and elsewhere. Canada's east-west trade patterns, which were artificially created through the National Policy, promoted a shift to overland trade (for which the three Maritime provinces were geographically ill-suited) and served to make the region essentially an "isolated extremity of Canada."[56] The emerging trade patterns were artificial in the sense that they were created, initially at least, by political decisions, not by market forces.

Many observers from the Maritimes and elsewhere have argued that the National Policy and protectionism have served to undercut the region's trading advantage in waterborne shipping. David Alexander summed up the impact of the National Policy on the region in this way: "In the Maritimes, underdevelopment seems a sorry descent from those heady days when the region possessed one of the world's foremost shipbuilding industries, the third or fourth largest merchant marine, financial institutions which were the core of many of the present Canadian giants, and an industrial structure growing as fast as that of central Canada."[57] In short, the National Policy is at least partly responsible for the region's economic decline.

The policy also encouraged American firms to establish branch plants in Canada. Here, geography clearly favoured Central Canada. When combined with the effects of the National Policy, Central Canada became the location of choice for foreign firms wishing to establish a presence in Canada. Maritimers can legitimately claim there was no place for them in the National Policy. From time to time, the federal government has come to terms with the fact that Confederation dealt the Maritimes a bad hand; however, it has come at a price. One keen observer of New Brunswick politics, for example, wrote in 1961 about the "enormous economic disabilities under which the region has been laboring since the inauguration of the National Policy," with the result that New Brunswick and, more generally, Maritime politicians have been cast in the role of supplicants pressing on whatever pretext can be devised for better terms from Ottawa.[58]

National Policy took on a life of its own, and its impact is still felt to this day. The answer to the question of the government's role in influencing where industry would be concentrated in the country has been straightforward, since the Maritimes simply could not compete with the vote-rich provinces of Ontario and Quebec. Ernest Forbes explains it soon became clear that whenever there was regional competition, Ottawa invariably opted for Ontario and perhaps also Quebec. He pointed out, for example, that Ottawa simply said, "We can't have a tariff on coal because Ontario needs to import it from the United States. They took the tariff off and were able to create an iron and steel industry in Ontario."[59] That decision alone shifted important economic power to Central Canada and served to eliminate the advantages previously enjoyed by Cape Breton coal producers. This is far from an isolated development.

Historians have produced a veritable catalogue of misguided federal policies to address the constitution's fundamental flaw when viewed from a Maritime perspective. Hugh Thorburn succinctly observed, "In the long run the federal government's tariff, transportation, and monetary policies have worked to the general disadvantage of New Brunswick."[60] Policies were struck in Ottawa to meet national objectives, which to a Maritimer became a code phrase meaning "the economic interests of Ontario and Quebec only." What was good for Central Canada was invariably perceived in Ottawa to be good for Canada as a whole, but the same reasoning would never apply in the Maritimes. Ottawa's monetary policy during the 1930s—and for that matter ever since—reflected economic circumstances in Ontario and Quebec and, only recently, Western Canada, often at the expense of the Maritimes. Canada refused to devalue its currency during the depression of the 1930s, while many other countries did. The Maritime region was "exposed to a two-way squeeze: from high and rigid prices for the manufactured goods she had to buy (from central Canada), and from difficult selling conditions in the export markets upon which she depended."[61]

Many policy-makers in Ottawa actually believed (and still do) that National Policy did not decide where wealth ought to be created. If so, why then were they only prepared to entertain special arrangements to redistribute wealth? Their concerns were tied to the national economy, and if it so happened that the bulk of the national economy was situated in vote-rich areas between Quebec City and Windsor, so much the better.

Equalization payments and special fiscal arrangements with the smaller provinces represented a quid pro quo for Ontario. But, as one student of Ontario politics wrote, the "quo was worth more than the quid." He noted:

> The time had come to build the St. Lawrence waterway, without delay. Not only would a deepwater canal open Ontario's ports from Cornwall to the Lake-head to international shipping, but the electricity produced by damming the St. Lawrence would satisfy Ontario's electrical needs for a generation. As part of the new spirit of cooperation...the seaway was an awesome undertaking and it boosted the economies of every province and state that bordered it, lowering the cost of Quebec iron ore that now supplied the Hamilton and Sault Ste. Marie steel mills, and opening western grain to eastern exports. The railroads and Halifax paid the price. Ontario reaped the benefit of so much new power that, by the advent of the 1960s, virtually all the province's electricity was generated by water.[62]

This, among many other developments, explains why Ontario has been loyal to Canada.

The "quo" continues to be worth more than the "quid." Indeed, our national political institutions now favour the "quo" more than ever. The number of Maritime seats in the Commons decreased from 43 in the 1870s to 31 in 1921. New Brunswick fell from 16 to 11. Yet, the size of the House of Commons increased from 206 seats in 1874 to 235 in 1921. In the 2015 election, there were 338 seats up for grabs. The three Maritime provinces combined accounted for 25 seats. Ontario gained 15 more seats from the previous election, Quebec 3 more, and Alberta and British Columbia 6 each. These newly gained seats alone accounted for more than the total seat allocation for the Maritime provinces in the 2015 election. All of this in the context of an upper house that has been remarkably ineffective in bringing a region's perspective to bear on National Policy–making and an unwillingness on the part of the larger provinces to balance the rep by pop power in the House of Commons with a capacity to speak for the interest of the smaller provinces.

The result is political leaders from the two largest provinces of the country—and now increasingly from Western Canada—can put in place a "national" policy that favours their own provinces over the others, establish Crown corporations in their own regions, establish tariffs that will benefit largely their own regions, concentrate investments in key infrastructure facilities in certain areas, all the time knowing they will never be called to account by an upper house speaking on behalf of regional interests.

The view that nation-building was essential for Canada to lessen its dependence on external conditions and that special measures were required given both its small population and its small manufacturing sector remains conventional wisdom. C. D. Howe, for example, favoured either private monopoly regulated in Ottawa by government controls or Crown corporations to create a strong manufacturing sector. Howe's decision during World War Two to locate virtually all the country's wartime production in Central Canada speaks to the underlying goal of the country's economic development policy. It also had wide-ranging implications for the Maritime provinces.

C. D. Howe was an extremely powerful minister in the governments of William Lyon Mackenzie King and Louis St-Laurent. He served in various departments between 1936 and 1957, including Transport, Munitions, Reconstruction, and Industry. At the start of World War Two, Canada had fifteen Crown corporations. Thirty-two were added during the war years, as Ottawa believed they were better suited to lure business people to manage war programs than a typical government department would be. In addition, Howe believed a successful war effort required a highly decentralized form of administration, such as that provided by the Crown corporation model.

Sir Robert Borden, who established Canadian National Railway as a Crown corporation in 1919, explained the advantages of such corporations: they were designed to promote business-like management, financial autonomy, and a degree of freedom from direct political interference.[63] Howe saw these attributes as being tailor-made for a successful war industry. At the same time, Crown corporations represented a significant new source of investments, with the potential to generate a great deal of new economic activity. Indeed, they would provide the basis for future development in the manufacturing sector in the postwar years.[64] For example, wartime Crown corporations gave rise to aircraft manufacturers, synthetic rubber producers, and an advanced technology company called Research Enterprises Limited. Virtually all the new corporations, however, were established in the Montreal-Windsor corridor; not a single one was located in the Maritime region.[65]

Although many of the Crown corporations established during the war were later disbanded, some continued, including Polysar and Canadian Arsenals Limited. Crown corporations served the war effort very well, but they also served in the long run to considerably strengthen Central Canada's manufacturing sector. And that was not all. The Department of Munitions and Supply made extensive new investments in Canadian industries, but by 1944, only about 3.7 per cent of these had been made in the Maritimes, mainly for aircraft and naval repair. In fact, even the bulk of the shipbuilding for the war was carried out elsewhere. Historians now recognize that "C. D. Howe and his bureaucrats favoured the concentration of manufacturing in central Canada,"[66] even though locating certain activities in the Maritime provinces made economic sense because of geography, the presence of entrepreneurial talent (e.g., K. C. Irving), and industrial bases in Saint John and Halifax.[67] This is one time when geography should have favoured the Maritime provinces; it was Central Canada, not Halifax or Saint John, that was far from the war theatre.

C. D. Howe was consistently focused on Central Canada in shaping the country's manufacturing sector. The Dominion Steel and Coal Corporation (DOSCO) was at one time one of Canada's big three steel producers and one of the largest employers in the Maritime provinces. Howe and his department decided to help steel producers modernize their operations for the war efforts. He offered subsidies to the Steel Company of Canada in Hamilton and the Algoma Steel Company in Sault Ste. Marie. He offered nothing to DOSCO, which prompted Arthur Cross, its president, to report that his firm was "the only primary steel producer in this country which is receiving no government assistance."[68] Howe's decision made sense to then prime minister Mackenzie King (from Ontario), the larger Ontario caucus, and Ottawa-based senior public servants.

The important point is that Canada's war effort and the measures in the immediate postwar period to reconstruct the country's economy were a product of government initiative, specifically the federal government's initiative. When the private sector could not deliver what the war effort required, Ottawa created Crown corporations. The capacity was created in Ontario and Quebec, while labour from the Maritimes was drawn to these two provinces.

Ottawa established the capacity in Central Canada, even when military considerations suggested otherwise. After a visit to Canada in 1940, the British Admiralty Technical Mission concluded, "Political issues weigh heavily" in military decisions. They underlined the problems with building ships in yards cut off from the Atlantic Ocean for five months and questioned the need for vessels to make the long trip down the St. Lawrence. American military advisors also made the same point.[69] The first ten ships built for Britain barely escaped getting trapped in the St. Lawrence in the winter freeze-up and "required substantial work in the Maritimes before they could risk an Atlantic crossing."[70] The British tried as best they could to convince Ottawa to make Halifax the logical naval headquarters for their Canadian convoys and as the repair centre for the larger vessels. They were not successful.[71]

In its first activities report tabled on April 30, 1941, the Department of Munitions and Supply made clear its bias for Central Canada. The Canadian and British governments had already committed $484 million to the war effort. Prince Edward Island and New Brunswick received nothing, while Nova Scotia recieved only $8.7 million, with $3 million of it allocated to a Montreal firm to build a floating dry dock for Halifax.[72]

Ottawa's postwar reconstruction efforts continued in the same pattern. Some of the Crown corporations continued operating, others were eventually privatized, and still others disbanded. Some 80 per cent of the funds earmarked for reconstruction were allocated to Ontario and Quebec firms. Firms looking for assistance had to be "profitable," and Ottawa often turned away from Maritime firms, arguing that the region lacked skilled workers, many of whom had moved to Central Canada to work for the war effort. Many other Ottawa decisions favoured Central Canada at the expense of the Maritime region industry, including Canadian National Railway's decision to establish a repair shop in Montreal, which in time would undermine the repair shop in Moncton and eventually cause its demise.[73]

Firms were lobbying hard for new business at the end of the Great Depression and at the beginning of the war. Large businesses located in major centres as well as those with political clout and close to Ottawa had an advantage. They knew who and how to lobby. C. D. Howe had his own economic interest in mind when deciding where to locate new activities and which businesses to support. Howe was strongly supportive of Algoma Steel and openly hostile to Nova Scotia–based DOSCO, Algoma's most important competition. It so happened that his good friend, Sir James Dunn, was Algoma Steel's major investor. We know that Howe destroyed his correspondence with Dunn. We also know that Howe was an active investor while he was a minister. Canada's former ethics counsellor wrote that Howe would manage his extensive stock portfolio according to government decisions and the information learned inside government during the week; however, Howe saw no contradiction between doing what seemed good for his country and doing well for himself.[74]

Thus, the Maritimes were essentially left on the outside looking in, as the country's wartime manufacturing sector started to take shape. The migration or the "assignment" of skilled labour to war industries in Central Canada, made it very difficult for the region to promote its own manufacturing sector in the postwar years. Here again, political decisions rather than market forces strengthened Central Canada's position in the manufacturing sector. It is important to stress that C. D. Howe, and others of like mind, set out to build a nation—not regions—and concentrating industrial development made sense from this perspective. That practice had a politically important bonus: it also made sense from a political perspective, given the concentration of industry would be in vote-rich Ontario and Quebec.

It is now well established that the manufacturing sector in the Maritimes stagnated during much of the twentieth century. In addition, though the region was fairly strong economically, relative to both national and international standards at the moment of Confederation, its position deteriorated during the first half of the century. We now know, for example, that with respect to Canada, the Maritimes accounted for 14 per cent of goods produced in 1880, for 9 per cent in 1911, and for only 5 per cent in 1939.[75] Today, it stands at 4.1 per cent.[76] More is said about this later.

In our ahistorical world, it is all too often overlooked that the federal government played a major role in promoting the country's manufacturing sector through tariffs and the establishment of Crown corporations. When decisions are made in Ottawa about where to locate a new research foundation, the Space Agency, or an R&D government unit, the debate nearly always turns on whether it should be located in Ottawa, other parts of Southern Ontario, or Montreal.[77] Only rarely will the Maritime provinces get, in the words of a former clerk and secretary to the Cabinet, a "breakaway" and draw the attention of Ottawa-based decision-makers.[78] Breakaways are increasingly rare, as both the region's political clout and the role of regional ministers have become increasingly marginalized.

It bears repeating that the mindset of Canada's national political and administrative institutions is to promote the country's economic engine (or Ontario) and to monitor national unity concerns (or Quebec). The Ontario and Quebec governments and opposition caucuses matter to the prime minister and to the leader of the Opposition because the two provinces are key to securing political power in Ottawa.

It is also worth repeating that without an effective voice speaking on behalf of the smaller regions, the prime minister and his key advisors are free to ignore regional concerns. An example will make the point clearer. I recall in the early 1980s, when DREE decided to launch an in-depth study to break down the federal government's expenditure budget by location (i.e., the regions), expense type (i.e., economic development measures versus transfer payments), cost of operations, and so on. The report divided government spending further into different categories: spending by point of outlay in terms of wages and salaries, economic development, social programs, investments in infrastructures, the purchase of goods, money spent for consultants and services, and here again the list goes on.[79] Before the study could get properly launched, word came from the Privy Council Office, which reports to the prime minister, that the department "had to" discontinue the project; PCO officials feared the study would have a negative impact on national unity and fuel regional tensions.

The study, if completed, would have provided a more thorough look at federal government spending by region. As it is now, there is a tendency to simply add up total spending in four or five regions without making a distinction between investments in R&D and transfer payments under Ottawa's Employment Insurance program. This approach implies that a dollar spent in the Maritime provinces on Employment Insurance is equal to a dollar spent in Ontario on R&D procurement, consulting contracts, and federal public service salaries.

An effective upper house responsible for bringing a regional perspective to bear on National Policy would have seen merit in an in-depth analysis of federal government spending in terms of where funds are spent and for what purpose. It could also have ignored such directives, as I've just described, from the prime minister or the PCO. One can also speculate that Ottawa's war and reconstruction efforts would have looked much different if an elected and effective upper house, free from the rep by pop bias, had been in place.

BRINGING HOME THE BACON

In a federation that lacks an effective upper house to speak on behalf of the smaller regions, who holds political power boils down to the number of constituencies a region has in the lower house. This matters because, as noted, our institutions concentrate power in the hands of the prime minister, who has a free hand in shaping policy or new initiatives, particularly with a majority mandate. The focus will naturally be on regions that offer more votes.

It does not end there. MPs bring home infrastructure investments, and those on the government side stand a better chance of bringing more bacon to their constituencies. A review of Ottawa's New Building Canada Fund, launched in 2013, reveals that some 83 per cent of the funding went to constituencies held by government MPs.[80] If infrastructure is a key ingredient in establishing the circumstances for economic success, then it is best for a region to have a lot of MPs and preferably on the government side—the regions with the most MPs have a better chance of seeing the bacon.

LOOKING BACK

To the Maritimes, whenever the federal government raises concerns about the national economy, it speaks to Ontario's economic interest, and when it raises concerns about national unity, it speaks to Quebec. I made this point to one of Canada's leading journalists; his response, "That is where people live."[81] This logic, if it applies at all, is better suited to a unitary state than to a federation. Federalism speaks to the need to accommodate different regional circumstances and perspectives. If Canadian delegates had made this point in 1864, we would likely have a different Canada or perhaps a similar Canada, but one equipped with national institutions truly capable of accommodating regional circumstances in shaping national policies.

Market forces and resource endowment are hardly the only factors shaping the location and pace of economic development. Public policy, government procurement, and infrastructure spending going back to canals, railways, and roads, also matter a great deal. In turn, how national politicians operate and decide matters to regional economies. When national political institutions in a federation covering a geographical region as large as Canada have a limited capacity to speak to the regional factor, small provinces go unheard when important government decisions are struck. Government policies and programs matter in giving rise to new economic activities, and they are rarely geographically neutral. More is said about this in the next chapter.

NOTES

1 Ibbitson, *Loyal No More*.
2 Starr, *Equal as Citizens*, 23.
3 Stephen G. Tomblin, *Ottawa and the Outer Provinces* (Toronto: Lorimer, 1995), 16.
4 Lysiane Gagnon, "A Senate Still Searching for Sober Second Thought," *Globe and Mail*, February 13, 2013, www.theglobeandmail.com/globe-debate/a-senate-still-searching-for-sober-second-thought/article8508777/.
5 Harry Bruce, *Down Home: Notes of a Maritimer's Son* (Toronto: Key Porter Books, 1988).
6 Jeffrey Simpson, "The Truth about Atlantic Canada's Economy," *Globe and Mail*, June 20, 2001, A7.
7 Canada, *2014–15 Federal Transfers to Provinces and Territories* (Ottawa: Office of the Parliamentary Budget Office, June 19, 2014), 8.
8 Jeffrey Simpson, "With Liberal Sweep, Political Stars Align for Atlantic Canada," *Globe and Mail*, October 22, 2015, http://license.icopyright.net/user/viewFreeUse.act?fuid=MjA4OTk1MDE%3D.
9 See, among others, John Ibbitson, "How the Maritimes Became Canada's Incredible Shrinking Rregion," *Globe and Mail*, March 20, 2015, www.theglobeandmail.com/news/national/how-the-maritimes-became-canadas-incredible-shrinking-region/article23554298/.
10 See, for example, Mark Milke, *Corporate Welfare at Industry Canada since John Diefenbaker* (Vancouver: Fraser Institute, July 2013), 7.
11 See, among others, Karen Howlett, "Muskoka Communities Cash in on G8," *Globe and Mail*, November 18, 2009, www.theglobeandmail.com/news/politics/muskoka-communities-cash-in-on-g8/article4263901/.
12 Edith Robb, "It's Now Time to Change Our Image," *Moncton Times & Transcript*, July 10, 2004, A3.
13 Ibid.
14 Timothy E. Cook, *Governing With the News: The News Media as a Political Institution*, 2nd ed. (Chicago: University of Chicago Press, 2005).
15 See, among others, Claire Morris, "The New Brunswick Experience," (remarks before the Ontario Management Forum, June 1995), 11–12.
16 I am thinking here of the work of F. H. Underhill, W. Y. Smith, J. M. S. Careless, and Donald Creighton.
17 Consultation with Nick Mulder, November 1997, Ottawa.
18 John Reid, quoted in Starr, *Equal as Citizens*, 286.
19 Quoted in Dirk Meissner, untitled article, Canadian Press, reporting on Hon. Paul Martin's trip to Vancouver, accessed on July 9, 2003, www.canada.com.

20 "Martin to Emphasize Regions," *National Post*, September 23, 2003, A1.
21 "Stephen Harper's Next Move," *National Post*, July 12, 2004, A11.
22 I note that after interim Liberal Party leader Bob Rae intervened, McGuinty apologized. See "Liberal MP McGuinty Apologizes for Comments; Resigns as Energy Critic," *Globe and Mail*, November 21, 2012, A3.
23 Canada, *Canadian Automotive Exports Recover* (Ottawa: Canadian Trade Commission Service, April 22, 2015).
24 See Canada, *Recent Trends in Canadian Automotive Industries* (Ottawa: Statistics Canada, June 20, 2013).
25 See Canada, Statistics Canada, *Total Manufacturing Jobs—Motor Vehicle and Motor Vehicle Parts*, table 2180024.
26 Ontario, "Automotive," accessed May 7, 2015, www.investinontario.com/automotive5.
27 Jim Stanford, "Canada's Auto Industry: Smokestack Sector or High-Tech Winner" (presentation to the Canadian Association of Business Economics, Kingston, August 2004).
28 See, among many others, "Project Would Secure about 4,000 Jobs at Plant," *Globe and Mail*, September 8, 2004, B18.
29 "Canada Auto-Bailout Funds Issued with Limited Research: Watchdog," *Wall Street Journal*, February 17, 2015, http://blogs.wsj.com/canadarealtime/2014/11/25/canada-auto-bailout-funds-issued-with-limited-research-watchdog/.
30 "Canadian Taxpayers Lose $3.5 Billion on 2009 Bailout of Auto Firms," *Globe and Mail*, April 7, 2015, www.theglobeandmail.com/report-on-business/canadian-taxpayers-lose-35-billion-on-2009-bailout-of-auto-firms/article23828543/.
31 See Donald J. Savoie, *Governing from the Centre: The Concentration of Power in Canadian Politics* (Toronto: University of Toronto Press, 1999).
32 Donald J. Savoie, *What Is Government Good At? A Canadian Answer* (Montreal and Kingston: McGill-Queen's University Press, 2015).
33 "Toronto Poised to be Powerhouse in Trudeau Cabinet," *Globe and Mail*, October 30, 2015, www.theglobeandmail.com/news/politics/toronto-poised-to-be-powerhouse-in-trudeau-cabinet/article27044986/.
34 "Stunning Liberal Gains in Quebec as Trudeau Wins Majority Government," CBC News (Montreal), October 19, 2015, www.cbc.ca/news/canada/montreal/quebec-results-federal-election-2015-1.3278830.
35 Donald V. Smiley, "Federal-Provincial Conflict in Canada," *Publius* 4, no. 3 (1974): 15.
36 Ronald L. Watts, "Final Comments," in *Regionalism: Problems and Prospects*, ed. Bertus L. Watts and Jabu Sindane (Pretoria: HSRC, 1993).
37 Donald V. Smiley and Ronald L. Watts, *Intrastate Federalism in Canada* (Toronto: Universtity of Toronto Press in co-operation with the Royal Commission on the Economic Union and Development Prospects for Canada

and the Canadian Government Publishing Centre, Supply and Services Canada, 1985), 29.

38 Roger Gibbins, *Regionalism: Territorial Politics in Canada and the United States* (Toronto: Butterworths, 1982), 195.

39 See Higgins, Hansen, and Savoie, *Regional Policy in a Changing World*, 195.

40 Matthew Mendelsohn, "Abolish the Senate? Forget it: Change the Senate? Maybe," *Globe and Mail*, May 24, 2013, www.theglobeandmail.com/opinion/abolish-the-senate-forget-it-change-the-senate-maybe/article12127063/.

41 Stéphane Dion, "Institutional Reform: The Grass Isn't Always Greener on the Other Side," in *Political Leadership and Representation in Canada: Essays in Honour of John C. Courtney*, ed. Hans J. Michelmann, Donald C. Story, and Jeffrey S. Steeves (Toronto: University of Toronto Press, 2007), 185.

42 Quoted in Colby Cosh, "Roger Gibbins Against Senate Reform? The Hell, You Say!" *Maclean's*, May 14, 2012, www.macleans.ca/authors/colby-cosh/roger-gibbins-against-senate-reform-the-hell-you-say/.

43 Cosh, "Roger Gibbins Against Senate Reform? The Hell, You Say!"

44 "Abolish the Senate Because Reform Is Never Going to Happen: Saskatchewan Premier Brad Wall," *National Post*, July 23, 2013, www.news.nationalpost.com/news/canada/canadian-politics/abolish-the-senate-because-reform-is-never-going-to-happen-saskatchewan-premier-brad-wall.

45 Preston Manning, "Reform, Not Abolition, Is in the East's Interest," *Globe and Mail*, June 10, 2013, A13.

46 See, for example, "New Brunswick's Premier Backs Harper's Senate Reform," CBC News Canada, October 1, 2011, www.cbc.ca/news/canada/new-brunswick-s-premier-backs-harper-s-senate-reform-1.988663.

47 Phillip A. Buckner, "The Transformation of the Maritimes: 1815–1860," 25.

48 Francis W. P. Bolger, "Prince Edward Island and Confederation 1863–1873," *Canadian Catholic Historical Association Report* (1961), 25.

49 Quoted in ibid., 27.

50 See, for example, Hansen, Higgins, and Savoie, *Regional Policy in a Changing World*.

51 Peter W. Hogg, *Constitutional Law of Canada* (Toronto: Carswell, Student Edition, 2010).

52 T. W. Acheson, "The National Policy and the Industrialization of the Maritimes, 1880–1910," *Acadiensis* 1, no. 2 (Spring 1972): 4.

53 Ibid., 7.

54 Ibid., 28.

55 D. A. Muise, "The 1860s: Forging the Bonds of Union," in E. R. Forbes and D. A. Muise, *The Atlantic Provinces in Confederation* (Toronto: University of Toronto Press, 1993), 39.

56 Ibid., 24.

57 Alexander, *Atlantic Canada and Confederation: Essays in Canadian Political Economy*, 4.
58 Thorburn, *Politics in New Brunswick*, 16.
59 Ernest Forbes, quoted in "Shafted," *Atlantic Progress* (Halifax), June 1999, 36.
60 Thorburn, *Politics in New Brunswick*, 16.
61 Ibid.
62 Ibbitson, *Loyal No More*, 87–88.
63 J. R. Mallory, *The Structure of Canadian Government* (Toronto: Macmillan, 1971), 124.
64 Donald J. Savoie, *The Politics of Public Spending in Canada* (Toronto: University of Toronto Press, 1990), chap. 10.
65 Ibid., 13.
66 Miller, "The 1940s: War and Rehabilitation," 325.
67 Savoie, *Visiting Grandchildren*.
68 Quoted in Bruce, *Down Home*.
69 Forbes, *Challenging the Regional Stereotype*, 174.
70 Ibid., 180.
71 Ibid., 181.
72 Ibid., 178.
73 Ibid., 174-98.
74 Howard R. Wilson, "The Constantly Rising Ethics Bar," (notes for a presentation to the Canadian Centre for Ethics and Public Policy, November 7, 2002).
75 Alexander, *Atlantic Canada and Confederation*, 68.
76 Statistics Canada, Gross domestic product, expenditure-based, provincial and territorial, CANSIM, table 384-0038.
77 Canada, Speech from the Throne to Open the First Session of the 38th Parliament of Canada, October 5, 2004, 4.
78 Gordon Osbaldeston made this observation at a meeting attended by the author in Ottawa in March 1982.
79 The study, confidential at the time, was labelled "A Perspective on the Regional Incidence of Federal Expenditures and Reserves and Revenues," Ottawa, Department of Regional Economic Expansion, n.d.
80 "Government Favours Infrastructure Projects to Conservative Ridings," *Globe and Mail*, July 14, 2015, A1.
81 Conversation over dinner with a leading Canadian journalist in Moncton, New Brunswick, October 7, 2015.

Chapter 6

GOVERNMENT AND ECONOMIC DEVELOPMENT

Government spending alone suggests that government has a strong influence in shaping the pace and location of economic activities. Canada's total Gross Domestic Prodcut (GDP) sits at around $1.89 trillion, while Canada's total government spending amounts to about $350 billion.[1] The public sector in Canada employs 3,631,837 and has a payroll of $194 billion.[2] But government spending tells only part of the story. The federal government is Canada's largest employer: It decides where staff is located, establishes tariffs and trade policies, manages regulatory regimes, puts in place procurement policies, supports R&D, and defines and administers immigration policies. It also offers incentives to the private sector, including tax incentives, and influences private sector decisions and investments by deciding when and where infrastructure investments occur, which enables businesses to move their goods and services to markets.

Many governments in the western world continue to embrace visionary investments to grow their economies. Nothing new here. In Canada, visionary investments began with canals, roads, and railways to ensure, among other things, that businesses could get their products to markets. In more recent years, the focus has been on R&D. This is what government is good at: putting in place the requirements for economic success rather than managing economic success.[3] This chapter reviews the government's visionary investments down through the ages and how the Maritime provinces have fared.

The important point is that market forces in Canada, or for that matter anywhere, have never been left to their own devices to shape the pace and location of economic activities. This has been true since Canada was born. Indeed, the potential for an increased infrastructure spending capacity to tap into new markets led many Fathers of Confederation to sign the Confederation deal. Railway construction and the building of canals dominated Canada's political and economic development agenda in the early years. Today, public spending in R&D and innovation are the new visionary investments. The other important point is that national policies have never been spatially neutral, and Ottawa has been anything but spatially blind when it comes to economic development.

THE RAILWAY

Every student of Canadian history knows the railway was a key factor in securing support for Confederation. The railway held considerable promise for both the military defence of the British colonies and promoting economic development. All the colonies saw merit in building a national railway system. However, the cost associated with building railways proved very difficult for individual colonies to sustain.

The importance of the railway was underlined by the explicit commitment made in Canada's constitution. Section 145 of the British North America Act reads:

> Inasmuch as the Provinces of Canada, Nova Scotia and New Brunswick have joined in a Declaration that the construction of the Intercolonial Railway is essential to the consolidation of the Union of British North America, and to the assent thereto of Nova Scotia and New Brunswick, and have consequently agreed that provision should be made for its immediate construction by the Government of Canada. Therefore, in order to give effect to that Agreement, it shall be the duty of the Government and Parliament of Canada to provide for the commencement within six months after the Union, of a Railway connecting the River St. Lawrence with the City of

> Halifax in Nova Scotia, and for the construction thereof without intermission, and the completion thereof with all practicable speed.

In hindsight, we know Canada's railway system did not benefit the Maritime provinces anywhere near the extent that it was envisaged at the time of Confederation. That said, politicians from the region and even managers of the Intercolonial Railway, initially at least, did seek to promote the region's economic development. The Intercolonial Railway was part of the Confederation deal, but it was also operated by the federal government. Accordingly, it did not have to produce a profit and held considerable flexibility in establishing freight rates. The government agreed, for example, to lower freight rates in 1887, essentially to attenuate the strength of the secessionist movement in Nova Scotia.[4]

Sir Charles Tupper, a Maritimer and the minister responsible for railways, explained the importance of managing freight rates on the Intercolonial Railway to promote development. He made it clear that he was prepared to make "distinctions in freight rates in favour of parties creating a great industry."[5] Tupper insisted the Intercolonial Railway was not built to make a profit; rather, much like the St. Lawrence canal, it was a public service to promote trade and a stronger economy. The St. Lawrence was costing some $100,000 a year to operate in 1885.[6] The argument went that, if the federal government could subsidize the St. Lawrence canal to establish the circumstances for economic success for businesses in Central Canada, it could do the same for the railways for businesses in the Maritime region.

Politicians and senior managers with the Intercolonial were able to hold down freight rates for long hauls from the Maritimes until 1915. Ernest Forbes notes that "between 1916 and the end of 1921, the transportation advantage in favour of a Toronto producer over an Amherst producer in the Montreal market increased by more than 66 percent. For the Montreal producer shipping to Toronto, the advantage over an Amherst producer had increased by 79 percent."[7] Although the region strongly protested, it lacked the political clout to do much beyond protesting at every opportunity. Ottawa responded by hiring an Ottawa-based firm to review the issue. James F. Hickling Consultants reported that if the rates remained high, it would lead to the loss of twelve thousand jobs in Atlantic Canada. The rates did not level down, and the region did indeed lose twelve thousand jobs in the manufacturing sector alone in the 1920s.[8]

The government decided to do away with the Intercolonial Railway in 1919; it later became part of the CNR. The loss to the Maritime region was substantial, not just in terms of keeping freight rates down; it also affected economic activities directly. The Intercolonial Railway head office was located in Moncton, and so were its machine shops.[9]

The CNR sought to introduce a more "business-like" policy to its operations in search of a profit, not wanting to follow in the same footsteps as the Intercolonial Railway.[10] There were several reasons for its demise. There were regional conflicts and charges of favouritism and patronage, particularly from Central and Western Canada. A key factor, however, was the decline of the Maritimes' political influence in the House of Commons. Representation in the Commons had fallen from 20 to 12 per cent by the 1920s, and the region did not have anywhere near a one-third representation in Cabinet, as it was promised in the negotiations leading up to Confederation. The Maritime provinces did not have the clout in either Parliament or Cabinet to hold their own in regional conflicts managed out of Ottawa, and the Senate was no help.

Notwithstanding their loss of political clout, Maritimers' discontent with Confederation soon made the railways an important focal point. To many Maritimers, railway policy demonstrated that the region could never get a fair deal from Confederation. A highly regarded minister from New Brunswick, A. G. Blair, resigned from the Laurier cabinet over the government's railway agenda and its impact on his region. Blair strongly opposed the construction of a rail line to Portland, Maine, which, he insisted, would undermine the ability of Maritime ports to play a significant role in the "national" economy. The deal was struck without Blair and he resigned, arguing that Laurier had undermined his credibility in dealing with the railways by having direct negotiations with their representatives.[11]

Things did not improve for the Maritimes until the Robert L. Borden government came to power, and only then for a short period. Borden's biographer wrote that Borden's railway policy, was, for a short period, "developed by a small group of Cabinet members" from Central and Western Canada on the advice of prominent businessmen.[12] It was under Borden that the Intercolonial Railway head office was moved from Moncton to Toronto in 1918. The federal Conservatives in the early 1900s were basically an Ontario party with aspirations in a growing West. Forbes wrote, "Each election saw majorities in Ontario, some breakthroughs in Western provinces and minorities only from the Maritimes. This pattern continued into the election of 1911, with the Conservatives winning 85 per cent of the seats in Ontario and their only other majorities coming from Manitoba and British Columbia. It was, then, the perspective of a caucus increasingly dominated by Ontario and the West that found expression in the government's suppression of the Intercolonial and the dismantling of its rate structure during and after the War."[13]

Maritime discontentment over Ottawa's railway policy only intensified in the aftermath of the demise of Intercolonial Railway. By the 1920s, special railway freight rates that applied to the Maritime region on such things as sugar were cancelled, and rates for other products rose between 140 to 216 per cent in the region, from 1916 to 1920, but only by 111 per cent in Ontario and Quebec. [14]

Integrating the Intercolonial into the "national" railway system had wide implications for all economic sectors in the Maritime region, including retail and wholesale businesses. It led to the rise of the Maritime Rights Movement and explains why all sectors and all classes in the Maritimes were supportive of the movement, which was non-partisan—no small achievement for the region. The point is worth repeating that the railway became a *bête noire* for the Maritimes and "probably the single most important source of anti-Ottawa animus."[15] Western farmers were able to obtain a renewal of the Crow's Nest Pass Agreement on freight rates in 1927, but Maritimers were unable to secure assistance to deal with a substantial increase in freight rates.[16] Maritimers also looked to Ottawa to explain the challenges confronting the ports of Halifax and Saint John.

The Maritime Rights Movement did, in the end, have an impact on Ottawa's railway policy. In 1922 the federal government announced a 7.5 per cent decrease in freight rates and the establishment of CNR's Atlantic regional office and regional operations in Moncton.

The Maritime Rights Movement would eventually die, but not the region's concerns with Ottawa's railway policy. As is well-known, the Maritime region experienced difficulty in making the transition from wartime to peacetime in the aftermath of World War Two. For one thing, Ottawa's decision to establish virtually all wartime production in Ontario and Quebec led many Maritimers to migrate where the jobs were. For another, Ottawa's decision to hike freight rates sharply and without notice, had a highly negative impact on the region's already weak manufacturing sector and economic development prospects.

Historian Stephen Henderson maintains "the national railway regulatory board seemed indifferent to the economic consequences to the outlying regions of the sudden jump in rates."[17] Provincial governments in the Maritime provinces were not, and they joined forces with their western counterparts in voicing strong opposition to the freight-rate increases, which also had a negative impact in Western Canada. Maritime premiers made the case, time and again, that centrally determined freight rates with no regard for regional consequences would continue to doom the region to an underdevelopment status.

The federal government had, in the past, sought to give assistance to western and eastern shippers. The Crow's Nest Pass Agreement between the federal government and Canadian Pacific in 1897 had reduced freight rates on grain shipments from the Prairies. The Duncan Commission, established as a result of the Maritime Rights Movement recommending an adjustment to freight rates, enabled Maritime producers to compete in the central Canadian market. The commission recognized that giving Maritime businesses access to markets in Central Canada was a condition of Confederation. Recommendations from the Duncan Commission gave rise to the Maritime Freight Rates Act, which funded westbound rates on freights from the Maritime provinces.

Notwithstanding the above, seven provinces decided to voice strong opposition to the proposed freight-rate increases before the Board of Transport commissioners in 1947. Ontario and Quebec said nothing, other than things were fine as they were, given their locational advantages. Stephen Henderson noted the hearings "descended into police court rows" because seven provinces voiced their displeasure in the strongest of terms. But nothing came of the hearings.[18] The seven provinces decided to appeal directly to the federal cabinet to stop the proposed freight-rate increases and voice criticism of the government's transportation policy; however, the Mackenzie King government rejected both the appeal and the seven provinces' recommendation that a Royal Commission on transportation policy be established.

Political pressure on the government persisted to address freight rates. The issue was hotly debated both in the Commons and within the two major political parties, both of which were in the middle of leadership conventions, and both accepted that some form of inquiry in the country's transportation policy was required. In addition, the seven provinces asked for a second meeting with the federal cabinet and again pushed for a Royal Commission. The government finally announced on October 12, 1948, that it would establish a Royal Commission on transportation. The government appointed Justice W. F. A. Turgeon, from Saskatchewan, to chair the commission, and Harold Innis (at the time Canada's leading economist) from Toronto and Henry Angus, an economist from British Columbia, as members. There was no commissioner from the Maritime provinces.

The commission could scarcely be called a success as dissension between two of the three commissioners became obvious. Angus dismissed out of hand any suggestion the country's transportation policy be designed to retain population in regions that no longer held the logic that had led to their settlement. He never addressed how and why the logic no longer held or if the logic could be corrected to assist slow-growth regions. Innis, meanwhile, argued the Board of Transport Commissioners lacked the resources and capacity to make impartial decisions, relying far too much on data provided by the railways. Innis even argued that freight rates in "central Canada created an imbalance that threatened Confederation."[19] He warned too much of the burden of the railways was being placed on the weaker regions of the country.[20]

The Turgeon Commission tabled its findings on February 9, 1951, and disappointed everyone, except the Board of Transport Commissioners and the two central provinces. Certainly, the commission did not deliver what the seven provinces were pushing for. As Henderson maintained, "The commissioners even refrained from concluding who bears the increases in railway freight rates, although the evidence presented by the seven provinces that their constituents paid the lion's share was voluminous and convincing. Beyond endorsing the principle of rate equalization and proposing the Western bridge subsidy, the Turgeon Commission made no significant recommendations."[21]

The Maritime provinces continued to press Ottawa for more favourable westbound freight rates. They had modest success until 1994. As noted, a special assistance program was introduced in 1927, establishing Maritime rates 20 per cent lower than rates elsewhere. It was revised in 1957 to 30 per cent, and in 1969 was extended to highway carriers. A further revision in 1974 provided an additional 20 per cent reduction for selected commodities moving to markets outside the region. A federal-provincial committee determined which products were eligible for the rate subsidy.

New products manufactured in the region could be added to the list. For example, wheel weights for automobiles were declared eligible when a firm in Nova Scotia began manufacturing them. Total payments under the freight assistance programs amounted to $60 million in 1980 and $63 million in 1981. By 1990–91, payments under the Maritime Freight Rates Act (railway) and under the Atlantic Region Freight Assistance Act (railway, marine, and trucking) amounted to nearly $100 million.[22] This program was killed in 1994, when the Chrétien government launched a major program review to repair Ottawa's balance sheet.

CANALS

The railway was by no means the only significant infrastructure needed to grow the economy in 1867. Canals connected communities, bypassed falls, and transported goods, which explains why they played an important role in the negotiations leading to Confederation. It also explains why the construction and maintenance of canals became a top priority with the new government in Ottawa. Canals were regarded as public goods and were for the most part financed by government. They held some strategic military importance, but they were used mostly for commerce.[23]

There was no shortage of possibilities in the negotiations for the construction of canals at the Quebec and London conferences. Delegates had their favourite projects. Maritime delegates had the construction of the Chignecto Canal at the top of their list. Since the railway and canals were the necessary ingredients of the day to establish the circumstances for economic success, the Chignecto Canal presented enormous potential for the Maritime region. Jacques de Meulles first suggested building a canal through the Chignecto Isthmus in 1686. Over the years, through twelve major engineering reports and three Royal Commissions, none of these studies disputed the engineering feasibility of building the canal.[24] There was an understanding between Canada and Maritime representatives that the construction of the Chignecto Canal was part of the Confederation deal. There was a consensus then, and for one hundred years later, that the "Isthmus of Chignecto" was a "barrier which has obstructed the full economic development of Canada, particularly that of the Atlantic region."[25]

But things took a different turn soon after Confederation. The building and rebuilding of canals remained a priority of the new federal government in Ottawa. The online *Canadian Encyclopedia* explained it this way: "Following Confederation in 1867, inland transportation in Canada was given high priority by the new government. The 1870s and 1880s were years of active canal rebuilding and improvements. The bottleneck locks on the Grenville, the third of the Ottawa River canals, were finally rebuilt; a new Carillon Canal replaced the original canal and the Chute à Blondeau single-lock canal. All the locks on the Lachine and St Lawrence River canals were rebuilt in this period to standard dimensions.... The third Welland Canal, a major rebuilding of the second, was finished by 1887."[26] Nothing is said about the Chignecto Canal in the encyclopedia.

Yet, until the mid-1960s, Maritime MPs continuously reminded the government of commitments made during the negotiations that led to Confederation. Amos Edwin Botsford, among other MPs from New Brunswick and Nova Scotia, told Parliament that delegates at the Quebec and London deliberations held the Chignecto Canal as an inducement to New Brunswick to agree to Confederation.[27] No one challenged his point.

Though Ottawa committed important resources to the building and rebuilding of canals soon after the country was born in 1867, and though the proposed Chignecto Canal figured in the discussions leading to Confederation, the canal never made it on the government's to-do list. All the major canals in Central Canada did. To deal with the various demands, the Macdonald government established a Royal Commission in 1870, chaired by Sir Hugh Allan, to look into canal building and establish priorities.

The Allan Commission divided its recommendations into works of first, second, third, and fourth classes. The first class embraced projects where "the general interest of the Dominion" was evident and to "be undertaken and proceeded with as fast as the means at the disposal of the government will warrant."[28] All canals, except one, that made it to the first list were quickly built. The Chignecto Canal, which was strongly endorsed by the Allan Commission, is the one that was never built.

The commission reported, "The evidence submitted points out with remarkable force and unanimity, the necessity of opening a highway for commerce between the Gulf of St. Lawrence and the head waters of the Bay of Fundy through the Isthmus of Chignecto dividing them."[29] The commission turned to expert advice on the feasibility of building the canal. G. S. Gzowski, the commissioner of canals, declared, "Having read all the existing reports referring to this canal, and given the subject my very best consideration, I am perfectly satisfied that Mr. Keefer's plan is quite practicable, with or without a supply of fresh water; and that a canal of the dimensions the Commissioners have decided on recommending, can be built for the amount estimated."[30]

There is evidence to suggest the Chignecto Canal got caught up in "conflicts and jealousies" in the Ottawa bureaucracy, and though tenders were called for its construction, it stalled in the Ottawa system. For whatever reason, it never made it to the drawing boards under the Macdonald government.

The Mackenzie government came to office in 1873, and it allocated funds in its spending estimates for the construction of the Chignecto Canal. However, the economic depression of the 1870s forced the government to cut spending, and the canal became a casualty.[31] MPs from the Maritimes, however, did not lose interest in Chignecto, and they kept pushing for its construction.

In response to ongoing pressure from the Maritime MPs, the government appointed another commission in 1875 to inquire into the feasibility of the Chignecto Canal. It is important to underline the point that the 1875 commission was only the second of many other commissions and reports on the Chignecto Canal through to the 1950s. All reported that the construction of the canal was possible on "climatic and engineering grounds."[32] There was always, however, a reason not to proceed with the project. Mostly, they had to do with cost, though somehow cost was never a problem for the construction of any other canals listed on the Allan Commission to-do list.

The Maritime provinces decided they could no longer wait for the federal government to make good on its commitment to build the canal. They asked leading engineer H. G. C. Ketchum to come up with a new proposal and to shop around for additional support. Ketchum raised funds from private sources and obtained a charter in 1882 to establish the Chignecto Marine Transport Railway. The federal government agreed to pay an annual subsidy of $200,000 for twenty years on the condition the project would be in operation within several years. This would enable Ottawa to turn over responsibility for the construction of the Chignecto Canal to the private sector—something it did not do for the other canals on Allan's A-list.[33]

Ketchum successfully raised funds in the United Kingdom and was able to commit $4 million to the construction of the Chignecto Canal. However, he did not have enough funds to complete the project on time. One of his British investors had to back out of the deal after the crash of the money market in England in 1890, and because some of the firm's investments had gone bad in Uruguay and Argentina. Ketchum asked for more time, but the House of Commons refused to extend the deadline for the subsidy; the project collapsed.[34] By 1896 Ketchum had raised and spent $3.5 million on the project and had something like 80 per cent of the work completed. He required another $1.5 million and about two more months of work to finish the project. The bill to extend the period for Ketchum to secure new funds was defeated in the Commons by a vote of fifty-five to fifty-four. The Senate played no role in the decision.[35]

Maritime politicians would still not let the project die. The Maritime economy was continuing to lose ground to Central Canada, particularly at the turn of the last century. One of the reasons that explains this is the prohibitive cost of moving goods to a protected market in Central Canada, as already noted. Many in the region looked to the Chignecto Canal as a solution.

The rise of the Maritime Rights Movement and repeated calls by Maritime MPs to address the issue led the House of Commons to adopt the following resolution in 1929: "Resolved, that in the opinion of this House, it is advisable that the government of Canada take immediate steps to further investigate said project as to feasibility, cost of construction, economic and national advantages to be gained by the construction of a ship canal across the Isthmus of Chignecto to connect the waters of the Bay of Fundy with the waters of the Gulf of St. Lawrence and further that the government be urged to make these surveys and investigations with the least possible delay."[36] Two years later, the Mackenzie King government responded by establishing yet another commission to look into the construction of the Chignecto Canal. The commission tabled its report in the Depression years of the 1930s, not good timing. Regardless, it did maintain, "As a result of our extended study we find that physically the project is feasible."[37] It also concluded the canal would have no negative impact on the region's fishery.[38]

The commission, however, had a number of reservations. One was cost. It estimated the cost at between $23 and $38 million, depending on the depth and width of the canal. Another was the canal's impact on Canada's railway system and loss of traffic; the commission reminded the government that the railway system was built at a considerable cost to taxpayers. Furthermore, the government was providing a subsidy to the region to provide railway services under the Maritime Freight Rates Act.[39] The commission considered the possibility of developing water power by harnessing the tides of the Bay of Fundy and concluded it was possible to combine navigation and power projects along the canal. But the cost would be very high, adding another $8 million to the total cost of the navigation project.[40] The commission—both chaired and managed from Central Canada—noted that its hearing in the region was "not largely attended and the interest displayed in the inquiry was not extensive."[41]

Arthur Surveyer, an engineer from Montreal, Quebec, chaired the commission. Other members included David Robb of Amherst, Nova Scotia, and John F. Sowards of Kingston, Ontario. Robb, the lone Maritimer on the commission who knew the region well, wrote a dissenting opinion, which is reported here by his colleagues: "Having had special opportunities to examine not only the previous engineering reports, but to look into the physical features closely as a life-long resident of the locality, he is of opinion that the Minudie-La Planche route would have considerable advantages over the Missiguash route recommended by the engineers and endorsed by his fellow commissioners. It is his belief that a canal on the Minudie-La Planche route could be built for much less than the present estimate."[42]

The commission's staff was drawn from the Ottawa bureaucracy. George W. Yates, the commission's secretary, was the assistant deputy minister in the Department of Railways and Canals. Other staff members came from the department's engineering department. The commission did acknowledge that the total cost of building the St. Lawrence-Great Lakes canal amounted to nearly $260 million, an amount much greater than the cost of developing the Chignecto Canal. It explained, however, that "in the case of the Great Lakes, the canals are a national necessity; in the case of Chignecto a canal would simply be a refinement of present facilities and largely of local significance."[43] It never explained what it meant by a "refinement of present facilities" or how it could separate "national necessity" from "local significance." In the end, the Chignecto Canal was not built.

This argument made sense to the chair who was from Montreal, the second member of the commission who was from Kingston, and all the commission's staff who were from Ottawa. It did not make sense to the lone voice from the Maritimes who wrote a dissenting opinion. Sitting in Ottawa, the St. Lawrence Seaway is a national project while the Chignecto Canal was only a regional project.

ONE LAST TRY

Maritime political and economic leaders were still not prepared to throw in the towel on the Chignecto Canal as late as the 1950s. Infrastructure spending was in vogue in the post-World War Two period. Construction began on the Trans-Canada Highway in 1950. In 1951 Parliament passed the International Rapids Power Development Act to enable Canada to start navigation works on the St. Lawrence River from Montreal to Lake Ontario. In 1954 the St. Lawrence Seaway Authority, a Crown corporation, was established by Act of Parliament to acquire lands and construct and operate a waterway between Montreal and Lake Erie. In the end, the cost was $470 million, with Canada assuming $336.5 million of the cost and the United States $133 million. In 1959 the St. Lawrence Seaway was completed, establishing a link between the Great Lakes and global markets. Other initiatives were later launched, including a realignment of the Welland Canal to bypass the city of Welland at a cost of another $300 million to Canada.[44] Canada and the UnitedStates spent an additional $600 million on hydroelectric development.[45] These developments all had a negative impact on Maritime ports, notably those at Halifax and Saint John.

Corey Slumkoski wrote that the proposed St. Lawrence Seaway once again sparked interest in the construction of the Chignecto Canal in the Maritimes. Like the St. Lawrence Seaway, the canal could provide a new source of hydroelectric power for the region by harnessing the tides. It would also shorten the distance between the eastern seaboard and the continental interior. Maritimers looked to past "massive" government investments in canals in Ontario and in the St. Lawrence—all funded by "federal coffers"—and asked why government investments could not be committed to the Chignecto Canal. The view from the Maritimes was that federal government spending continued to be earmarked for projects of "national importance" as defined by Ottawa.[46] The difference, of course, is that one region—Ontario-Quebec—had the political clout and the bureaucratic influence to decide what was of national importance and what was regional.

Maritimers were paying careful attention to what Ottawa was doing in Central Canada and not doing in their region. C. C. Avard, the editor of the *Sackville Tribune-Herald*, wrote, "Ontario has its canals, why not the Maritimes?"[47] New Brunswick MP Alfred J. Brooks rose in the Commons on June 9, 1948, to make the point that "it was all very well for Ontario to have pleasure excursions, scenic beauty and places for the boys to go swimming, but we in the Maritime provinces are asking for canals which would be of benefit to the Maritime provinces and to the whole of Canada."[48] Progressive Conservative MP Percy Black from Nova Scotia declared, "The members of this house are not averse to spending $500 million in order to build the St. Lawrence canal but Nova Scotia, Prince Edward Island and New Brunswick are given the brush off."[49]

Local business and community leaders established a Chignecto Canal Committee to promote the project[50] and commission studies to make the case for the canal before the federal government. The committee proposed to build the 30.5-kilometre canal on a narrow strip of land that separates Nova Scotia from New Brunswick. Studies showed the canal would shorten shipping routes between the continental interior and the eastern seaboard of the United States by some 650 kilometres. Support for the committee's work came from many quarters in the four Atlantic provinces, starting with the two adjoining communities, Sackville, New Brunswick, and Amherst, Nova Scotia, local boards of trade, and leading businessmen from the region, notably K. C. Irving.

Local business leaders made the case that national tariffs and trade barriers made it difficult for them to sell their products in international markets. They had to push their products "uphill" to markets in Central Canada while businesses in Central Canada only had to nudge their goods downhill to the Maritime provinces.[51] The Chignecto Canal Committee made the case that all sectors of the Atlantic economy would benefit from the canal: essentially, the canal would establish the required circumstances for economic success in the region, much like the St. Lawrence Seaway was doing in Central Canada. The committee also noted the canal would generate new activities around large zinc and copper deposits in northern New Brunswick, in the forestry, fishery, coal, and manufacturing sectors. Since transportation disadvantages to the eastern seaboard of the United States and to markets in Central Canada would be considerably attenuated, the region's economic performance would improve. This, combined with new sources of energy, would provide important economic benefits not only to the three Maritime provinces but also to Newfoundland and Labrador. K. C. Irving and other business leaders pledged to invest $105 million in new economic activities in the Bay of Fundy area alone if the canal was built.[52]

The committee was also careful to highlight benefits that would flow to Central Canada. The canal, it argued, would open up new markets for Ontario- and Quebec-based businesses by cutting shipping costs between Central Canada and the eastern seaboard of the United States. The committee reminded Ottawa that out of the ten surveys of the Chignecto Canal since Confederation, "all" agreed that it "was feasible."[53] It reminded Ottawa that the 1870 Hugh Allan Royal Commission had divided its recommendations into works of first, second, third, and fourth classes. The first class included "all these works" that were in "the general interest of the Dominion" and should be "proceeded with as fast as the means" will warrant. As already noted, the Chignecto Canal was one of twelve placed in the first category and the only one that was never built.[54]

The estimated cost of building the canal in 1957 stood at $90 million, a figure substantially lower than the construction of the St. Lawrence Seaway. The committee listed, in detail, the benefits flowing from the Chignecto Canal:

> 1) The Canal would be the direct cause for the investment of over $105 million in new industries in the Fundy area.... The stimulus that this new investment would give to the regional industry would make the Chignecto Canal a primary major development project of the Atlantic region. New plants constructed as a result of the existence of the Chignecto Canal would result in a permanent increase in annual production of the Atlantic Provinces estimated at $280 million.
> 2) The construction phase of the Canal could result in a temporary increase of $300 million in Canadian incomes, of which $160 million might be spent in the Atlantic Provinces.
> 3) The net cost to Canada of this step to relieve the depressed conditions of the Atlantic Provinces could be more than counterbalanced by increased revenues from the region.

4) The Canal would be a natural extension of the St. Lawrence Seaway, linking it with a sheltered route for Atlantic coastal shipping. For the new waterway a laker-type boat could be used, which would be cheaper to build and to operate than the ships normally used in ocean travel.
5) It appears probable that the very large tidal power potential of the eastern portion of the Bay of Fundy will be economically developed in the future. This can be achieved without conflict with the construction and operation of the Canal.
6) The Canal would create a new economy in Atlantic Canada.[55]

As we know, Ottawa did not buy the committee's arguments. Lionel Chevrier, the powerful Transport minister from Quebec, made clear his opposition to Chignecto at every opportunity. If the responsible minister—particularly one with Chevrier's influence—representing a province that was also home to the prime minister did not support a project that came under his jurisdiction in the 1950s (and before governing from the centre became how things work in Ottawa), the chances of the project seeing the light of day were slim. Chevrier was convinced the Chignecto Canal would take away from his St. Lawrence Seaway project, and he embraced all arguments against the Chignecto Canal, insisting the cost was too high.

Chevrier would also report that not all of Atlantic Canada was four squares behind the project. Certainly, New Brunswick, Prince Edward Island, and Newfoundland and Labrador made clear their support, at least publicly. The Angus L. Macdonald Nova Scotia government, however, never made its support publicly known—something those in Ottawa opposed to Chignecto would often point out. Macdonald had lobbied Ottawa to help pay for the construction of two bridges, including the Canso Causeway.

Macdonald and Chevrier teamed up in September 1952 to announce the construction of the causeway. Macdonald, a Cape Breton native, attached considerable importance to linking his home island to mainland Nova Scotia. He pledged to have one hundred pipers march across the causeway, playing "The Road to the Isles." The causeway was officially opened in December 1954 with a gala parade, but the one hundred pipers were silent.[56] Chevrier and those of like mind in Ottawa much preferred committing funds to two bridges and other Nova Scotia projects, which had no negative impact on Central Canada and represented no competition for the St. Lawrence Seaway, than supporting the Chignecto Canal.[57]

All that is left of the proposed Chignecto Canal are eleven engineering and feasibility reports and the remnants of the work carried out by Ketchum. The canal will never be built. K. C. Irving, who knew a thing or two about pulling himself up by his bootstraps, did not hesitate to point the finger at Ottawa for the canal always remaining on the drawing board. He said the construction of the Chignecto Canal was a project Ottawa "owed to this part of the country."[58] K. C. Irving once observed, "Let's not forget that in some cases, Upper Canadians are the worst type of foreigners."[59]

Once more, key political figures in Ottawa did not accept the arguments in favour of the Chignecto Canal, convinced that the Chignecto Canal, which they deemed a regional project, could create problems for the St. Lawrence Seaway, which they saw as a national project. Power established by national political institutions—notably the House of Commons operating on a rep by pop basis—was free (and remains free) to define what is national and what is regional. The Senate had little influence on the Chignecto Canal issue.

RESEARCH AND DEVELOPMENT, THE NEW INFRASTRUCTURE

R&D and innovation are to the new economy what railways and canals were to the old one. The word from government think tanks and economic development specialists is that a country, a region, or a community either innovates or dies. If there is a consensus among the specialists, it is that "innovation underpins growth in productivity and productivity is the key to a better standard of living."[60] It is no coincidence the countries that fared better in the aftermath of the 2008 recession were those that invested more in R&D. Governments continue to contribute more to R&D and innovation than is generally assumed. Of course, high-performing national economies have a strong entrepreneurial private sector, but they also have a public sector heavily involved in R&D activities and in putting together visionary funding, which would otherwise not take place.[61]

Governments, for example, had a direct hand in developing the Internet, GPS, and nuclear power. In Canada, the government can claim to have played a pioneer role in developing the country's aerospace industry and a number of pharmaceutical products.[62] In its early years, BlackBerry benefitted from assistance and procurement contracts from the government of Canada and still does, since federal public servants are equipped with a BlackBerry, rather than an iPhone. In the United States, the National Science Foundation provided a grant that produced the algorithm that led to the search engine Google. A partial list of commercial products that flowed out of the space program include freeze-dried food, Dustbusters, Speedo swimsuits, hand-held high-density LED units, scratch-resistant lenses, improved radial tires, and solar cells.[63]

R&D—IT'S A NATIONAL THING

There is a mindset in Ottawa that "national" centres of excellence should be located in Central Canada and that it is important to ensure a degree of balance between Ontario and Quebec. The same mindset applies to national museums and to the manufacturing sector.

In March 2013 I had a conversation with David Parsons, a recently retired Ottawa-based business owner. I told him about Paderno, a well-known, innovative, and successful manufacturer of cookware from Prince Edward Island. I pointed out that the company had even produced the cookware for Air Force One. He had never heard of Paderno, and he had a puzzled expression. "Somehow," I said, "you don't think that Paderno should be located in PEI?" "Yes," he responded. That is the perception in Central Canada due to a variety of causes that have accumulated over the years.

As for national museums, it seems only Central Canada can properly be home to them. New museums are established in the Ottawa-Gatineau area with some regularity (e.g., the Canadian Museum of Civilization in 1989, now known as the Canadian Museum of History, the National Gallery of Canada in the 1980s, and the Canadian War Museum in 2005) and with minimal political controversy in the national media. Things were different when the Asper family applied for federal government funding to help build a Canadian Museum of Human Rights in Winnipeg.[64]

The mindset is that when it comes to national initiatives the focus should be on the Toronto-Ottawa-Montreal corridor, because that is where they properly belong and to meet international competition. This corridor is looking to compete with New York, London, and Tokyo, not with other Canadian regions, and particularly not with the Maritime provinces. Ottawa is located in the middle of the corridor where both political power and bureaucratic influence come together. The observation of a Toronto-based advertising executive whose firm produced a prominent commercial for the Super Bowl was revealing: "The fact that we're from Toronto, a relatively small place, the international exposure will hopefully help us."[65] If Toronto is considered a relatively small place to compete in the global economy, one can only imagine what residents of the Toronto-Ottawa-Montreal corridor must think of Halifax or Moncton.

In recent years, Ottawa has introduced new measures to isolate important national programs and its investments in economic development from political and regional considerations. In February 2002 the government of Canada launched a ten-year innovation strategy designed "to move Canada to the front rank of the world's most innovative countries"[66] by turning to arm's-length foundations to deliver the programs. That previous politically inspired decisions enabled firms and institutions to develop an R&D capacity and position them to access funding from arm's-length foundations did not seem to be a factor in the eyes of the Ottawa-based officials who established the new policy. It made sense that, although the first step was politically inspired, future decisions should now be struck by arm's-length considerations. Good for Ontario and Quebec; not so good for the Maritime provinces.

Lucienne Robillard, Industry minister in the Martin government between December 2003 and July 2004, looked to the United States and to key sectors located in Ontario and Quebec to guide the work of her department. It is worth quoting her at length:

> The department's analysis indicates that U.S. productivity growth has outpaced productivity growth in Canada for the following reasons. On average, U.S. firms invest more strongly in capital equipment, which translates directly into higher productivity. There is a large Canada-U.S. innovation gap, reflected in higher levels of R&D spending in the U.S. relative to the size of their economy.... Canadians have every right to be confident in our economy. We have innovative leaders on the cutting-edge in areas like ICT, biotechnology and nanotechnology. Our automotive industry continues to demonstrate that it has what it takes to attract new investment. We possess an aerospace industry that is of global prominence.[67]

Like other Industry ministers, she views things from a national perspective, and here read Ontario and Quebec.

Ottawa's 2002 "innovation strategy" set a target of developing at least ten internationally recognized technology clusters in Canada by 2010. Existing strengths and clusters already in various stages of maturity were noted, including "wine in Niagara, aerospace in Montreal, new media in Vancouver, agricultural biotechnology in Saskatoon, information and communication technologies in Ottawa, Toronto and Kitchener-Waterloo...and a well-established financial services cluster in Toronto."[68] These constituted important bootstraps for the named regions to participate in the new economy. Nothing was said then, or since, about innovation clusters in the Maritime provinces.

Responding to pressure from MPs from Atlantic and Western Canada, Industry Canada produced a report on regional perspectives on innovation. The January 2003 report argued that "industrial R&D worker per capita is highest in Central Canada where opportunities have historically been the greatest" and that "business investment in R&D is relatively weak in most regions with only Ontario and Quebec being above the national, per capita average." In the case of the Maritime provinces, the report said that "private sector R&D performance lags [behind] the rest of the country, industry receptor capacity is a critical challenge and cluster development is in early stages." It added that "the [Maritime] region's small and medium-sized universities have difficulty competing for R&D programming as currently designed and provincial governments have limited capacity to invest in university growth." It concluded, however, that ACOA's Atlantic Innovation Fund (AIF) "has had positive impact, encouraging key industry stakeholders to act in a coordinated fashion."[69]

The "national" innovation strategy has invested billions in R&D, in the new economy, and in the creation of at least ten internationally recognized technology clusters. The bulk of the investment is now being delivered through arm's-length agencies or foundations operating free from political interference. As a senior federal official and a key architect of the strategy explained, "The problem when you launch a new program is that ministers and MPs are always on the lookout to get their share of the spending. The innovation strategy is vitally important to Canada's economic future and we decided to isolate it from this problem. We created foundations where decisions are made strictly on the basis of merit."[70]

There was a time, however, when Central Canada started from scratch in innovation, and MPs were on the lookout for a helping hand from the federal government. A retired Industry Canada official explained, "I was there when we developed Shirleys Bay. We built the place and grew a strong ability to carry out research in civilian telecommunications and military research. We started from scratch. Now when we introduce new initiatives in these areas, we add new program architecture on the existing capacity. Resources go there. The Maritime region missed the boat back then and continues to miss it now. New measures are designed for what is there, what exists, not for the Maritimes to catch up or to start where central Canada started in the 1960s."[71] There were federal government start-up resources available in the 1960s to get started, to grow a capacity, but those are no longer available. The focus now is on helping existing capacities develop further.

In addition to the innovation strategy, the federal government has established and funded a number of independent bodies over the past several years, and today they operate completely free of political direction. They include the Canada Foundation for Innovation (CFI) (over $3 billion), the Canada Research Chairs, the Canada Millennium Scholarship Foundation ($2.5 billion), Canada Health Infoway ($500 million), Genome Canada ($435 million), the Canadian Health Services Research Foundation ($126 million), the Trudeau Foundation ($120 million), and the Canada Foundation for Sustainable Development Technology ($100 million). Much like the head offices and activities of the thirty-two Crown corporations established during World War Two, these foundations, their head offices, and their activities have little impact on the economy of the Maritimes. And, much like the Crown corporations, these foundations will continue to have a significant impact on the economies of Ontario, Quebec, and now, albeit to a lesser extent, Alberta and British Columbia.

The foundations are part of neither the private nor the public sector; they operate in a kind of no man's land. For instance, the former head of the CFI, David Strangway, described the foundation as "a non-governmental organization."[72] He is right, given that ministers, the government, and Parliament have no authority to direct, control, hold to account, or impose sanctions on them. Yet, these foundations are also not part of the private sector, because they are not subject to market forces. They are, in fact, self-governing entities that spend public funds but are accountable to no one other than themselves. They are free to operate away from political requirements and regional considerations, and that is precisely what they have done.

The foundations have concentrated their innovation strategy and spending program efforts in Southern Ontario, Montreal, to some extent Vancouver, and in some instances in Alberta. The Maritime provinces have been virtually left out. The CFI, for example, has allocated "less than 3 per cent of its resources to research activities in the three Maritime provinces, the Canadian Institutes of Health Research about 2.5 percent, the Canadian Space Agency less than 3 percent, and the Networks of Centres of Excellence less than 2 percent."[73] Per capita spending by the CFI reveals that Quebec secured $63.41 per person and Ontario $51.07. Compare this to $35.37 per person for Prince Edward Island, $33.08 for Nova Scotia, and $15.34 for New Brunswick.[74] Again, the head offices of these foundations are located in the Toronto-Ottawa-Montreal corridor. Given this situation, it is difficult to imagine how the Maritime provinces will ever catch up or, more to the point, why Maritimers would ever favour a strong role for the federal government in economic development.

Ontario has done very well under all foundation programs. The province was awarded over 40 per cent of the funding under the Canadian Institutes of Health Research, 34 per cent under Networks of Centres of Excellence, and 38 per cent under the CFI. It also secured 39 per cent of the funding in natural science and engineering research. This and other evidence suggest those who argue free trade and the north-south economic pull are such that Ontario's economic interests are now less tied to east-west economic relations may well have overstated their case. Interprovincial trade remains important to Ontario, accounting for about 30 per cent of its total trade. Ontario is the centre of Canada's financial services industry, it houses the bulk of Canadian companies' head offices, and the national government and its public service are in tune with Ontario's economic interests. Ontario firms draw more from Canada's network of embassies, and its strong diplomatic presence in the United States, than any other region.[75]

Ontario and Quebec are also faring very well under the Canada Research Chairs. Together, they have 1,141 Canada Research Chairs out of a total of 1,880, or 60.7 per cent.[76] Ontario alone has been allocated 703 chairs (37.4 per cent), while the universities in the three Maritime provinces combined were allocated 93 chairs, or 4.9 per cent of the total. The three Maritime provinces accounted for 5.2 per cent of Canada's population in 2014 (see table 1 on the next page).

Table 1. Regional distribution of the Canada Research Chairs

	Number	%	% of the population
Maritimes provinces	93	4.9	5.2
Quebec	438	23.3	33.2
Ontario	703	37.4	38.5
Other provinces	646	34.4	23.1
Total	1,880	100.0	100.0

Figure 1

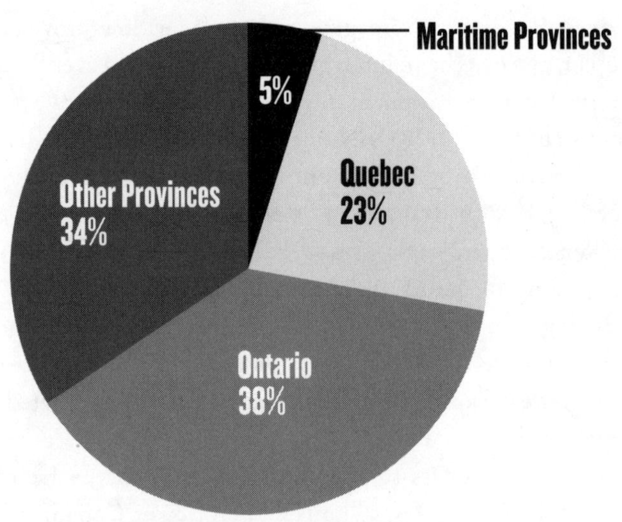

After hearing numerous complaints from Atlantic MPs, the Prime Minister's Office acknowledged the government's innovation strategy was bypassing the Atlantic region. As we saw earlier, ACOA produced a $300 million, five-year program designed to strengthen the economy of the four provinces by accelerating the development of knowledge-based industries. The AIF was political in the sense that the initiative was in response to pressure from Atlantic MPs on the government side only a year or so before the next election. In addition, the initiative was funded in part by reallocated funds from existing economic development programs for Atlantic Canada. Other R&D activities, including the foundations, were funded with new money exclusively. However, it served to leave the national innovation agenda intact, free from having to deal with regional considerations. The AIF has been no less successful than CFI or other national efforts in this regard. To the extent evaluation reports in government hold much merit, a mid-term evaluation audit of the AIF conducted in 2004 by an Ottawa-based consulting firm concluded that the program was successful, that it had supported some hundred projects with a total value of more than $625 million, and that it was "meeting a need that is not met by any other federal program."[77]

DEUX POIDS, DEUX MESURES

There is evidence that Ottawa's approach to visionary investments also applies to other sectors. As noted, Ottawa's procurement policies during World War Two, which helped transform Canada's economy from agricultural-based into an industrial economy and helped shape Canada's modern manufacturing sector, strongly favoured the two most populous provinces and largely ignored the three Maritime provinces. This approach was also evident in Ottawa's shipbuilding efforts in the early 1980s. The federal government approved plans to build six Halifax-class frigates in 1983, and another six in 1988. The Saint John shipyard was awarded the contract through a competitive building process with some restrictions tied to Canadian content.

Shortly after the contract was awarded, Ottawa forced Saint John Shipbuilding to subcontract three vessels to MIL-Davie Shipbuilding located in Sorel, Quebec. Quebec ministers led by Marc Lalonde intervened to ensure Quebec received its share of the procurement contract. The Quebec facility could not compete in the open bidding process and was only awarded the work through political intervention. New Brunswick's Roméo LeBlanc, then senior cabinet minister, told me that "Marc Lalonde and André Ouellet got to Trudeau and that was that. I had little say in that decision."[78] The Quebec shipyard had difficulties meeting production targets and ran into delays. Saint John Shipbuilding sued MIL-Davie Shipbuilding for non-performance. The suit was dropped only after Ottawa compensated Saint John Shipbuilding for $323 million for problems at MIL-Davie. For its part, Saint John Shipbuilding delivered the frigate program "on time and under budget."[79]

Quebec minister for the Economy, Jacques Daoust, told the media in May 2015 that he was "begging" Ottawa to give a shipbuilding contract to the Davie Shipyard now that "British Columbia and the Maritimes' shipyards have well-filled order books." He neglected to add that the Maritimes won the competition in an arm's-length tender process.[80] Begging works, particularly when it comes from a province with seventy-eight MPs in Parliament. In June 2015 the minister of Defence announced the government was initiating "exclusive negotiations" with Davie Shipyard to provide a supply ship for the Canadian navy.[81] The announcement came four months before the 2015 general election. Political intervention, it seems, is fine when it involves Ontario or Quebec with their large number of MPs, but less so when it comes to the Maritime provinces. The Senate, meanwhile, played no part in speaking to the regional perspective on this or other major procurement decisions.

The previous example is far from the only one where national political institutions have let down outer Canada. The Mulroney government awarded the CF-18 maintenance contract to Canadair after Bristol Aerospace, from Winnipeg, won the bid.[82] The head of Bristol told then Manitoba premier Howard Pawley, "If this is the way Canada wishes to do business, we will avoid smaller provinces; they have too little political clout. It's better for us to choose provinces like Quebec or Ontario; they can pull the political strings."[83]

Jeffrey Simpson suggested Stephen Harper learned the lesson and put in place an arm's-length bidding process for the 2011 decision to build new navy ships. He wrote that government "defined the ships it wanted, and the money it would pay. It asked a group of civil servants to assess the shipyards interested in bidding. It hired an international firm to cross-check their work. It published the results, and lived by them, whatever the political consequences."[84] Politicians were only told of the choice minutes before the announcement was made public.[85] The Halifax-based Irving Shipyard won the bulk of the contract. The point is, when Ottawa embraces an open, transparent, and fair bidding process free of political interference, the Maritime region is able to compete and win. It is interesting, if not revealing, to note that Harper is from Western Canada and Trudeau and Mulroney are from Central Canada.

Ottawa's *deux poids, deux mesures* is evident in other procurement projects, revealing that ACOA has had difficulty pursuing its advocacy mandate within the federal government. In the 1980s, Germany's Thyssen Industries called on the federal government, wishing to establish a manufacturing plant in Bear Head, Cape Breton. Thyssen wanted to establish a heavy industrial manufacturing plant in eastern Nova Scotia to produce military vehicles and a range of environmental protection products. What Thyssen asked of the government was a sole-sourced start-up order from the Department of National Defence to design and build 250 Light-Armoured Vehicle (LAV) units from the department's 1,600 LAV requirements. ACOA strongly endorsed the proposal.[86] Thyssen was able to secure an "understanding in principle" with the federal government in 1988.

The project, however, did not go beyond the understanding in principle. The proposal ran into stiff opposition from Ontario ministers in the federal cabinet, senior public servants in Ottawa, and the Ontario-based defence industries. The *Toronto Star* reported the proposal "sparked a split within Mulroney's cabinet, between ministers from Atlantic Canada—the proposed site of the Bear Head plant—and the manufacturing heartland of Ontario."[87] Whenever such opposition arises, the Atlantic region is no match against Ontario's political weight in the House of Commons. And the Senate is relegated to the sidelines.

Senior public servants in the Privy Council Office, the Industry department, and Foreign Affairs teamed up to oppose the project. Industry officials feared that it would "undermine existing domestic manufacturer General Motors." PCO and Foreign Affairs officials argued the proposal "could jeopardize Canadian foreign policy by selling military vehicles to volatile areas such as the Middle East." Robert Fowler, who was then a senior PCO official, explained, "At bottom this is a moral choice, a point of principle, a decision not to build a stall in the Middle East arms bazaar."[88] The project never advanced beyond the discussion stage in Ottawa.

Now, fast forward to 2015. Somehow, moral choices and points of principle are thrown out the window. The government of Canada agreed to a multi-billion dollar deal to sell "made-in-Canada light armoured vehicles" to Saudi Arabia. The deal was approved by the federal government's Canadian Commercial Corporation in support of General Dynamics Land Systems Canada, based in London, Ontario. The government has refused to make public the requirements of the deal, insisting it needs to protect the "commercial confidentiality" of General Dynamics Land Systems Canada.[89] Departmental emails revealed that the Department of Foreign Affairs issued no red flags over the proposed deal and that "General Dynamics has little to fear concerning official approval of its export permits." The *Globe and Mail* observed, "Selling General Dynamics light-armoured vehicles to the Saudi government will help sustain more than 3,000 jobs in Canada, including many in London, Ont., where the factory is located. There are 10 federal ridings in the London region, many of them held by Conservatives, and the Tories are eager to retain this foothold in the October election."[90] The federal government refused "to divulge how it was justifying this massive sale to Saudi Arabia under Ottawa's strict export control regime" given that "rules oblige Ottawa to examine whether arms shipments would further endanger the civilian population in countries with poor human-rights records."[91]

The newly elected Justin Trudeau government had an opportunity, shortly after it came to power, to cancel the contract. Its Global Affairs department has a responsibility to audit requests to export military goods to countries "whose governments have a persistent record of serious violations of the human rights of their citizens."[92] Stéphane Dion, the minister responsible, declared, "The contract is not something that we will revisit."[93] Political and business leaders in London jumped to the defence of the contract to Saudi Arabia, insisting it was "a pivotal component of the region's effort to become a major hub for defence-industry manufacturing."[94] No federal minister and no senior federal public servant spoke about "a moral choice" or building a "stall in the Middle East arms bazaar."

Controversy over the Saudi arms deal negotiated by the previous Harper government dogged the Justin Trudeau government for months. The United Nations released a report documenting human rights violations by Saudi Arabia.[95] The Foreign Affairs minister, Stéphane Dion, described Saudi Arabia's human rights record as "terrible."[96] No matter, the government announced the contract "will be exempt from the global arms deal"—a standard practice for countries that sign the treaty—and stood firm in its decision.[97] The *Globe and Mail* explained why: "The $15 billion deal will keep 3,000 Canadians employed for 14 years—many of them in Southwestern Ontario."[98] It later added in an editorial that cancelling the contract "would be a futile gesture because another country would simply supply the combat vehicles."[99] That logic does not apply, it seems, to the Maritime provinces.

This instance speaks to *deux poids, deux mesures,* and it speaks once again to the inability of our national political institutions to deal with regional circumstances. If anyone needed examples in which provincial premiers can never play the role the Senate ought to be playing, one need look no further than this case or Ottawa's decision to award the CF-18 maintenance contract to a Montreal-based firm even if Winnipeg-based Bristol won the bid, or to the ability of Ontario MPs, federal cabinet ministers, and senior public servants in Ottawa to turn a blind eye to "a moral choice, a point of principle" when it comes to Ontario's economic interests.

LOOKING BACK

Ottawa has always been able to count on the three Maritime provinces as it sought to strengthen its role in the federation. Why would the region want to support a strong central government, given that Ottawa has consistently left the Maritime region wanting under its national economic development agenda, and given that national political institutions—unlike the case in other federations—have little capacity to accommodate regional interests, notably those from the smaller provinces? History suggests that a strong central government has favoured the more populous provinces in establishing circumstances for economic success. This should come as no surprise to anyone, since the rep by pop basis for establishing political power has never been challenged.

Certainly, the Maritime provinces have fared extremely well under Ottawa's various transfer payment schemes from the Equalization program to Employment Insurance. The trade-off for the Maritimes was to let Ottawa focus on promoting economic development in Central Canada in return for sharing some of the benefits through federal transfers in the form of guilt money to both Maritime governments and Maritimers. But even that is changing now, as we will see in following chapters.

As noted, there is a tendency in Ottawa, in some think tanks, and in the national media, to add up all federal government spending and argue that the Maritime region continues to receive more than its share. This perspective conveniently overlooks the fact that a dollar spent in R&D, in an attempt to establish the circumstances for economic success, can hardly compare to, say, a dollar spent in Employment Insurance.

Politicians, and even public servants, tend to view Canada through regional lenses. Politicians define their work through the region they represent and the region that holds the most potential to gain and retain power. Nearly all public servants who hold influence are located in the National Capital Region, or NCR. They bring to their work the perspective and biases of regional stereotypes, the economic interests of the NCR, and particularly the ambitious ones will follow the lead of central agencies, notably the PCO and the Finance department in focusing on the national interest—in reality the interest of Ontario and Quebec. This explains, for example, why the F-18 contract was awarded to a Montreal firm, and as we have seen, why moral choices and points of principle apply to the Maritime provinces but are cast aside when it comes to the economic interest of Southern Ontario. Other federations have an effective upper house in their national political institutions to bring a broader and more balanced regional perspective to these lenses. Canada does not.

NOTES

1 Statistics Canada, CANSIM, table 384-0038. This is total government spending and does not take into account the impact of transfer payments. Accordingly, total government spending is lower than $350 billion.

2 Canada, *Public Sector Employment* (Ottawa: Statistics Canada, 2011).

3 See Savoie, *What Is Government Good At?*

4 See E. R. Forbes, "The Intercolonial Railway and the Decline of the Maritime Provinces Revisited," *Acadiensis* 24, no. 1 (Autumn 1994): 3-24.

5 Canada, *Debates*, House of Commons, 1879, 157-9, http://eco.canadiana.ca/view/oocihm.9_07185.

6 Forbes, "The Intercolonial Railway," 8.

7 Ibid., 14-15.

8 Ibid., 17.

9 "New Brunswick's Railways of the Past," Provincial Archives of New Brunswick, 2016, http://archives.gnb.ca/Exhibits/archivalportfolio/TextViewer.aspx?culture=en-CA&myFile=Railways.

10 See, for example, Ken Cruikshank, "The People's Railway: The Intercolonial Railway and the Canadian Public Enterprise Experience," *Acadiensis* 16, no. 1 (Autumn 1986): 78-100.

11 D. M. Young, "Blair, Andrew George" in *Dictionary of Canadian Biography*, vol. 13, University of Toronto/Universite Laval, 2003–, www.biographi.ca/en/bio/blair_andrew_george_13E.html.

12 Colin Howell, "The 1900s, Industry, Urbanization and Reform," in *The Atlantic Provinces in Confederation*, ed. E. R. Forbes and D. A. Muise (Toronto: University of Toronto Press, 1993), 167.

13 Forbes, "The Intercolonial Railway," 24.
14 E. R. Forbes, "The Origins of the Maritime Rights Movement," *Acadiensis* 5, no. 1 (1975): 57.
15 Rawlyk and Brown, "The Historical Framework of the Maritimes and Confederation," 26.
16 Frank, "The 1920s: Class and Region, Resistance and Accommodation," 253.
17 T. Stephen Henderson, "A Defensive Alliance: The Maritime Provinces and the Turgeon Commission on Transportation, 1948–1951," *Acadiensis* 35, no. 2 (Spring 2006): 46-63.
18 Ibid., 51.
19 Ibid., 60.
20 Ibid., 61.
21 Ibid., 62; and Canada, *Report of the Royal Commission on Transportation* (Ottawa: King's Printer, 1951), 42.
22 Savoie, *Regional Economic Development: Canada's Search for Solutions*, 167.
23 See, for example, Robert F. Legget, "Canals and Inland Waterways," *The Canadian Encyclopedia*, last edited March 4, 2015, www.thecanadianencyclopedia.ca/en/article/canals-and-inland-waterways/.
24 Donald E. Armstrong and D. Harvey Hay, *The Chignecto Canal* (Montreal: Economic Research Corporation Limited, April 1960), 6; and Chignecto Canal Committee, *The Story of the Chignecto Barrier* (1950).
25 Ibid., 5.
26 Legget, "Canals and Inland Waterways."
27 Armstrong and Hay, *The Chignecto Canal*, 14.
28 Ibid., 6.
29 Canada, *Canal Commission*, Ottawa, February 24, 1871, 79.
30 G. S. Gzowski quoted in ibid., 84.
31 See, for example, "Commission to Investigate the Nature and Extent of the Commercial Advantage to be Derived from the Construction of the Baie Verte Canal," Archives Canada, CAIN no. 257773, http://www.archivescanada.ca/.
32 See, for example, Armstrong and Hay, *The Chignecto Canal*, 5.
33 Ibid., 13.
34 Ibid.
35 Ibid., 6. For a contrary view, readers should consult C. R. McKay, "Investors, Government and the CMTR: A Study of Entrepreneurial Failure," *Acadiensis* 9, no. 1 (1979): 71-94. McKay maintains the Ketchum proposal did not make economic sense.
36 Canada, *Report of the Chignecto Canal Commission* (Ottawa: Printer of the King's Most Excellent Majesty, 1939), 16.
37 Ibid., 5.
38 Ibid., 11.
39 Ibid., 9.

40 Ibid., 11.
41 Ibid.
42 Ibid., 12.
43 Ibid., 10.
44 See "Seaway History," Great Lakes St. Lawrence Seaway System, 2016, http://www.greatlakes-seaway.com/en/seaway/history/.
45 Viktor Kaczkowski and Gordon C. Shaw, "Saint Lawrence," *The Canadian Encylopedia*, February 17, 2009, www.thecanadianencyclopedia.ca/en/article/st-lawrence-seaway/.
46 Corey Slumkoski, *Inventing Atlantic Canada: Regionalism and the Maritime Reaction to Newfoundland's Entry into Canadian Confederation* (Toronto: University of Toronto Press, 2011), 97.
47 G. S. Gzowski quoted in ibid., 99.
48 Ibid.
49 Ibid.
50 Members of the committee included Mayor N. S. Sanford, G. Fuller, and A. R. Lusby of Amherst, NS, and Mayor H. A. Beale and E. R. Richard of Sackville, NB.
51 Arthur Irving tells me that K. C. Irving made this point at various public meetings.
52 Chignecto Canal Committee, *The Story of the Chignecto Barrier*, 9.
53 Ibid., 15.
54 Ibid., 8.
55 Ibid., 5 and summary, 1.
56 See T. Stephen Henderson, *Angus L. Macdonald: A Provincial Liberal* (Toronto: University of Toronto Pres, 2007), 191.
57 See, among others, Slumkoski, *Inventing Atlantic Canada*, 97–106.
58 Quoted in ibid., 100.
59 K. C. Irving quoted in Jacques Poitras, *Irving vs. Irving: Canada's Feuding Billionaires and the Stories They Won't Tell* (Toronto: Viking, 2014), 19.
60 *Issues, Recommendations and an Action Plan* (Halifax: 4Front Atlantic Conference, 2013), 7.
61 See, among others, Mariana Mazzucato, *The Entrepreneurial State: Debunking Public vs Private Sector Myths* (New York: Anthem Press, 2013).
62 National Aeronautics and Space Administration, NASA *Spinoff 2002* (Washington, DC: National Aeronautics and Space Administration—Commercial Technology Division, 2002).
63 OECD regularly produces studies in R&D from a comparative perspective. See, for example, *Innovation in Science, Technology and Industry: Research and Development Statistics* (Paris: OECD, 2013).
64 "Museum Caught in Backlash: Some Disdainful Media Writers Toss Poison Darts at Asper's Stunning Project in Winnipeg," accessed April 25, 2005, www.thestar.com.

65 "Super Bowl Viewers Love Canadian Ad," *Globe and Mail*, February 3, 2004, B1.
66 Canada, *The Innovation Agenda* (Ottawa: Department of Industry, February 2002).
67 "Robillard Says Industry Is a Top Priority under PM Martin," *Ottawa Hill Times*, January 12–18, 2004, 16.
68 Canada, *Innovation Target 13* (Ottawa: Industry Canada, n.d.), 1.
69 Canada, *Achieving Excellence: Regional Perspectives on Innovation* (Ottawa: Industry Canada, January 2003), 10–12.
70 Consultation with a senior federal government official, Ottawa, April 2004.
71 Consultation with a former Industry Canada official now resident of Shediac, New Brunswick, December 18, 2014.
72 Canada, Parliament, House of Commons, Standing Committee on Industry, Science and Technology, *Evidence*, April 3, 2001 (Ottawa: Public Works and Government Services Canada, 2001), 8.
73 See, among others, Donald J. Savoie, *Pulling against Gravity: Economic Development in New Brunswick During the McKenna Years* (Montreal: Institute for Research on Public Policy, January 2001), 181. The section is also based on data obtained from the Treasury Board Secretariat and ACOA.
74 Data received from the head of the Canada Foundation for Innovation, Moncton, New Brunswick, September 20, 2004.
75 See "Notes for an address by the Hon. Stéphane Dion, President of the Privy Council Office and Minister of Intergovernmental Affairs," Distinguished Speaker Series, Faculty of Law, University of Western Ontario, September 21, 2001, 2.
76 This information was provided to me by officials with the Canada Research Chair Secretariat on May 6, 2015.
77 See "Audit Recommends Boost in Funding for Innovation Fund," *Moncton Times & Transcript*, August 11, 2004, A1.
78 Roméo LeBlanc made this comment to me in 1985.
79 Poitras, *Irving vs Irving*, 248.
80 Martin Ouellet, "Davie Shipyard: Quebec Tired of 'Begging' Ottawa for Contracts," *Montreal Gazette*, May 14, 2015, http://montrealgazette.com/news/quebec/davie-shipyard-quebec-tired-of-begging-ottawa-for-contracts.
81 Steven Chase, "Tories Begin Talks with Quebec Shipyard to Build Navy Supply Ship," *Globe and Mail*, June 23, 2015, http://www.theglobeandmail.com/news/politics/tories-lease-commercial-supply-ship-for-navy-from-quebec-shipyard/article25075797/.
82 Howard Pawley, "Mulroney, Me and the CF-18," *The Winnipeg Free Press*, March 19, 2011.
83 Ibid.
84 Jeffrey Simpson, "At Last, a Cure for Government Procurement," *Globe and Mail*, October 26, 2011, www.theglobeandmail.com/globe-debate/at-last-a-cure-for-government-procurement/article4403540/.

85 Poitras, *Irving vs. Irving*, 287.

86 I attended a briefing in Ottawa on November 28, 1989, where the proposal was outlined in detail.

87 "Beatty Baffled by Millions in Bear Head Lobby Fees," *Star*, April 29, 2009, www.thestar.com/news/canada/2009/04/29/beatty_baffled_by_millions_in_bear_head_lobby_fees.html.

88 Elizabeth Thompson, "Mulroney Didn't Promote Bear Head, Exec Testifies," TheWhig.com, April 22, 2009, www.thewhig.com/2009/04/22/mulroney-didnt-promote-bear-head-executive-testifies.

89 See Steven Chase, "Ottawa Aims to Keep Lid on Details of Saudi Arms Deal," *Globe and Mail*, May 27, 2015, www.theglobeandmail.com/news/politics/ottawa-wont-release-assesment-of-arms-deal-with-saudi-arabia/article24634202/; and Steven Chase, "Canada's Arms Deal with Saudi Arabia Shrouded in Secrecy," January 21, 2015, www.theglobeandmail.com/news/politics/canadas-arms-deal-with-saudi-arabia-shrouded-in-secrecy/article22547765/.

90 Steven Chase, "Foreign Affairs Found No Red Flags for Israel in Saudi Arms Deal," August 27, 2015, www.theglobeandmail.com/news/politics/foreign-affairs-found-no-red-flags-for-israel-in-saudi-arms-sale/article26121923/.

91 "The Harper Government Won't Divulge How it Is Justifying the Sale to a Region Notorious for Human Rights Abuse," *Globe and Mail*, May 29, 2015.

92 Steven Chase, "Critics Push Ottawa to Explain Justification for Saudi Arms Deal," January 5, 2016, www.theglobeandmail.com/news/politics/critics-push-ottawa-to-explain-justification-for-saudi-arms-deal/article28029875/.

93 Ibid.

94 Richard Blackwell, "London, Ont. Defends Saudi Arms Deal as Integral to Region's Economy," January 7, 2016, www.theglobeandmail.com/news/national/ontario-city-defends-saudi-arms-deal-as-integral-to-regions-economy/article28063630/.

95 Steven Chase, "Liberals Committed to Saudi Arms Deal Even After Concerning UN Report, Dion Says," January 28, 2016, www.theglobeandmail.com/news/politics/liberals-committed-to-saudi-arms-deal-even-after-concerning-un-report-dion-says/article28438488/.

96 Steven Chase, "Liberals Mum on Dion's Rationale for not Cancelling Saudi Arms Deal," *Globe and Mail*, February 19, 2016, www.theglobeandmail.com/news/politics/liberals-mum-on-dions-rationale-for-not-cancelling-saudi-arms-deal/article28825839/.

97 Steven Chase, "Saudi Arms Deal Exempt from Global Treaty, Ottawa Says," *Globe and Mail*, February 9, 2016, www.theglobeandmail.com/news/politics/saudi-arms-deal-exempt-from-global-treaty-ottawa-says/article28688598/.

98 Steven Chase, "The Big Deal," *Globe and Mail*, February 5, 2016, www.theglobeandmail.com/news/politics/the-saudi-arms-deal-why-its-a-bigdeal/article28568660/.

99 Steven Chase, "Cancelling Saudi Arms Deal Would Have No Effect on Human Rights: Dion," *Globe and Mail*, March 29, 2016, www.theglobeandmail.com/news/politics/cancelling-saudi-arms-deal-would-have-no-effect-on-human-rights-dion/article29427814/.

Part 3

WHAT HAS BEEN DONE?

Chapter 7

DROVE DREE TO THE LEVEE, BUT THE LEVEE WAS DRIE

Don McLean's "American Pie," well-known to baby boomers, is about the tragic death of three young rising rock and roll musicians in an airplane crash. McLean's song suggests the tragic deaths held an important message for my generation, making the point that we had lost a great deal more than three popular singers. Baby boomers were slowly coming of age on February 3, 1959, when Buddy Holly, Ritchie Valens, and the Big Bopper (J. P. Richardson Jr.) were killed. Baby boomers were, for one thing, witnessing a fast-expanding role for government. Many applauded politicians of the day when they declared war on poverty or called for a "great" or "just" society. They saw government accomplishing great things. For example, the United States responded victoriously to then president Kennedy's call to land a man on the moon and bring him back safely to earth within a decade and Canada's successful implementation of an ambitious publicly funded universal health-care system.

The government had the green light to grow, and grow it did in the immediate post–World War Two period. Not only did the Allies win the war, but also governments had planned the war effort and run the economy very well. Unemployment had fallen to zero, and yet prices had been held down, at least when the goods were available. It became clear that national governments were able—at least in moments of crisis and when moved by an overriding goal—to lead their countries to accomplish great things. The concern now turned to the postwar economy, with many fearing that the end of the war would trigger a recession, if not another depression. Canadians' confidence in the ability of government to accomplish great things could not have been stronger.

The Canadian government presented a major policy paper to Parliament toward the end of World War Two, which was clearly Keynesian in outlook: "The Government will be prepared, in periods where unemployment threatens, to incur deficits and increases in the national debt resulting from its employment and income policy...in periods of buoyant employment and income, budget plans will call for surpluses."[1] When the war ended, everyone was prepared for measures to avoid a return to the Depression years. But the expected severe economic downturn did not materialize and the measures proved unnecessary. Still, the Canadian government was now convinced it possessed a new arsenal of economic policies to achieve high employment and generally manage the economy.[2] If governments could successfully manage a war effort and avoid another economic depression, they could do almost anything. Alleviating regional economic disparities was only one of many things policy-makers of the day felt they could successfully tackle.

The war years, if anything, also served to solidify Keynesian economics in government treasuries and growth in government programs. John Maynard Keynes and a strong number of his disciples on both sides of the Atlantic served in key positions in government. Classical economists everywhere were on the defensive. They proved unable to come up with solutions for the expected postwar recession or to compete with the new intellectual forces increasingly being felt on university campuses. In addition, classical and neoclassical economists have never been comfortable dealing with regional aspects of national economies. Keynesian economists, meanwhile, did not hesitate to come forward with fresh thinking and take centre stage in government offices. They also did not hesitate to expand the role of government at a time when regional economic development came into fashion on university campuses. As noted, many universities started to offer specialized courses in regional planning and regional studies.

In Canada, Bob Bryce was promoting the message of Keynes's *General Theory* inside government. He had studied at the feet of Keynes while at

Cambridge and had returned to Canada via Harvard, where he introduced Keynesian economics to both faculty and students. Bryce went on to work in the Department of Finance in October 1938, on the eve of the Munich Crisis. He discovered that "some limited policy work" was being done in the office of the deputy minister and by a handful of senior clerks (six in all) there and in the Treasury Board. This was about to change dramatically in both central agencies and line departments. Some forty years later, there were 2,400 economists in the Canadian public service.[3]

But that was not all. Between the postwar period and the 1970s, the government of Canada expanded in all sectors: new departments and agencies were created, units were added in line departments, new Crown corporations were established, and central agencies expanded. Royal Commissions were also established to identify how to promote more even economic development. The belief was strong that if there were problems in society, then governments could solve them. The generation that grew up on Buddy Holly's music saw government as a positive force in society. Many wanted to join its ranks, be part of the action, and many did.

Governments in Canada were able to carve out new roles in every sector of the economy during this period. They introduced new programs in health care, social services, industrial development, the environment, post-secondary education, economic development, arts and culture, agriculture, the fishery, regional economic development, and the list goes on. Again, governments grew and grew. As a proportion of GDP, the combined expenditure of all three levels of government in Canada increased from 20 per cent in 1951, to 32.5 per cent in 1961, and again to 49 per cent in 1992. In addition, between 1947 and 1995, total government spending rose 114 per cent faster than did GDP.[4] In 1941 there were 49,709 federal public servants. The number grew to 180,325 in 1951; to 281,834 in 1961; to 382,775 in 1971; to 427,093 in 2011; and were slightly down to 423,850 in 2014.[5]

Regional development measures, meanwhile, enjoyed the support of some politicians but senior public servants were less enthusiastic, even in the heyday of regional development. Such measures have to be sustained at the political level. It is worth repeating Tom Kent's observation: "From the point of view of almost all conventional wisdom in Ottawa, the idea of regional development was a rather improper one that some otherwise quite reasonable politician brought in like a baby on a doorstep from an election campaign."[6]

Senior public servants in the departments of Finance, Industry, and in the PCO focus on national economic efficiency, on national policies, and see regional development measures as playing havoc with national economic efficiency models. It is exceedingly difficult to find documents produced by these departments or their officials that are supportive of regional development efforts.

They are many in Ottawa who speak to Kent's observation. Arthur Kroeger, a widely respected former senior federal public servant who served as deputy minister in several departments, including Industry, gave a presentation in 2003, praising the Department of Industry since its inception. He was, however, critical of Ottawa's regional development efforts. He wrote that the Department of Regional Economic Expansion had a wide array of policy and program instruments and "had a substantial budget—$600 million in the early 1970s—translate that to the present day, probably a couple of billion."[7] DREE's actual budget in 1970-71 totalled $317,708 million and $328,060 million in 1971–72.[8] When it comes to regional development, facts and evidence-based advice do not seem to carry much weight with senior Ottawa-based officials; the so-called baby on the doorstep has never been accepted at the senior bureaucratic level. From an Ottawa perspective, it was quite appropriate for the Department of Industry to spend $350 million in 1972-73 and today $1.2 billion mostly in Southern Ontario and the Montreal region, but somehow spending on regional development has never measured up. (The $1.2 billion at Industry does not include funding for the three regional development agencies for Ontario and Quebec.)[9]

REGIONAL ECONOMIC DEVELOPMENT: THE PLAYERS TRIED FOR A FORWARD PASS

Pierre E. Trudeau came to power at the very moment when belief in the government's good potential was very high. The federal government had successfully launched a number of national programs and initiatives, notably medicare and the construction of the Trans-Canada Highway. Trudeau decided to enter the political arena to strengthen national unity, and he claimed his concerns extended beyond Quebec's place in the Canadian family, though his focus was on his home province.

Trudeau boldly declared, "Economic equality...is just as important as equality of language rights....If the underdevelopment of the Atlantic provinces is not corrected, not by charity or subsidy, but by helping them become areas of economic growth, then the unity of the country is almost as surely destroyed as it would be by the French-English confrontation."[10] In Trudeau's early years, regional economic development would enjoy an unprecedented, though short-lived, priority status on the National Policy agenda.

Trudeau did not, however, have to start from scratch. Canada's first regional development programs, introduced in the late 1950s and early 1960s, were designed to promote development in slow-growth rural areas. They were not, however, nearly as ambitious as the early Trudeau efforts. The measures applied to a highly limited number of areas and programs, and were restricted to a narrow band of activities, notably infrastructure spending. I have reviewed these programs in detail in my earlier work.[11]

Trudeau's measures were not only far more ambitious, but they also targeted both rural and urban areas in slow-growth regions. For several years, they were tied to an economic strategy based on the literature of leading economists, including François Perroux and Jacques Boudeville and the growth pole concept.[12] Trudeau also established a new department, the Department of Regional Economic Expansion, and gave DREE a mandate to promote development in slow-growth regions. He appointed his most trusted political lieutenant, Jean Marchand, from Quebec, to head the new department and gave it substantial financial and human resources.

DREE programs have already been reviewed in detail in other works.[13] Suffice to make two points. First, the department had a full arsenal of programs designed for slow-growth regions. Second, the government, initially at least, had one overriding goal in mind: alleviating regional disparities. The focus was on the four Atlantic provinces and eastern Quebec. DREE's legislation called on the department to implement measures to promote development in areas of "exceptional inadequacy of opportunities for productive employment."[14] The legislation was clear, the department's policy was clear, and the goal was clear: create employment in slow-growth areas. Politicians and residents from slow-growth regions saw DREE as their federal government department, headed by a powerful minister and a close associate of the prime minister, and believed it should combat regional disparities.

In DREE's early years, the department looked mainly to urban areas located in slow-growth regions that showed some promise in order to apply Perroux's growth pole concept. Perhaps the most quoted sentence in the study of regional development was Perroux's observation: "Growth does not appear everywhere and all at once; it reveals itself in certain points or poles, with different degrees of intensity; it spreads through diverse channels."[15] From a regional development perspective, then, efforts must be made to strengthen these focal points in slow-growth regions and start a process of self-sustained economic growth.

The theory held promise even for some government officials, at least for a brief period. For one thing, it had the potential to give rise to a "no-cost" regional development policy. Past efforts to deal with economically depressed rural areas had proven costly in the eyes of central agency officials and yielded no apparent progress. By concentrating efforts on selected growth centres, employment opportunities would be created that would not only lead to other opportunities, but would also mop up surplus labour from surrounding rural areas. The thinking was regional development efforts would now lead to self-sustaining economic activity, and they would not, as in the past, constitute an ongoing drain on the Treasury.

DREE introduced a Special Areas program together with a regional Industrial Incentives program. One program would build the infrastructure and the other would offer financial incentives to lure businesses to selected regions and encourage local entrepreneurs to expand their businesses. Both were also designed to target designated growth areas within slow-growth regions. The DREE legislation provided considerable flexibility to the minister to shape measures and to designate which regions would qualify. It gave the department a variety of instruments, from loan guarantees to the private sector, cash grants support for community groups, and agreements with provincial governments. The legislation, however, did not establish clear objectives or performance requirements, which is precisely what politicians on the government side prefer. No sense providing fuel for the blame game or giving reasons for the opposition parties and the media to clobber the government for not meeting its objectives.

The legislation enabled the DREE minister to designate a region after simply "consulting" the relevant provincial government but did not spell out how, or in what format, DREE should consult the provinces. Here again the minister and the department had considerable flexibility. Anthony Careless, in his review of DREE's early days, maintained Ottawa had a take it or leave it approach to federal-provincial relations in introducing regional development measures, with slow-growth provinces having little choice but to take what was put forward.[16] The approach provided maximum flexibility for the minister and his colleagues to decide who would and—more importantly—who would not benefit from regional development measures and what measures ought to be pursued. In other words, DREE's first minister, Jean Marchand, and his department were given a free hand not only to shape new initiatives but also to decide where they should apply.

Marchand was able to limit the number of designated areas to twenty-three which, at the time, was seen as a victory for him and regional development programming.[17] Looking back, however, the number was a far cry from what François Perroux envisaged in his work on growth poles. Perroux saw large, sprawling, strategically located urban centres that had economic ties with other large urban centres in other parts of the world. Certainly, Perroux did not have Bathurst, New Brunswick, or Sydney, Nova Scotia, in mind as he developed his growth pole theory. But Marchand and senior DREE officials did.

Marchand's limited designations, however, motivated provincial governments to push for more of their regions to garner DREE's attention. They became convinced that what stood between some of their communities and economic development was a DREE growth pole designation. The pressure on the Trudeau government to designate more regions increased month after month.

Initially, DREE was able to target only six regions for "faster industrial growth" in urban centres in the Atlantic provinces and Quebec: St. John's, Halifax-Dartmouth, Saint John, Moncton, Quebec City, and Trois-Rivières. The Special Areas program, meanwhile, sponsored a great variety of projects in virtually every sector. They provided for industrial parks, highway construction, water and sewage systems, tourist attractions, schools, and the list goes on. Money for DREE was no problem in the department's early years. Marchand along with Tom Kent, a powerful mandarin in his own right, were able to secure from the Treasury Board all the funds the department would need and then some. Indeed, the newly formed DREE could not spend all the funds it was given.[18] In the early 1970s, DREE's budget was around $320 million. In contrast, ACOA's budget was about $300 million in 2014–15.

Trudeau and Marchand stood firm on one point: DREE's goal was to alleviate regional disparities. Marchand famously said that if federal regional development programs do not spend something like 80 per cent of the funding east of Trois-Rivières, they will fail.[19] Trudeau saw regional development from a national unity perspective, convinced the right policy would strengthen bonds between Canada's regions.

But as time would reveal, it was a great deal easier to say it than to do it. Politicians from all parties and from both the federal and provincial governments were unrelenting in pressuring Trudeau and Marchand to designate more and more regions. The rise of the sovereignty movement in Quebec would also add substantially to the pressure on Trudeau and Marchand to designate more communities. Tom Kent, DREE's first deputy minister, wrote, "The depressed economy of Montreal was considered to be a breeding ground for separatist sentiment."[20]

Both Trudeau and Marchand were very sensitive to their home province Quebec's place in Canada and to national unity concerns. Cabinet ministers and MPs from Quebec soon began to push for designation of Montreal as a special area, arguing that if DREE was truly serious about applying a growth pole strategy, it would deem Montreal applicable as a special area under its Industrial Incentives program. No other community in the province, including Quebec City and Trois-Rivières, could possibly generate as many new economic activities as Montreal could, if given a helping hand.

By the late 1960s, Montreal's growth was no longer keeping pace with other regions, notably Toronto, and the government had to deal with the expectations of a large contingent of Liberal MPs from Montreal, which included the prime minister. At Confederation, Montreal was the dominant urban centre, home to more than 90,000, while Toronto's population was 44,000.[21] In 1961 Montreal's population stood at 2,215,627, nearly 300,000 more than Toronto's. However, by 1971, Montreal was only ahead by 100,000.[22] Montreal area MPs, of which Trudeau was one, wanted to arrest Montreal's slide in relation to Toronto. They insisted the best way to nip the sovereignty movement in the bud was to see Montreal return to a reasonable rate of growth, which required special measures. A helping hand from the federal government to Quebec to grow its economy would also show its residents that federalism was the most viable option. Toronto and Bay Street were fast becoming Canada's banking and financial sector, supplanting Montreal and famed St. James Street. The pressure on Ottawa to somehow show Quebec that federalism could benefit the province became intense and protracted. The Quebec caucus, with the prime minister and several senior ministers as members, held a powerful position in the government, having won fifty-six seats and 54 per cent of the province's popular vote.[23]

In the end, Trudeau and Marchand designated Montreal as a special region, known as "region C," which consisted of southwestern Quebec, including what was then Hull (now Gatineau) and Montreal, and three counties of eastern Ontario, as a concession to Ontario MPs. The maximum incentive grant in region C was lower than elsewhere in eastern Quebec and the Atlantic provinces. The grant could not exceed 10 per cent of approved capital costs, plus $2,000 for each direct job created. Elsewhere in the designated regions of eastern Quebec and Northern Ontario, the maximum incentive grant was fixed at 25 per cent of approved capital costs and $5,000 for each new job created. A third level of assistance was established for the Atlantic region, which called for a maximum grant of 35 per cent of capital costs and $7,000 per job created. Finally, the changes stipulated that region C's special designation was to be for two years only, a period deemed sufficient to help Montreal return to a "reasonable rate of growth."[24] The changes, however, resulted in an expansion of the coverage of the designated regions to about 40 per cent of Canada's population and almost 45 per cent of manufacturing employment and established a three-level hierarchy of incentive grants.

Tom Kent saw the changes as highly detrimental to regional development efforts elsewhere. He explained that the changes "took much of the force out of the regional development programme because if companies could get sizable subsidies for projects close to the country's industrial heartland, they were not going to be induced to go to more remote locations for the sake of marginally bigger subsidies." The situation, Kent argued, was made worse because Quebec DREE officials awarded incentives "close to the maximum" in Montreal, while DREE officials in the Maritimes made offers "far below the theoretical maximum."[25]

Designating Montreal opened the floodgates for other ministers and MPs to push the government to designate their constituencies to qualify for federal regional development programs. If Montreal could qualify, why not Winnipeg, Regina, or Calgary? Money was not the problem. It soon became obvious that DREE could not possibly spend all the money it had been allocated.[26] Rather, the problem was Marchand's commitment that spending less than 80 per cent of Ottawa's regional development budget east of Trois-Rivières would compromise the government's regional development objective, alleviating regional disparities. Designating Montreal so soon after DREE was born effectively did in the overall objective. By the early 1970s, or just a few short years after DREE was established, it became clear that the department was in serious political difficulty. Regions not designated became increasingly vocal in their criticism, arguing the federal government was discriminating against them; how could they possibly compete with regions getting a helping hand at every turn? If their communities were not growing at the anticipated rate, it was all too easy to point the finger at DREE as the culprit.

Politicians, even on the government side, became exasperated with Perroux's growth pole concept; they insisted it was not working. Provincial governments, even in slow-growth regions, also became highly critical of Ottawa's approach to regional development. The federal government, they insisted, was playing political and economic havoc within their jurisdictions, deciding which regions would qualify for assistance and which would not. They argued that for voters, government is government and they had to defend decisions that had a serious impact in their jurisdiction but for which they could not be held responsible because they had very little or no say in the decision-making process. They also made the case that designating Montreal for federal regional development purposes had a profoundly negative impact, effectively rendering Ottawa's regional development efforts for their province of limited value.

In summary, viewed from Ottawa, regional development efforts became an important part of the national unity debate, at least as it was playing out in Quebec. Viewed from the provincial governments' perspective, however, federal regional development efforts were found lacking on several fronts, and several provincial governments, including those that benefitted from the efforts, notably the Atlantic provinces, called for a fundamental review.

The approach became politically unsustainable. Something had to give and it did in the immediate aftermath of the 1972 general election. The Trudeau government barely hung on to power, winning only 109 seats to the Conservatives' 107 seats. Trudeau and his advisors concluded one of the things that had gone wrong was the government's regional development policy. Trudeau transferred Marchand to Transport and appointed another powerful minister from Newfoundland and Labrador, Don Jamieson, as the DREE minister. Trudeau and Jamieson also launched an ambitious review of the government's regional development policy, convinced the status quo had cost them significant political support.

The growth pole concept was thrown out—never properly understood and never given a chance to see if it could work. Better relations with provincial governments became important, at least politically, and the pursuit of "developmental opportunities" became the new password to access federal regional development funding. The difference was that the password was given to all provinces, have and have-less.

There is no need to review the details of the General Development Agreement (GDA) approach, which my early work on regional economic development offers in considerable detail.[27] The point is that DREE was now everywhere in the economic development field: in urban and rural areas, in every economic sector, and in every region of the country, be it have or have-less. The new approach held strong political appeal. For one thing, it meant turning provincial governments into partners, since, under the GDAS, nothing could be done without their approval. It was left to the provincial governments to come up with proposed initiatives that suited the provinces. For another, initially at least, it enabled the Liberal government to be visible in regional development in all provinces with regional development initiatives. This, it was felt, would recapture votes lost in the 1972 election.

The approach also led to the decentralization of DREE. Decision-making was pushed down to provincial capitals where a director general was now leading a relatively large provincial DREE office to negotiate economic development agreements with the provinces and to deliver a regional industrial incentive program. Large regional DREE offices were also established in Atlantic Canada, Quebec, Ontario, and Western Canada.[28] However, Ottawa's regional development efforts would henceforth be focused almost exclusively on the provinces, essentially redefining *regional* to mean *provincial* development. In short, the federal government was joining provincial governments in pursuing a province-building agenda.

Marchand's commitment to see 80 per cent of Ottawa's regional development budget allocated east of Trois-Rivières was now history. DREE still favoured the four Atlantic provinces and eastern Quebec in its programming, but its budget would now be increasingly spread throughout Canada. Provincial governments became very strong supporters of DREE and the GDA approach. They had an important say in developing initiatives, and the focus of the GDAS was provincial, not regional as in Atlantic

Canada, the Maritime provinces, or sub-provincial areas, as was the case under the growth pole or special areas approach. GDA programming gave provincial premiers and their respective governments strong positive visibility: they were seen as responsible for delivering economic development projects on the ground with the federal government paying an important share of the cost, in some instances up to 90 per cent.

In time, however, having provincial governments play the lead role in delivering programs would also lead to DREE's downfall. Federal cabinet ministers did not look kindly on provincial politicians—often from a different political party—enjoying considerable political visibility with federal dollars. Roméo LeBlanc, then minister of Fisheries, even went so far as to publicly voice his criticism of DREE: "I resisted the DREE agreement in fisheries because I found it difficult...to accept that...what I could not do in my defined area of responsibility, I find another department...doing through the provincial governments."[29] Other federal ministers, notably Eugene Whelan, joined in the public criticism. Whelan argued that DREE had lost the ability to coordinate activities to support new economic development in a province that would not compete with an existing business in the same sector in a neighbouring province.[30]

Senior public servants in central agencies became no less critical of DREE and the GDA approach. They felt that provincial DREE officials had gone "native," identifying with the interests of provincial governments and unable to bring a national or even a regional perspective to their work. They saw a hodge-podge of DREE projects and could not discern an economic development strategy. DREE, it seems, supported rural development if the provincial government wanted it or a tourism project, the construction of a new road, or whatever else struck the fancy of provincial governments.[31] The thinking in Ottawa was that DREE had been turned into little more than a funding agency for provincial governments.

DREE's last minister, Pierre De Bané, bluntly told the department, within weeks of his arrival, he would not support the status quo. He told a DREE staff conference, "To preserve the status quo, I would have to devote all my efforts and energies over the next twelve months to convince my colleagues of the appropriateness of DREE as we now know it. A very fundamental problem here is that I am not prepared to do that."[32] He called for a comprehensive review of Ottawa's regional development efforts and sought the prime minister's support. When Cabinet ministers and senior central agency officials share a similar concern, something has to give, and it did. It would be the end of DREE.

A NEW APPROACH

On January 12, 1982, Prime Minister Trudeau unveiled a major government reorganization for economic development. The new organization did not, however, square with De Bané's wishes. De Bané's letter to the prime minister had called for a stronger DREE and a stronger emphasis on alleviating regional disparities. Trudeau, knowing it was his last chance at doing what he had set out to do when he entered politics—patriate the constitution and secure Quebec's place in Confederation—essentially left central agencies on their own to define a new approach to regional development. De Bané, a relatively junior minister, did not have the clout of a Jean Marchand, a Marc Lalonde, or a Lloyd Axworthy, and so, he had little say in shaping the new machinery of government for regional development.

Though Pierre De Bané and his colleagues from the Atlantic provinces looked to regional development to alleviate regional disparities, central agency officials in Ottawa did not, nor did many politicians from the have regions. PCO officials had the upper hand in shaping the new machinery, given that it fell under the prerogative of the prime minister, not Cabinet. Central agency officials, notably in the Finance department, became convinced in the early 1980s that there was a different economic environment emerging in Canada. They saw the manufacturing sector in Central Canada weakening at the same time as mega energy projects were poised to transform the economies of both Atlantic and Western Canada.

During his 1981 budget speech, Allan MacEachen tabled a document titled *Economic Development for Canada in the 1980s*, which maintained that regional balance was changing as a result of buoyancy in the West, optimism in the East, and unprecedented softness in key economic sectors in Central Canada. Something had to be done to come to the rescue of Central Canada, while Western and Atlantic Canada were poised for economic growth. Underpinning this view were the economic prospects associated with resource-based megaprojects.

According to central agency officials, the Atlantic region, in contrast to historical economic trends, was expected to enjoy a decade of solid growth, largely as a result of offshore resources. The West, meanwhile, would capture over half of the investment in major projects. Ontario and Quebec would face problems of industrial adjustment, brought about by increased international competition. Yet, opportunities were thought to exist there as well. If properly managed, the economic spinoff from major projects could create numerous employment opportunities in Central Canada. Some 60,000 person-years of employment would be created in Ontario alone from major pipeline projects in Western Canada. Thus, the regional challenge in the 1980s would take a new direction. Regions that had previously enjoyed strong growth were confronted with problems of adjustment, while those that had traditionally lagged behind were enjoying strong prospects for expansion. All in all, both problems and opportunities existed in all regions. The minister of Finance explained, "Regional economic development will be central to public policy planning at the federal level."[33] Ottawa's goal of alleviating regional disparities was now history.

The policy direction was designed to take advantage of major economic forces working on the Canadian economy and to spread the benefits to all regions. The policy document pointed to some $440 billion of potential projects, predominantly in energy and resources, which would be launched before the end of the century. By and large, these major projects would be located in the West, in the North, and on the East Coast and were expected to bring about a new wave of comparative advantages and economic growth not seen in these regions in the twentieth century. They would also provide an important source of income, improve provincial revenues, and generate new economic activity. Cabinet ministers began to voice a similar message of economic optimism, notably for the future of the Atlantic provinces. The minister of Energy, Marc Lalonde, commented, "What offshore oil and gas provides [*sic*] in Atlantic Canada is the opportunity for an accelerated, more dramatic economic turnaround than would otherwise have been thought possible. The basic strength is here. And now we must build on that strength."[34]

There was also an anticipated growth in income from grains and other food products, including fisheries. The Department of Finance's policy document noted, "Rapid population growth in the world is placing new demands on food, and in response to rising world prices further expansion and modernization of the agricultural and food sectors throughout Canada is in prospect."[35] This development, it was felt, would again favour both the western and Atlantic provinces. In Central Canada, the competitive pressure on manufacturing would require adaptation, regeneration, and adjustment. The policy document thus stressed reorienting and restructuring Central Canada's manufacturing sector. The restructuring "must both reduce the pressure for costly support to less competitive industries and at the same time provide alternative employment opportunities in higher productivity and higher wage sectors."[36] The Department of Finance policy document argued that megaprojects in Western and Atlantic Canada would help restructure Ontario manufacturing. More to the point, the Atlantic provinces, Ottawa officials now believed, were poised to look after themselves. The new regional problem was the weakening manufacturing sector in Ontario and Quebec, and the federal government would now focus more of its resources to that end. The message, produced and packaged by Ottawa-based central agency officials, did not fall on deaf ears in a Cabinet chaired by a prime minister from Quebec with a strong majority of its members from Ottawa and Quebec sitting in a House of Commons dominated by MPs also from Ontario and Quebec, free to ignore a largely ineffective Senate.

WHAT TO DO?

The next challenge was to reform the machinery of government in the economic development sector to give life to the emerging economic circumstances. Trudeau announced the establishment of a new central agency, the Ministry of State for Economic and Regional Development (MSERD), responsible for overseeing the economic development function in government, particularly its expenditure budget. Trudeau simply added a regional policy and coordination responsibility to the work of the existing central agency and small regional offices in provincial capitals; however, it had a very short life. MSERD was dismantled a few years after it was established, in June 1984. It disappeared without leaving much of a trace, at least in the regional economic development field.

Problems surfaced with MSERD shortly after it was created. It could not reconcile its national and regional mandates. It saw the need to accommodate regional circumstances or deal with regional disparities to be in conflict with its national mandate. MSERD's deputy minister warned his minister against "balkanizing Canada's economic space. In other words, the clause (to assist disadvantaged areas) could put us into conflict with our own objectives."[37] He had to choose between competing objectives, and the regional mandate stood no chance against the national mandate for the deputy minister and the central agency. The balkanizing of Canada's economic space looks very different in Ottawa and in Central Canada than it does in the regions.

Trudeau also established a new line department, the Department of Regional Industrial Expansion (DRIE), which survived longer than MSERD. He appointed Ed Lumley, Member of Parliament for Stormont-Dundas, as DRIE's first minister. From the very start, Lumley made it clear the government was no longer in the business of alleviating regional disparities. His concerns were directed at Central Canada's manufacturing sector, where he expected job losses.

Lumley rose in the House of Commons on June 27, 1983, to unveil a new economic development program. He cautioned that "combatting regional disparities is difficult even in good economic times....It is much more difficult in a period when, because of a worldwide downturn, Canada's traditional industries are suffering from soft markets, stiff international competition, rapid technological change and rising protectionism from the countries that make up our market."[38] For Lumley and for the "Ottawa system," there was never a good economic time to combat regional disparities.

A new program to meet these circumstances would have to be one that he could "clearly recommend to the business community, to the Canadian public, and to all Members of Parliament." DRIE, Lumley insisted, had come up with such a program. It was a "regionally sensitized multifaceted programme of industrial assistance in all parts of Canada....This is not a programme to be available only in certain designated regions. Whatever riding any Member of this House represents, his or her constituents will be eligible for assistance."[39] Federal regional economic development had come full circle and could now be found in all areas of the country, including downtown Toronto. The program was also able to accommodate a variety of needs, including investment in infrastructure, industrial diversification, the establishment of new plants, and the launching of new product lines.

DRIE came under heavy criticism soon after it was established. Brian Mulroney, then leader of the opposition, was critical of the government for having abolished DREE. He outlined a series of measures during the 1984 election campaign to promote economic development in slow-growth regions. He pledged to introduce a "specific legislative mandate to promote the least developed regions" and "every department will be required to submit to the Standing Committee of Parliament on Economic and Regional Development annual assessments of the effect of departmental policies on specific regions."[40] Once in power, however, the Mulroney government was slow off the mark in introducing new regional development measures. In fact, his government did not pursue commitments made while his party was in opposition or during the election campaign. To this day, federal government departments and agencies are not required to submit an assessment of the effects of their policies on specific regions to a Standing Committee of Parliament or anywhere else.

DRIE was also intensely criticized by slow-growth provinces. The press was reporting that the bulk of spending under DRIE was being directed to Ontario and Quebec. For example, over 70 per cent of DRIE's spending under the Industrial and Regional Development Program (IRDP) was going to Ontario and Quebec. By contrast, at least 40 per cent of DREE's budget had been consistently spent in Atlantic Canada.[41]

DRIE had other problems. It was viewed as a large, cumbersome, and bureaucratic department, largely insensitive to the economic circumstances of the Maritime provinces and Newfoundland and Labrador. Both the local business community and provincial governments in the region became openly critical of the bureaucratic nature of the DRIE approval process. One official revealed that a decision under a signed DRIE subsidiary agreement on a given project had to go through some twenty-two federal "vetting centres."[42] In fairness to DRIE, it must be noted there was a tendency in Atlantic Canada to compare the effectiveness of DRIE to DREE, which was much like comparing oranges and apples. One major difference, of course, was that DRIE did not have the clear, unencumbered mandate to promote regional economic development that DREE had. This difference probably explains the main criticism directed at DRIE: that it was essentially an industry department and not a regional development department.

Many federal officials were very candid about the seemingly inherent conflicts in DRIE's dual mandate to promote industrial and regional development. It was often referred to as the shotgun wedding of DREE and the Department of Industry Trade and Commerce (IT&C), and many concluded the marriage had not worked. One frequently heard about the pulling and shoving inside DRIE over whether to concentrate on high-growth industries and to build on Canada's existing industrial strength (often located in Central Canada) or on regional development. Former IT&C officials in DRIE were convinced that DREE issues dominated in the department, while former DREE officials were equally convinced of the opposite.[43] In the end, DRIE embraced an industry perspective and concentrated its efforts on Central Canada's manufacturing sector and its growing IT firms. It never pursued its regional development mandate.

It did not take long for the Atlantic and western premiers to view DRIE as part of the problem rather than part of the solution. The point was made that DRIE programming had, in fact, increased rather than alleviated regional disparities. The programs for which DRIE controlled the funds, such as IRDP and the Defence Industry Productivity Program (DIPP), applied to a far greater extent in Southern Ontario and southern Quebec than they did in either eastern or western Canada. A province such as Prince Edward Island, for example, had virtually no hope of taking full advantage of these programs because it lacked the appropriate economic and industrial base. DRIE had no interest in building such a base outside of Ontario and Quebec.

Some provincial government officials in the Maritime provinces also observed that on occasion, firms thinking of establishing a plant in either their region or Southern Ontario, received more generous offers from DRIE to locate in Southern Ontario.[44] It was true that under IRDP's tier system, the slow-growth regions were favoured. Since its tier system only established maximum levels of federal assistance, however, it was possible for DRIE to offer a more generous grant to set up in a more developed region in Ontario simply by offering the maximum level available under that particular tier and which was less than the maximum under other tiers that applied to slow-growth regions.

DRIE also became involved in other widely reported political controversies. Sinclair Stevens, the DRIE minister, was forced to resign over charges that he had been in a serious conflict of interest. The new DRIE minister, Michel Côté, was also forced to resign from Cabinet over a conflict of interest, after securing an undeclared loan from a friend while in Cabinet.[45] The ministers' resignations opened up a new wave of criticism from slow-growth regions. Mulroney, hearing criticism from the Atlantic and western provinces and seeing the department creating political problems in the media following the resignation of two high-profile ministers, had had enough. He disbanded the department and launched a new approach to regional development.

LOOKING BACK

Ottawa's regional economic development efforts (circa 1969–1985) speak more to a political agenda rather than to a strategic economic development plan. The efforts had more objectives—at times conflicting ones—than a policy could possibly deliver. The goal of alleviating regional disparities was short-lived and replaced by a confusing set of shifting policy goals. In the process, Ottawa redefined regional development to pursue provincially designed priorities and thus joined provincial governments in promoting a province-building agenda.

In less than twenty years, the goal of Ottawa's regional policy underwent three distinct phases. It was initially conceived to alleviate regional disparities with the focus on eastern Quebec and the four Atlantic provinces. The focus shifted when regional development efforts were enlisted to combat the sovereignty movement in Quebec. It shifted once again when Ottawa decided the more important regional challenge had moved to Ontario and Quebec's manufacturing sector.

National Policy and the war efforts had driven Central Canada's manufacturing since the 1880s. The difference going forward was the effort would now be assisted by the government's regional development policy. Ottawa-based policy-makers actually believed in the early 1980s that Central Canada's manufacturing sector would be confronting serious adjustment problems while Western and Atlantic Canada would flourish on the basis of major energy projects. Within a few years, however, it became obvious that the difficult circumstances confronting Central Canada's manufacturing were short-lived, and optimism in the East, because of energy-driven megaprojects, was no less short-lived.

Partisan political considerations were always an important part of the calculations as was the need, at least occasionally, to have smooth federal-provincial relations. Yet, at other times, the goal was to bypass provincial governments and secure more federal government visibility by federal dollars spent in the regions. Partisan political considerations dictated when to bypass or when to work closely with provincial governments.

The political pressure of the day often appeared to be the dominant force shaping and reshaping Canada's regional development policy. At the same time, the policy, however defined, was never fully accepted in key central agencies in Ottawa. In the end, what truly matters is the overall economic health of the country and the inherent bias of a largely Central Canada bureaucracy (at least at the senior levels) supported by the political and economic interests of Ontario and Quebec. The pattern—albeit with an important recent nod to Western Canada—continues, as we will see in the next chapter.

NOTES

1 Canada, Department of Reconstruction and Supply, *Employment and Income with Special Reference to the Initial Period of Reconstruction* (Ottawa: King's Printer, 1945), 21.

2 A. W. Johnson, *Social Policy in Canada: The Past as It Conditions the Present* (Halifax: Institute for Research on Public Policy, 1987).

3 J. L. Granatstein, *The Ottawa Men: The Civil Service Mandarins, 1935–1957* (Toronto: Oxford University Press, 1982), 279.

4 R. M. Bird and revised by M. Smart, "Public Expenditure," *The Canadian Encyclopedia*, February 7, 2006, http://www.thecanadianencyclopedia.ca/en/article/public-expenditure/.

5 See, among others, David K. Foot, ed., *Public Employment and Compensation in Canada: Myths and Realities* (Ottawa: Institute for Research on Public Policy, 1978).

6 Canada, *Proceedings of the Standing Senate Committee on National Finance*, no. 12, March 22, 1973, 14–24.

7 Arthur Kroeger, "Reflections on the Evolution of the Federal Industry Department Prior to 1993," presented at the Industry Canada 2003 Executive Conference, Ottawa, May 2003, 5.

8 Canada, *Annual Reports* (Ottawa: Department of Regional Economic Expansion 1969-70 through 1971–72).

9 See Canada, *Planning and Performance Reporting—Industry Canada, 2015–16*, https://www.ic.gc.ca/eic/site/017.nsf/eng/07520.html.

10 Quoted in Richard W. Phidd and G. Bruce Doern, *The Politics and Management of Canadian Economic Policy* (Toronto: Macmillan, 1978), 324.

11 See, among others, Savoie, *Visiting Grandchildren*.

12 François Perroux, "A Note on the Notion of Growth Pole," *Économie appliquée*, nos 1–2 (1955), 6.

13 See Savoie, *Regional Economic Development: Canada's Search for Solutions.*
14 Ibid.
15 François Perroux, *L'Économie au* XX*e siècle* (Paris: Presses universitaires de France, 1969), 45.
16 Anthony Careless, *Initiative and Response: The Adaptation of Canadian Federalism to Regional Economic Development* (Montreal and Kingston: McGill-Queen's University Press, 1977).
17 See Savoie, *Visiting Grandchildren.*
18 Ibid.
19 Ibid., 85.
20 Tom Kent, *A Public Purpose: An Experience of Liberal Opposition and Government* (Montreal and Kingston: McGill-Queen's University Press, 1988), 424.
21 Richard Starr, *Equal as Citizens,* 22–23.
22 Canada, Population des régions métropolitaines de recensement (Ottawa: Statistique Canada, Annuaire du Canada, 1986), table 2.6, 2-24.
23 See John English, *Just Watch Me: The Life of Pierre Elliott Trudeau, 1968–2000* (Toronto: Vintage Canada, 2010).
24 Canada, *Annual Report, 1971–1972* (Ottawa: DREE, 1973), 21.
25 Kent, *A Public Purpose,* 424.
26 Savoie, *Visiting Grandchildren,* 95.
27 Donald J. Savoie, *Federal-Provincial Collaboration: The Canada-New Brunswick General Development Agreement* (Montreal and Kingston: McGill-Queen's University Press, 1981).
28 Canada, Department of Regional Economic Expansion, *The New Approach* (Ottawa, 1976).
29 "No Fisheries Accord—LeBlanc," *Moncton Times,* February 11, 1977, 1.
30 Savoie, *Visiting Grandchildren,* 104.
31 Canada, Proceedings of the Senate Standing Committees on Agriculture, *Minutes of Proceedings* (Ottawa, 1977), 11-19.
32 Canada, DREE, Senior Staff Conference, Ottawa, June 17 and 18, 1980, 22.
33 Canada, *Department of Finance, Economic Development for Canada in the 1980s* (Ottawa, November 1981), 11.
34 Canada, Department of Energy, Mines and Resources, "Notes for an Address by the Honourable Marc Lalonde, Minister of Energy, Mines and Resources to the Second Atlantic Outlook Conference," Halifax, February 18, 1982, 2.
35 Canada, Finance, *Economic Development for Canada in the 1980s,* 17.
36 Ibid.
37 Memorandum from the Secretary of MSERD to the Minister, the Honourable H. A. Olson, *Government Organization Act, 1982,* June 14, 1982, mimeo.
38 Canada, DRIE, "Speaking Notes—The Honourable Ed Lumley to the House of Commons on the Industrial and Regional Development Program," June 22, 1983, 1 and 2.

39 Ibid.

40 Savoie, *Visiting Grandchildren,* 130.

41 Donald J. Savoie, *Establishing the Atlantic Canada Opportunities Agency* (Ottawa: Office of the Prime Minister, May 1987), 14.

42 Ibid., 14.

43 Savoie, *Visiting Grandchildren,* 137.

44 Savoie, *Establishing the Atlantic Canada Opportunities Agency,* 34.

45 "Party Comes First, Unhappy Côté Says in Deciding to Quit," *Globe and Mail,* August 23, 1988, A1.

Chapter 8

"INFLICTING PROSPERITY ON ATLANTIC CANADA"

My focus remains on economic development in the Maritimes; however, Ottawa continues to look to Atlantic Canada rather than the Maritimes in its regional development programs, and I have to report on these programs. I was directly involved in shaping two major phases of Canada's regional development. The first, when the Department of Regional Economic Expansion (DREE) was abolished and the Department of Regional Industrial Expansion (DRIE) was established, and the second, when Atlantic Canada Opportunities Agency (ACOA) was created. In 1981 I was employed as a senior policy analyst with DREE when the department loaned me to Minister Pierre De Bané's office. I had met De Bané on a few occasions, and he told me he had read and enjoyed my recently published book on regional development.[1] He asked that I join his office as senior policy advisor for a two-year period. I agreed to his request, and so did the department.

Though De Bané liked the book, I knew several senior departmental officials did not. I was critical of the status quo, arguing that the federal government had abdicated its responsibility for regional development to the provinces and to a single-line department. Far too many in Ottawa, I argued, were washing their hands of any responsibility for regional development, insisting it was DREE's responsibility instead. I also argued DREE was little more than a treasury board for the provinces, with provincial governments submitting proposals and the federal government, for the most part, agreeing to fund them. DREE rarely took the lead in shaping new measures and had little to no influence with other federal government departments and agencies.

De Bané and a number of his cabinet colleagues from Atlantic Canada agreed with this assessment.[2] Shortly after I arrived in his office, he asked me to draft his speech to an upcoming senior DREE staff conference. As noted, De Bané served notice in his talk to his officials that he was not prepared to defend the status quo before the prime minister and his colleagues. He wanted a stronger DREE and a much stronger federal government presence in regional development. He asked senior departmental officials for ideas; however, little came of his request. The department did not wish to rock the boat at a time when the prime minister, senior cabinet ministers, and central agency officials were focused on P. E. Trudeau's agenda of patriating the constitution. The goal of senior DREE officials was to survive by not drawing attention to the department.

De Bané, encouraged by his cabinet colleagues from Atlantic Canada, decided to push for an overhaul of the government's approach to regional development. A month after the conference, De Bané asked me to draft a letter to the prime minister, making the case that DREE needed a stronger mandate. Trudeau agreed and told De Bané he would soon initiate the process; it would be carried out jointly between the Privy Council Office and DREE.

The machinery of government unit in PCO managed the process in relative secrecy—nothing new here. The review was carried out solely by PCO and with very little consultation with DREE officials. PCO insists that all machinery of government issues need to be managed in relative secrecy at the centre. The prime minister has the prerogative to organize the machinery as he wishes, without referring the matter to Cabinet. The argument goes it is not possible to turn things over to Cabinet for fear that ministers would be concerned only with protecting or expanding their departmental turf. In any event, it is now well accepted in Ottawa that the prime minister and PCO will, with little consultation, decide on all-important machinery questions. Ministers and departments have no choice but to play by the rules of the game as established by the prime minister and PCO.

The head of the machinery of government at the time, Steve Rosell, would meet me for lunch from time to time or call to brief me in the broadest of terms on the DREE review. In turn, I would brief De Bané, but I had few details on the proposed changes. I note once again the prime minister was, at the time, dealing with an issue that mattered to him a great deal more than regional development—patriating the constitution and incorporating a charter of rights in it. My sense was the prime minister turned the steering wheel over to senior PCO officials and in effect said, "Here, you drive De Bané's request."

On January 12, 1982, Trudeau unveiled a major machinery of government change, which is outlined in the previous chapter. Trudeau had a meeting with De Bané shortly before announcing the changes, essentially to tell him what was about to be announced and that he would be moved over to the fishery portfolio. I had objections to the changes, but the die was cast. I served in the newly established MSERD as a senior policy advisor but only for a brief and unproductive period.

I returned to the Maritimes in 1983 to establish the Canadian Institute for Research on Regional Development at the Université de Moncton. I published a paper in *Canadian Public Policy*, "The Toppling of DREE and the Prospects for Regional Economic Development," which was highly critical of the machinery of government changes.[3] I later published a book titled *Regional Economic Development: Canada's Search for Solutions* that took stock of Canada's regional development efforts. In it, I made the case that recent machinery and policy changes had further weakened Ottawa's commitment to regional economic development.

Several measures tied to the 1982 machinery of government changes and the overhaul of the government's regional policy had a particularly short life. I am referring to the establishment of a "regional fund," which disappeared a few years later without leaving a trace. In addition, the central agency established to give voice to the regions within the federal government was also disbanded within a few years.[4] The remnants of the 1983 Trudeau machinery of government changes only served to worsen matters. There was no one at the centre of government charged with promoting regional development, and DRIE, in DREE's stead, limped along with a confused mandate.

HATFIELD AND REGIONAL DEVELOPMENT

New Brunswick premier Richard Hatfield called in late August 1986 to invite me to lunch. He told me he had just returned from Toronto, where an Ontario cabinet minister urged him to read my most recent book on regional development. I had no idea whether he read the book, but he asked me to summarize it, which I did over lunch. He added that any time an Ontario politician recommends a book on regional development, he worries!

Hatfield expressed strong reservations about the work of both DRIE and MSERD. I agreed. He told me the four Atlantic premiers also had serious reservations about Ottawa's approach to regional economic development. He asked if I could suggest solutions and if I could produce, over the next few days, a "five- or six-pager" speaking note with ideas about what to do. He explained that the following week he was meeting with the prime minister, who planned to stop in Fredericton to meet with him on his way to Newfoundland and Labrador, where he was scheduled to chair a Cabinet committee meeting. I spent the Labour Day weekend working on the document, and I was able to send it to him by late Monday. I was later told Hatfield simply handed the note to the prime minister and urged him to read it.

Mulroney travelled to Charlottetown, Prince Edward Island, a few weeks later to meet with the Atlantic premiers. He informed them that he would be asking me to prepare a report on establishing a new economic development agency for Atlantic Canada. He also told the premiers that I would be consulting them, as well as a cross-section of Atlantic Canadians, in preparing the report.[5]

WHAT TO DO?

The prime minister's mandate letter essentially gave me the green light to explore any issue and come forward with whatever recommendations I felt appropriate. I was told to consult Atlantic Canadians, including federal cabinet ministers, the four premiers, leading representatives of the region's business community, representatives of the academic community, and community leaders, and then come up with a plan. Mulroney also asked that I brief Dalton Camp, a senior official in PMO and PCO, on my work, as well as Fred Doucet and Charles McMillan from PMO. I did. Camp, in particular, retained a strong interest in my work and the eventual agency, Doucet and McMillan much less so.

I initiated communications with senior officials at PCO, and I was in frequent contact with them. I knew my way around the federal public service and in political circles, having worked in a line department and served as senior policy advisor in a minister's office. I had learned that PCO officials would be asked to pick up the pieces, when it came to machinery of government issues, draft the legislation with Justice department officials, and orchestrate the changes. More to the point, I had learned from the De Bané experience that PCO would hold the key to all machinery of government changes. I developed a very strong relationship with John (Jack) L. Manion, then the associate clerk of the Privy Council, who proved very helpful in my work. I was in frequent contact with him and made a point of briefing him on the consultations and my progress. We became and remained friends until he passed away in 2010.

I worked on the initiative full-time between October 1986 and February 1987 and continued work on it between March and the day the prime minister unveiled the agency. I consulted over one hundred Atlantic Canadians. The consultations were helpful, up to a point. My experience is that once you have carried out several consultations in each sector, you start hearing the same message. Provincial government officials made the point, time and again, that DRIE had little to offer the region in sharp contrast to DREE, and that DRIE needed to be scrapped. Representatives of the business community called for less bureaucracy and more proactive government programs, representatives of the region's business schools called for new programs to encourage entrepreneurship, and representatives of sectoral or special interest groups all stressed the importance of their sectors to the region's economic future. Representatives of community economic groups, meanwhile, argued economic development should always start at the community level.

What about the economic development literature? I had, along with my colleague and friend Benjamin Higgins, organized a conference in the summer of 1985 to honour François Perroux and his work. Perroux attended the conference and presented a paper, the last he would write; he passed away in June 1987. As noted, Perroux's growth pole concept had fallen out of fashion by the 1970s. However, he defended his work with conviction and enthusiasm at the conference. Certainly, his paper still holds merit, but it was of limited value in preparing my report.[6] We managed to attract some of the world's leading scholars of economic development to the Perroux conference. William Alonso (Harvard University), John Friedmann (University of California, Los Angeles), Niles Hansen (University of Texas), Karen Polenske (MIT), Harry Richardson (University of Southern California), Lloyd Rodwin (MIT), and Thomas Courchene (at that time from the University of Western Ontario), among others, gave seminal papers. I was able to draw important insights from them in preparing my report, which remains accessible in Canada's two official languages.[7]

THE REPORT

The report on the establishment of ACOA is structured in four parts: 1) Past Efforts; 2) Observations from the Consultations; 3) Solutions and Instruments; and 4) Organizing the Agency for Regional Development. The report is constructed around the theme "solid and self-sustaining economic development in Atlantic Canada must in large part be endogenous. Atlantic Canadians themselves will have to provide the energy, the skills and the imagination to conceive and organize economic activity if the region is to prosper."[8]

I drew from lessons of the cargo cult to make the point that Atlantic Canadians need to look to their own energy, innovations, and entrepreneurs to grow their economy. As William Alonso explained at the conference in honour of Perroux, "During the Second World War, natives of some Pacific islands saw the arrival of American troops. The Americans cleared and leveled an oblong piece of the jungle, set lights along the edges, and lo! After a while, a giant silver bird arrived, bearing all manner of valuable things. This gave rise to a cargo cult among the natives, who, having seen what the Americans had done to attract the silver bird, similarly set about clearing portions of the jungle and then waited by their fires, patiently and reverently, for the arrival of the bird."[9] I wanted to bring home the point that it was not sufficient to rely solely on building industrial parks and offering cash grants to lure outside investors and simply sit back and wait for the big silver bird of economic development to arrive from Ottawa.

The consultations in preparing the report made the case that Atlantic Canada had lost its place in Ottawa's regional development policy, existing federal programs constituted a veritable Tower of Babel, and government policies should focus on promoting innovation and entrepreneurship. Past efforts, I argued, never lived up to expectations, because they were always pushed aside to a single-line department and because the objectives were neither clear nor lasting, and often conflicting.

Representatives of the business community, for the most part, insisted they did not need another cash grant to help them promote economic growth. They called for better coordination between programs, better information on trade opportunities, better measures to promote R&D, and easier access to existing government programs. Many made the point that the local business community was small and unable to support an in-house capacity to undertake R&D, explore trade opportunities, and navigate different bureaucratic layers to access programs.[10] They also argued the machinery of government had become too big and too complex, making it difficult for them to access helpful measures.

Several provincial government officials argued that regional development was getting "bad press" in Ottawa. Others, meanwhile, insisted the federal regional development bureaucracy had become too cumbersome. Federal cabinet ministers from the region argued there was a "need for solid data and analysis of the impact of national policies on the region."[11] They pointed out they needed facts and arguments to make the case in Ottawa that the existing national political policy was inhibiting growth in the region.

Many raised as an issue the role of politicians in regional development. They argued politicians from the Atlantic region are "regional development's best friends in Ottawa," but they can also play havoc with programs.[12] The problem is politicians want to respond to the wishes of the voters in their riding, and this pressure often calls for misguided initiatives. The machinery of government, they maintained, should be designed to protect or, if possible, even isolate program delivery from politicians.

I made a series of recommendations. The emphasis, I argued, should be on promoting a strong private sector. I suggested the new agency should not create new cash grants for businesses but rather rely on existing federal-provincial programs. I urged the establishment of a small number of centres for entrepreneurial development to encourage learning institutions to develop entrepreneurship and small-business courses.

I recommended a new tax incentive for the region, one designed for aspiring entrepreneurs. Atlantic Canadians, I argued, should be allowed to accumulate capital tax-free to start a new business in their region, a kind of RRSP for aspiring entrepreneurs. I also urged the government to locate the agency's head office in Atlantic Canada and added that a deputy-minister-level official should lead the agency. It should have a distinct organizational status to ensure it enjoys more autonomy than a typical government department without being a Crown corporation. The agency should implement measures to promote market development, human resource development, and R&D.

I recommended three additional mandates for the agency: play an advocacy role for the region in Ottawa; coordinate the activities of other federal departments and agencies in Atlantic Canada; and promote federal-provincial co-operation. I recommended the agency should not have its own programs, but rather rely on those of other federal departments and provincial governments. Government programs and money in the regional development field were sufficient, and there was no need to add more. I insisted there was no shortage of government programs handing out grants.

Additionally, I recommended the government limit the size of ACOA to one hundred top-flight officials. Given the agency would rely on other government programs, I saw no need to create a large bureaucracy. I envisaged an agency that had the capacity to influence other federal departments and agencies to strengthen their role, presence, and activities in Atlantic Canada. I saw an agency with a limited number of high-profile officials, with some borrowed from the private sector for a period of time, who would, in concert with the business community, identify economic and trade opportunities.

I concluded the agency should play a catalyst role, not only to identify opportunities but also to make them happen. I recommended the establishment of a $250 million fund to be drawn from existing government departments and agencies, notably DRIE, which was being disbanded. Again, I saw no need for "new money." For one thing, federal government was dealing with a stubborn deficit problem at the time. For another, I felt there were enough financial resources for regional development already available—the challenge was to make better use of them.

The theory behind the agency model for regional development called for more policy and administrative independence, greater effectiveness, a more accurate process to assess performance, a stronger ability to deal with non-government actors, better suited nationally inspired measures to mesh with regional circumstances, and better accountability requirements. All of this squared quite nicely with what I heard in the consultations.

THE RESPONSE

Prime Minister Mulroney decided to unveil the new agency on June 6, 1987, in St. John's, Newfoundland. The timing and location were opportune for Mulroney, given that a by-election was to be held in St. John's East a month later. Never one to understate good news, Mulroney declared, "We begin with new money, a new mission and a new opportunity," adding, "the Agency will succeed where others have failed," and predicting it would "inflict prosperity on Atlantic Canada."[13]

Mulroney accepted a number of my recommendations. The agency's head office would be located in Atlantic Canada—in Moncton—not in Ottawa, and it would be headed by a deputy-minister-level official. It would not be a Crown corporation, but it would have an independent advisory body of prominent Atlantic Canadians. As my report called for, the agency was given four mandates: play a coordinating role with other federal departments, the four provinces, and the private sector; play an advocacy role in Ottawa on behalf of Atlantic Canada; play a lead role in promoting co-operation between the federal government and the four Atlantic provinces; and promote entrepreneurship development in the region. In addition, former MSERD and DRIE responsibilities in Atlantic Canada were transferred to the new agency together with their budgets.[14]

Mulroney rejected two important recommendations. First, he decided to give ACOA an additional $1.05 billion in new money over five years, rather than relying on MSERD and DRIE's existing budgets. Second, Mulroney directed ACOA to launch new cash grant programs, rather than relying on existing federal and provincial government programs.[15] While the government did establish an advisory board to guide ACOA, it was later disbanded. The board had very little impact on the agency's policy direction and none over its operations.[16] Though ACOA, like its sister agencies, retains the agency model, it is only for political and administrative purposes, and it operates like any other federal government line department.

The legislation establishing ACOA gave it substantial authority to plan, coordinate, and implement all manner of economic development measures in the region, including full authority to promote "economic opportunities and development in Atlantic Canada over which Parliament has jurisdiction."[17] As well, ACOA "shall coordinate the policies and programs of the Government of Canada in relation to opportunity for economic development in Atlantic Canada."[18] With regard to program authority, the legislation enabled ACOA to "enter into agreements with the government of any province or provinces in Atlantic Canada respecting the carrying out of any program or project of the Agency."[19] In addition, the agency "may, by order, establish as a designated area, for the period set out in the order, any area in Atlantic Canada where, in the opinion of the Minister, exceptional circumstances provide opportunities for locally based improvements in productive employment."[20]

IT'S ABOUT POLITICS

Mulroney saw clear political advantages in unveiling a new regional development agency, locating its head office in Moncton, allocating over $1 billion of new money, and directing the agency to deliver its own cash grant program. New money holds more political appeal than a reprofile of existing budgets. All of the above provided opportunities to cast the government in a positive light and generate visibility. The announcement came a little over one month from a by-election and a little over one year before the next general election. From a partisan political perspective, the timing was excellent.

Mulroney and his advisors took comfort in the reaction to the announcement, which was greeted with enthusiasm by many everywhere in Atlantic Canada. The local media gave it two thumbs up. The *Fredericton Daily Gleaner*, for example, ran a highly positive article with the headline "Atlantic Canada Gets Big Boost."[21] The announcement was even praised by Liberal politicians from the region. In New Brunswick, for example, then Opposition leader Frank McKenna warmly welcomed the announcement and observed, "I believe with the composition of the Agency and terms of reference, there is reason to be optimistic."[22] Nova Scotia Liberal leader Vince MacLean echoed McKenna's sentiments.[23] That was likely enough for Mulroney to declare the ACOA initiative a success and a job done for Atlantic Canada. He was off to deal with other more pressing issues from a "national perspective."

I had been asked to be available to brief the prime minister in St. John's for the June 6 announcement. Mulroney had only one question for me:

how was Atlantic Canada, and in particular, how were Acadians reacting to his proposed Meech Lake agreement? I had little to offer at this point other than what the local media were reporting. I was not prepared for the question. I expected questions about economic circumstances in Atlantic Canada and my report, and I was well prepared to answer any questions on these two topics. In hindsight, I can appreciate why Mulroney would have at the top of his political agenda his proposed Meech Lake Accord to bring Quebec into the Canadian constitutional family (which he had negotiated with the ten provinces). It had far more crucial political consequences for him and his government than the establishment of an economic development agency for Atlantic Canada. Though the day belonged to Atlantic Canada, Ottawa's political and national agenda, as always, had other more pressing and politically important matters to address.

However, there was considerable political pressure on senior ACOA officials to come up with a new cash grant program, given the election was a year away. ACOA officials delivered. A new program, labelled the Action Program, was formally introduced on February 15, 1988. The response was overwhelming, no doubt partly because so many types of economic activities became eligible and partly because of the high-profile publicity campaign heralding its introduction, but also because the region was finally coming out of the deep recession of the early 1980s. It was also one of the most generous regional development programs ever introduced in Canada. For whatever reason, the Action Program was quick off the mark. After less than two years, ACOA had reviewed over 34,000 inquiries, processed 6,800 applications, and approved 2,700 projects under the program.[24] Applications, initially at least, came in at ten times the rate of any predecessor programs.

The Action Program was in full swing by fiscal year 1988-89, and during that year alone applications totalled 9,634, of which nearly 5,000 were approved. The greatest number of approved offers involved modernization and expansion, followed by the establishment of new facilities and studies. ACOA also reported that the program assisted over 400 first-time entrepreneurs. Although only about 80 innovation projects had been supported, this level of assistance was reported to be five-fold the rate of support provided by previous programs.[25]

Over 15 per cent of approved projects fell under the Business Support element of the program or activities aimed at improving the quality of entrepreneurial skills in Atlantic Canada, including business database improvement,

Atlantic case studies, and counselling. About 80 per cent of all studies supported under the Action Program were valued at less than $25,000.[26]

The focus in ACOA's early years was on the Action Program at the expense of its other mandates, if only because politicians insisted on it. The Action Program, much more than other initiatives, provided ample opportunities to generate positive visibility. But federal-provincial agreements for regional development no longer enjoyed the priority status they had under DREE, and ACOA quickly served notice it would only consider an agreement that was supportive of its overall strategy. The Mulroney government wanted to end the practice of provincial governments announcing initiatives as being subject to obtaining federal participation, thus putting federal ministers in the difficult position of going along with the provincial government or being held responsible for the measure not proceeding. The political tide was turning at the provincial level in Atlantic Canada, and Liberal premiers would form government in two of the four provinces within six months. Political visibility for federal spending became as important under Mulroney has it had become under P. E. Trudeau.

ACOA's focus on its Action Program meant it was not able to prioritize its advocacy and coordination mandates. As all government bureaucracies are want to do, ACOA insisted it had little success on either the coordination or advocacy front because it was never given the resources to be effective in these areas. ACOA argued that obtaining new money was only part of the equation. It also required sufficient staff or, in the parlance of bureaucracy, a sufficient number of person-years, to carry out its four mandates. ACOA was given 320 person-years; this, the agency argued, was barely sufficient to implement the Action Program properly. Indeed, ACOA maintained it had to hire some 50 people on special contracts to deal with the backlog of applications under the Action Program. For a few years, central agencies, particularly the Treasury Board, resisted ACOA's attempts to secure more staff. The Treasury Board had another agenda to pursue: it had to implement a 15,000 person-year cut in the federal public service, which the Mulroney government had announced as part of a broad policy of restraint in government spending.[27]

ACOA, however, had another reason for its lack of success in pursuing its advocacy mandate, pointing out it "may appear somewhat unusual for an Agency that is part of a federal system to be given a statutory role in advocating the interests of a particular region within that system." It added, however, that past experience had shown "regional interests cannot be adequately protected without an effective ongoing direct link to the central decision-making structure."[28] That effective link never existed before ACOA, still does not exist, and is unlikely to ever exist unless fundamental changes are made to our national political institutions. This state of affairs was left unattended by the Fathers of Confederation. A relatively small agency, at least by federal government standards, operating a thousand kilometres away from Ottawa, with no institutional capacity to influence other federal government departments, can not nearly repair a fundamental flaw in our constitution. The emergence of governing from the centre in Ottawa has only made matters worse.

Advocating for regional development or for the economic interests of Atlantic Canada goes against the grain in the federal government. The idea of establishing ACOA came from the prime minister, not the bureaucracy. Central agency officials focused on ACOA's generous Action Program rather than on its own work on the impact of other federal government departments' policies on Atlantic Canada. I know of no central agency taking on the task of assessing the impact of so-called national policies or programs on the regions. Central agency officials did not see it as a problem; however, central agencies felt the Action Program was too open-ended and supported far too many projects, creating an overcapacity in many sectors. Arguments arose that some new businesses supported by the Action Program simply put existing enterprises, which did not have government-supported modern facilities, out of business.[29] Central agencies, all firmly entrenched in the Ottawa system, are in the business of assessing the work of line departments and agencies, never their own.

Don McPhail, ACOA's first deputy minister and president, was placed on early retirement a few years after the agency was established. Dalton Camp, a former senior PMO and PCO advisor, who kept a close eye on the agency in its early months, left government in 1989. In a column with the *Toronto Star*, Camp argued ACOA had become so successful operating outside of the Ottawa system that senior mandarins were out to do it in. He insisted McPhail's firing was a result of "a bureaucratic coup in the national capital." He added, "The small bores in Finance, Treasury Board and latterly in the Prime Minister's Office, who have opposed ACOA from the outset, should not be allowed to make McPhail the first victim in their long campaign to destroy the Agency."[30] Camp later told me the Ottawa system has a well-honed capacity to send off "antibodies" to fight regional considerations and regional development.

LOOKING WEST

One of the most powerful regional ministers in the Mulroney cabinet was Don Mazankowski, the deputy prime minister. And one of his most important goals was to do for Western Canada what Trudeau, Marchand, and Pelletier had done for Quebec. He was determined to place the Western agenda front and centre on the national political agenda. His agenda was economic; he sought to put in place measures to diversify the Western economy. He, like other westerners, was convinced that the West needed to develop sectors other than agriculture, oil, and gas.

In addition, by early 1987, the Mulroney government was in serious political difficulty in the West. Public opinion polls showed the government was struggling to maintain a narrow lead, and, at one point, it trailed the New Democratic Party. In 1986 the government had nearly lost a by-election in Pembina, Alberta, hitherto regarded as one of its safest seats in the country. Worse still, that same year the government, as already noted, had awarded the CF-18 maintenance contract to a Quebec firm, although a Winnipeg firm had submitted the lowest bid. The public outcry in western Canada against this decision resonates in the region to this day. A general election was expected in 1988, and it was important for Mulroney to solidify his Western base quickly if he was to have any hope of winning a second mandate.

Mulroney went to Edmonton to announce the details of the new Western Economic Diversification Canada (WD) initiative.[31] The agency would administer a $1.2 billion fund of new money and, like its sister agency ACOA, WD would assume responsibility for DRIE's A-base budget in Western Canada, thus adding still more financial resources to the announcement. The prime minister explained his government's regional policy was designed to provide "federal leadership for each region, tailored to its unique potential and needs. At the same time, we want to ensure that regional perspectives are front and centre in the development of national priorities, and that regional economic development is backed by strong national centres of industrial and technological expertise."[32] No mention was made of alleviating regional disparities.

Mazankowski explained that WD would be similar in many ways to ACOA and that it represented in reality the second phase of a multi-step redefinition of Ottawa's regional development policy. "We think it is very important," he said, "to develop economic programs that fit a particular region and for the decision-making to take place in that region. We believe that to establish a uniform policy across the country, administered out of Ottawa, is not the answer. Clearly, the approach we've had in the past, in terms of addressing regional economic expansion, has not worked."[33] However, nothing was done to ensure the machinery of government in Ottawa would be able to accommodate regional economic circumstances in planning future economic development efforts.

NORTHERN ONTARIO

On July 15, 1987, the federal government unveiled yet another special agency to promote economic development, this time in Northern Ontario. In announcing the Federal Economic Development Initiative in Northern Ontario (FedNor), the federal minister for the region, James Kelleher, pointed out the government had consulted the business community and the provincial government to determine what was needed. The reaction to the announcement was much less positive than that following the decisions to establish ACOA and WD respectively. The Ontario government, for example, made it clear it had not been involved in the consultations; indeed, a deputy minister declared, "There haven't been any senior level discussions yet and it is not clear what FedNor is for."[34]

QUEBEC AND SOUTHERN ONTARIO

In time, Quebec and, more recently Southern Ontario, would also secure their own federal regional economic development agency. Harper established the Federal Economic Development Agency for Southern Ontario (FedDev Ontario) in August 2009 and—not to be outdone—gave the agency a $1 billion budget of new money over five years. He later added another $920 million for a second five-year period, beginning in April 2014. On December 9, 2013, the Harper government also announced the establishment of a $200 million Advanced Manufacturing Fund to promote innovation in the manufacturing sector. FedDev Ontario is charged with implementing the fund, which suggested that from Ottawa's perspective, the centre of Canada's advanced manufacturing sector is in Southern Ontario.[35] Knowing how government bureaucracies operate, it would go against the grain for FedDev Ontario to support an initiative outside its region, much like ACOA would not wish to support an initiative in, say, Manitoba. Ontario now has two federal regional development agencies and a third one, if you include Industry Canada, which is largely concerned with Central Canada, in addition to a specific regional development program under the Advanced Manufacturing Fund.

THE NORTH

In August 2009 Harper unveiled a new regional development agency for Canada's north, the Canadian Northern Economic Development Agency (CanNor). It is worth repeating that every postal code in Canada, even the ones on Bay Street, in the heart of Canada's financial district and one of the world's economic hotspots, has access to a federal regional development agency. All of the above is done under the regional development banner. The point is that political logic can always be adjusted to meet the partisan political requirements of the day, and this is particularly true when it comes to regional development policy. Harper had strong reservations about the work of federal regional development agencies while in Opposition. But his view changed once in power—he created two new such agencies and a regional program to assist the manufacturing sector in Southern Ontario. Interestingly, all regional development agencies were established by Progressive Conservative or Conservative governments.

Table 1. Canada's Six Regional Development Agencies

Atlantic Canada Opportunities Agency (ACOA)
Canada Economic Development for Quebec Regions (CED)
Canadian Northern Economic Development Agency (CanNor)
Federal Economic Development Agency for Southern Ontario (FedDev Ontario)
Federal Economic Development Initiative for Northern Ontario (FedNor)
Western Economic Diversification Canada (WD)

Source: Regional Development Agencies across Canada, http://feddevontario.gc.ca/eic/site/723.nsf/eng/01690.html.

ACOA OVER THE YEARS

Mulroney won a majority mandate in the 1988 election and won 12 seats in Atlantic Canada—more seats than he initially expected. He also won more seats in Western Canada than public opinion surveys had predicted the year before: 169 seats for his party, 83 for the Liberals, and 43 for the NDP.[36] He and his advisors had every reason to think the decision to establish regional development agencies was a political success.

Once back in office, however, Mulroney quickly unveiled a series of spending restraint measures. ACOA was one of the targets. The government froze the agency's expenditure budget to the level of the previous year and directed that the $1 billion of new money be spent over a seven-year period rather than five. If the expenditure level is the test for a government's commitment to regional development, then ACOA's best days were in the months following the June 6, 1987, announcement leading up to the November 21, 1988, general election.

The Mulroney government had other issues on the front burner in the immediate aftermath of the 1988 election, starting with the need to address the political fallout from the failed Meech Lake Accord, pursuing the Canada-United States Free Trade Agreement, and implementing a controversial HST tax. It may well be that from Mulroney's perspective, he had dealt with regional development by setting up a string of regional economic development agencies, and nothing more was required.

THE CHRÉTIEN APPROACH

Jean Chrétien decided to make regional economic development one of five major policy priorities in his 1990 bid to lead the federal Liberal Party. He asked me to hold the pen for his policy statement on regional development while Rod Bryden, Senator Michael Kirby, and David Dingwall would provide political guidance. I recall Chrétien praising DREE and Ottawa's decision to decentralize a number of units to the regions. I cautioned him on the first: DREE may have been fine at some point, but it was yesterday's solution. I agreed fully with him on the benefits of decentralizing federal government units to slow-growth regions. Chrétien gave his policy statement in St. John's, Newfoundland, and spoke about the need to move more units to the regions, and to my delight, said that he would not abolish

ACOA or return to the days of DREE. He also called for new investments in infrastructure, R&D, and tourism for Atlantic Canada.[37]

In 1975 Chrétien, as Treasury Board president, had led the charge in relocating units of the federal bureaucracy away from the NCR and other major metropolitan centres to slow-growth areas. Chrétien explained at the time that relocating both "federal jobs and salaries" constituted another important instrument "for the promotion of economic activity in the less advantaged regions of this country."[38] The initiative's first effort relocated 4,503 permanent and 6,080 temporary jobs from the NCR to twenty-four communities in all ten provinces between 1977 and 1982. The jobs were distributed as follows: 2,235 permanent and 630 temporary for the Atlantic provinces; 1,091 permanent and 1,900 temporary for Quebec; 626 permanent and 1,680 temporary for Ontario (outside of the NCR); and 551 permanent and 1,870 temporary for the western provinces.[39]

The program had few friends in Ottawa. Senior public servants never saw merit in the territorial de-concentration of government units, better known in Ottawa as the decentralization program. For one thing, it meant less control over government operations. For another, they saw first-hand the program's impact on the Ottawa real estate market. Politically, the Ontario and Ottawa caucuses were also opposed to the program. When the Progressive Conservative Party came to power in 1979, Sinclair Stevens, a senior Ontario minister and Treasury Board president in the short-lived Clark government, immediately announced a review of the program. He explained his decision was prompted by the need to restrain government spending.[40]

The program never recovered. It continued to meet stiff opposition from senior public servants, from public-sector unions, and from the Ontario and Ottawa caucuses. The program, to have any chance of success, required a strong commitment from the prime minister. When he returned to power, Trudeau decided to focus his energy on patriating the constitution and did not relaunch the decentralization program.[41]

The Mulroney government did look to the decentralization program to deal with the closure of the Canadian Forces base in Summerside, Prince Edward Island. It did not, however, transfer any existing unit. Rather, it decided to establish a new administrative unit there to process the goods and services tax. Mulroney also moved the Canadian Space Agency to Montreal and an Ottawa medical laboratory to Winnipeg. The Quebec caucus and some key Mulroney ministers were adamant that the Space Agency be located in the Montreal area to shift some federal spending in science and technology away from Ontario, where it had been traditionally concentrated. The laboratory's move to Winnipeg, meanwhile, was widely perceived to have been, in part, compensation for losing the CF-18 maintenance contract to a Montreal firm, even though Winnipeg-based Bristol Aerospace had submitted the lowest tender.[42] However, Mulroney never pursued government decentralization with any degree of enthusiasm or commitment. Transferring newly established units to the regions became a convenient way to deal with a political problem in an ad hoc fashion, but he saw no reason to re-establish the decentralization program.

Chrétien, for his part, lost interest in decentralization shortly after he became prime minister and he never relaunched the program, contrary to what he had promised. He did locate the newly created gun registry centre (Canada Firearms Centre) in Miramichi (formerly Chatham), New Brunswick, to assist the community in dealing with nearly a thousand job losses after the federal government decided to close CFB Chatham and move its activities to Quebec and Alberta air bases. No one from Ottawa ever explained why it made more military sense to locate activities in Quebec than in Miramichi. The Miramichi gun registry office employed about two hundred workers, including casual and term employees.[43]

There are reasons why Chrétien, once in power, never embraced the program as he had committed to do in his party leadership campaign. Senior public servants insisted the program was too costly. More importantly, the "Ontario factor" became extremely important to Chrétien. Ontario was the single most politically important region for Chrétien in all three general elections he fought. He knew better than anyone, given his longevity in federal politics, that Ontario was invariably the key to maintaining a Liberal majority, and he was not about to jeopardize it.

A former minister in the Chrétien government maintained the reason Chrétien lost interest in government decentralization had everything to do with Liberal-dominated Ontario and the Ottawa caucus. He observed that decentralization was a "complete nonstarter" with John Manley, an Ottawa MP and Chrétien's powerful Industry minister, and later deputy prime minister and Finance minister.[44] In a pre-budget consultation session in Moncton in November 2002, Manley simply dismissed out of hand a suggestion by one participant that Ottawa should look at decentralization to promote regional development, insisting "it would not work," without further explanation.[45] Manley did not even want to entertain the question. No one else, for that matter, has ever explained why it would not work, but the comment essentially means it would not work politically in a rep by pop political world.

Andy Scott, former cabinet minister in the Chrétien and Martin governments, insisted a "study of the superannuation directorate...has confirmed that there are economic gains to be had in pursuing such a program."[46] No sooner had Scott made clear his views than a public service union (the Public Service Alliance of Canada) issued a press release, arguing that "moving jobs from Ottawa doesn't save money through salaries because, as opposed to moving jobs overseas, federal employees in Canada receive the same salary."[47] That probably made sense in the NCR, much less so in other regions.

Senior public servants in Ottawa have invariably pointed to cost to undermine the program. However, not all factors are taken into account when assessing the program's cost. There is strong evidence that the decentralized units function more efficiently in the regions than in Ottawa. The Cheque Redemption Control Directorate (Department of Supply and Services), located in Matane, Quebec, in the economically depressed Gaspé region, processes the same number of cheques with 275 employees that it processed with 300 employees when it was in Ottawa. The director of the unit explained one reason for the increased productivity was that he was able to select the 275 employees from 3,500 applicants, while in Ottawa he had considerably fewer applicants to choose from. He added that staff turnover at Matane is practically non-existent, compared to the high turnover experienced earlier in Ottawa. The director of the Supply and Services unit in Shediac, New Brunswick, reported similar findings, claiming his unit is far more efficient than when it was located in Ottawa.[48] Because it is not in its interest to do so, Ottawa has never calculated the savings realized from efficiency when establishing the total cost in decentralizing government units and jobs. Evidence-based policy advice be damned, particularly when it may threaten the interest of Ottawa-based public servants. They see only plenty of reasons not to support a decentralization program.

Harper had no interest in decentralization, and little was done under its banner during his tenure in office. Shortly after the Justin Trudeau government came to power, Dominic LeBlanc, the minister from New Brunswick, pledged to reactivate Ottawa's decentralization program.[49] Officials in Ottawa said LeBlanc was "flying solo"; the "system" had not considered the issue, and there was no plan to do so.[50] Given the weight of Ontario in the Liberal caucus, there is little hope the program will be reactivated.

The federal public service is increasingly concentrated in the Ottawa-Gatineau region. Thirty years ago, 72 per cent of federal public servants worked in regional and field offices. Today, the percentage is down to 57. Leaving aside the handful of policy units in regional agencies, all policy and coordinating units are located in Ottawa, as are all central agencies. Recent developments only serve to reinforce Ottawa-Gatineau as the region to secure federal government employment. The Chrétien and Harper program reviews—notwithstanding firm commitments to the contrary—have been much harder on government employment in the regions than in the National Capital Region. Federal government jobs now account for about one in five workers in the NCR. The decline in federal employment has taken place outside the NCR. In August 2014 Statistics Canada reported a decline of 16,200 federal public servants outside of the NCR over a one-year period, compared with an increase of about 8,000 in the NCR during the same period. More specifically, the number of federal government workers in Ottawa-Gatineau increased by 6.1 per cent, while it dropped by 7.3 per cent in the rest of the country between 2013 and 2014.[51] There is a disconnect between what governments say in launching program reviews and what the numbers actually reveal when the dust settles. The regions always lose more than the NCR.

CHRÉTIEN AND ACOA

Canada became the focus of scrutiny by international financial markets because of its high accumulated debt. In early January 1995, the *Wall Street Journal* described the Canadian dollar as a "basket case," and on January 12 an editorial titled "Bankrupt Canada?" in the same publication declared, "Mexico isn't the only U.S. neighbour flirting with the financial abyss." The contributor went on to argue, "If dramatic action isn't taken in the next month's federal budget, it's not inconceivable that Canada could hit the debt wall and have to call in the International Monetary Fund to stabilize its falling currency."[52] This editorial made a significant impact on those in the Cabinet still hesitant to accept the general expenditure stance advocated by Finance. Indeed, the Deputy Minister of Finance David Dodge later described it as a "seminal event" in the politics of the 1995 budget, and an ambitious program review exercise was launched.[53]

Chrétien, together with Finance minister Paul Martin, launched a comprehensive program review exercise; the results are well-known.[54] The review was guided by the following six questions: 1) Does the program area or activity continue to serve the public interest; 2) Is there a legitimate and necessary role for government in this program area or activity; 3) Is the current role of the federal government appropriate, or is the program a candidate for realignment with the provinces; 4) What activities or programs should or could be transferred in whole or in part to the private or voluntary sector; 5) If the program or activity continues, how could its efficiency be improved; 6) Is the resultant package of programs and activities affordable within the fiscal restraint? If not, what programs or activities should be abandoned? More importantly for line departments, central agencies decided they would be divided into three categories of spending cuts: large (25 per cent, or in some cases more), substantial (15 per cent), and token (5 per cent). The assigned reductions were to be implemented over a period of three years.[55]

ACOA answered the six questions and made the case that its programs served a critical role in Canadian society, that its role was necessary to promote national unity, and that there was little opportunity for moving its activities to the provinces or the private sector. Notwithstanding the arguments, the agency would fall under the large 25 per cent category. The ACOA minister of the day, David Dingwall, did appeal to Chrétien to reduce ACOA's cuts, but to no avail. To comply with the cuts, ACOA ended all grants to private businesses and reduced its budget by $173 million over a three-year period. The agency also announced it would no longer fund resource agreements with provincial governments under its co-operation agreements. Federal-provincial agreements in fisheries, agriculture, and mineral development had been part of Ottawa's regional economic development efforts going back to the General Development Agreements in the early 1970s.[56] Dingwall, however, reported a victory of sorts in his battle to protect ACOA during the program review exercise. As he told the Gomery Commission, "On the Atlantic Canada Opportunities Agency there was a full campaign inside the government to get rid of the regional agencies, and we had to fight very, very hard to maintain those agencies."[57]

The government did not get rid of ACOA, but Chrétien put in place a machinery of government change that saw the agency becoming part of the Industry portfolio under then minister John Manley. Many inside ACOA felt betrayed, interpreting the decision as a clear signal of Ottawa's desire to establish greater political and administrative control over the agency. To make matters worse, John Manley became the senior minister responsible for ACOA. Senior ACOA officials who had a first-hand look at Manley's priorities and his interventions inside the government widely perceived him as parochial and largely concerned with Ottawa, its suburbs, and the high-tech sector.[58] A good number of senior ACOA officials told me that, for Manley, federal government spending for economic development, particularly in the high-tech sector, made sense in the Ottawa region but rarely in other regions, notably Atlantic Canada.

Changes to the Employment Insurance program, among other decisions flowing fom the Chrétien-Martin program review, were a hard sell for Chrétien in the Maritime provinces. His government suffered heavy losses in the region in the 1997 election, including two senior cabinet ministers, Doug Young and David Dingwall. He even saw hand-picked candidate Dominic LeBlanc lose in his former New Brunswick riding of Beauséjour. Chrétien's Liberal Party also lost all eleven seats in Nova Scotia. Ever the politician, he knew Ontario, not the Maritime provinces, would remain the key to a majority in the next election. As the Maritime provinces had turned away from his government, the best the region could expect from this seasoned politician was benign neglect, and that is precisely what it received. Chrétien would turn his back on the region, much like the region had turned its back on him.

Liberal MPs and senators from the Maritimes had every reason for their concern that their region was falling off the government's radar. In the post-program review exercise of the late-1990s, budget speeches provided for new spending and new economic development measures, but none seemed to resonate in the Maritime provinces. The 1999 budget, for example, added $200 million to the Canada Foundation for Innovation, $75 million to the Natural Sciences and Engineering Research Council of Canada, $6 million for National Research Council Canada, $55 million for biotechnology R&D, $50 million for Networks of Centres of Excellence,

$150 million for Technology Partnerships Canada, and $430 million for the Canadian Space Agency. There was very little here that would benefit the Maritime region. The Technology Partnerships Canada program was viewed for what it was, a program designed for the economic circumstances of Ontario and Quebec, which always secured the bulk of the program's budget, while the Canadian Space Agency was seen as mostly benefitting Ottawa and Montreal.[59] Though few government MPs said so publicly, they were taken aback when Chrétien continued to have ACOA report through the Industry department and John Manley. They knew Chrétien well and were very aware of his capacity to send out political messages; in this case, the message was that he owed the region precious little after losing two of his senior ministers and every seat in Nova Scotia in the 1997 general election.

The 2000 federal budget held no greater promise for the region. It established a $60 million Canadian Foundation for Climate and Atmospheric Sciences but located its head office in Ottawa; provided $46 million for national pollution enforcement and the Great Lakes Action Plan; and added $900 million to the Canadian Foundation for Innovation. It also gave the Montreal-based Business Development Bank of Canada an $80 million injection of new money to support its financing activities.[60] Again, the budget offered nothing new to the Maritime provinces.

Two Liberal MPs—Joe McGuire from Prince Edward Island and Charles Hubbard from New Brunswick—teamed up with Senator Wilfred Moore from Nova Scotia and Senator John Bryden from New Brunswick to produce a report on possible future economic development efforts in Atlantic Canada. They retained an outside consultant to work with caucus research staff to produce *Atlantic Canada: Catching Tomorrow's Wave*, which they tabled on May 31, 1999. The report explored new opportunities in biotechnology, aquaculture, health sciences, food processing, and oceans technology and urged the government to look at promoting clusters in these sectors. It also looked to more traditional sectors, notably shipbuilding. It pointed the finger directly at Industry minister John Manley and reported that an analysis of the "shipbuilding industries in the United States, Denmark, France, Germany and Spain" revealed "Canada is the only country to not provide any direct construction grants, loan guarantees, preferential rate export financing, research and development grants, preferential tax treatment or customs duties on imported ship materials."[61]

But Manley had no interest in promoting a shipbuilding policy, describing it as a sunset industry.[62]

Sunset industries are dealt with differently, depending on where they are located. Manley could dismiss shipbuilding as a sunset industry and incur little political cost for the government or his party. Its direct economic impact was limited to a handful of seats in Atlantic Canada, British Columbia, and around Quebec City. Many observers view the automobile industry, at least from a Canadian perspective, as a sunset industry.[63] It cannot compete with Mexican and Asian manufacturers, and regional trade agreements have made a difficult situation even worse.[64] The government of Canada was, however, not throwing in the towel on the auto sector. Fearing that the Trans-Pacific Partnership (TPP) would hurt the industry, Prime Minister Harper pledged to invest $1 billion in an "Automotive Innovation Fund," in addition to a $58 million repayable loan to Toyota and a $200 million Advanced Manufacturing Fund for Ontario.[65] All of this against the backdrop of Denis DesRosiers's (arguably Canada's leading authority on the auto industry) prediction that "Canada will continue gradually to lose its production base until somewhere between 2030 and 2040, we'll be Australia, where the last carmaker with a factory in the country is scheduled to close its gates by 2018."[66]

When former New Brunswick premier Frank McKenna decided to enter into the debate, he echoed the findings of the caucus report on shipbuilding. He claimed that, had the shipbuilding industry been located in Ontario, Ottawa would have hurried to define a shipbuilding policy.

> Shipbuilding belongs to us on the Atlantic Coast of Canada. But friends, this is not an artificial creation, we've been building ships for hundreds of years; before this country was ever created, we were building ships. This is the land of the *Marco Polo* and the *Bluenose*. This is the story of our civilization as we developed here. We build ships, and we build good ships. Unfortunately, we live in the only country in the industrialized world that does not have a shipbuilding policy to support those who build ships. And—this may sound a little bit cynical—but I think if you could get ships in Oshawa, Ontario, or Ottawa, they would have shipbuilding policy for this country.[67]

Only after Manley left the department for Foreign Affairs did Industry Canada come up with a shipbuilding policy that, on June 19, 2001, provided some assistance for that sector.

Manley saw no need for the federal government to intervene and assist the shipbuilding industry but had a different view when it came to an Ottawa-based professional hockey team: he sought to assemble a federal financial package to come to the rescue of the Ottawa Senators in 2000. He and the federal government backed down after it raised "a storm of criticism from tax payers." Three years later, Manley created another political firestorm when, as minister of Finance, he called the President-CEO of the Canadian Imperial Bank of Commerce in support of a proposed refinancing deal for the Ottawa Senators.[68]

NEW ATLANTIC INVESTMENT PARTNERSHIP

Five months before the 2000 federal election, then prime minister Chrétien had a change of heart about economic development in the Maritimes. He went to Halifax on June 29, 2000, to announce what he described as a "fresh approach to regional economic development." He explained, "The Atlantic Investment Partnership is a bold plan designed to ensure not only that Atlantic Canadians can take their rightful place in the new economy, but that they can make their place at home—in Atlantic Canada." He announced $700 million would be committed to the region over a five-year period to strengthen its ability to compete in the global knowledge-based economy. Major investments under the partnership would include:

- $300 million for the Atlantic Investment Fund (AIF), which would make strategic investments to strengthen innovation capacity, increase the region's competitiveness, and encourage the region's transition to a more knowledge-based economy. The investment was to be overseen by an advisory board made up of academics and business leaders in the R&D and high-technology fields;
- $110 million for the expansion of National Research Council facilities in Atlantic Canada; and
- $135 million for the Partnership for Community Economic Development to strengthen economic planning at the local level and improve access to funding for strategic community-level projects.[69]

At first, the Chrétien initiative was well received in the region. However, it soon became clear that $300 million of the $700 million promised was recycled ACOA money, all of which was earmarked for the Atlantic Investment Fund. The other $400 million was simply reallocated from the existing ACOA budget for different things. In addition, ACOA would continue to report through the Industry minister. Also, at the time, Chrétien ignored a key recommendation produced by the Liberal Atlantic caucus committee of MPs and senators: to come up with a new shipbuilding policy.

The reallocation meant the formal end of federal-provincial agreements for economic development. These were ratified in 1974 under the General Development Agreements (GDAs), continued in 1982–83 under the Economic and Regional Development Agreements (ERDAs), and then by ACOA, this time under co-operation agreements. These agreements came to an end in Atlantic Canada in 2002–03. Thus, both cash grants and federal-provincial agreements as instruments of regional economic development died under Chrétien's watch.

HARPER AND ACOA

Stephen Harper, the first leader of the newly amalgamated Conservative Party of Canada, had been highly critical of ACOA while in Opposition. In his leadership bid, he tabled what he called "an Economic Revitalization Plan for Atlantic Canada," in which he said almost nothing about ACOA. He did pledge to "redirect inefficient corporate subsidies...to lower taxes." He also pledged to give the region "full access to non-renewable resource wealth," to invest in "infrastructure," and to support the military, which, he argued, would (somehow) benefit the Maritime provinces.[70] Shortly after winning the leadership of his party, Harper declared he had not "decided what we do with ACOA per se....You know, I think it's an open debate whether we would want to deliver legitimate federal programs through a regional agency or not. I'm not closed to that."[71] This scarcely constituted a ringing endorsement for ACOA or its programs.

At the 2005 Conservative Party policy conference in Montreal, Harper insisted the party mirror his own view on regional development by emphasizing "general infrastructure development." In a plenary session, the party rejected a proposal that would have abolished regional development agencies and replaced them with a targeted business-tax reduction in the designated regions.[72]

Harper essentially pursued a policy of deliberate neglect toward ACOA. Unlike previous governments, including the Chrétien government and its modestly funded AIF program, the Harper government never launched a major ACOA-led initiative for the region. He simply allowed ACOA to run on its tracks, neither adding resources nor fundamentally redirecting its efforts. Like other departments and agencies, the agency was subjected to program expenditure or strategic reviews under Harper. The reviews squeezed ACOA programs but did not generate a fundamental overhaul of its approach. Harper avoided machinery of government changes in the regional development field that could strengthen both policy and programming in slow-growth regions.

He did, as noted, establish a new regional development agency in vote-rich Southern Ontario and another for Canada's north, the only two regions that did not have their own federal development agency. He also established a new program for Ontario's manufacturing sector, as noted earlier. This is all about political calculations. ACOA's expenditure budget for 2014–15 totalled $284 million. The agency for Southern Ontario's budget for the same year amounted to about $210 million, in addition to the budget for FedNor (the federal agency for Northern Ontario), the $1.1 billion budget for Industry Canada, and the $200 million for Ontario's manufacturing sector, which was turned over to the agency for Southern Ontario to administer. The federal regional development agency for Canada's north, meanwhile, had a budget of $31 million.[73] Combined, Canada's regional development agencies spend over $1 billion annually, employ some 1,600 public servants, and account for 0.4 per cent of the government of Canada's program spending.[74]

JUSTIN TRUDEAU AND ACOA

Justin Trudeau's Liberal Party had very little to say about regional economic development in its 2015 election platform. The party stressed the importance of infrastructure investments to stimulate the economy.[75] The commitment overlooked the fact that while some regions need infrastructure investments (e.g., Southern Ontario, Montreal, and Vancouver), other regions (e.g., the Maritimes) do not need more roads or mass transit investments. Trudeau often spoke of traffic gridlock problems during the 2015 election campaign. I have seen precious few gridlock problems in any of the three Maritime provinces. It is another case of a Quebec- or Ontario-based politician viewing problems through a national lens. What the Maritimes need to promote economic development is quite different, as the concluding chapters suggest.

In naming his cabinet, Trudeau did not appoint a minister from Atlantic Canada to lead the agency. He gave that responsibility to the minister of Innovation, Science and Economic Development, Navdeep Singh Bains, MP from Mississauga–Malton in Ontario. This is the first time that ACOA reports solely to a minister from outside the Atlantic region. Even when John Manley was the minister of Industry with responsibility for ACOA, he was advised by a junior minister or a minister of state to assist him (Lawrence MacAulay from Prince Edward Island, later Fred Mifflin from Newfoundland and Labrador, and later still George Baker, also from Newfoundland and Labrador).

Early reports from ACOA officials suggest the Trudeau approach is not working well. The minister has a line department and a dozen agencies, including six regional agencies reporting to him, all vying for his attention. Senior ACOA officials report they are having great difficulties securing time with their minister.[76] They also report that all their briefings and proposals are channelled through bureaucratic echelons in the Department of Innovation, Science and Economic Development, where efforts are made to have "all" regional agencies address the same issues and have a common template. Some ACOA officials believe this spells the end of the agency model, given that the regional perspective is now managed in the Ottawa bureaucratic system.[77] One can easily appreciate the minister will have a stronger interest in the economic agency for Southern Ontario and his line department, and he will wish to view his role and responsibilities through a national lens. ACOA officials were not reassured when Bains appointed a senior Bay Street lawyer as his chief of staff and the prime minister named Greg Fergus, MP for Hull-Aylmer, as parliamentary secretary.[78]

ACOA no longer signs federal-provincial agreements for regional development and no longer has cash grant programs for the private sector. The agency centres its activities around innovation, trade and international business, community infrastructure development through sunset programs, advocacy measures from its 1987 mandate, coordination (also from its original mandate), entrepreneurship, and business development.[79] If budget allocation reflects priorities, ACOA attaches importance to innovation, entrepreneurship, and business development, which account for about 50 per cent of its budget. Measures to promote advocacy and coordination account for about 5 per cent. Like other federal departments and agencies, ACOA allocates an important part of its budget to overhead and operating expenditures, accounting for nearly 25 per cent of its budget. It is also home to 566 Full-Time Equivalents (FTES), a far cry from the 100 person-year recommendation I made in my report to the prime minister in 1986–87.[80]

ACOA has been a model of bureaucratic stability since it was established in June 1987. It has outlasted all previous regional development departments or agencies. DREE lasted only thirteen years. Established by Mulroney, ACOA survived the Chrétien-Martin program review (1994–97), which eliminated cash grants and federal-provincial agreements as instruments of regional economic development, and Harper's lack of interest in its operations. There have been no major twists and turns in its approach or programs and, like other departments, its expenditure budget has been squeezed from time to time. The major innovations in the regional development field under Harper's watch were the establishment of two new sister regional development agencies, and under Justin Trudeau, it was having the agencies report through a line department.

There is little evidence that ACOA has been successful in influencing other federal government policies, one of its four mandates. I can think of no area where ACOA tried with any degree of success to shape the policies or measures of other departments to reflect the economic circumstances of the Maritime region.

However, I can think of many areas that cry out for a regional perspective. Tax incentives, for example, can constitute a key economic development tool. Nothing has changed in this area over the years. The Department of Finance produces evaluation reports with an elaborate breakdown of all its tax expenditures.[81] The department still does not provide a regional breakdown of tax expenditures, though Finance officials report that Ontario, Quebec, Alberta, and British Columbia traditionally earn the lion's share of tax expenditures—over 80 per cent of all corporate tax spending. The three Maritime provinces trail these provinces significantly, and tax expenditures play only a negligible role in Ottawa's fostering of regional economic development. One federal Finance official speculated that tax expenditures with a specific regional development purpose never amount to more than 2 per cent of the total federal tax expenditure budget.[82] We also know that non-taxation of capital gains on principal residences total well over $1 billion a year, and this favours urban areas like Toronto, Vancouver, and Ottawa. Unlike federal transfer payments, tax expenditures are hardly visible, so it is difficult, without Ottawa's co-operation, to produce a regional breakdown to establish winners and losers.

ACOA readily admits it has not been successful in pursuing its advocacy mandate. Senior ACOA officials report that, given their limited resources, it is best to employ them where they have an opportunity to make an impact. The advocacy mandate offers no such opportunities.[83] This is the standard response from government bureaucracies when they fail to meet objectives. They are then able to ask for more resources. However ACOA, a relatively small agency by federal government standards with its head office in Ottawa, can never successfully pursue what properly belongs to political institutions to resolve.

Evidence also suggests that central agencies do not believe ACOA is up to standard in providing sound policy advice. I received an email in 2014 from a consultant who had been retained by the PCO, asking for advice to prepare a report on prospects for future co-operation between the four Atlantic provinces.[84] I was puzzled as to why the PCO had not turned to ACOA for such a report and advice. ACOA, according to its 2013–14 report on plans and priorities, has seventy-two FTEs working in its policy, advocacy, and coordination unit, with a mandate to provide "intelligence, analysis and well-grounded advice on a broad range of issues and topics."[85] One can only conclude that from a PCO perspective, a consultant is better at providing advice than are seventy-two public servants about an issue that goes to the heart of their agency's mandate.

LOOKING BACK

The single most important element in shaping and reshaping federal regional economic development policy remains partisan political considerations. In Canada, regional development policy has always been more about partisan politics, and at times national unity, than about regional development. Regional development agencies spread out to all corners of

Canada, enabling federal politicians to tell all Canadians in all communities, large and small, economically strong and weak, that they are doing something for them through regional development. That is what Canada's regional development policy now stands for.

There was only a brief period (circa 1968–72) when regional development policy was anchored in something more than political considerations. The period saw a focus on slow-growth regions, on attenuating regional economic disparities, and a reliance on Perroux's growth pole concept; however, the concept was soon deemed a political failure.

Political visibility—or rather a lack of visibility—led the federal government to kill federal-provincial agreements as an instrument of regional development. Assistance to the private sector is now in the form of instruments such as soft loans, loan guarantees, or support for trade missions. Whatever measures are currently available for regional development, are now available everywhere in Canada. Mulroney and Harper added one regional development agency after another, and regional development has now come to mean all things to all regions. Justin Trudeau has brought the regional agencies and the regional perspective under the direct ambit and control of a line department.

Do the Maritime provinces have their place in Ottawa's regional development policy? The short answer is no more, no less than other regions. If regional development policy is designed to assist slow-growth regions, to help them deal with long-standing regional problems, or to adjust national policies to correspond better to regional economic circumstances, then Ottawa's policy is seriously lacking from a Maritime perspective. It has become a political tool to gain votes, as this chapter demonstrates.

Regional development policy has few friends in Ottawa other than those planning political campaigns. Having a federal regional development agency in every postal code in Canada speaks to this reality. Senior public servants in Ottawa have resigned themselves to the fact that politicians will drive regional policy for partisan purposes; they simply do as they are told. They see politicians who, like them, once had strong reservations about regional development measures change their tune once in power, like Stephen Harper.

In the process, all theoretical considerations underpinning the agency model are thrown out the window. Given the Justin Trudeau changes, ACOA no longer enjoys much policy or administrative independence. If anything, the Justin Trudeau machinery of government reforms suggest that the regional perspective will likely become murkier still in Ottawa.

Past regional development efforts in Atlantic Canada, however, have been numerous and in place for some sixty years. In the next chapter, I discuss whether Canada still has a regional development problem.

NOTES

1 Donald J. Savoie, *Federal-Provincial Collaboration: The Canada–New Brunswick General Development Agreement* (Montreal and Kingston: McGill-Queen's University Press, 1981).

2 I am referring to Cabinet colleagues Roméo LeBlanc and Allan J. MacEachen.

3 Donald J. Savoie, "The Toppling of DREE and the Prospects for Regional Economic Development," *Canadian Public Policy* 10, no. 3 (1984), 328–37.

4 See, among others, Donald J. Savoie, *Visiting Grandchildren.*

5 Canada, *Release Announcing my Appointment* (Ottawa: Office of the Prime Minister, October 28, 1986).

6 François Perroux, "The Pole of Development's New Place in a General Theory of Economic Activity," in *Regional Economic Development*, ed. Higgins and Savoie, 48–76.

7 The report is available on the website of the Donald J. Savoie Institute at www.djsi.ca.

8 Savoie, *Establishing the Atlantic Canada Opportunities Agency*, 2.

9 William Alonso, "Population and Regional Development," in *Regional Economic Development*, ed. Higgins and Savoie, 138.

10 Savoie, *Establishing the Atlantic Canada Opportunities Agency*, 31.

11 Ibid., 32.

12 Ibid., 35–36.

13 "PM Launches New Agency for Atlantic Canada," *Halifax Sunday Herald*, June 7, 1987, 1.

14 "Atlantic Canada Gets Big Boost," *Fredericton Daily Gleaner*, June 8, 1987, 1.

15 Ibid.

16 See, among others, R. Harley McGee, *Getting It Right: Regional Development in Canada* (Montreal and Kingston: McGill-Queen's University Press, 1992), 154.

17 Canada, An Act to increase opportunity for economic development in Atlantic Canada, to establish the Atlantic Canada Opportunities Agency and Enterprise Cape Breton Corporation and to make consequential and related amendments to other acts, assented to August 18, 1988, chapter 50, 7.

18 Ibid.

19 Ibid., 4.

20 Ibid., 3.
21 See, among many others, "PM Launches New Agency for Atlantic Canada," *Halifax Sunday Herald*, June 7, 1987, 1; and "Atlantic Canada Gets Big Boost," *Fredericton Daily Gleaner*, June 8, 1987, 1.
22 "Hatfield, McKenna Voice Support," *Fredericton Daily Gleaner*, June 9, 1987, 2. See also "Region's Leaders' Reaction Positive," *Fredericton Daily Gleaner*, June 8, 1987, 2.
23 CBC Radio News (Halifax), June 8, 1987, MIT Media Tapes and Transcripts.
24 Canada, *Report of the Minister for the Fiscal Year 1988–89* (Moncton: Atlantic Canada Opportunities Agency, August 31, 1989), 31.
25 Ibid., 32.
26 Ibid.
27 See, for example, Savoie, *The Politics of Public Spending in Canada*, chapter 7.
28 Canada, *Report of the Minister for the Fiscal Year 1988–89*, 33.
29 See Speaking Notes for Peter O'Brian, Director, Canadian Federation of Independent Business (for a presentation to the Consultation Session on ACOA, Halifax, September 11 and 12, 1989).
30 "Petty Bureaucrats Pull Shabby Coup," *Toronto Sunday Star*, July 20, 1989, B3.
31 Canada, Western Economic Diversification Canada Initiative (news release, Office of the Prime Minister, August 4, 1987).
32 Canada, "Notes pour une allocution du Premier Ministre Brian Mulroney sur le développement régional devant les Chambres de Commerce d'Edmonton et de l'Alberta," (Office of the Prime Minister, August 4, 1987), 3 (author's translation).
33 "Aid Package Focus of PM's Trip," *Globe and Mail*, August 1, 1987, A6.
34 "Tory Activists, Friends Fill New Board," *Globe and Mail*, November 21, 1987, B3.
35 See Canada, www.feddevontario.gc.ca/eic/site.
36 Election 1988, www.thecanadianencyclopedia.ca/en/article/election-1988-feature/.
37 I report on this and other activities in Donald J. Savoie, *I'm from Bouctouche, Me: Roots Matter* (Montreal and Kingston: McGill-Queen's University Press, 2009), 205-6.
38 Canada, "Statement by the Honourable Jean Chrétien, Minister Responsible for the Federal Government Decentralization Paper" (October 3, 1977).
39 Ibid.
40 Canada, "Statement by the Honourable Sinclair Stevens, President of the Treasury Board" (August 15, 1979).
41 See, among others, John English, *Just Watch Me: The Life of Pierre Elliott Trudeau 1968–2000* (Knopf Canada: First Edition, 2009).
42 See Savoie, *The Politics of Public Spending in Canada*, chapter 8; and "Ottawa Loses to Winnipeg as Site for World-class Lab," *Ottawa Citizen*, October 8, 1987, 1.
43 "Where Did Gun-Registry Money Go?," *Chronicle-Herald* (Halifax), December 11, 2002, 1.

44 See, among many others, John Geddes, "The Ontario Factor," *Maclean's*, March 22, 2004, 21.

45 Savoie, *Visiting Grandchildren*, 1. Manley made this comment during a consultation session held at the Hotel Beauséjour, Moncton, November 22, 2002.

46 "Region to Land Federal Jobs as Part of Liberal Plan, Says MP," *Saint John Telegraph-Journal*, October 28, 2004, 1.

47 "Relocating Federal Jobs Won't Save Cash," Canada.com News, accessed October 23, 2004, http://www.canada.com.

48 "Productivité accrue," *Le Soleil* (Quebec), August 5, 1978, 1. The director at Shediac made his observation at a federal officials' meeting to which I was invited. The meeting was chaired by the FEDC for New Brunswick. See also Donald J. Savoie, "Le programme federal de decentralisation: un réexamen," *Canadian Public Policy* 12, no. 3 (September 1986).

49 Adam Huras, "Dominic LeBlanc Says New Position Is Central Role in the Machinery of Government," *Saint John Telegraph-Journal*, November 6, 2015, www.telegraphjournal.com/telegraph-journal/story/44563272/dominic-leblanc-says-new.

50 Consultations with central agency officials, January 8, 2016.

51 James Bagnell, "Public Admin Jobs Rising in Ottawa Despite PS Cuts Elsewhere," *Ottawa Citizen*, September 5, 2014, http://ottawacitizen.com/news/public-admin-jobs-rising-in-national-capital-region.

52 Quoted in Peter Aucoin and Donald J. Savoie, "Launching and Organizing a Program Review Exercise" (paper prepared for the Canadian Centre for Management Development, Ottawa, 1988), 2.

53 See, for example, Amelita Armit and Jacques Bourgault, eds., *Hard Choices or No Choices: Assessing Program Review* (Toronto: Institute of Public Administration of Canada, 1996).

54 See, among others, Arthur Kroeger, "The Central Agencies and Program Review" (paper prepared for the Canadian Centre for Management Development, Ottawa, n.d.), 2.

55 See, among others, Donald J. Savoie, *Court Government and the Collapse of Accountability in Canada and the United Kingdom* (Toronto: University of Toronto Press, 2008), chapter 12.

56 *Action Plan—Program Review* (Moncton: Atlantic Canada Opportunities Agency, September 22, 1994). Senior ACOA officials made this document available to me.

57 Canada, Commission of Inquiry into the Sponsorship Program and Advertising Activities, Hon. David Dingwall, January 21, 2005, vol. 60, 10549.

58 Consultations with senior ACOA officials, Moncton, various dates, 1995-2004.

59 Canada, *Budget Speech* (Ottawa: Department of Finance, February 16, 1999).

60 Canada, *Making Canada's Economy More Innovative* (Ottawa: Department of Finance, February 28, 2000).

61 Canada, *Atlantic Canada: Catching Tomorrow's Wave* (Ottawa: Liberal Party, Atlantic Caucus, May 31, 1999), 91.

62 Bea Vongdouangchanh, "There Is No Question People Wanted Harper Gone, I Just Didn't Think He'd Take Me with Him: Stoffer," *Hill Times*, November 2, 2015, www.hilltimes.com/2015/11/01/there-is-no-question-people-wanted-harper-gone-i-just-didnt-think-hed-take-me-with-him-stoffer/34009.

63 See, among many others, Jim Stanford, "You Call This an Auto Strategy?," *Globe and Mail*, April 30, 2015, www.theglobeandmail.com/globe-debate/you-call-this-an-auto-strategy/article24181049/.

64 John Ivison, "Harper's Aversion to Government Intervention in the Economy is Both Political and Personal," *National Post*, September 1, 2015, http://news.nationalpost.com/news/canada/canadian-politics/harpers-aversion-to-government-intervention-in-the-economy-is-both-political-and-personal.

65 Jane Taber, "Amid Election Rumours, Tories Hurry a Toyota Funding Announcement," *Globe and Mail*, July 30, 2015, www.theglobeandmail.com/news/national/ottawa-insisted-on-moving-up-toyota-funding-announcement-source/article25776732/; and Steven Chase, Greg Keenan, and Gloria Galloway, "Harper Pledges $1 billion in Grants for Auto Sector in Wake of TPP Deal," *Globe and Mail*, October 6, 2015, www.theglobeandmail.com/news/politics/harper-offers-1-billion-to-help-auto-sector-after-tpp-deal/article26677638/.

66 Scott Barlow, "Expert Says Domestic Auto Sector Will Be Dead by 2040," *Globe and Mail*, April 13, 2015, www.theglobeandmail.com/globe-investor/inside-the-market/top-links-expert-says-domestic-auto-sector-will-be-dead-by-2040/article23895147/.

67 Premier Frank McKenna speech at the Atlantic Vision Conference, Moncton, New Brunswick (October 9, 1997), 5.

68 "John Manley Is on Thin Ice," Opinion, *Globe and Mail*, January 7, 2003, www.theglobeandmail.com/globe-debate/john-manley-is-on-thin-ice/article748047/.

69 See "Atlantic Innovation Fund," Atlantic Canada Opportunities Agency, last modified November 27, 2015, www.acoa-apeca.gc.ca/eng/ImLookingFor/ProgramInformation/AtlanticInnovationFund/Pages/AtlanticInnovationFund.aspx.

70 Stephen Harper, "Harnessing the Potential: An Economic Revitalization Plan for Atlantic Canada," (n.d.), 1–7.

71 "Harper Questions ACOA," PEI-CBC, accessed April 6, 2004, www.pei-cbc.ca (site discontinued).

72 "Harper Pledges Strategy to Boost Region," *Saint John Telegraph-Journal*, March 21, 2005, 1.

73 Canada, *2014–15 Estimates Parts I and II. The Government Expenditure Plan and Main Estimates* (Ottawa: Treasury Board Secretariat, 2014).

74 Canada, *Regional Development Agencies: A Tool for Regional Development*, a presentation to the OECD, Paris, April 29, 2015.

75 "The Platform," Liberal Party of Canada, www.liberal.ca, n.d.

76 Consultations with senior ACOA officials, Moncton, various dates in December 2015–January 2016.

77 Consultations with senior ACOA officials, Moncton, various dates in December 2015–January 2016.

78 "Bay Street Corporate Lawyer Hired as Chief of Staff to Innovation Minister," 2 HTTP://WWW.THEGLOBEANDMAIL.COM/news/politics/globe-politics-insider/bay-street-corporate-lawyer-hired-as-chief-of-staff-to-innovation-minister/ARTICLE28048362/

79 Canada, *Atlantic Canada Opportunities Agency, Program Activity Architecture* (Moncton, ACOA, undated), 1–7.

80 Canada, *2014–15 Estimates Parts I and II.*

81 Canada, *Tax Expenditures and Evaluations* (Ottawa: Department of Finance, 2013).

82 Savoie, *Regional Economic Development: Canada's Search for Solutions*, 184.

83 Consultations with senior ACOA officials, June 2014. See also Donald J. Savoie, *Rethinking Canada's Regional Development Policy* (Moncton: Canadian Institute for Research on Regional Development, 1997), 15–26; and Canada, ACOA *Five-Year Report to Parliament, 1998–2003* (Moncton: ACOA, October 2003), chapter 4.

84 I do not have the authority to release the name of the consultant. His email is dated February 2, 2014.

85 Atlantic Canada Opportunities Agency, *Section II: Analysis of Programs by Strategic Outcome—2013–14 Report on Plans and Priorities* (Moncton: Atlantic Canada Opportunities Agency, 2014).

Chapter 9

DO WE STILL HAVE A PROBLEM?

I recall, as a young public servant in Ottawa, discussing a departmental proposal with a deputy minister from a central agency. He remarked the proposal looked like "a solution looking for a problem."[1] He explained far too many public servants are busy devising solutions to a problem that is never properly defined or, in some cases, may not even exist.

Regional economic development is particularly vulnerable to solutions looking for problems. Certainly, politicians representing slow-growth regions will always be on the lookout for solutions to what ails their region and ask that something be done. They also have a sense of urgency to their search, given that elections now come every four years at a minimum. Politicians view the world from a spatial or regional perspective. They represent people and constituencies, not economic sectors, and they look to them both for guidance and a verdict on their performance. The world of politicians is defined by geography, and party leaders will look for solutions to problems in regions offering the greater prospect for winning and retaining power.

Senior public servants—now, for the most part, working in the National Capital Region—have quite a different take. They view the world from a sectoral or departmental perspective or, if working in a central agency, from the perspective of their agency's mandate. They do not represent constituencies. Their interests are tied to the interests of their departmental sectors, the wishes of their political masters, and their own interests.[2] Public servants look to hierarchy not to geography for guidance and a verdict on their performance. They, at least those operating outside a regional agency, view regional development essentially as a political problem best left to politicians to sort out. I remind readers of Tom Kent's pertinent observation: "From the point of view of almost all conventional wisdom in Ottawa, the idea of regional development was a rather improper one that some otherwise quite reasonable politicians brought in like a baby on a doorstep from an election campaign."[3] Kent served in the Prime Minister's Office, as deputy minister in a line department and as head of a Crown corporation.

It is scarcely an exaggeration to assert that, when it comes to regional development, federal public servants have essentially turned the steering wheel over to the politicians and said, "You drive and you come up with solutions." The result, as we have seen, is a series of regional development agencies covering all of Canada and a policy that cries out for coherence and clarity. Canada's regional development policy, in some ways, can only make sense to politicians who have a capacity to view the world from where they sit—the region they represent—and the need to secure support from the regions that will give them the best chance of winning a mandate to form the government.

The government of Canada has, since the early 1960s, committed substantial financial resources to regional development measures in the Maritime provinces and increasingly in other regions. As previous chapters illustrate, the first phase started slowly with modest measures to promote rural development in carefully selected regions. The second phase was highly ambitious, introducing many measures between the late 1960s and the early 1970s, and committing more resources than could be properly spent. The focus, we may recall, was clearly on alleviating regional disparities and on regions east of Trois-Rivières. The third phase shifted focus to national unity concerns. We are now in the fourth phase of Ottawa's regional development efforts. This phase essentially washes its hands of regional disparities and the focus is on *all* regions. More to the point, the Maritime region together with Newfoundland and Labrador and eastern Quebec has lost its place under the regional development sun. The government of Canada itself has admitted it has not been combatting regional disparities for some time. It reported the obvious to OECD with the remark that it had initiated a "shift from correcting regional disparities to encouraging the development of regional potential in the 1980s and 1990s."[4]

Notwithstanding the vast amount of resources committed to regional development over the years and the goal of developing the potential of all regions, the federal government has never been able to determine how to assess a region's economic potential. How could it, given all the variables at play at any one time? The value of the Canadian dollar, monetary policy, the price of oil in world markets, and the state of the American and global economies, among many other factors, all have a profound impact on a region's economic potential, even in the short term. It is even less clear how the government can possibly determine when a region has attained its economic potential. This lends itself to solutions looking for problems and to politicians wanting to be seen unveiling measures to promote economic development in the regions they represent. It is much easier for politicians to determine the political potential of regions. In a federation where only rep by pop decides who holds effective political power in national institutions, politicians will focus on regions that offer the most potential for accessing the levers of power.

Canada is now 150 years old. Time to take stock of how well the Maritime region, which includes two of the four original provinces that formed the federation, has performed in relation to other regions. Notwithstanding Ottawa's muddled regional policy, many efforts have been launched over the past sixty years or so under the regional development banner in all three Maritime provinces. How then does today's Maritime economy compare to sixty years ago? How well has the regional economy performed recently in relation to other regions? Has the region made progress in narrowing the economic development gap with other regions? This chapter seeks to answer these and other questions and to assess the progress the region has made in its development.

THE PROBLEM IS POLITICAL

Mackenzie King, Canada's longest serving prime minister, in a 1936 speech to the House of Commons said, "If some countries have too much history, Canada has too much geography." He knew regionalism had dominated and would continue to dominate Canada's political agenda. If all politics in the United States is local, in Canada, all politics is both local and regional. And Mackenzie King, better than anyone, knew how to assuage regional conflicts and patch things up, while leaving the operation of our national political institutions intact—he of the famed comment, "Conscription, if necessary, but not necessarily conscription."[5]

Political boundaries are political constructs that give life to political communities and, in turn, political demands. Boundaries define a political space and politicians view their work directly tied to the political space they represent. Nothing new here. That is what politicians in a representative democracy do, are expected to do, and have done since responsible government came into fashion in Canada some 170 years ago. The important questions are: Do governments influence the pace and location of new economic activities, and who has the upper hand in shaping policy and initiatives? More importantly, what is the problem policy-makers are trying to fix? Is it one of alleviating regional disparities, and if so, how does one measure it? Is it one of promoting economic activities at the regional level, and if so, what regions and how do you measure success?

As is so often the case on policy issues, the answers to the questions depend on where one sits. A Member of Parliament from Rosedale, an affluent suburb of Toronto, is very likely to have a different take on regional development than one from Cape Breton. Some politicians may well have unreasonable expectations of what governments can actually accomplish. Gérard Veilleux, a former senior official in the Department of Finance in Ottawa, reports that he once attended a federal-provincial meeting of Finance ministers, where one provincial Finance minister insisted the government of Canada should never rest until "all provinces have a higher economic growth rate than the national average."[6] He, of course, offered no solution on how to accomplish it! He had a solution looking for a problem.

MEASURING THE PROBLEM

As a lifelong resident of the Maritime provinces, I have seen first-hand the progress my region has made on many fronts since the 1960s. The infrastructure is much improved, new universities have been established and existing ones strengthened considerably, the urban structure is more mature, new businesses able to compete in the global economy have been launched, and the quality of public services in all sectors is also much improved. Maritimers have attained a much higher level of education than in years past. The list goes on. However, Maritime politicians do not compare the state of their economy with years past, but rather with the economies of other Canadian regions.

Progress does not answer Galbraith's question either. Indeed, one can make similar observations about other Canadian regions, which have all outperformed the Maritimes, with the exception of Newfoundland and Labrador. We now have many ways to assess the economic health of a region. By virtually any measure, however, for well over one hundred years, the Maritime provinces have lagged—and continue to lag—behind other Canadian regions. This chapter takes stock of the region's economic health. We begin with arguably the most important factor: the people factor.

THE PEOPLE FACTOR

One of the most telling signs that a community or a region is in economic decline is when it loses population and is unable to attract new residents. Vibrant and growing economies are always able to attract people in search of economic opportunities. The Maritime provinces have fallen short on both fronts for over a century—a loss of population combined with an inability to attract new Canadians. The impact is evident on many fronts. All in all, the Maritime region scores poorly on the people factor. In short, the region is unable to attract new residents, its population age structure is cause for concern, and its level of urbanization is low—at least when compared with other regions.

The size of a region's population matters for several reasons. To prosper, a region needs a growing workforce, from unskilled labourers to highly skilled knowledge workers. New residents often bring with them a determination to do better and to pursue whatever economic or employment opportunities are available or create new ones. New arrivals are also more willing to challenge the status quo. The size of a region's population matters even more in Canada than in other federations, because all of Canada's political power at the federal government level is based solely on representation by population. A loss of population automatically translates into a loss of political power.

The people factor, however, encompasses a much larger agenda than population growth. It speaks to the number of people in the workforce, levels of unemployment, dependence on Employment Insurance, age structure, skills, and education levels. It also speaks to where people live—urban versus rural—which is important because many economic opportunities now surface in urban areas rather than rural ones, and young university graduates prefer moving to urban areas over rural ones.

Tables 9.1 to 9.11 sum up the economic challenges confronting the Maritime provinces, which are all linked in one way or another to the people factor. They also speak to the uncertain progress the Maritime region has made on the heel of Ottawa's various regional development measures.

As noted, the region has not been as successful as other Canadian regions in retaining its population and attracting Canadians from other regions or new Canadians. Table 9.1 outlines in stark terms the region's economic struggles and suggests these are not over. As recently as 1961, the three Maritime provinces accounted for 7.9 per cent of Canada's population. In 2014 the percentage dropped to 5.2 per cent and Statistics Canada reports that it will drop further to 4.3 per cent by 2038. Leaving aside the three provincial premiers occasionally highlighting the region's economic challenges in the media and for their constituents, the region will become increasingly marginalized on the national political agenda.

Table 9.1. Population Growth, Maritimes and Canada, Starting in 1961–2014 and 2038

		PEI	Nova Scotia	New Brunswick	Maritimes	Canada
1961	(n.)	104,629	737,007	597,936	1,439,572	18,238,247
	(%)	0.6	4.0	3.3	7.9	
1991	(n.)	129,765	899,942	723,900	1,753,607	27,296,859
	(%)	0.5	3.3	2.7	6.5	
2014	(n.)	146,283	942,668	753,914	1,842,865	35,540,419
	(%)	0.4	2.7	2.1	5.2	
Growth 1961–2014		39.8	27.9	26.1	28.0	94.9
2038	(n.)	178,300	933,900	752,500	1,864,700	43,490,100
	(%)	0.4	2.1	1.7	4.3	
Growth 1961–2038		70.4	26.7	25.8	29.5	138.5

Source: Statistics Canada, CANSIM, *table 051-0001, 052-0005.*

Table 9.2. Interprovincial Migrants, Maritimes and Canada, 1971–2013

	Maritimes					Canada		
	Net inter-provincial migration	Net immigration	Net migration	Average population for the period	Net population migration	Net migration	Average population for the period	Net population migration
1971–1975	30,278	11,358	41,636	1,584,261	2.6%	494,209	23,971,123	2.1%
1976–1980	-14,280	5,956	-8,324	1,664,592	-0.5%	309,251	22,370,060	1.4%
1981–1985	7,113	1,781	8,894	1,708,890	0.5%	220,338	25,350,495	0.9%
1986–1990	-8,000	3,802	-4,198	1,759,909	-0.2%	672,930	26,861,309	2.5%
1991–1995	-6,306	10,726	4,420	1,803,638	0.2%	945,200	28,679,284	3.3%
1996–2000	-12,903	7,578	-5,325	1,819,997	-0.3%	802,253	30,151,671	2.7%
2001–2005	-14,191	5,555	-8,636	1,823,085	-0.5%	924,637	31,640,202	2.9%
2006–2010	-14,540	22,473	7,933	1,825,176	0.4%	975,646	33,267,610	2.9%
2011–2013	-17,431	12,444	-4,987	1,845,005	-0.3%	607,320	34,749,729	1.7%
Total	**-50,260**	**81,673**	**31,413**			**5,951,784**		
As a percentage for the period 1971–2013	**1.8%**					**20.8%**		

Source: Statistics Canada, Estimates of population, CANSIM II*, tables 051-0017, 051-0004, 051-0001; compiled by the author.*

One does not need to look much further than interprovincial migration to appreciate the challenge. The region welcomed over 81,000 new Canadians between 1971 and 2013, but lost over 50,000 residents to other provinces. Contrast this with the Canadian average: Canada has witnessed strong population growth since 1971, fuelled in large part by immigration (see table 9.2). While the Maritime provinces saw their population grow by 260,744 between 1975 and 2014, Canada witnessed an increase of 11,569,296.

Table 9.3 traces in more detail the population growth for the Maritime provinces between 1961 and 2014 and provides a comparison with Canada. As noted, the region accounted for nearly 8 per cent of Canada's population in 1961, but fell to 5.2 per cent by 2014. The table again starkly underscores the region's inability to grow and to attract and retain population. The population of the Maritime region grew by 28 per cent between 1961 and 2014, in sharp contrast to Canada's 95 per cent growth in the same period.

Table 9.3 Population Growth, Maritimes and Canada, 1961–2014

	PEI	Nova Scotia	New Brunswick	Maritimes	Canada
1961	104,629	737,007	597,936	1,439,572	18,238,247
Share of Canada 1961	0.6%	4.0%	3.3%	7.9%	100%
1971	111,641	788,960	634,557	1,535,158	21,568,311
1981	122,510	847,445	696,405	1,666,360	24,343,180
1991	129,765	899,942	723,900	1,753,607	27,296,859
2001	135,294	908,007	729,498	1,772,799	30,007,094
2011	144,038	944,469	755,530	1,844,037	34,342,780
2014	146,283	942,668	753,914	1,842,865	35,540,419
Share of Canada 2014	0.4%	2.7%	2.1%	5.2%	100%
Growth 1961–2014	39.8	27.9	26.1	28.0	94.9

Source: Statistics Canada, Census of Population.

Maritimers continue to go down the road, and their choice of destination makes the case that urban Canada holds a particularly strong appeal. Halifax is the urban centre of predilection for New Brunswickers and Prince Edward Islanders, while Toronto is for Nova Scotians. Rural Nova Scotians, however, also look to Halifax as their first urban destination of choice. This and other factors suggest Halifax continues to be well positioned to lead the Maritime region in economic development. This matters, or should matter, to government officials as they plan economic development efforts for the region. I note that Toronto, Ottawa, and Calgary are also strong magnets for Maritimers in all three provinces. (See tables 9.4, 9.5, and 9.6.) I also note that Ottawa ranks in the top seven choice destinations for Maritimers leaving the region and at number two in the case of Nova Scotians. This may well be a result of Ottawa's decision to locate more and more of federal government personnel in the NCR since the 1980s and the rise of the lobby industry and consultant firms migrating to Ottawa, where they have easy access to government officials.

Table 9.4. New Brunswick Interprovincial Migration, May 2010–May 2011: Top Ten Destinations

	Total	Gender		Status	
		Male	Female	Non-immigrant	Immigrant
Halifax RGM	1,080	500	580	1,020	60
Edmonton	445	345	100	430	15
Calgary	410	225	185	335	75
Toronto	375	205	170	245	130
Ottawa	325	185	140	50	275
Montreal	280	175	105	215	65
Quebec	265	170	95	255	10
Gatineau	180	80	100	170	10
Charlottetown	175	120	55	140	35
Shannon, ME	165	60	105	165	0

Source: Statistics Canada, Special Order.

Table 9.5. Prince Edward Island Interprovincial Migration, May 2010–May 2011: Top Ten Destinations

	Total	Gender		Status	
		Male	Female	Non-immigrant	Immigrant
Halifax	205	85	120	160	45
Toronto	160	40	120	65	95
Calgary	120	85	35	115	5
Pembroke*	95	67	28	95	0
Fredericton	65	20	45	65	0
Surrey, CY	55	25	30	0	55
Ottawa	50	20	30	40	10
Hamilton	35	35	0	0	35
Red Deer	35	35	0	35	0
Northampton *	30	30	0	30	0

Source: Statistics Canada, Special Order.

Table 9.6. Nova Scotia Interprovincial Migration, May 2010–May 2011: Top Ten Destinations

	Total	Gender		Status	
		Male	Female	Non-immigrant	Immigrant
Toronto	1,150	515	635	820	330
Ottawa	835	405	430	745	90
Edmonton	525	290	235	435	90
Calgary	455	225	230	375	80
Montreal	350	205	145	310	40
Moncton	340	145	195	320	20
St. John's	325	180	145	320	5
Vancouver	255	110	145	225	30
Fredericton	255	135	120	250	5

Source: Statistics Canada, Special Order.

Another telling population indicator is the region's age structure. All of Canada is facing a demographic challenge, but leaving aside Newfoundland and Labrador, this is clearly evident in the Maritime provinces. Richard Saillant documents the challenge confronting New Brunswick in his *Over the Cliff? Acting Now to Avoid New Brunswick's Bankruptcy*.[7] He is not alone. As far back as 2005, Ottawa's Department of Finance highlighted Canada's looming demographic challenge. It argued that over the next twenty-five years, Canada is expected to register one of the largest increases in the ratio of the elderly to the working-age population of all the G7 countries.[8] As Saillant documented, the demographic challenges increase demands on social services and health-care facilities and place a downward pressure on economic activity. The important point, and one that Saillant underlines, is that the Maritime region's population is aging at a much faster clip than other Canadian regions, and this entails daunting challenges for economic development, the delivery of public services, and the fiscal capacity of the region's three provincial governments.

Table 9.7 provides a breakdown of population by age, comparing the three Maritime provinces with Canada. The trend for the three Maritime provinces should be cause for deep concern for policy-makers at all levels. If projections from Statistics Canada are correct, some three out of ten Maritimers will be sixty-five or over by 2038. I draw attention to the region's aging rate between 2014 and 2038, compared with the national average for the sixty-five years and older generation: 30.7 per cent for the Maritimes, compared with 24.0 per cent for Canada. The region's already weak economic structure and the difficult fiscal situation of all three provincial governments suggest the region is particularly ill-prepared to meet the demographic challenge in comparison to other Canadian regions.

The region's demographic challenge will force the hand of the three provincial governments to rethink their priorities in key sectors. It will add pressure to spend more on health care and less on education. This, in turn, will force the hand of the three governments to pursue strategies to address pressure from residents to maintain the status quo. Closing a school in many rural communities sends out a signal that their future is uncertain and that the provincial government does not hold out much hope for the community. The challenge for politicians in the three Maritime provinces will be much greater than in other regions because of the region's fast-aging population.

Table 9.7. Population by Age, Maritimes and Canada, 1961, 2014, and 2038

	Total (n.)	0–14 (n.)	%	15–64 (n.)	%	65+ (n.)	%
1961							
PEI	104,629	37,701	36.0	55,419	53.0	11,509	11.0
Nova Scotia	737,007	256,328	34.8	414,348	56.2	66,331	9.0
New Brunswick	597,936	227,187	38.0	322,914	54.0	47,835	8.0
Maritimes	1,439,572	521,216	36.2	792,681	55.1	125,675	8.7
Canada	18,238,247	6,191,922	34.0	10,587,265	58.0	1,459,060	8.0
2014							
PEI	146,283	23,228	15.9	96,847	66.2	26,208	17.9
Nova Scotia	942,668	132,789	14.1	637,082	67.6	172,914	18.3
New Brunswick	753,914	109,924	14.6	505,750	67.1	138,240	18.3
Maritimes	1,842,865	265,941	14.4	1,239,679	67.3	337,362	18.3
Canada	35,540,419	5,708,667	16.1	24,246,495	68.2	5,585,257	15.7
2038							
PEI	178,300	25,800	14.5	102,800	57.7	49,700	27.9
Nova Scotia	934,000	119,900	12.8	525,800	56.3	288,300	30.9
New Brunswick	752,500	98,200	13.0	418,900	55.7	235,400	31.3
Maritimes	1,864,800	243,900	13.1	1,047,500	56.2	573,400	30.7
Canada	43,489,900	6,724,900	15.5	26,309,400	60.5	10,455,600	24.0

Source: Statistics Canada, Estimates of population, CANSIM II, tables 051-0001, 052-0005; compiled by the author.

Only between 1971 and 1991 did growth in the region's labour force match Canada's (see table 9.8). Though it is not possible to establish a direct correlation between the two, it is worth pointing out that this period squares with the time when Ottawa's regional development efforts were the most ambitious and when the focus was still clearly on Atlantic Canada (i.e., the later DREE years and early ACOA years). It is also important to note, however, that the baby boom, which came of age during that period, may well be a better explanation for the growth in the region's labour force between 1971 and 1991 than Ottawa's regional development efforts. The reader will note, however, that the region's labour force actually shrank between 2011 and 2014 by 0.4 per cent, while Canada saw a 2.7 per cent increase.

A shrinking labour force holds other obvious and important negative implications for a region. It points to a shrinking tax base, slower economic growth, lower productivity, and skill shortages. It is now widely accepted that businesses look to a strong labour force and skilled workers when deciding which new opportunities to pursue and where to locate economic activities. The OECD, for example, ranks a skilled workforce as one of the top ingredients for both business and economic growth.[9]

Table 9.8. Labour Force, Maritimes and Canada, 1966–2014

	Maritimes	Growth %	Canada	Growth %
1966	484,000		7,242,000	
1971	526,000	8.7	8,639,000	19.3
1981	851,160	61.8	14,682,980	70.0
1991	1,002,240	17.7	17,203,560	17.2
2001	1,084,380	8.2	19,312,880	12.3
2011	1,165,980	7.5	22,343,490	15.7
2014	1,160,900	-0.4	22,949,350	2.7

Source: Statistique Canada, CANSIM, *table 282-0007.*

The region's employment record mirrors its labour force participation role. The Maritime provinces saw impressive employment gains between 1971 and 1991 that were close to the Canadian average and even surpassed it between 1981 and 1991 (see table 9.9). Again, while it is not possible to establish a distinct link between the two, the periods coincide with when Ottawa's regional development policy had a much clearer focus on Atlantic Canada (i.e., the later DREE years and early ACOA years). But things have taken a turn for the worse recently, with the region actually registering a drop of 0.5 per cent between 2011 and 2014, while Canada saw a gain of 3.4 per cent.

Table 9.9. Total Employment, Maritimes and Canada, 1966–2014

	Maritimes	Growth (%)	Canada	Growth (%)
1966	460,000		7,242,000	
1971	490,000	6.5	8,104,000	11.9
1981	759,810	55.1	13,566,030	67.4
1991	875,150	15.2	15,420,830	13.7
2001	970,990	11.0	17,918,760	16.2
2011	1,056,400	8.8	20,665,240	15.3
2014	1,050,640	-0.5	21,362,690	3.4

Source: Statistics Canada, CANSIM, table 282-0007.

As noted earlier, Richard Florida stimulated a wide-ranging debate in the regional development literature and in government circles with his work on the merit of the creative class. An important element of a region's creative class is the education level of the workforce. Table 9.10 reports on the percentage of the population over fifteen who have at least a bachelor's degree. The three Maritime provinces have consistently trailed the Canadian average, and still do. One can assume the region continues to export our better educated to urban centres, notably Toronto and Ottawa. It is also important to note all three provinces have made substantial gains on the education front since 1961. This suggests high growth regions have benefitted greatly from welcoming new residents educated in the Maritime provinces, a benefit that is all too often overlooked when calculating which regions benefit the most from federal government spending.

Table 9.10. Percentage of the Population over 15 who Have a Bachelor's Degree or Higher, Maritimes and Canada, 1961–2011

	1961	1971	1981	1991	2001	2011	1961–2011
Canada	2.9	4.8	8.0	11.4	15.1	20.9	720
PEI	1.5	3.2	6.1	8.5	11.0	13.9	926
Nova Scotia	2.3	4.1	7.4	10.4	13.5	18.9	821
New Brunswick	1.8	3.4	6.0	8.4	10.8	15.4	856

Source: Statistics Canada, Census of Population.

The region does not fare any better when other socioeconomic indicators are considered. The region has the most residents in Canada with no high school diploma or a trade school certificate (see table 9.11). This too speaks to the quality of the human resources and the substantial discrepancy between the Maritime region and the rest of Canada.

Table 9.11. Percentage of the Population without a High School Diploma or Trade Certificate, 2011

	%
Prince Edward Island	2.0
Nova Scotia	2.3
New Brunswick	2.1
Maritimes	2.2
Canada	1.7

Source: Statistics Canada, 2011 National Household Survey, catalogue number 99-012-x2011044.

The Maritime region has more employees belonging to a union than other Canadian regions (see table 9.13). The fact that the region relies heavily on public sector employment may well explain this phenomenon. Table 9.12 reveals the extent to which public sector employees belong to a union and reports on the stability in membership over time. In 2004, 75.5 per cent of public sector employees in Canada belonged to a union, only slightly more than 74.8 per cent in 2014. In contrast, the percentage of private sector employees belonging to a union in 2014 was 16.8, down from 19.0 in 2004.

When we look to the regional level, the Maritime region clearly has a stronger attachment to unions than other regions do. This is particularly true for the region's public-sector employees: in New Brunswick, 76.2 per cent of public-sector employees belong to a union, 75 per cent in the case of Nova Scotia, and 82.1 per cent in Prince Edward Island. Public-sector employees often have a greater desire and ability to embrace the status quo and make it stick. They operate outside of market forces, and globalization has not had anywhere near the impact on the public sector as it has had on the private sector. This holds important implications for a region that will need to challenge the status quo in all sectors, but particularly in the public sector, given its aging population.

All of the above contribute to the people factor and all paint a less than positive portrait for the Maritime region. Given the importance of the people factor to economic development, this will require attention from the region's policy-makers. The people factor, however, is broader still and speaks to attitude and confidence to create, pursue, manage, and deliver knowledge, products, or services. I return to these factors later.

Table 9.12 Percentage of Employees Belonging to a Union

	Public Sector	Private Sector
2004	75.5	19.0
2005	75.0	19.3
2006	74.8	18.9
2007	74.5	18.7
2008	74.6	17.8
2009	74.9	17.8
2010	75.4	17.5
2011	74.5	17.3
2012	75.0	17.7
2013	75.2	17.5
2014	74.8	16.8

Source: Statistics Canada, table 282-0223.

THE URBAN STRUCTURE

If the growth pole or the creative class concepts are to have any meaning, one needs to look to a region's urban structure. Indeed, many economists insist the economic health of a region is directly tied to the maturity of its urban structure.[10] At the turn of the twentieth century, the Maritime economy had an urban-rural structure that resembled somewhat the one found in Ontario and Quebec. But things began to change around that time. By the 1920s, Ontario and Quebec were already making strides toward a mature urban structure; not so for the Maritime provinces. Ontario and Quebec were passing the halfway point in their urban-rural split at the end of World War One, while the Maritime provinces were only one-quarter of the way up.

Table 9.13. Percentage of Employees Belonging to a Union, by Province

	Sector	2004	2005	2006	2007	2008	2009	2010	2011	2012	2013	2014
Newfoundland & Labrador	Public	76.0	74.4	76.3	75.8	74.8	76.4	77.6	77.8	75.6	77.3	74.3
	Private	22.7	21.3	20.7	20.5	20.9	21.3	20.8	19.8	20.8	22.5	22.2
Prince Edward Island	Public	80.2	79.4	77.2	77.4	78.4	78.9	79.2	78.0	80.5	82.4	82.1
	Private	9.4	10.2	9.5	10.2	8.6	9.0	8.5	8.5	9.8	10.3	8.9
Nova Scotia	Public	72.2	72.1	69.1	71.5	71.5	72.6	72.7	74.5	74.0	74.0	75.0
	Private	12.5	13.3	13.2	13.7	12.6	13.8	12.8	13.2	13.3	13.2	13.8
New Brunswick	Public	73.5	71.5	71.4	71.3	71.6	70.8	71.1	72.4	73.3	74.5	76.2
	Private	12.5	12.1	12.4	12.3	12.8	12.4	12.4	13.1	12.0	12.2	11.2
Quebec	Public	81.9	80.9	82.1	81.6	81.5	82.5	82.8	81.9	81.8	82.8	81.7
	Private	26.7	27.1	27.1	26.4	26.0	25.9	24.9	25.3	25.8	25.6	25.1
Ontario	Public	70.7	71.7	70.8	70.5	71.3	71.0	71.0	69.9	71.3	71.5	70.6
	Private	16.7	17.5	16.6	16.6	15.3	15.1	14.9	14.9	15.3	15.0	14.4
Manitoba	Public	77.4	77.7	78.1	78.1	78.4	77.9	78.7	77.3	78.4	78.6	77.0
	Private	20.6	20.0	20.0	19.7	18.8	18.6	18.9	18.1	17.9	18.1	18.0
Saskatchewan	Public	75.7	75.3	76.3	75.6	75.0	75.7	76.0	75.9	75.4	74.7	74.5
	Private	17.7	17.7	18.2	17.2	17.9	17.7	18.1	17.3	17.5	17.0	16.0
Alberta	Public	69.7	67.5	68.6	68.1	69.3	70.2	70.9	70.4	70.5	68.1	68.8
	Private	12.4	12.2	12.9	12.3	12.1	12.2	12.1	11.3	11.4	11.2	10.8
British Columbia	Public	81.4	79.2	77.4	77.3	76.0	76.0	77.3	75.8	75.2	76.1	76.9
	Private	20.1	19.9	19.1	19.5	18.1	17.8	17.8	17.5	18.0	18.0	16.5

Source: Statistics Canada. Table 282-0078.

Today, the Maritime region's urban structure is only slightly better than Ontario and Quebec were about one hundred years ago (New Brunswick is 48 per cent rural, Nova Scotia 43 per cent, and Prince Edward Island 53 per cent). Western Canada has also made the transition to a more mature urban society over the past forty years or so (Alberta is now only 17 per cent rural, Saskatchewan 33 per cent, and British Columbia 14 per cent). Canada is 19 per cent rural.[11]

Table 9.14. Urbanization of Canada, 1891 and 2011

	Rural population (%)	
	1891	2011
Canada	69	19
Newfoundland and Labrador	n/a	41
Prince Edward Island	87	53
Nova Scotia	83	43
New Brunswick	85	48
Quebec	66	19
Ontario	61	14
Manitoba	73	28
Saskatchewan	n/a	33
Alberta	n/a	17
British Columbia	62	14

Source: Statistics Canada, Census of population.

INNOVATION AND PRODUCTIVITY

If most economists agree on one thing in the economic development literature, it is that innovation and productivity drive self-sustaining economic growth, which explains why the government of Canada has kept innovation and productivity at the very top of its economic development agenda for the past fifteen years or so.[12]

Public and private sector investments in R&D are crucial to innovation and productivity. Statistics Canada defines R&D as creative work undertaken on a systematic basis to increase the stock of scientific and technological knowledge and to use this knowledge in new applications.

Expenditures in R&D are thus an important indicator of the efforts devoted to creative activity in science and technology. In provinces with a strong R&D performance—Ontario, Quebec, Alberta, and British Columbia—the business sector and governments are both very active. The private sector in the Maritime region does not invest nearly as much, even in per capita terms, in R&D activities as do private firms in Ontario and Quebec.

This is also true for the federal government, which, while being a major R&D player in Ontario and Quebec, is scarcely present in this sector in the Maritime provinces. It may well be that one influences the other, and that federal programs designed to encourage R&D are tied to private sector participation. This would explain, at least in part, why federal R&D programs have had so little impact in the Maritime provinces. In other words, we may well be dealing with a catch-22, a kind of vicious circle from which the region cannot escape. Whatever the reason, in 1981 the Maritime provinces had only secured 3.1 per cent of the federal government funding in R&D, and the percentage dropped to 2.6 per cent in 2012 (see table 9.15), notwithstanding ACOA's new efforts in this area. In 2001, 78.4 per cent of federal government spending in the natural sciences, engineering, social sciences, and the humanities went to Ontario and Quebec, while 2.5 per cent went to the three Maritime provinces.

Table 9.15. Provincial Distribution of Total R&D Expenditures from All Sources in Natural Sciences, Engineering, Social Sciences, and Humanities, 1981–2012 (Canada = 100)

	1981	1985	1991	1995	2001	2005	2011	2012
NL	0.9	1.0	1.0	0.7	0.6	1.0	1.0	1.2
PE	0.2	0.1	0.1	0.1	0.2	0.2	0.2	0.2
NS	2.1	2.4	2.2	1.9	1.6	1.7	1.6	1.6
NB	0.8	1.3	1.1	1.0	0.7	0.9	0.9	0.8
QC	18.6	22.8	26.7	27.0	27.7	25.9	26.5	25.9
ON	3.8	44.5	49.5	50.3	50.7	48.8	45.6	45.4
MB	3.1	2.9	2.6	2.1	2.0	2.1	2.1	2.1
SK	1.9	2.5	2.0	1.8	1.7	1.6	1.8	1.8
AB	10.7	8.9	7.3	7.1	6.9	8.6	10.4	1.1
BC	6.0	7.0	7.3	7.8	0.8	8.6	9.5	9.4

Source: Statistics Canada, CANSIM II, table 358-0001.

We are often told innovation, ideas, knowledge, and scientific discoveries drive the modern economy, and a good number of economists increasingly look to patents to assess the economic health of a country or a region.[13] The Conference Board of Canada and the C. D. Howe Institute, among others, have carried out studies on patents as indicators of a strong innovative culture. The C. D. Howe Institute insisted, "Patents reward the innovation and creativity drive economic growth."[14] In 2010 the Conference Board reported that Canada is not performing well compared to international averages. It ranked Canada fourteenth among sixteen peer countries when it comes to patenting and gave it a D grade.[15] Meanwhile, the C. D. Howe Institute looked at the performance of Canada's provinces and concluded, "Across Canada, Alberta and Ontario consistently outperform national averages in domestic patent applications per capita, while the Atlantic Provinces are dramatically below average" (see table 9.16).[16]

Table 9.16. Domestic Patent Applications: Average Annual Applications per Capita, by Province

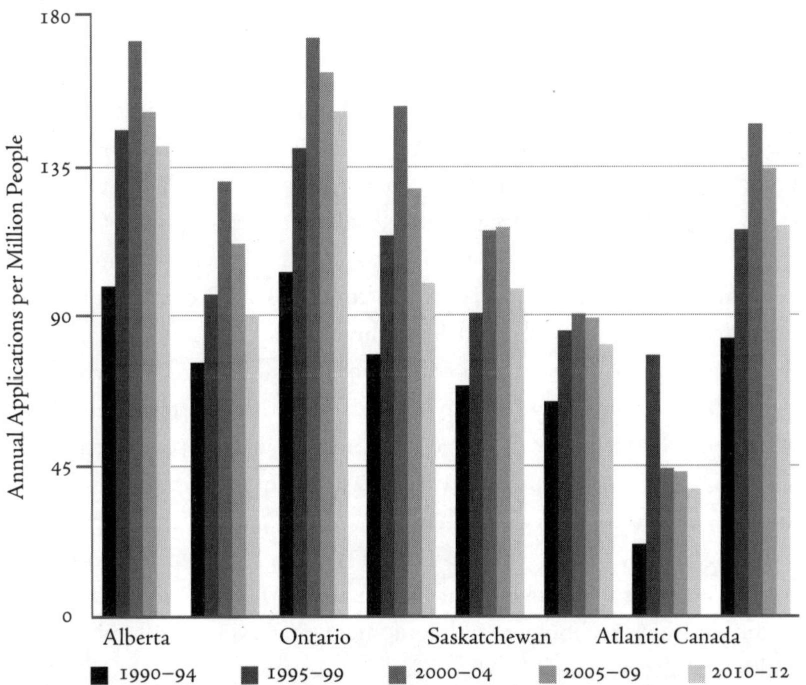

Source: C. D. Howe, E-Brief, Measuring Innovation in Canada.

Labour productivity in the three Maritime provinces continues to trail the national average by a wide margin. Productivity also reveals a great deal about the health of either a national or a regional economy. It is the amount of value that a worker can produce for unit of time worked, so that a higher productivity equals a higher value of product. A higher productivity also equals a more competitive economy and more wealth creation, which explains why Ottawa policy-makers have stressed its importance since the 1980s. Aside from Prince Edward Island, there has been little improvement in recent years on the productivity front in the Maritime region. Indeed, both New Brunswick and Nova Scotia have gone in the opposite direction and lost ground, as table 9.17 reveals.

Table 9.18 presents a more comprehensive look at productivity and GDP by hours worked. The government of Canada has been preoccupied for years by the country's trailing productivity level in relation to the United States (by some 25 per cent). The focus in Ottawa has been on comparing levels between the United States and Canada and not between regions.[17] There are, however, sharp differences between the Canadian regions, as table 9.19 reveals. In 2013 for example, Alberta was Canada's most productive province, with a productivity level twice as high as the least productive, Prince Edward Island.

The tables below make the case that Maritimers work harder than the average Canadian but are substantially less productive. This makes the point that the region's productivity challenges are not for want of a work ethic. A review of call centre jobs in New Brunswick and other Canadian regions reveals that New Brunswick workers are "eager, determined and uncomplaining." It also reports that in contrast to call centre workers in Toronto, New Brunswick workers embraced the "professionalization" of their work. The difference: call centre workers in Toronto view the work as marginal, a temporary stopgap job until something better comes along, while New Brunswick call centre workers view it as a permanent job.[18] The point: the work ethic of Maritimers does not explain the lower productivity levels in the region. There are various reasons that explain the difference: productivity per hour worked is much higher in certain sectors such as energy some provinces are better than others in promoting innovation and new technology and equipment that boost productivity (see tables 9.18 and 9.19).

Table 9.17. Manufacturing Labour Productivity, Defined as Value Added Divided by Total Hours Worked, 1996–2013 (Canada = 100)

	1996	1997	1998	1999	2007	2008	2009	2010	2011	2012	2013
Newfoundland & Labrador	82.7	75.4	73.4	68.8	76.2	85.5	83.0	88.4	82.7	106.1	99.8
Prince Edward Island	56.7	55.2	73.4	60.0	69.6	66.3	77.9	73.1	65.9	66.2	77.0
Nova Scotia	67.4	67.7	72.5	69.7	64.3	64.2	67.1	70.0	73.4	73.8	70.4
New Brunswick	83.6	80.8	83.9	74.0	92.2	88.5	91.7	96.2	97.0	88.0	86.8
Quebec	102.4	101.3	103.7	100.6	101.6	103.4	106.3	100.8	100.0	99.3	100.6
Ontario	102.6	103.4	103.0	106.6	102.5	101.0	99.4	101.3	101.3	103.5	100.7
Manitoba	73.5	76.7	78.3	59.7	78.5	79.7	79.3	77.3	78.6	83.0	88.6
Saskatchewan	89.5	99.5	102.3	80.1	101.9	105.2	114.0	115.3	114.9	118.9	122.1
Alberta	120.9	116.1	108.7	107.4	119.8	122.6	117.8	120.2	116.9	110.9	111.8
British Columbia	88.5	88.3	84.8	90.5	86.8	87.4	87.8	89.9	90.1	89.8	92.8

Source: Statistics Canada, CANSIM II, *tables 051-0001 and 383-0029.*

Table 9.18. Labour Productivity and Related Variables, Canada and Provinces, 2007 and 2013

	2007		2013	
	Annual average number of hours worked for all	Labour productivity	Annual average number of hours worked for all	Labour productivity
Canada	1,783	46.7	1,745	48.7
NL	1,917	79.8	1,875	69.9
PE	1,851	28.4	1,784	28.2
NS	1,805	33.5	1,734	35.4
NB	1,833	36.2	1,808	36.0
QC	1,735	42.9	1,703	44.0
ON	1,773	44.1	1,724	44.6
MB	1,783	40.0	1,741	45.1
SK	1,838	53.8	1,839	58.5
AB	1,895	65.6	1,873	70.4
BC	1,747	42.6	1,708	45.1

Source: Statistics Canada, CANSIM table 383-0029, "Labour productivity and related variables by business sector industry, consistent with the North American Industry Classification System (NAICS) and the System of National Accounts (SNA), provinces and territories, annual."

Table 9.19. Labour Productivity and Related Variables, By Province, 2007 and 2013 (Canada = 100)

	2007		2013	
	Labour productivity	Annual average number of hours worked for all	Labour productivity	Annual average number of hours worked for all
NL	171	108	144	107
PE	61	104	58	102
NS	72	101	73	99
NB	78	103	74	104
QC	92	97	90	98
ON	94	99	92	99
MB	86	100	93	100
SK	115	103	120	105
AB	140	106	145	107
BC	91	98	93	98

Source: Statistics Canada, CANSIM table 383-0029, "Labour productivity and related variables by business sector industry, consistent with the North American Industry Classification System (NAICS) and the System of National Accounts (SNA), provinces and territories, annual."

TRADE

Chapter 3 highlights trade as key to a region's economic development. I note that Douglass North, a widely read economic historian, argues that the timing and pace of economic development is tied to the success of the export sector, and that regions tied to a single export commodity very often fail to achieve sustainable economic expansion. Trade agreements between Canada and the United States (FTAS) and later between Canada, the United States, and Mexico (NAFTA) have altered trade patterns and the dynamics of economic integration. More to the point, free trade agreements have had a profound impact on trade patterns at the regional level, and this is also true for the Maritime provinces. International trade has grown faster than interprovincial trade, and the three Maritime provinces have fared quite well in recent years at the international level. The region now exports more, *toute proportion gardée*, to the United States than at any time since Canada's National Policy was implemented. This makes the case that the region should support trade agreements whenever Ottawa puts them on the agenda.

Table 9.20 reports on the region's exports to the United States since 1976 from a comparative perspective and shows the growth of such exports from New Brunswick and Prince Edward Island was greater than the Canadian average from 1976 to 2001. Key export sectors include food manufacturing and crop production in Prince Edward Island, plastic and rubber products manufacturing and paper manufacturing in Nova Scotia, and paper manufacturing, food processing, and wood product manufacturing in New Brunswick. However, this list suggests that, since a large proportion of the region's exports remains closely linked to its natural resources, the region has not been successful in making a transition away from resource-based activities. This, as North suggests, is key to strong economic development. The reliance on natural resources also explains why rural exporters outperform urban exporters in the four Atlantic provinces. The opposite is true in other regions of Canada.

Table 9.20. Exports to the United States, as a Percentage of National or Provincial GDP

	1976	1981	1991	2001	2005	2011	2013	Growth 1976–2013
Canada	12.7	15.1	15.3	31.9	24.3	17.3	17.7	39.4%
Prince Edward Island	1.9	3.7	4.3	17.3	15.4	9.5	11.0	478.9%
Nova Scotia	9.1	9.7	8.4	17.9	14.1	8.5	7.9	-13.2%
New Brunswick	10.6	22.3	14.8	36.8	38.3	39.7	40.9	285.8%

Source: Statistics Canada, Provincial Economic Accounts and Catalogues 65-003.

Table 9.21 makes the case that growth in trade is now centred more on international trade than interprovincial trade in all regions of Canada except the Yukon, where a sharp decline in gold mining had a profound impact on one of the territory's key exports. International exports accounted for 25 per cent of the GDP of Nova Scotia and 43 per cent of New Brunswick's in 2002, compared to 19 and 26 per cent respectively in 1992.

VENTURE CAPITAL

The government of Canada often underlines the importance of venture capital, insisting that it underpins innovation and enables small- and medium-sized firms to grow.[19] Industry Canada regularly produces reports on the state of venture capital by sector and regions.[20] In 2014 it reported that Ontario and Quebec led the country with respect to firms receiving venture capital. British Columbia and Alberta followed, reporting solid growth over previous years. The three Maritime provinces, together with Manitoba and Saskatchewan, trailed badly (see table 9.22).

Table 9.21. Interprovincial and International Exports as a Share of GDP, Canada, Provinces and Territories, 1992, 2000, 2002, and 2011

	Interprovincial exports/GDP				International exports/GDP				Total exports/GDP			
	1992	2000	2002	2011	1992	2000	2002	2011	1992	2000	2002	2011
Newfoundland & Labrador	10	15	20	26	19	41	40	40	29	56	60	66
Prince Edward Island	30	26	26	25	14	29	28	18	44	55	54	43
Nova Scotia	19	21	21	22	17	26	25	18	36	47	46	40
New Brunswick	26	31	32	38	26	39	43	44	52	70	75	82
Quebec	19	20	20	20	21	40	35	24	40	60	55	44
Ontario	19	19	19	18	31	51	46	31	50	70	65	49
Manitoba	25	32	32	20	19	29	28	25	44	61	60	45
Saskatchewan	23	27	28	24	28	42	37	25	51	69	65	49
Alberta	23	24	24	22	27	41	35	32	50	65	59	54
British Columbia	13	15	14	17	24	33	27	21	37	48	41	38
Yukon	11	17	15	17	47	15	13	11	58	32	28	28
Northwest Territories & Nunavut	19	25	22	28	20	30	29	33	39	55	51	61
Canada	19	20	20	20	26	43	38	29	45	63	58	49

Source: Statistics Canada, CANSIM, *table 384-0038 and Provincial Economic Accounts.*

Table 9.22. Number of Companies Receiving VC (Venture Capital) by Province, 2013 and 2014

Province	2013	2014	Growth (%)
British Columbia	51	60	18
Alberta	26	27	4
Saskatchewan	4	4	0
Manitoba	1	1	0
Ontario	139	142	2
Quebec	154	151	-2
New Brunswick	14	19	36
Nova Scotia	12	9	-25
Prince Edward Island	0	1	n/a
Newfoundland and Labrador	1	2	100
Territories	n/a	n/a	n/a

Source: Thomson Reuters Canada 2015.

INCOME

Per capita income also reveals a great deal about a region's economic health, speaking to both the region's economic vitality and the well-being of its residents. In the 1960s and 1970s, governments turned to per capita income as one of the main criteria for establishing both regional development policy and measures to assess the economic health of regions, if only because income levels are an easily understood indicator of regional disparities. Tables 9.23 and 9.24 report on progress made in attenuating disparities in income. Certainly, progress has been made, but transfer payments account for some of it. The argument, as we saw earlier, is that income based on government transfer payments promotes economic dependency on government rather than self-sustaining economic development. Table 9.24 reveals the region remains dependent on EI benefits, which also serve to strengthen per capita income.

Provincial governments can also become dependent on federal transfers, as some economists have long contended.[21] Have provinces will argue the federal government has been too generous in transferring money from have

Table 9.23. Personal Income Per Capita, Selected Years, 1961-2001; Relationship to National Average (Canada = 100)

	1961	1965	1971	1975	1981	1985	1991	1995	2001	2006	2011
Newfoundland & Labrador	62.0	61.4	67.7	71.6	72.5	73.3	82.8	80.6	81.1	83.5	78.8
Prince Edward Island	62.2	54.7	66.3	70.8	73.5	74.9	82.0	86.8	83.2	82.9	86.1
Nova Scotia	78.0	74.5	78.0	78.8	81.9	86.7	86.4	90.0	91.1	90.4	90.0
New Brunswick	68.4	69.0	74.6	75.6	76.4	79.6	82.6	87.9	87.3	87.5	84.1
Quebec	91.2	91.6	91.5	91.0	89.6	91.0	92.4	91.9	91.4	90.2	91.5
Ontario	116.5	114.6	115.2	110.6	104.1	108.1	108.8	107.8	106.8	102.2	108.9
Manitoba	94.2	94.4	93.9	95.9	95.7	98.2	93.2	94.4	92.8	90.7	93.5
Saskatchewan	72.8	90.4	84.3	103.9	102.2	89.5	85.8	88.0	86.7	91.6	88.0
Alberta	101.3	97.8	96.5	102.0	115.9	110.8	102.1	103.2	115.1	126.8	104.0
British Columbia	115.2	112.8	105.7	107.0	112.6	102.7	103.6	103.2	96.1	100.8	103.2

Source: Statistics Canada, Provincial Economic Accounts, 2002.

provinces to have-less provinces. Former Ontario premier Dalton McGuinty repeatedly warned Ottawa and other provincial governments against adding new funding for have-less provinces: "My concern is that it's very important that the provinces understand that they have to protect the golden goose here. If there is more money available from the federal government, we'd rather that it be distributed in such a way that it benefits all of us, including supporting, for example, post-secondary education in the province of Ontario, which contributes to the strength of our economy and increases our capacity to make contributions to the federal government."[22] McGuinty never questioned how Ontario became Canada's golden goose or the impact Ottawa's policies had on economic development in his and the other nine provinces. McGuinty also never made reference to the fact that the Maritime provinces invest a great deal in post-secondary education only to see a high number of their graduates move to Ontario for work. This too contributes to the strength of the Canadian economy. When the time came, however, McGuinty did not hesitate to launch a high-profile campaign to secure a greater share of federal transfers for Ontario, notably under the Equalization program.

Melville McMillan, with the Department of Economics at the University of Alberta, has challenged widely believed assumptions about Ottawa's Equalization program. He reports that the provincial governments of the five core Equalization recipient provinces have not become more dependent on Equalization over the past twenty-five to thirty years. Contrary

Table 9.24 Total Regular EI Benefit Payments ($M), Selected Years, Maritimes, Quebec, and Canada, 1972–2010

	Maritimes	% of total	Quebec	% of total	Canada
1972	136.1	7.0	521.7	30.7	1,700.2
1975	282.6	9.7	1,011.8	34.8	2,907.7
1981	497.3	12.1	1,643.4	39.9	4,115.8
1985	938.5	10.5	2,885.0	32.1	8,975.3
1991	1,475.6	10.0	4,716.5	31.9	1,4783.3
1995	1,157.5	11.8	3,337.4	33.9	9,838.2
2001	1,078.7	13.3	2,665.0	32.9	8,089.4
2005	1,126.6	13.3	2,808.9	33.2	8,451.0
2010	1,449.6	10.9	3,631.7	27.2	1,3351.7

Source: Statistics Canada, Employment Insurance Statistic, CANSIM II*, table 276-0005.*

to Dalton McGuity and Brad Wall, he insists the program benefits both recipient and non-recipient provinces: "We expect net out migration from Equalization recipient provinces. Those migrants carry with them a bundle of human capital—human capital that largely represents the investments of the provincial governments from which they come. Education is the most obvious factor but healthcare is another consideration. To the extent that Equalization improves provincial public services, and so education and healthcare, migrants bring with them more human capital than they would otherwise. That improvement in human capital benefits those provinces with a net inflow of interprovincial migrants. Greater productivity and higher tax revenues are economic benefits."[23] He also points out that all provinces have received Equalization at some time, and he calculates this net provincial immigration has likely provided "Alberta with about $20 billion annually of human capital financed by other provinces."[24]

As we know, Ottawa put the Equalization program on a downward track in 1982, when it decided to dump the ten-province formula in favour of a five-province formula that excluded Alberta, thereby saving billions over the years for the federal treasury. But this was not the only reason for Ottawa's decision to move to a five-province formula. Escalating resource revenues pushed the ten-province formula so high that all provinces, with the exception of Alberta, would have qualified to receive Equalization payments. In addition, Ottawa decided to take the four Atlantic provinces, those with the weakest tax bases, out of the formula, which would serve to soften the blow to all the receiving provinces. By at least one estimate, the five-province formula reduced revenues to the receiving provinces to about 92 per cent of what they would have received under the ten-province formula.[25]

We also may recall that Ottawa overhauled its transfers to provinces for health care, post-secondary education, and social services in 1996–97 as part of its program review exercise. Ottawa merged two existing programs—the Canada Assistance Plan (CAP) and Established Programs Financing (EPF)—to create the Canada Health and Social Transfer (CHST) program. The CHST included both a transfer of cash and tax points, and the initial transfers were below levels established in earlier programs. In addition, EPF and CAP had an equalization component that provided additional cash to have-less provinces. The new program, which once again divides funding between health and social transfers, moved to an equal per capita payment, which still favoured provinces with expanding populations, notably Alberta

Table 9.25. Federal Transfer Payments as a Percentage of Provincial Revenues, 1961–2013

	1961	1965	1971	1975	1981	1985	1991	1995	2001	2013
Newfoundland and Labrador	63.0	60.8	58.5	52.8	48.4	49.4	44.0	43.0	43.1	15.7
Prince Edward Island	60.0	54.3	59.6	59.6	52.4	49.6	42.5	39.7	42.5	39.1
Nova Scotia	51.1	45.8	46.0	49.7	47.1	40.3	36.9	40.3	37.9	37.2
New Brunswick	50.0	49.7	48.2	49.7	44.3	42.9	36.0	35.1	36.2	37.0
Quebec	23.3	21.7	28.9	25.3	23.0	24.3	17.7	19.9	16.3	20.1
Ontario	25.9	16.0	19.5	22.1	19.9	16.9	14.5	15.4	11.4	19.2
Manitoba	44.2	30.9	34.7	38.9	33.5	31.0	31.6	29.7	27.4	26.4
Saskatchewan	34.4	24.6	37.5	34.6	28.3	29.9	33.8	33.5	34.0	14.2
Alberta	33.8	19.0	22.6	15.8	7.9	12.2	13.7	11.6	8.7	14.9
British Columbia	34.4	15.3	19.9	18.6	15.0	18.8	12.7	11.5	12.3	17.2

Source: Statistics Canada, Provincial Economic Accounts.

and Ontario. New funding adjustments were subsequently made ($11.5 billion over five years announced in 1999, $21 billion in 2000, and a further $35 billion over five years in 2003).[26] In addition, a high-profile First Ministers' Conference on health care, held in September 2004, added $41 billion of new money over a ten-year period under CHST. All these adjustments translated into $16.5 billion in federal transfers for health care in 2005-06, an amount that grew to $24 billion in 2009-10.[27]

The Harper government, however, decided not to renew Martin's ten-year health accord with the provinces. It agreed to continue to increase health transfers to 6 per cent for six years, but then tie all further increases to the rate of nominal GDP, which measures economic growth, including inflation.[28]

Tables 9.25 and 9.26 make the point that all provinces receive federal transfers, some more than others.[29] The tables also reveal, however, that all provinces have become less dependent on federal transfers than was the case in 1961 or 1971 and, leaving aside Newfoundland and Labrador, nowhere is this more evident than in the three Maritime provinces. If Ottawa's objective is to make the three Maritime provinces less dependent on federal transfers, then it is on the right track as the two tables below reveal.

Table 9.26. Equalization Payments as a Percentage of Provincial Government Revenue, Maritimes, 1961-2013

	Prince Edward Island	Nova Scotia	New Brunswick
1961	25.0	19.5	21.1
1965	28.6	21.9	22.1
1971	22.5	20.2	19.5
1975	26.2	25.2	21.7
1981	31.5	27.0	25.4
1985	28.3	20.5	22.6
1991	26.0	20.0	22.2
1995	23.5	23.8	20.7
2001	24.7	31.8	21.6
2006	23.6	19.0	21.5
2011	20.7	13.5	19.0
2013	21.4	16.6	19.5

Source: Statistics Canada, Provincial Economic Accounts, and ACOA.

LOOKING BACK

This chapter cannot be a happy read for Maritimers. It documents the difficult economic situation that continues to confront the region; there are precious few bright spots and many worrisome ones. Looking ahead, the region's aging population and its impact on both economic growth and the cost of public services, notably health care, will add to the region's economic woes at a time when federal transfers are on a downward trend. Though it is difficult to link Ottawa's approach to regional development and the state of the Maritime economy, the chapter reports that the region performed better when Ottawa's regional policy was clearer and its focus was on Atlantic Canada.

The data suggest that where the government can claim some degree of success in alleviating regional disparities is through its various transfer payments schemes. The transfers have also ensured, to some degree, a national level of public services and some degree of parity in per capita income. However, this has come at a price, making both individuals and governments dependent on federal transfers. The data also suggest, however, that Ottawa is slowly but surely shifting away from ensuring a comparable level of public services between regions, given changes to the Equalization program and to other transfers to the provinces with a greater reliance on per capita criteria. There is evidence that the federal government is also slowly attenuating its commitment to achieve some degree of parity in per capita income. It has been unable to come up with an approach to make regions less dependent on its transfer payments other than by slowly turning off the tap.

This chapter reveals the region has underperformed in virtually all key economic indicators. The people factor is cause for concern, not only because the region has been unable to attract new residents, but also because the region's population is aging at a faster pace than that of other regions. The one bright spot for the Maritime provinces is on the international trade front since NAFTA was signed.

Given uncertain messages coming out of Ottawa over the past twenty years or so, it is becoming increasingly difficult to identify Canada's regional development problem, let alone solutions. It seems Canada's regional development problem is now part political, part economics, part history, part geography, and part regional envy—with the part political always dominating the agenda.

NOTES

1 Gérard Veilleux, then secretary for Federal-Provincial Relations.
2 See the vast literature on public choice theory.
3 Canada, *Proceedings of the Standing Senate Committee on National Finance*, no. 12, March 22, 1973, 14–24.
4 Canada, *A Longstanding Commitment to the RDA Model* (Ottawa: Regional Agencies, April 29, 2015), 3.
5 "Dodging a Political Bullet," *Canada: A People's History*, CBC Archives, www.cbc.ca/history/EPISCONTENTSE1EP14CH3PA4LE.html.
6 Consultations with Gérard Veilleux, various dates.
7 Richard Saillant, *Over the Cliff? Acting Now to Avoid New Brunswick's Bankruptcy* (Moncton: CIRPPPA, 2014).
8 Canada, *Canada's Demographic Challenge—Annex 3 of the Budget Plan 2005* (Ottawa: Department of Finance, 2005), 1-4.
9 *A Skilled Workforce for Strong Sustainable and Balanced Growth* (Paris: OECD, 2010).
10 See, for example, Paul Bairoch, *Cities and Economic Development From the Dawn of History to the Present* (Chicago: University of Chicago Press, 1988).
11 Canada, Population, Urban and Rural, by Province and Territory, *2011 Census of Population* (Ottawa: Statistics Canada, last modified February 4, 2011).
12 See, for example, Canada, *The Innovation Agenda* (Ottawa: Department of Industry, February 2005).
13 I note not everyone agrees that patents are "indicators of a strong innovative culture." See, among many others, L. Zucker, M. Darby, and M. Brewer, "Intellectual Capital and the Birth of U.S. Biotechnology Enterprises," *American Economic Review* 88, no. 1 (1998): 290-306.
14 Robbie Brydon et al., "Measuring Innovation in Canada: The Tale Told by Patent Applications," e-brief, C. D. Howe Institute, November 28, 2014, 1.
15 Canada, *Patents Index* (Ottawa: Conference Board of Canada, 2016), www.conferenceboard.ca/hcp/details/innovation/patents-index.aspx.
16 Brydon et al., "Measuring Innovation in Canada," 1.
17 See Richard Saillant, *A Tale of Two Countries: How Canada's Great Demographic Imbalance is Pulling the Country Apart* (Halifax: Nimbus Publishing, 2016).
18 Ruth Buchanan, "1-800 New Brunswick: Economic Development Strategies, Firm Restructuring and the Local Production of Global Services," in *Globalizing Institutions: Case Studies in Regulation and Innovation*, ed. Jane Jenson and Boaventura de Sousa Santos (UK: Ashgate, 2000).
19 See, among others, Venture Capital Action Plan, *Canada's Economic Action Plan*, n.d., www.actionplan.gc.ca/en/initiative.
20 Canada, *SME Research and Statistics* (Ottawa: Industry Canada, Q4, 2014).

21 See, among others, R. Boadway and F. Flatters, "Efficiency and Equalization Payments in a Federal System of Government: A Synthesis and Extension of Recent Results," *Canadian Journal of Economics* 15, no. 4 (1982): 613–33.

22 Quoted in "Rich and Poor Provinces Split," *Globe and Mail*, October 26, 2004.

23 Melville L. McMillan, "Alberta and 'Equalization': Separating Fact from Fiction or Sorting Out Some Implications and Options in Canadian Fiscal Federalism," *Information Bulltetin*, no. 155 (Edmonton: Western Centre for Economic Research, January 2012), 23 and 25.

24 Ibid., 70.

25 "The Equalization Program and Atlantic Canada," in *Atlantic Provinces Economic Council Report* 35, no. 4 (Winter 2001): 1–6.

26 Canada, "Address by Prime Minister Paul Martin at First Ministers' Meeting" (Office of the Prime Minister, December 13, 2004), 5–7.

27 "New Federal Investments on Health Commitments on 10-year Action Plan on Health" (Health Canada news release, September 16, 2004). It should be noted that, combined with CHST tax points, the total transfer stood at $30.6 billion in 2005–06.

28 "Health Transfer Payments: Flaherty Announces Reduction of Growth in Spending by 2018," *Huffington Post*, December 19, 2011, http://www.huffingtonpost.ca/2011/12/19/health-transfer-payments-flaherty_n_1158072.html.

29 For a brief history of Canada's transfers to provinces, see Paul Boothe, "Finding a Balance: Renewing Canadian Fiscal Federalism" (Benefactors Lecture, C. D. Howe Institute, October 30, 1998).

Part 4

WE ARE TO BLAME

Chapter 10

THE UNFINISHED AGENDA

We recall the Charlottetown Conference was originally called to promote political and administrative union of the three Maritime provinces. Delegates from Canada crashed the party and a few years later Canada was born, or rather reborn, with the expectation that the Maritimes would break the impasse between Canada West and East or between Ontario and Quebec. Maritime union was thrown out the window, although the idea has resurfaced from time to time, with no success.

The Maritime provincial governments prefer to talk about Maritime co-operation rather than political union. But even here progress has been spotty and slow. There is a sign on the Nova Scotia-New Brunswick border that rankles me every time I see it. The sign prohibits the importation of honeybees into Nova Scotia. I once asked former premier Darrell Dexter what happens if a bee from the New Brunswick side decides to fly over the border. Is it expected to see the sign and turn around? Dexter explained there are a lot of small-scale beekeepers in Nova Scotia who fear being swamped by large operations from away, and they have put up strong resistance to change. That sign speaks to both the inability (or unwillingness) of the three Maritime provinces to embrace economic co-operation and to the pressure from many Maritimers on political leaders to protect the status quo.

This chapter explores attempts to unite the Maritime provinces and to promote greater co-operation between the three provinces. Maritimers and their governments are ultimately responsible for progress, or lack of progress, on this front. To be sure, Ottawa, national political institutions, and National Policy can share some of the blame, but they are not the primary culprit. We Maritimers and our provincial governments are.

Best to report my bias at the outset. I favour Maritime union, and I have made my views clear for some time. In the summer of 2014, I was invited to Frank McKenna's annual Atlantic business, government, and academic networking meeting in Fox Harbour, Nova Scotia. Then Prince Edward Island premier Robert Ghiz, an excellent golfer (much better than I am), was in my foursome for a round. He approached me and said, "Donald, let's have a good time today. We won't talk about Maritime union today, OK?" "Fine by me," I replied, except that a few minutes later, one of the region's leading businessmen walked up to Ghiz and said, "There is something I don't understand here. Nova Scotia produces excellent wine. I like it. But I am having a hell of a time buying it in New Brunswick. Why is that?" Touché, I thought. A year later, when I saw Ghiz at the same event, I told him, "I suppose you still do not want to talk about Maritime union?" "No," he replied, "let's talk about it. I am no longer premier." As I understood him, Ghiz was saying that as premier he had provincial interests to protect, which is no different from any other Canadian premier. Ghiz was also no different from current (and many past) Maritime premiers in his unwillingness to embrace Maritime political union.

Why do I favour union or, failing that, much stronger co-operation between the three provinces? There are three reasons. First, I believe the Maritime provinces constitute a political community with shared values and a common history. Second, political union would reduce the cost in program operations and in the delivery of public services. Third, we would have a greater capacity to initiate self-sustaining economic development by pooling limited resources, avoiding counter-productive competition among the three provinces, and creating a larger market for Maritime businesses.[1]

Not enough Maritimers agree with me on Maritime union, and I hold little hope that I will ever see it. Murray Beck had a point when he wrote, "Over two centuries the people of each province have developed such an attachment to their own political entity, its capital, and its institutions that they look with suspicion, even hostility, upon any attempt to tamper with them."[2] Politics and province-building in a slow-growth region, combined with a tendency in the Maritimes to focus on a province's identity, history, and competition with neighbouring provinces, explain in large measure why progress in promoting co-operation has been slow and political union impossible. Of course, there are also a number of thorny issues that will not be easy to resolve, for example, how best to deal with the language rights of the francophones in a new Maritime jurisdiction.

Maritimers, their politicians, and their provincial governments are no different than other Canadians and their provincial governments. Our Maritime political and bureaucratic institutions are as path-dependent as are other institutions. Politicians and their values are influenced by the institutions within which they are embedded. As March and Olsen maintained, the "logic of appropriateness" is shaped by institutions.[3] Luke Flanagan, who studied attempts at Maritime union and co-operation between 1960 and 1980, put it best: "Political leaders will make decisions within and according to the political setting that was established at an earlier point in time. Political change cannot be readily achieved because the political leaders who operate within the setting are vested as the core beneficiaries."[4]

The above explains, in no small measure, why competition for economic development between the three provinces remains intense and promoting a regional perspective remains, at best, work in progress. One can only assume that the three provinces believe they can accomplish more working independently than they can working collectively or as a whole. I have had two personal experiences that speak to this point.

As part of the consultations in preparing my report on the establishment of ACOA, I met with ten local business leaders over lunch in Sydney, Nova Scotia. One of them said, "If there is a choice between creating jobs in Halifax or Toronto, send them to Toronto. Halifax has had more than its share." No one in the room challenged him, and I was left speechless. Why, I thought, would a Maritimer say this? I hasten to add that the individual may not represent the Cape Breton business community. I only heard it once, and I note that it was a Cape Bretoner, Harvey Webber, who launched the Atlantic Canada Plus campaign designed to encourage Atlantic Canadians to think more about their region and to purchase locally made products.

Later, I interviewed former Nova Scotia premier John Savage to discuss regional economic development policy. As noted, among the first points he made in the interview was that one of the biggest obstacles in promoting economic development and attracting new investments in his province was interprovincial competition with New Brunswick. As I reported in the Introduction of this book, Savage said, "When I go to Toronto to meet with chief executive officers to promote Nova Scotia as a place to invest, I very often discover that Frank McKenna has already been there. We need to coordinate our activities better."

I can add that Frank McKenna told me one of the most controversial decisions he made while in office was awarding a contract to manufacture the province's licence plates to an Amherst, Nova Scotia, firm rather than a New Brunswick one. Amherst is only a few kilometres from the New Brunswick border. No matter, many New Brunswickers insisted the contract should have been awarded to a New Brunswick firm, even if it did not have the lowest bid, because it employed New Brunswickers who paid taxes in that province.

McKenna and Savage are not the only former Maritime premiers to lament the lack of regional co-operation. Former Prince Edward Island premier Alex Campbell maintains the region never made the "decision to develop as a region. We are...separate, competitive, jealous and parochial provinces. We fight each other for industrial development. We fight each other for subsidies and we bicker about energy and transportation. And too often, the lines of battle are drawn on purely political grounds or selfish local considerations. I believe that we must come together collectively to develop the region on a sound economic basis. We must set aside jurisdictional jealousies for the bigger goal of regional unity and strength."[5]

We are no closer today to Maritime political union, and competition between the three provinces is as intense as it ever was. Why? Certainly, the federal government has not helped matters. If anything, it has made matters worse by focusing its regional development efforts on federal-provincial agreements, by having regional ministers, in the past, who have designated political responsibilities to individual provinces rather than the region, and by continuing bilateral exchanges between prime ministers and premiers. However, if blame is to be assigned for a lack of progress on regional co-operation, then—as I have said—we need to look first to our provincial governments and ourselves. It was not the federal government that put up the sign on the Nova Scotia border, prohibiting honeybees from crossing the border. It is not the federal government saying no to Maritime political or economic union.

MARITIME UNION: A NONSTARTER THROUGH THE AGES

Maritime union is an idea whose time never comes. It is often debated and, at times, even gains currency, particularly when Canada's national unity is threatened. When the threat recedes, so does interest in Maritime union. This suggests that if Maritime union were ever to see the light of day, it will happen on the heel of a major crisis brought about by forces outside the region rather than by Maritimers themselves deciding that union would make more economic sense. In short, Maritime union will require "a special kind of trauma" such as being cut off "physically and psychologically from the rest of Canada" because of Quebec leaving the federation or a financial crisis confronting all three provincial governments at the same time.[6]

Leaving aside former New Brunswick premier Louis J. Robichaud, no provincial premier has been willing to champion Maritime—or even less, Atlantic—union. Former Nova Scotia premier Donald Cameron had this to say: "We shouldn't waste our time and energy trying to get people to accept the idea of one Atlantic province."[7] Former Prince Edward Island premier Robert Ghiz was no less blunt. He remarked that Maritime union "would be a large mistake," and Prince Edward Island "should have no part of it."[8] From time to time, a premier or two, never three, will raise the possibility of Maritime political union while business community representatives will often voice support for it. But nothing comes of the notion.

And yet, the idea of Maritime union never dies. There have been a number of attempts to bring about political union from 1864 to the 1970s. Former New Brunswick premier Louis Robichaud put forward the idea of political union of the four Atlantic provinces during the 1964 federal-provincial constitutional conference held in Charlottetown. He told the conference, "Perhaps Premiers Stanfield, Smallwood, Shaw and I may get together today and, on this centennial of the first meeting in Charlottetown, decide to reduce the number of Canadian provinces from ten to seven. Should that occur, the focal point of progress and activity in the nation would unquestionably and rapidly take a marked shift to the east."[9] Robichaud explained why he was issuing such a challenge: "The new pressures of the mid-20th century, the problems of national unity, and the growth in governmental responsibilities, combine in calling for a re-examination of proposals for the union of these four Atlantic provinces."[10] The next step, he suggested, "was a 'serious' study to look into all facets of the matter, since the subject is too serious to permit the discussion of it to be clouded or subverted by prejudices or pettiness of any nature."[11]

The proposal, initially at least, did not meet with much enthusiasm from Robichaud's Atlantic colleagues. Then premier Walter Shaw, of Prince Edward Island, dismissed the idea and said the chances for political union "were extremely limited."[12] Then premier Smallwood pointed out that Newfoundland was not on the mainland, and so could not be considered a "Maritime" province. In any event, he maintained that Newfoundland much preferred dealing directly with Ottawa and not as part of the Maritime provinces.[13] Perhaps for good measure, Smallwood attended only one more Atlantic Premiers' Conference, and it was later disbanded. Then Nova Scotia premier Stanfield did not shut the door on the proposal but expressed some caution: "We are prepared to consider it, provided provision is to be made for proper safeguards. On a per capita basis, we have a higher standard of income than the three other provinces and we wouldn't want to have that brought down. We would only be prepared to consider it on a basis of everybody else being pulled up rather than Nova Scotia being pulled down."[14] Despite his reservations, Stanfield obviously saw merit in Robichaud's proposal; he later suggested that Robichaud and he ask their respective legislative assemblies to decide through a free vote whether the two provinces should proceed with a joint study to determine the feasibility of a political union.

In early 1965 the Nova Scotia and the New Brunswick legislative assemblies unanimously agreed to launch "a study to inquire into the advantages and disadvantages of a union of the province of Nova Scotia and the province of New Brunswick to become one province within the nation."[15] Though the study was slow in getting started, certain developments gave it a major boost. When Alex Campbell was elected premier of Prince Edward Island, he immediately announced that his province would like to join the study. John Deutsch, chairman of the Economic Council of Canada and principal of Queen's University, agreed to head up the study. The national media were highly supportive of efforts to promote more co-operation between the Maritime provinces.[16] Newfoundland, however, showed no interest in participating in the study. Not only did its premier stop attending the Atlantic Premiers' Conference, but also a pattern emerged in the 1960s in which Newfoundland was less and less willing to develop "a regional" voice even in federal-provincial relations or to promote an Atlantic perspective on sectoral issues.[17]

With Prince Edward Island now a full partner in the Maritime Union Study, few doubted the study's importance and its potential impact. The three premiers issued a joint statement in their respective legislatures, reporting their commitment to public consultation and to the "direct participation...of interested organizations and bodies."[18] The study also received a number of "public briefs" and commissioned some twenty studies.[19]

Not long after the Deutsch study was formally launched, it became clear it would shift away from the issue of political union and toward identifying ways to promote greater co-operation between the three provinces. This is not to suggest there was no support among the Maritime population for political union. A public opinion survey sponsored by the study "indicated a favourable attitude to complete union of the three provinces... on the part of approximately two thirds of the people 16 years of age and over. One quarter of the people are not in favour of such union and the balance, approximately 10 percent, is not sure....The people of Prince Edward Island are the least in favour while those in New Brunswick are somewhat more than those in Nova Scotia. English respondents favour union more so than do the French."[20] Still, the officials directing the study concluded advocating co-operation that would lead to political union would be less threatening than to recommend outright and immediate union. Public opinion polls were one thing, but convincing politicians and the three bureaucracies to overlook their self-interest was quite another. Moreover, for citizens to agree via a public opinion survey on some vague notion of what Maritime political union might be and what it could entail was quite different from doing so after a full-blown debate in which the merits and drawbacks were fully aired.

The Maritime Union Study was made public on November 27, 1970, by then premier Campbell and two newly elected premiers, Richard Hatfield of New Brunswick and Gerald Regan of Nova Scotia. There was little doubt the study's ultimate objective was political union; however, it urged that the region move only gradually toward this goal by a series of new cooperative arrangements. Still, the study pointed to eventual political union as the preferred option because of the "uncertainties" confronting the region, "which...arise from two dangers—the possible political disintegration of the nation and continued substantial economic disparities in relation to the remainder of the country."[21] The study also made clear why it did not recommend immediate political union, despite the favourable response reported in the public opinion surveys:

> The historical and traditional loyalties to the individual provincial entities are strong; the attachments to local diversities and interests are more intense than elsewhere in the country....The resistance to change in existing political structures is reinforced by the established relationships and interests that are associated with governments; these tend to be particularly intimate and strong. It can be expected that various influential groups, the holders of franchises and concessions, the bureaucratic apparatus, and many who have vested interests in the existing arrangements would be apprehensive of changes that might bring uncertainties....There is no question that in the Maritimes many of these forces weigh heavily in the direction of the status quo.[22]

NEW MACHINERY TO PROMOTE CO-OPERATION

The Maritime Union Study looked to new measures for the machinery of government to encourage greater co-operation, and eventually, political union. The new machinery would be charged with the responsibility of promoting "regional economic planning, regional negotiations with federal authorities, establishing common administrative services, developing uniform legislation, co-ordinating existing provincial policies, preparing a constitution for a single provincial government for the Maritimes and implementing steps leading to political union."[23] Inspired by the European Economic Community, the study recommended three new organizations to undertake the various tasks. It urged the establishment of a Council of Maritime Premiers, a Maritime Provinces Commission, and a Joint Legislative Assembly.

The Council of Maritime Premiers would consist of the three premiers, meet at least quarterly, consider recommendations coming from the new Maritime Provinces Commission, approve joint submissions, and negotiate with Ottawa on behalf of the region.[24] The commission, meanwhile, which would consist of five members, would be responsible for preparing a long-term development plan for the region, for recommending common regional policies, and for preparing proposals for joint administrative policies and a unification of the three public services, a constitution for a single Maritime province, and a timetable for political union.[25] The Joint Legislative Assembly would bring together all members of the three provincial legislatures in a joint session once a year to review the work of the council and commission. It would also be charged with determining the method by which the final step of political union would take place.[26] The study urged that a thorough review be undertaken in five years on the progress realized toward full political union. If it were to report progress is not being made and "political union cannot be accomplished within a further five years, the entire program should be reconsidered."[27]

The three premiers quickly declared their support for much of the Maritme Union Study's recommendations. The director of the study explained, "It was staggering to submit a report on November 21, 1970, in the Confederation Chamber in Charlottetown, and then have it adopted within two months. I do not think there has been a Royal Commission in this country that has ever had that happen. Taken further, within four more months there was a formal and enforceable agreement between the three provinces. Then, lo and behold, we even have it accepted by the Legislatures and formal institutions of regional co-operation were established."[28] Then premier Hatfield even gave his support for political union, so long as the federal government provided financial assistance to implement it. The other two premiers were much more lukewarm on the issue, with Regan arguing that co-operation was possible without union and Campbell suggesting that union was not necessary at "this time."[29] Though the premiers took immediate steps to establish the Council of Maritime Premiers, they put off a decision on the Maritime Provinces Commission and the Joint Legislative Assembly. The power to constitute the commission was built into the legislation establishing the council; however, the premiers have never pursued the matter. The power to constitute the assembly remains the prerogative of the three provincial legislative assemblies, and this too has not been pursued.

The Council of Maritime Premiers can point to a number of initiatives that have led to new regional institutions and cooperative measures.[30] There are now a host of regional institutions in place, including the Atlantic Veterinary College, the Maritime Provinces Higher Education Commission, and the Maritime Land Registration and Information

Service, along with a wide array of interprovincial committees that operate joint programs or provide services. The council could also report that it successfully promoted a "Maritime" position in dealing with Ottawa. Indeed, it is not difficult to get the three Maritime premiers to gang up on Ottawa, to agree that the federal government should be doing more in, say, regional economic development and transportation or that it should not be cutting transfer payments to the provinces.

Though the council has had some successes, it also has had its failures, including attempts to cooperate on trade and investment promotion, which has been stymied by continuing competition. Also, in the aftermath of Canada's energy crisis in the 1970s, the three premiers agreed to put in place an energy agency to encourage regional planning, a pooling of capital, and the allocation of regional or Maritime energy resources. However, the proposed Maritime Energy Corporation failed to get off the ground.[31] There are a number of cases where co-operation did not take place, cases where a slight political nudge should have worked. I am thinking here of motor vehicle licensing, where economic benefits could be easily achieved given economies of scale in program administration.[32]

The reasons for the failure of the Maritime Energy Corporation are not difficult to pinpoint: province-building overshadowed region-building. Indeed, in time, each province found one reason or another to lose interest in a joint energy corporation. New Brunswick was able to secure federal financing to construct its own nuclear power plant; a new government in Prince Edward Island declared its firm opposition to nuclear power; and Nova Scotia saw coal-generated power as a way to create new jobs in economically depressed Cape Breton. The three provinces also accused the federal government of reneging on its initial commitment to support the Maritime Energy Corporation. The federal government did raise issues that enabled the three provincial governments to back out of their participation in the corporation.

The Council of Maritime Premiers together with the follow-up to the Deutsch Commission has never lived up to expectations, however modest. A united Maritime region remains a region of the imagination, rather than a region shaped by physical boundaries and political jurisdictions and institutions. The council has had no regional body to initiate policy. No one with the council is responsible to any one government, and this matters a great deal in the "control and command" world of government bureaucracies.[33]

Murray Beck argued that the Council of Maritime Premiers was "unable to develop a backbone." It is difficult to grow a backbone when you have no capacity to cut across jurisdictions and institutions to pursue common problems or opportunities.[34] The Joint Legislative Committee (JLC), the intended umbrella for Maritime co-operation, was disbanded after only a few meetings. Luke Flanagan maintains the JLC failed "because of the lack of a concrete mandate and a lack of political will from the premiers to give it a mandate or some form of oversight over executive decisions. This underscored the fact that the premiers were fully in control of the regionalism process and were not willing to cede their power to extra-provincial actors and institutions."[35]

THE COUNCIL OF ATLANTIC PREMIERS

In the aftermath of the failed Meech Lake Accord, then Newfoundland and Labrador premier Clyde Wells made a plea for an Atlantic rather than a Maritime perspective on regional co-operation. The media reported that Wells even favoured full political union of the four Atlantic provinces. Wells subsequently retracted his support, saying he had been misquoted—and later shifted to the more traditional and cooler Newfoundland posture.

At one of its regular meetings, on October 27, 1999, the Council of Maritime Premiers extended a formal invitation to Newfoundland and Labrador to join the council as a full partner.[36] Several months later the four Atlantic premiers met in Moncton to sign a memorandum of understanding, establishing the Council of Atlantic Premiers. The four premiers made it clear the focus of the new council would be "to promote Atlantic Canadian interests on national issues...to establish common views and positions and work to ensure Atlantic Canadians and their interests are well represented in national debates."[37] They set the co-operation bar low, much lower than the Deutsch commission did some thirty years earlier: calling on four provincial governments to apply pressure on Ottawa was the easy part, requiring no political will and no difficult decision to pursue the objective.

A former senior official with the Council of Maritime Premiers reported the three Maritime premiers agreed to extend the invitation to the premier of Newfoundland and Labrador to strengthen their hand with the federal government, based on a profound desire for more clout in Ottawa. He explained, "There was deep frustration over their inability to influence the federal government. All three were Progressive Conservative premiers. They looked to Brian Tobin, a former Liberal cabinet minister in Ottawa with Jean Chrétien and concluded that he could help a great deal in their dealings with Ottawa. The Council of Atlantic Premiers is a lot about dealing with Ottawa, not as much about regional cooperation." He added, "Tobin, meanwhile, saw an opportunity to become spokesperson for all of Atlantic Canada rather than just Newfoundland and Labrador."[38] An official with the council, however, readily acknowledged that interprovincial co-operation is far more difficult with "Newfoundland and Labrador in the mix."[39]

The council's first meeting set the tone for what was to come. The four premiers discussed the upcoming annual premiers' conference. They also "identified regional priorities," notably "securing adequate funding for health care, identifying and pursuing key investments to strengthen economic growth, including infrastructure and highways, and seeking improvements to the national fiscal transfer system."[40] With respect to strengthening economic growth, the premiers "called for the federal government to invest in a new shared-cost highways program for Atlantic Canada to further economic development to reduce disparity and increase opportunities."[41] The agenda spoke to what Ottawa could do for the region, but had very little to say about what the region itself ought to be doing to promote economic development.

It is important to emphasize the central purpose of the Council of Atlantic Premiers is to lobby the federal government on behalf of the four provinces and to influence national policies. The work of the council differs from that of the Council of Maritime Premiers in that the Atlantic council is much more of a lobby group. The council itself reported, "The work of the Council of Atlantic Premiers will be in addition to the ongoing work of the Council of Maritime Premiers, which has been in existence for more than twenty-five years. All premiers have recognized the need for continued concerted co-operation on a Maritime basis. The Maritime provinces do have specific ties and interests which are distinct from Atlantic concerns."[42] These range from interprovincial flows in post-secondary education and health to the development of closer economic relationships.[43]

That the Council of Atlantic Premiers sees itself as little more than a lobby association working Ottawa on behalf of the four Atlantic provinces is made clear by the list of accomplishments it has made public:

- advocating for the sustainability of health care;
- calling for reform of the federal Equalization program;
- defending the Atlantic Canada-US softwood–lumber agreement;
- requesting that the federal government pass new airline regulatory legislation to encourage competition;
- urging the federal government to establish a national shipbuilding and marine-fabrication policy;
- harmonizing the framework for regulating the licensing and sale of insurance products in the region; and
- collectively building international trade opportunities for Atlantic businesses through the Team Canada Atlantic trade partnership.[44]

All in all, having Newfoundland and Labrador in the mix has made it extremely difficult for the region to do much beyond forming a club to lobby Ottawa. Even in this capacity there have been some significant disagreements among the four provincial governments, notably on fishery policy and federal Equalization payments. The four Atlantic premiers can agree that "the fiscal capacity of the Atlantic provinces falls short of the national average even after equalization. These shortcomings in the Equalization Program must be corrected."[45] However, they agree on little else about equalization. There is precious little evidence to suggest the council has ever influenced how national policies are shaped. The fact is that the council and its members have minimal clout in Ottawa's political and bureaucratic circles.

It is important to stress that until former premiers Wells and Tobin came on the scene, Newfoundland and Labrador had consistently shunned closer co-operation with the three Maritime provinces—so much so that its government passed an order-in-council in the late 1970s prohibiting any government department from signing a regional agreement with the Maritime provinces without first securing full Cabinet approval. Newfoundland and Labrador effectively killed the Atlantic Premiers' Conference when it decided in the mid-1960s to no longer attend meetings. The government of Newfoundland and Labrador also stopped its annual contribution to the operation of the Atlantic Provinces Economic Council in the early 1980s, arguing its economy was so different that it made no sense to speak of an Atlantic economy. It later established its own Newfoundland and Labrador Economic Council. Patrick O'Flaherty of Memorial University recently explained, "Newfoundland's economy is more tied into that of Central Canada.... I don't think Maritime union represents any real alternative for Newfoundland. It is not a big issue here. I would say that if there is any kind of option that Newfoundlanders would entertain, if Canada does break up, the first one that they will want to explore will be independence. There is still a strong subterranean nationalist feeling in Newfoundland."[46]

It is important to remember that Newfoundland has had a distinct political and economic history. The province was not populated by Loyalists and Acadians, and its ties to the rest of Canada are relatively recent. A former secretary to the Council of Maritime Premiers explained, "It's hard enough to get three sovereign governments to cooperate on anything and that's in the good times. When you add a fourth, who is further away, whose history is different, whose culture is different and whose aspirations are different, it gets even harder to negotiate anything."[47] Former premier Wells quickly backtracked on his earlier call for greater co-operation and economic integration, on the grounds that he did not know quite what "economic co-operation and integration" meant. St. John's *Evening Telegram* ran an editorial titled "A Boat to Miss?" at the height of the discussion, and argued, "The real reason behind Mr. Wells' reluctance to get involved in the scheme may lie in the simple fact Newfoundland has little to gain by it.... This may be one boat the province will only be too glad to miss."[48]

If the Maritime region was to have healed itself through political union, or even through close economic co-operation, it has thus far failed to do so. Of course, there are many reasons for this lack of success; some are self-inflicted, others are not. One can question the merit of having three or four provincial governments coming together to lobby Ottawa. Given that Ottawa draws its political power from the more populous regions, it can ignore the positions of these small provinces, whether they speak with one, three, or four voices. Such an association of small provinces is not likely to fix Canada's constitutional flaw.

There has been little progress in developing new instruments to promote interprovincial co-operation since the 1980s. Existing instruments, such as the Maritime Provinces Higher Education Commission, have been allowed to limp along with minimal influence on the three provincial governments. In virtually all sectors, the commission plays a very modest role simply because provincial governments prefer it that way. One of the more important ways the Council of Maritime Premiers has been able to promote co-operation is through the creation of regional organizations.[49] The council has, however, created few regional organizations since the 1970s.

From time to time, two or three provincial governments will unveil a new measure to promote co-operation. The premiers of New Brunswick and Nova Scotia signed an agreement in 2015, pledging to establish a Joint Office of Regulatory and Service Effectiveness to promote "a modern, consistent and fair regulatory environment in both provinces."[50] Nothing was said then about Prince Edward Island, and time will tell if this office can overcome resistance from the two provincial bureaucracies; however, a few months later, Prince Edward Island joined the initiative.[51] Newfoundland and Labrador remains on the sidelines.

The four Atlantic provinces signed the Atlantic Memorandum of Understanding Concerning Apprentice Mobility in 2015. The agreement makes it easier for apprentices to gain on-the-job training and work experience required to complete certification. It did not require the four provincial governments to spend much political capital to secure an understanding that held no political cost for the four premiers.[52]

The above is a modest report card some fifty years after the Deutsch Commission report. There are several reasons inhibiting co-operation among the three Maritime provinces, and more is said about this later. Suffice to note it never happens that the three Maritime premiers are elected on the same day, and this is even less the case with the four Atlantic premiers. The three or four premiers pursue different political agendas at different times. They are content with making vague references to Maritime co-operation, but even this does not hold much appeal leading up to and during a provincial election campaign.

OTTAWA AND MARITIME CO-OPERATION

The federal government could have played a much greater role in promoting a "Maritime" perspective on economic development, and it still can. Many in Ottawa insist they favour greater regional co-operation, but they maintain there are limits to what they can do. They readily admit bewilderment that three such small political entities—with the largest, Nova Scotia, having a population base not much greater than the NCR—are not already united economically and politically.

The federal government has, however, made only a few tangible efforts to promote Maritime co-operation. For example, it shared the costs of the Maritime Union Study and seconded Edgar Gallant, a senior federal bureaucrat, to set up the Council of Maritime Premiers. Such isolated gestures aside—and despite the vast number of individuals in Ottawa who claim to favour Maritime political union, or at a minimum, greater co-operation, particularly in economic development—there is little evidence to suggest federal policies are geared to promote this.

On the contrary, evidence suggests they have actually worked against it. Otherwise, how do we explain, for example, Ottawa's change of position with regard to the establishment of the proposed Maritime Energy Corporation? Ottawa never made its second thoughts clear. Rumours circulated that it did not want to hold a minority position in the corporation. The newly elected Joe Clark government simply declared it wanted to put everything on hold and carry out a review of the proposed Maritime Energy Corporation. The review provided an excellent opportunity for some of the provinces, notably Prince Edward Island, to back out of commitments.[53] Such second thinking certainly did not help matters and probably gave the three provinces a *porte de sortie* from the proposed deal.

There are other examples, but perhaps none more telling than those found in federal regional development efforts overhauled in 1972, when the General Development Agreement (GDA) was introduced to implement regional development programs. The GDA, and later ERDA, sponsored programs and projects totalling billions of dollars in the Maritime region between the mid-1970s and the mid-1990s. They sponsored measures in agriculture, fisheries and aquaculture, transportation, industrial development, energy, mineral development, local development, forestry, ocean-related industries, rural development, pulp and paper, urban development, tourism, and the list goes on. In short, these measures went to the heart of economic development efforts in the three Maritime provinces over a thirty-year period. The agreements—with Ottawa sharing between 50 and 90 per cent of the cost—were almost all exclusively *provincial* in scope. Only in the case of tourism and trade did the federal government attempt to introduce a *regional* focus. There have even been instances where local federal offices were actually in competition with one another to secure a project for "their" province, much as provincial governments have been accused of doing.[54] More to the point, federal regional development efforts continue to be geared to a "province-building" agenda as much as their provincial counterparts.

The bulk of past and current federal government regional development efforts in the region have served to fuel competition between provincial governments. A province-building agenda may well make sense for the three Maritime provincial governments and also from a political perspective in Ottawa, but much less so from an economic development perspective. When a choice has to be made between political and regional economic development interests, the political interest always seems to win.

The federal government's organizations for economic development also speak to a national perspective (see, for example, the departments of Industry and Finance) or, failing that, a provincial perspective, rarely a regional one. Many federal government departments have small "provincial" offices and, dating back to 1972, continue to promote a largely provincial perspective under ACOA. The focus of ACOA's efforts is driven by provincial offices located in the three provincial capitals.

Federal Crown corporations that have a strong presence in the region also have a provincial perspective. I am thinking here of CBC's evening newscasts all produced along provincial lines rather than from a Maritime perspective. These supper-hour programs produced in large office studios in all three provincial capitals tend to reinforce provincial perspectives on both politics and economic development. More to the point, the federal government Crown corporation fuels a provincial perspective every morning and evening on its newscasts, thus making it more difficult for provincial politicians to define and pursue a "Maritime" agenda.

In the case of New Brunswick, CBC Radio has three morning news shows, one for Moncton, another for Saint John, and yet another for Fredericton. I note, however, that Radio-Canada only has one office studio in the region and brings a multi-province perspective to its work.

Michael Kirby, former secretary to the Cabinet for federal-provincial relations with the government of Canada, made it clear that if blame has to be assigned for a lack of co-operation between the Maritime provinces, one should look to the three Maritime premiers. He explained, "If we try to produce a program for the region which we believe is in the regional interest, each province counts the number of dollars going within its boundaries and if they are not equal, Ottawa is accused of playing favourites. If two provinces want the same project, God help us if we, in Ottawa, make the choice of location; that's outside interference." He illuminated a catch-22:

> Put simply, asking the federal government for its position on regional cooperation puts it in a no-win position. If the federal government encourages the Maritime provinces to get together, it can be, and is, criticized for applying unnatural and unwanted pressure to force the provinces to act in ways other than those they would prefer. If the federal government does not encourage regional cooperation, it can be, and is, criticized for setting the provinces against each other and for failing to support and encourage what is perceived by many people both inside, and particularly outside, the region as a good thing.[55]

Kirby expressed the view widely held in Ottawa that if interprovincial co-operation is found lacking in the Maritimes, the Maritimes should look to the political will of provincial political leaders for answers. Kirby insisted, "It is not an appreciated role for Ottawa to take the lead on Maritime cooperation."[56]

He has a point. If blame is to be assigned, the bulk of it must be directed at Maritimers and their politicians. Murray Beck put his finger on the problem nearly forty years ago, when he wrote, "Although the Maritime provinces may have some sort of empathy for one another because they share the same economic misfortunes, they fall short of having the capacity to respond jointly to common problems which cut across established institutions or interests."[57]

It should come as no surprise that provincial premiers view the world through provincial lenses, more specifically, their respective provinces. As noted, provincial premiers are elected to promote the interests of their provinces. These interests are defined by provincial boundaries, by geography, and by voters living in a defined physical space. Province-building is rooted in this provincial reality for all the provinces, but more so in the case of the Maritimes.[58] Shortly before he left government, former Prince Edward Island premier Robert Ghiz dismissed the idea of political union out of hand, calling it "preposterous."[59] As mentioned, Robert Ghiz felt a responsibility to oppose Maritime political union as premier, but felt no such responsibility once out of power.

We can blame provincial premiers for not doing enough and Newfoundland and Labrador for putting the brakes on regional co-operation since the province joined the region's premiers' council. But, again, we Maritimers are ultimately to blame. Former Nova Scotia premier Gerald Regan had a point when he wrote,

> It is a curious fact of political life that if three premiers were to meet to discuss a matter of little importance, they would probably be applauded for working together—at minimum for creating good will. Of course, in such a situation, few if any important concerns or interests are threatened. However, should three premiers meet to explore some concrete and substantive issues; should they begin to explore serious joint or corporate enterprise; should they seriously examine proposals which may lead to changed public policy with a potential saving in costs; should they spend money, hire staff, and develop a real capacity to act—then the critics are legend. They are convinced that time is being wasted and therefore maintain that time is too valuable for such futile exercises, and dire warnings about loss of sovereignty, loss of flexibility, loss of money, loss of independence, and loss of just about everything are heard on all sides. The basis of this curious state is quite obvious—so long as nothing is done no one is threatened; once one attempts serious discussion on any matter, some part of the existing fabric is challenged and it quite naturally reacts.[60]

Regan then catalogued the reasons why Maritime premiers hesitated to go much further than talking in general terms about the merit of regional co-operation and generating a united voice to call on Ottawa to do more for the region. It is worth quoting him again at length on this point.

> A decision to act jointly on a matter of public policy can result in: (1) concern by the legislature that its power and authority is being challenged and even destroyed; (2) concern by the cabinet that its power and authority is being eroded; (3) concern by the minister responsible (and sometimes the cabinet) that he must subject his actions to an additional constraint; (4) concern by the civil service that its procedures (and maybe its jobs) are at stake; (5) concern by special interests groups; (6) concern by the critics of government that what is proposed

is delivering the province into the hands of competitors or "outsiders"; (7) concern by the taxpayer that he will have to carry a greater and greater burden—and see his taxes spent in other provinces.[61]

Regan went to the heart of the matter when he observed that Nova Scotia premiers pursue co-operation only "when it is beneficial to the taxpayer of Nova Scotia."[62]

Although Regan wrote these words forty-four years ago, they apply no less today than in 1972. During this period, potential savings on the delivery of public services have been lost and potential opportunities to cooperate on economic development matters have been left unattended.

LOOKING TO WESTERN CANADA

The three most western provinces, all dealing with some of the same challenges as Regan outlined above, have been able to pull together to promote economic development. On April 30, 2010, British Columbia, Alberta, and Saskatchewan signed an economic development partnership agreement designed to create a free-trade zone. They set out to abolish barriers to trade, investment, and labour mobility. They also have concrete plans to cooperate further on trade, investments promotion, innovation, and joint purchasing agreements. It is important to underline that the New West Partnership Trade Agreement establishes obligations binding the three parties and outlines, in specific terms, the machinery that will be implementing the various initiatives.[63] It is revealing that three of the strongest provincial economies have sufficient self-confidence to pursue co-operation in economic development, while three of the weakest do not. It makes the point once again that attitudes and the people factor matter in economic development, and more is said about this below.

LOOKING BACK

The idea of uniting the three Maritime provinces is older than Canada, and it remains an idea that refuses to die. It resurfaces every decade or so, particularly when a national unity or fiscal crisis is on the horizon. The most recent attempt was by three Maritime senators in November 2012, one from each province.[64] The attempt again went nowhere.

It appears many proponents of political and administrative union of the three Maritime provinces have thrown in the towel. Much like tigers do not part easily with their stripes, as the saying goes, provincial premiers and provincial bureaucracies, for the most part, see no merit in a political union. If it is not possible to get leadership from key community leaders, then it is unlikely solid progress can be made. Ottawa, meanwhile, has essentially stayed on the sidelines, unwilling to play a leadership role on the issue. In fact, it has (unwittingly or not) often done the opposite, putting in place policies, programs, and organizations—particularly in regional development and other fields—that promote a provincial perspective.

Premiers and their senior officials much prefer talking about co-operation than political union. But even here progress has been halting. Where the three premiers, and now four under the Council of Atlantic Premiers, have been successful is in coordinating their effort to take aim at federal government policies. But that is the easy part. Success has been elusive when it comes to restructuring provincial programs to promote close interprovincial co-operation, promoting economic development, or streamlining existing government programs to capture savings.

The culprit? We are all to blame. In the end, we can all share blame for a lack of progress in promoting regional co-operation. Ottawa could have done much more through its economic development policies and the work of Crown corporations and line departments. Provincial premiers could have shown more leadership in Maritime co-operation. We Maritimers could have asked our political leaders and governments to do more. Our political institutions are also responsible. The federal and provincial governments have a national and provincial focus. Donald Smiley pointed to the Senate to explain why the "federal government is unrepresentative of Canada's regional diversities" and why "provincial government assumes the almost exclusive franchise of speaking for regional interests."[65] The regional perspective has no political home in Canada's national political and administrative institutions, and therein lies the problem.

The flaw in Canada's constitution is that the federal government does not provide "an adequate channel for territorial demands," either in Parliament or in the executive in Ottawa. Provincial premiers have filled the vacuum as the spokespersons for territorial demands at the national level, because someone has to fill the void. The result is that we have strong executives—or governing from the centre—at both levels of government, which promotes government-to-government relations. No one inside the two executives is able to articulate an "imagined" regional community like the Maritime region.[66]

NOTES

1 David M. Cameron, "Regional Integration in the Maritime Provinces," *Canadian Journal of Political Science* 4, no. 1 (March 1971): 24.
2 J. Murray Beck, "The Maritimes: A Region or Three Provinces?," Royal Society of Canada, *Transactions* 4, no. 15 (1977): 313.
3 James G. March and Johan P. Olsen, "The New Institutionalism: Organizational Factors in Political Life," *American Political Science Review* 78, no. 3 (1984): 735; and B. Guy Peters and Jon Pierre, "Institutions and Time: Problems of Conceptualization and Explanation," *Journal of Public Administration Research and Theory* 8, no. 4 (1998): 567.
4 Flanagan, "The Political Union Debate in Canada's Maritime Provinces," 39.
5 MacLauchlan, *Alex B. Campbell.*
6 Ralph Surette, "Atlantic Progressive Image New Twist in Unity Debate," *Globe and Mail,* March 17, 1977, 8.
7 Quoted in "The Hunt for Economic Union," *Commercial News* (Bedford, NS), April 1991, 19.
8 "Premier Robert Ghiz Says Maritime Union Would Be a Mistake," *The Guardian,* January 26, 2013, 1.
9 Quoted in "Atlantic Union Suggested," in *Chronicle-Herald* (Halifax), September 2, 1964, 1.
10 New Brunswick, "Proposal Regarding the Political Union of the Atlantic Provinces Submitted to the Atlantic Premiers Conference" (September 1964), 1.
11 Ibid., 3.
12 Quoted in notes for an opening address by Honourable Hugh John Flemming, Premier of New Brunswick, at the Atlantic Premier's Conference held in Fredericton, July 9, 1956, 4.
13 Ibid.
14 Quoted in Paul H. Evans, *Report on Atlantic/Maritime Interprovincial Cooperation between 1950 and 1971* (Halifax: Council of Maritime Premiers, 1985), 2.
15 *The Report of the Maritime Union Study* (Fredericton: Queen's Printer, 1970), 1.
16 Evans, *Report on Atlantic/Maritime Interprovincial Cooperation*, 94.
17 Ibid., chap. 3.
18 *Report of the Maritime Union Study*, 2–3.
19 Ibid., see appendix A.
20 Ibid., 108–9.
21 Ibid., 9.

22 Ibid., 66–67.
23 Ibid., 75.
24 Ibid., 76.
25 Ibid., 77.
26 Ibid.
27 Ibid., 79.
28 Notes for an address by Fred Drummie to the annual meeting of the Institute of Public Administration of Canada, Halifax, September 13, 1976, 2.
29 See "Premiers Accept Three Union Study Proposals," in *Chronicle-Herald* (Halifax), January 27, 1971, 1.
30 See, for example, Council of Maritime Premiers, "The Future of Maritime Cooperation" (news release, June 2, 1981).
31 See "The Record of Cooperation in the Maritimes" (notes for remarks by Emery M. Fanjoy to the conference "Regional Cooperation in the Maritimes: The Recent Issues and Prospects," Halifax, April 21, 1981). It is also important to note there are now over two hundred regionally funded post-secondary programs, including a common medical school, a dental school, and a forest technology school, among others.
32 See, for example, MacLauchlan, *Alex B. Campbell*, 232.
33 See, for example, Savoie, *Court Government and the Collapse of Accountability*.
34 Beck, "The Maritimes: A Region or Three Provinces?," 311.
35 Flanagan, "The Political Union Debate in Canada's Maritime Provinces," 214.
36 "Premiers Committed to Regional Cooperation?" (Council of Maritime Premiers, news release, October 27, 1999).
37 Council of Atlantic Premiers, "Establishment of Council of Atlantic Premiers" (Halifax, May 15, 2000).
38 Consultations with a former official with the Council of Maritime Premiers, Moncton, May 18, 2004.
39 Consultations with an official with the Council of Atlantic Premiers, Moncton and Halifax, May 17, 2004.
40 Council of Atlantic Premiers, "Establishment of Council of Atlantic Premiers."
41 Ibid., 2.
42 Interprovincial co-operation was a great deal easier when there were only the three Maritime provinces involved. See, for example, Emery M. Fanjoy, "The Record of Cooperation in the Maritimes" (remarks to the Conference on Regional Cooperation in the Maritimes: The Record, Issues and Prospects, Halifax, April 21, 1981).
43 See Backgrounder, in ibid., 3–4.
44 Council of Atlantic Premiers, "CAP Initiatives," (Halifax, n.d.), 1.
45 "Atlantic Premiers Discuss Equalization" (Council of Atlantic Premiers, news release, December 4, 2000).
46 Quoted in "Is Newfoundland Part of the Maritime Family?," *Chronicle-Herald* (Halifax), May 23, 1991, A2.

47 Quoted in "Newfoundland's Role in Maritime Union Key Item for Talks," in *Evening Telegram* (St. John's, NL), May 22, 1991, 1.

48 "A Boat to Miss?," *Evening Telegram* (St. John's, NL), May 26, 1991, 4.

49 See www.cap.cpma.ca (site discontinued).

50 "New Brunswick and Nova Scotia to Cooperate on New Office," (Government of New Brunswick news release, March 24, 2015).

51 "Prince Edward Island Joins Regional Office (news release, July 22, 2015), www2.gnb.ca.

52 *Atlantic Premiers Advance Agenda for Sustainable Growth in the Region* (Halifax: Council of Atlantic Premiers' meeting communiqué, June 28, 2015).

53 Donald J. Savoie, "Interprovincial Cooperation in the Maritime Provinces: The Case of Electricity" (Moncton: CIRRD, 1991), 8.

54 Donald J. Savoie, *Federal-Provincial Collaborations: The Canada–New Brunswick General Development Agreement* (Montreal and Kingston: McGill-Queen's University Press, 1981), chap. 9.

55 Michael J. L. Kirby, "Regional Cooperation: The View from Ottawa" (remarks to the Conference on Regional Cooperation in the Maritimes, Halifax, April 21–22, 1981), 19–20.

56 Ibid., 21.

57 Beck, "The Maritimes: A Region or Three Provinces?," 313.

58 Savoie, *Visiting Grandchildren*, 211.

59 Quoted in Mika Rekai, "Maritime Union an Unwelcome Proposal," *Maclean's*, December 9, 2012, www.macleans.ca/news/canada/an-unwelcome-proposal/.

60 An address by the premier of Nova Scotia to the twenty-fourth annual conference of the Institute of Public Administration of Canada, Fredericton, NB, September 5–7, 1972.

61 Ibid.

62 Quoted in Flanagan, "The Political Union Debate in Canada's Maritime Provinces," 214.

63 "New West Partnership," April 30, 2010, http://www.newwestpartnershiptrade.ca/.

64 The three senators were Stephen Greene from Nova Scotia, John Wallace from New Brunswick, and Mike Duffy from Prince Edward Island. See Tim Harper, "Senators Revive Maritime Union Proposal, thestar.com, November 30, 2012, www.thestar.com/news/canada/2012/11/30/senators_revive_maritime_union_proposal.html.

65 Donald Smiley, *An Elected Senate for Canada, Clues from the Australian Experience* (discussion paper, Institute of Intergovernmental Relations, 1985), 21.

66 James Bickerton, "Seeking New Autonomies: State Rescaling, Reterritorialization and Minority Identities in Atlantic Canada" (paper presented to annual meeting of the Canadian Political Science Association, Concordia University, Montreal, June 1–3, 2010. 1–7), accessed October 19, 2015, www.cpsa-acsp.ca/papers-2010/Bickerton.pdf.

Chapter 11

SO, WHO IS TO BLAME?

Given the findings of earlier chapters about the Chignecto Canal, National Policy (circa 1878), decisions tied to developing Canada's war effort, the chosen location of Ottawa's visionary investments, the concentration of power in the hands of the prime minister (who has to look to the more populous provinces to gain and secure power not counter-balanced by an upper house in Parliament and the clustering of senior public servants in the NCR), one can easily understand why many Maritimers would point to Ottawa and say, "You are to blame, end of the story." Maritimers know that what can happen along the St. Lawrence Seaway and between Quebec City and Windsor, Ontario, is considered in Ottawa "of national importance," but what happens in their own region is deemed regional and, consequently, of less importance. The Senate—the one institution that should bring balance between provincial power produced by rep by pop and the smaller provinces—has never been a credible actor. Contrary to advantages in the Quebec-Montreal-Ottawa and Toronto corridor, Maritimers have to consistently pull against gravity to generate economic activities.

How does one answer Galbraith's question? Who, or what, is to blame for the region's relative underdevelopment? Certainly, Ottawa and national policies have to shoulder some of the blame. But they are not solely responsible. Geography, natural resources, and our urban-rural structure also matter, and we Maritimers also need to look in the mirror, as I've discussed. Though it would simplify things for many Maritimers, we cannot answer Galbraith's question simply by pointing to Ottawa. Just as other Canadians telling Maritimers to pull themselves up by their bootstraps absolves them of any responsibility, Maritimers insisting the national government and national policies are responsible for their region's underdevelopment also absolves them of responsibility for their region's struggles.

In this chapter, I seek to assign blame for my region's underdevelopment. It is necessary to bring closure to this debate for several reasons. In economic development, the blame game offers nothing to the Maritime provinces. We can keep on blaming national policies, but no one where it matters is listening, and with the region losing political clout in a federation that relies solely on representation by population to decide who holds political power in Ottawa, the blame game is fast losing currency. A more competitive and globally integrated economy is also pushing the blame game to the sideline. In short, there is no longer any market for the blame game and we need to put it to rest. But, before we do, it is equally important for both Maritimers and Canadians to understand one of the most significant reasons for the region's economic woes.

One can also easily appreciate why "national" politicians, Ottawa-based officials, and the national media would focus on what matters in Ontario and Quebec, and now, increasingly, Alberta and British Columbia, the latter given their growing economic and political importance. Canadian politics is all about winning. The overriding goal of all party leaders and their advisors is to win power, and good politics does not always equate with good public policy. The observation of a sitting Member of Parliament in a planning session leading up to the 2011 election campaign sums it up well: "If we have to keep our promises, it means we won."[1]

National politicians understand better than anyone that to win power you promise what you need to and focus on regions with the most seats and, once in power, look after those who brought you there. A combination of geography and national policies have concentrated Canada's economic strength in a narrow corridor between Quebec City, Montreal, Ottawa, Toronto, and Windsor. The country's political, bureaucratic, media, and economic elites are also concentrated in this corridor. This is where Canada's political, bureaucratic, and economic gravity begins.

As I have discussed, the three Maritime provinces are not much of a factor in Canadian politics. A national political leader and accompanying advisors no longer need to concentrate much of their efforts on any of the three Maritime provinces, or the region as a whole, to gain and retain power. Even senior Maritime politicians on the government side are now openly telling their constituents that the Maritime region needs to understand it is fast losing political clout in Ottawa.[2]

Justin Trudeau's cabinet also reflects this trend. The Maritime provinces gained three Cabinet ministers with portfolios of limited influence (i.e., the Treasury Board, Fisheries and Oceans, and Agriculture and Agri-Food), Quebec gained six, and Ontario eleven. Ontario secured all the key economic development portfolios (i.e., Finance, Innovation, Science and Economic Development—to which ACOA reports—Indigenous and Northern Affairs, Small Business and Tourism, International Trade, Immigration, Refugees and Citizenship). Recall that Trudeau's political party won every seat in the Maritime provinces in the 2015 election, the first time in history any political party was able to do so.

I also note that Trudeau's transition team consisted of four Ontario-based individuals.[3] The role of transition teams is to assist incoming prime ministers in assuming power, including providing advice on Cabinet-making, new policy initiatives, and machinery of government issues.[4] It was the Trudeau transition team that recommended against appointing a minister from Atlantic Canada to be responsible for ACOA and having all regional agencies report through a line department traditionally preoccupied with the economic interest of Central Canada.

All key actors in the Prime Minister's Office are also Ontario-based individuals with ties to the Ontario government. Justin Trudeau's chief of staff worked at Queen's Park, as did his principal secretary. This is true "going down the line." The national media pointed to the lack of francophone representation in the PMO, with only one Quebec official holding a mid-level position. Nothing was said about having the absence of representation from the Maritime provinces or Atlantic Canada in the PMO.[5] Chiefs of staff to ministers occupy an important place in Ottawa's political circles. They are often the link between these ministers, the line departments, and central agencies, notably the Prime Minister's Office, which has the final say in the chief of staff appointment process. Chiefs of staff in the Justin Trudeau government are from Ontario, Quebec, and Western Canada—only one from the thirty-one total is from the Atlantic provinces. I know that Ontario ministers were able to secure their chiefs of staff from their province, but not so with any of the three Maritime cabinet ministers.[6]

Chiefs of staff are politically partisan, and they look after the political interests of their ministers and the government as a whole. As mentioned, the political interest of the government is tied to vote-rich Ontario and Quebec. My own experience in government suggests that political and policy actors bring conscious and unconscious bias to their work, and where you come from matters.

The Justin Trudeau government also announced that the former head of Ontario government-supported think tank Mowat Centre would join the Privy Council Office as deputy secretary of the Cabinet responsible for results and delivery.[7] He will be working with an Ontario-Quebec centric public service with virtually all of its policy-advising capacity located in the NCR. All are linked to Parliament which, in turn, is guided solely by rep by pop with a largely discredited upper house unable to speak with any authority on behalf of regions.

Ottawa-based senior public servants view the country in national aggregates and, increasingly, in a global setting. Their concern is the health of the "national" economy, the highly competitive nature of the global economy, the government's fiscal health, and the state of public service. Ottawa-based officials took great pride in having played a key role in managing the war effort and in turning Canada into the world's second largest defence production exporter, after the United States.[8] Their efforts were deliberately concentrated in the narrow Quebec-Windsor corridor, where the country's political and bureaucratic powers are concentrated. In many ways, it made their efforts easier, knowing the political power of the day would agree.

The rise of court government and its courtiers has made Ottawa even more Ottawa-centric than in years past. Peter Aucoin wrote about the tendency of senior public servants in Ottawa to demonstrate "enthusiasm" for the government's agenda. This as a tactic to advance their careers or in the mistaken notion that neutral public servants should all be, as one British scholar observed, "promiscuously partisan," that is, partisan to the government but quite willing to change when a different party takes power.[9] All to say that in the era of court government, senior public servants are increasingly seen supporting the government's agenda, which is tied to political power and the exercise of gaining it and securing it.

The national media will want to speak to a national agenda. No one in the national media (with most of their columnists located in Ottawa) highlighted the fact that the Ottawa-based public service is growing at the expense of the regions. We saw earlier that the national media tend to stereotype the Maritimes, projecting an image of a region that is patronage ridden and economically dependent, unable to properly manage its natural resources such as the fishery. The media will not ask why this state of affairs persists or why much of Canada's fishery policy is struck in the Langevin Block, which houses both PMO and PCO, and in the head office of the Department of Fisheries and Oceans on Kent Street in downtown Ottawa—both far from the country's fishing grounds.

No one in Ottawa, it seems, speaks with any influence for the Maritime provinces. Strong, powerful regional ministers have become a thing of the past since governing from the centre became *de rigueur* in Ottawa. Justin Trudeau did away with regional ministers altogether. The local or regional media are largely ignored. Provincial premiers do speak to the interests of their provinces but to whom? Ontario, Quebec, and Alberta premiers may be heard by the national media and by the prime minister, but not so for the premiers of three small provinces. Federal-provincial conferences of First Ministers have lost their appeal, but even when they are held, their focus is on national unity and national financial or economic issues, rarely, if ever, on regional economic development.

Maritimers will always be able to point the finger at Ottawa and national policies when assigning blame for their region's relative underdevelopment, so long as the country relies solely on rep by pop to establish political power at the national level. Politicians who want to win power—and most do—will "care" more for regions that can bring them power than for those at the margin. The Maritime provinces were shunted to the margin shortly after Canada was born. It did not take long for understandings struck in the negotiations leading to Confederation, such as a commitment to see the Maritimes hold one-third of the Cabinet and the notion that the region would be the arbiter between the interests of Ontario and Quebec, to become meaningless.

PARTITIONING BLAME: THE STATE

As noted, if we have learned anything about economic development, it is that the state will never stand by and let market forces run the day. This is as true in Canada as it is elsewhere. As we saw earlier, from the day it was born the government of Canada has had a direct hand in promoting economic development.

Though there is no market left for the argument, particularly outside of the region, I continue to argue that the federal government holds some responsibility for the Maritime's underdevelopment.[10] As we know, the Maritime region had a thriving economy before Confederation. It had natural advantages in the production of fish, coal, lumber, and shipbuilding. It also had strong exports. At the time of Confederation, at least some believed the Maritime provinces would actually become the centre of Canada's manufacturing sector because of its natural resources and its proximity to markets in Europe, the West Indies, and the eastern seaboard of the United States. This even appeared to be the case in the 1880s, with employment and production in the manufacturing sector at more than double what it was in 1870. In New Brunswick alone, growth in both employment and production increased by 40 per cent between 1870 and the 1880s.[11]

Given the deteriorating state of the Maritime economy since the 1890s, one can easily appreciate why Maritimers would point the finger at the federal government, and in particular at National Policy, for their region's relative underdevelopment. During the 1880s the impact of the National Policy began to be felt. We know that population growth in the region, for example, began to slow by the 1880s, about the same time as the National Policy started to have an impact. Population growth from 1881 to 1891 grew by only 1.1 per cent, and then only by 1.5 per cent between 1891 and 1901.[12]

Certainly, our national political institutions have a lot to answer for when it comes to how they operate and decide. Virtually from the day Canada was born, the Maritime region has not been able to give voice to its economic interests in the country's national political institutions, as I have pointed out time and again in this book. This is in sharp contrast to Ontario and Quebec. The western provinces, meanwhile, were strong proponents of a Triple-E Senate, until they gained both economic and political clout. The argument that provincial premiers can play the role the Senate ought to perform in support of the regions is a nonstarter. Yet, it is increasingly heard. Saskatchewan premier Brad Wall, for one, maintained, "The Senate was to be a voice for the regions, specifically the provinces. We have that without the Senate, constitutionally known as the provinces."[13]

Wall's argument does not hold water, as Montreal mayor Denis Coderre made clear. Wall pressed Coderre to support the Energy East Pipeline, suggesting it was in the interest of the national economy. Coderre dismissed Wall's position out of hand by saying metropolitan Montreal has a population of 4 million, Saskatchewan has 1.1 million—end of story.[14] No mayor or elected politician from a large city or state within a federation having an effective upper house would likely make this argument. In any event, there would be an important component in the country's national political institution to challenge the mayor's view.

Wall and others of like mind have also never answered why other federations, like the United States, Australia, Russia, India, and Germany, have incorporated into their national political institutions a strong political capacity to speak to the regional perspective. They also have not answered Donald Smiley's call for a capacity in national political institutions to accommodate the requirements of intrastate federalism. Without such a voice where policy decisions are actually struck and legislation is drafted and passed, the smaller regions will always be on the outside looking in as national policies take shape.

Over the years, the executive has had a relatively free hand to strike decisions favourable to the economic interests of Ontario and Quebec. As we have seen, this was the case for the railways and canals; for the concentration of virtually all investments in the war effort and of R&D spending in Central Canada; for the concentration of the federal public service in the NCR; for initiatives inside a government department to document government spending (not only by region but also by category) getting killed before they get off the ground; and the list goes on. It is worth stressing that there is no legitimate political body to bring a regional perspective to bear on how policies and major initiatives are struck.

Provincial premiers are not part of national political institutions and have little, if any, influence on the machinery of government in Ottawa. Premiers can be ignored and most times they are, particularly those representing small provinces. It is up to the federal government, specifically the prime minister, not provincial ministers, to call a First Ministers' Conference. Stephen Harper did not call a meeting for several years between 2009 and 2015. The federal government, not provincial premiers, sets national policies, establishes national programs, and defines national economic strategies with, or without, consulting provincial governments.

Where were the provincial premiers when Ottawa decided to transfer, by stealth, more and more public servants from the regions to the NCR? Recall that some thirty-five years ago, 27 per cent of federal public servants worked in the NCR while today the number is 43 per cent. Where were the provincial premiers when Ottawa's program review exercises cut spending disproportionally in the regions, despite senior federal politicians insisting they would not? The federal government created 18,700 public service jobs in Ottawa and eliminated 15,200 in the regions between 2006 and 2015.[15] Where were the provincial premiers when tax incentive policies were designed in the Department of Finance in Ottawa? Where were the provincial premiers when the PCO instructed DREE to stop working on a regional breakdown of federal spending by function? Where was the premier of Manitoba when Ottawa decided to award the CF-18 maintenance contract to a Montreal firm, though a Winnipeg firm had the lowest bid? I can add to the list.

In all the above cases, the premiers were thousands of kilometres away from Ottawa, working on their own priorities, dealing with their own political challenges, and coping with the details of the day. The federal government's machinery is not in the business of telegraphing to provincial premiers what it is working on. Provincial premiers do not have privileged access to the proposals public servants are developing or to discussions in Cabinet committees, Cabinet itself, and the Prime Minister's Office. As one federal government deputy minister observed, "He who controls the first draft of a policy proposal often controls policy."[16] When it comes to influencing national policies and programs, it is no exaggeration to contend that premiers are at their best when issuing press releases suggesting the federal government is not doing enough for their provinces. These press releases may serve a political purpose back home, but they have very little influence in Ottawa.

As mentioned earlier, in the past, the Maritimes were able to secure the odd "breakaway." The motive was political. I am thinking here of Mulroney's decision to establish ACOA one year before a general election or Chrétien's decision in June 2001 to establish a new Atlantic Investment Fund five months before a general election. Even as recently as twenty years ago, the region mattered more politically than it does today. As noted, more new seats were added for the 2015 general election in Ontario, Quebec, and western Canada than the combined total of seats in the three

Maritime provinces. Breakaways are fast becoming a thing of the past. The region is losing whatever political clout it had during the Maritime Rights Movement and when powerful regional ministers mattered in Ottawa. The region does not have much of a political counterweight to the concentration of political power in Ottawa.

All to say Ottawa and national policies explain, in part, the Maritimes' relative underdevelopment. In future, the region is likely to secure less attention and even less favourable policies and will have to deal as best it can with national political institutions that are not designed to accommodate regional circumstances. This will have a profound impact not only on economic development, but also on the quality of public service. The signs are there, including the recent government decision to calculate federal transfers on a per capita basis, which assumes that all regions have similar demographic challenges.

There are important lessons for the region. It is not—and never has been—in the region's economic interest to have a strong central government. From the day Canada was born, whenever the federal government has intervened to promote economic development, it has favoured Ontario and, albeit to a lesser extent, Quebec and left the Maritime provinces on the outside looking in. Maritimers bought into the argument for a strong central government, thinking it was part of a bargain that gave Ottawa a free hand to decide where wealth was to be created in return for a distribution of some of the wealth to sustain a level of public service somewhat comparable between regions. As Luke Flanagan pointed out, the objective of the three Maritime provinces in the 1950s was to "make the region more dependent on the federal government so that they could develop their public service."[17] Even that bargain no longer holds. Moreover, when the bargain was in place, transfer payments to provincial governments and individuals in the Maritime region were hardly the way to promote economic development.

National economic development policies, visionary investments, and tariffs have strengthened the economy of Central Canada while inhibiting economic development in the three Maritime provinces. There has never been an effective voice in Ottawa to speak on behalf of the economic interests of the Maritime region. The Maritimes have been left to rely on a small contingency of MPs from the region and a handful of ministers (a far cry from the one-third of Cabinet that was promised at Confederation) to articulate the region's economic interests and influence national policies. They now matter even less in a government dominated by the prime minister and carefully selected advisors. In a federation like Canada, which combines a Westminster-style Parliament system with a dominant executive, this scenario has come to matter more and more as the region continues to lose population and as political power continues to shift away from the region. This, combined with a complete reliance on rep by pop to decide who holds power and how to shape public policy, constitutes the fundamental flaw in Canada's constitution. This flaw answers, but only in part, Galbraith's question.

OTTAWA IS NOT SOLELY TO BLAME

Problems in the economy of the Maritime provinces began to surface before Confederation. The region began to bleed population to other regions by the 1860s, a development that has continued to this day. By 1881 some 100,000 individuals born in the Maritime provinces had moved to the United States. Between 1881 and 1890 the flow of out-migration to the United States continued, and the out-migration tide to other regions in Canada began. Canada's two central provinces and the western region saw a sharp increase in population in relation to the Maritime region starting in the 1880s.[18]

Several powerful forces came together around Confederation that had a negative impact on the economy of the Maritime provinces. First, the sea and sail era was fading fast. Prosperity in many communities throughout the region was evident in the shipbuilding boom across the Maritimes. The region had plenty of wood, easy access to excellent harbours, and a skilled workforce—all key ingredients for a thriving industry. Demand was strong for well-crafted sailing ships, and even small communities from St. Martins, New Brunswick, to Pictou County, Nova Scotia, had their own shipbuilding industry.

The region was a world leader in the shipping industry of its day. Samuel Cunard launched his business in Nova Scotia. Indeed, both shipbuilders and shipowners prospered, as investments continued to pour into the region. The industry was highly competitive, with regional businesses able to build ships between $25 and $40 per ton, which compared favourably with any other region.[19] Their products sold both locally and in the export market, particularly in the eastern seaboard of the United States and Britain. But the industry was about to come to a screeching halt, and Confederation would not be to blame.

Isambard K. Brunel's invention in shipbuilding would revolutionize the industry, and the Maritime region would pay a heavy price. In 1845 Brunel designed the first iron-hulled propeller-driven ship to cross the Atlantic Ocean. He later designed a larger ship capable of moving goods to Australia and India much more efficiently than wooden sailing ships.[20] Slowly but surely the shift away from wooden sailing ships was underway. The heyday of the Golden Age of Sail was at an end by the 1880s; the transition would be particularly challenging in the Maritime region.[21]

But that was not all. The United States ended its reciprocity treaty with the British North American colonies in 1866. Maritimers can point their finger only at Washington for this, not Sir John A. Macdonald or other Fathers of Confederation. It was the United States that killed the treaty, convinced that Britain and its colonies had sided with the Southern Confederacy. The colonies, including the Maritime colonies, began the search for new markets. At the time, uniting the British North American colonies made economic sense to everyone, because there were few other opportunities for new markets. It would lay the groundwork for a transcontinental economy and market and the construction of a national railway system. Sir John A. Macdonald's dream to see a Canada that would stretch from sea to sea would, above all, serve to strengthen the transcontinental market. The Prairie provinces, rich in agricultural land, would be able to supply an easily accessible market in other Canadian regions.

The emerging transcontinental market defined by geography also favoured producers in Central Canada. Again, Ontario and Quebec saw no alternative to the transcontinental market with the collapse of the US reciprocity trade agreement. S. A. Saunders summed it up best: "The prospects that Confederation would provide a large market were brighter for the people of the colony of Canada than they were for the people of the colonies by the sea."[22] In short, geography conspired against the Maritimes, and Canada's political institutions only made things worse for the region.

Would the Maritime provinces have prospered more if they had continued with their traditional economic relationship with Britain, the United States, and the West Indies? Would the region have been better off with a political and economic union with the United States rather than sign on to the Canadian confederation? One can easily deal with the first question: Britain was four squares behind a union of the British North American colonies and had little interest in maintaining the status quo. The decision, in many ways, belonged to Britain, not to the Maritime provinces. Indeed, we saw earlier that Britain made it clear, in both subtle and blatant ways, it strongly favoured a political union of the colonies as a way to lessen its financial commitment.

Would the Maritime provinces be better off economically had they joined the United States? We will never know. Certainly, the political institutions in the United States are better able to accommodate regional circumstances than Canada's institutions. Power derived from rep by pop in the United States is counterbalanced in several ways, notably by a Triple-E Senate. The country's economic and political elites also come from many regions, and no state or region dominates the federation. Unlike Canada, there are major urban centres in the regions that serve to spread political power around the country—New York, Chicago, Atlanta, Miami, Los Angeles, and Houston, among others. One can speculate that Halifax would have become a major US naval facility and that the World War Two efforts would have been spread more evenly, given the work of the US Senate.

It is also unlikely that the Maritime provinces would be as dependent on transfers from the federal government had they joined the United States. Transfer payments are not nearly as valued as tools of public policy in the United States as they are in Canada. Federal transfers to the Maritime provinces, however, have come in the form of guilt money from Ottawa or compensation for the impact of National Policy and national initiatives on slow-growth regions. In some ways, it is the price Ottawa has had to pay to enable it to establish the circumstances for economic success in vote-rich Ontario and Quebec.

Of course, Britain wanted a union of North American colonies, but the colonies, including the Maritime provinces, were in no mood to join the United States. The collapse of the reciprocity treaty with the Americans, the Fenian raids on the Maine-New Brunswick and Canada West borders, and deep political ties with Britain all precluded political or commercial union with the Americans. S. A. Saunders explained, "The colonies had a common allegiance, in that they were British.... The likelihood of union with the United States seems now to have been remote, except through conquest. The possibility of conquest by the United States helped to quicken and strengthen the feeling of unity among the colonies."[23] In essence, joining the United States was not on anyone's agenda, including the Maritime colonies.

THE REGION'S ECONOMIC SECTORS AT CONFEDERATION IN THE BRITISH NORTH AMERICAN COLONIES

The Maritime provinces had their own problems and challenges at the time of Confederation, some of them self-inflicted, some not. Key economic sectors did not hold sufficient comparative advantages to compete with Central Canada, and the emerging transcontinental market served to worsen matters.

In the years leading to Confederation, the economy of the Maritimes was built on the export of a few staples. Four sectors underpinned the region's economy at that time: lumbering, farming, fishing, and mining. Fish were important to Nova Scotia, forest products to New Brunswick, and some agricultural products to both colonies. Prince Edward Island did not focus on the export market, but when it did, it looked to shipbuilding and agriculture.[24] All these sectors, however, were confronting important challenges at the time.

The forestry sector, concentrated in New Brunswick, had been mismanaged from the very beginning by Europeans with indiscriminate cutting of the most desirable timber. W. S. MacNutt provides an excellent account in his *New Brunswick, A History 1784–1867* of how *not* to manage the forestry sector, which is precisely how New Brunswick managed it during the nineteenth century. He explains that there was too much cutting of timber, in particular of the species most in demand. The goal was not to manage the sector but rather to exploit it as quickly as possible, looking to maximize profit over the shortest period possible.[25] First come, first served, cut what you can, and maximize profits in the short term in an unregulated market sum up how things worked for everyone in the province's key economic sector.

As the wood shipbuilding industry peaked in 1864, there was no emerging industry on the horizon to take its place. Forest products went mostly to Britain and fish and forest products to the West Indies and the United States. Potential for growth in the forestry sector at the time of Confederation was limited.

The agricultural sector essentially enabled early settlers to own land and feed their families, which suited the times. Agriculture would never hold the same economic promise in the Maritime provinces that it did, and still does, in the other regions. The problem is a scarcity of arable land. Where there is fertile arable land, the plots are small and widely scattered.[26] The opening of the West also had a profound impact on the agricultural sector. A number of Maritimers, notably agriculturists, either sold or abandoned their farms to claim better land in the Prairies and British Columbia. It was not long, for example, before British Columbia apples captured market share in both the Prairies and Central Canada and away from Nova Scotia growers.[27] Saskatchewan is home to some 40 per cent of Canada's farmlands.[28] Maritimers cannot blame Confederation or national political institutions for this.

Agriculture in the Maritime provinces also had to compete with other sectors, notably forestry and the fishery, which offered better prospects for a quick financial return. Historian Robert Cooney became convinced that the economic future of the colony was threatened by too much attention paid to lumbering and not enough to agriculture. He offered this advice to New Brunswickers, "Lumber moderately, fish vigorously and farm steadily."[29] The advice was not heard, in part because the province's agricultural sector held only limited opportunities.

Good agricultural land in the region remains concentrated in small scattered plots along the St. John River Valley in New Brunswick and across the northern part of Nova Scotia. Prince Edward Island has some excellent agricultural land but has a small surface area of only 5,700 square kilometres, making it only Canada's twenty-third largest island. The region's limited arable land has in turn inhibited innovation in the agricultural sector and the adaptation of new equipment. Indeed, for a long time, farming in our region was limited to family-owned self-sufficient farms. To sum up the main challenge, the agricultural soils of the Maritime provinces are not fertile when compared with the rich agricultural soils of Western Canada and parts of Ontario and Quebec, and thus, offer limited opportunities.[30]

The region's potato industry, however, till holds a comparative advantage. The United States and the Caribbean markets have been important export markets for Maritime potatoes, going back 150 years. Even this sector has faced challenges that have little to do with Confederation. For example, the United States' decision to kill the reciprocity treaty with the British colonies to the north added a tariff of fifteen to twenty-five cents per bushel of potatoes.[31] This forced producers to search for new markets in places like Cuba, but the new markets could never replace the rich US market.

The fishery sector lured early Europeans settlers to the Maritime region: first the French, then the English, Scottish, and Irish settled in communities near the shoreline to fish and farm. It seems that every "creek and cove" along the shore had an abundance of cod.[32] Leaving aside British Columbia and Newfoundland and Labrador, the fishery sector essentially belongs to the Maritime provinces; however, the sector has been plagued by two problems. On one hand, we can point the finger at Maritimers and, on the other, at the federal government. Maritime fishers overfished a number of species, and for this they have no one to blame but themselves. There is also a consensus that the federal government has not been able to manage the fishery well. A review of the fishery by a parliamentary committee made a stark conclusion— "In our view, the major factor was clearly mismanagement"— and pointed the finger at the federal government.[33]

For a long time, the region's fishery was populated by small fishing establishments that saw little merit in innovation. They also found new equipment too costly to acquire and operate.[34] Contrary to British Columbia, the fishery sector in the Maritimes is spread around small, relatively isolated communities. From the very beginning, the region's fishing industry showed a strong tendency to decentralization. The region's many natural ports favoured a decentralized fishery without imposing a fiscal burden on governments to build elaborate infrastructure facilities. However, fishers operating in small, relatively isolated communities with limited transportation facilities did not keep up with new technology and processing facilities to incorporate more value-added products and pursue markets outside their own and neighbouring communities.

The region's coal, iron, and steel industry was slow to mature, but mature it did by the early 1900s. At one point, one employee in five in Nova Scotia worked in the coal and coal-related industries.[35] Nova Scotia, and to a much lesser extent New Brunswick, had large coal deposits with easy access to deep-water ports. The region's development of the iron and steel industry grew in tandem with railway construction.[36]

The coal industry ran into difficulties with the development of fossil fuels and hydroelectric power. In addition, new blast furnaces built in the United States were designed to burn American coal, which made it difficult for the coal industry in the Maritimes to compete. In time, the region's iron and steel industry lost its competitive edge to other jurisdictions. Transportation was an issue but so were tariffs imposed by Ottawa. We know that Ottawa-imposed tariffs had a highly negative impact on Cape Breton's mining industry at a critical moment in its development but served to strengthen that in Ontario.[37] We also saw earlier that during the war years, C. D. Howe helped the two Ontario-based steel plants with government subsidies and let DOSCO, in the Maritimes, wither away without support.

However difficult it may be to see today, there was a widespread belief in some quarters at the time of Confederation that the Maritime provinces would become the manufacturing centre of Canada. We saw earlier this belief held until the 1880s. Employment and productivity increased twofold in the manufacturing sector in the early years after Confederation. During this period, the region saw business start-ups and business expansions in sawmills, textiles, and metalworking and held its own with other regions.[38]

Things became considerably more difficult for the region's manufacturing sector by the turn of the century, so that by 1935 employment in the manufacturing sector in both Nova Scotia and New Brunswick was about half of what it had been in 1890.[39] A good number of manufacturing businesses closed, not because of competition from within the region but because of competition from central Canadian manufacturers. The region's inability to keep pace with the manufacturing sector in Central Canada became even more evident after 1920.[40] Size of market, proximity to markets, and transportation costs came to matter a great deal more than they had in the early years after Confederation, and the Maritime region was at a disadvantage in all three factors.

Though I do not wish to minimize the importance of national policies and Ottawa's decision to concentrate its efforts to promote the manufacturing sector in Central Canada, it does not tell the complete story.[41] The country's infrastructure quite naturally favoured an east-west trade pattern. Investments in manufacturing logically migrated to areas that stood a better chance of success for economic development. Central Canada manufacturers were better positioned than those in the Maritimes to produce and sell goods to expanding markets in Western Canada, in addition to the growing markets in Central Canada.

As the manufacturing sector began to turn to consumer goods, from home furnishing to canned foods, proximity to markets became even more critical. Leaving aside the expanding markets to the West, Ontario and Quebec alone had almost four times the population the Maritime provinces had as early as 1871. When foreign investors, notably Americans, looked to establish branch plants in Canada, they looked to the regions that would generate the best return on investments. Firms producing consumer goods had every reason to locate in Central Canada because of its proximity to markets and lower transportation costs to access markets in both western and eastern Canada.

As observed on several occasions here, success breeds success in all things and this is particularly evident in economic development. For instance, Waterloo, Ontario, has become a breeding ground for successful start-ups in the IT sector. Waterloo made BlackBerry as much as BlackBerry made Waterloo. Though there are occasional breakaways, success in the IT sector rarely happens by chance. Geography matters.

The new economy did not deal well with the Maritime region's two liabilities—size and geography. Even more so than traditional industries, the new economy has an "inherent tendency toward geographical agglomeration."[42] An entrepreneur wishing to launch a new IT enterprise will have a better chance of success in Waterloo than in my home town of Bouctouche, New Brunswick. An entrepreneur will find in Waterloo, among other things, a leading university in the computer science field, a highly skilled workforce, and access to venture capital.

Who can Maritimers blame for this state of affairs? They can by no means blame University of Waterloo for developing a world-class computer science program or the entrepreneur looking to Waterloo to launch an IT business. Can Maritimers blame Ottawa and national policies for concentrating economic development efforts in the Montreal-Windsor corridor over the years? Can Maritimers blame geography for locating Waterloo in the middle of Canada and in the middle of the two most populous provinces? Yes, they can, but the blame game will not generate new economic activities in their region nor will it attenuate Waterloo's economic potential. The blame game may help Maritimers deflect some of the responsibility for their region's poor economic performance, but it will serve no other purpose.

MEA CULPA

There are things we do not do that also explain our region's underdevelopment. Much of it relates to culture or attitudes that have evolved over the years. The Maritime region has witnessed its share of failures over the last century and a half, and while there is some comfort in blaming others, whether it is the federal government or big businesses, for our region's economic woes, it does not tell the whole story. I argue that Maritimers cling to the status quo more than others. The region cries out for greater interprovincial co-operation in all sectors, particularly in economic development, but progress has been painfully slow. Maritimers—in particular the premiers—should be advocating Senate reform, but very little is said either because they fear losing the little influence they may have in Ottawa or because they want to remain in tune with their party leaders at the national level. Though they carry less political clout at the national level, Maritimers will continue to punish politicians who attempt to introduce change. Consider changes to the Employment Insurance program, which the majority of economists have long advocated. When a panel of Canada's leading social scientists came together to review it, they concluded the program is not as effective as it could be and has not kept pace with changes in the economy and the labour market.[43]

The Maritime region punished the Chrétien government in the 1997 election, after it had introduced changes to the EI program. Two senior cabinet ministers from the region and close associates to Chrétien, Doug Young and David Dingwall, went down to defeat.[44] Chrétien lost every seat in Nova Scotia and won only three in New Brunswick, where Chrétien's hand-picked candidate, Dominic LeBlanc, also went down to defeat. Four years earlier, Chrétien had won nine out of ten seats in New Brunswick and eleven out of eleven in Nova Scotia.

The Harper government introduced further changes to the Employment Insurance program in 2013. The changes met with stiff and vocal opposition, and the four Atlantic premiers responded by commissioning a review of the changes and their impact on their region. The review was not critical of the changes, essentially arguing that much of the fear concerning the changes arose from the way they were introduced. The problem, it seemed, was essentially one of communications, not substance. Still, the Conservative Party lost all constituencies in the Maritime provinces, including two Cabinet ministers who went down to defeat in the 2015 election. The region's then senior minister Peter MacKay had earlier decided not to run.

LOOKING BACK

The relative underdevelopment of the three Maritime provinces is due to geography, history, national policies produced by national political institutions that have a blind spot when it comes to incorporating the regional factor, misguided provincial government policies, a weak urban structure, and the region's people factor. It is not possible to single out one factor among these and argue that it explains everything or that it is the most important. In short, no single factor alone answers Galbraith's question.

Certainly, the Canadian state holds some responsibility for the economic underdevelopment of the Maritime provinces. The region still holds some comparative advantages in several key sectors, from the fishery to forestry, which have been mismanaged or left unattended by Ottawa. The country's national political institutions hold a distinct bias in favour of the more populated provinces, and decisions flowing from them have often placed the Maritimes at a disadvantage. Visionary investments from Ottawa have very rarely made it to the Maritime provinces, which have traditionally turned to exportation and the sea for new markets and economic opportunities, while Ottawa still looks, albeit less and less, to policies that favour developing a national continental market.

But Ottawa and national policies are not solely to blame, far from it. Geography matters and manufacturers quite naturally will look to locate new activities with easier access to market. There are thus three answers to Galbraith's question in order of importance: 1) geography, the national railway, and the intercontinental markets; 2) national political institutions and National Policy; and 3) the people factor, attitudes, attachment to the status quo, and the policies of our provincial governments. Though I cannot establish the relative impact of the three factors, I can only repeat what I wrote earlier, "Geography explains two-thirds of everything" in national and regional development.

This chapter also contends that the region has generated its own problems and challenges in key sectors. There are many things the region has not done and still does not do to promote economic development. The next chapter explores this issue.

NOTES

1 Consultations with Dominic LeBlanc, Moncton, August 6, 2011.

2 See, for example, Valcourt, "L'Atlantique doit se prendre en main," *Acadie Nouvelle*, April 14, 2015, 3.

3 Kathleen Harris, "Justin Trudeau's Team Begins Transition to Power," CBCNews, October 22, 2015, www.cbc.ca/news/politics/canada-election-2015-trudeau-liberal-transition-1.3282909.

4 See, among others, Donald J. Savoie, ed., *Taking Power: Managing Government Transitions* (Toronto: Institute of Public Administration, 1993).

5 Adam Radwanski, "Meet the PMO: All Pearson, no Pierre: Inside Trudeau's Inner Circle," *Globe and Mail*, January 12, 2016, www.theglobeandmail.com/news/politics/inside-trudeaus-inner-circle/article28079401/.

6 "Cabinet Chiefs of Staff," iPolitics.ca, February 7, 2017.

7 Christina Spencer, "Mowat Centre Head Appointed Deputy Secretary to Cabinet," *Ottawa Citizen*, December 23, 2015, http://ottawacitizen.com/news/national/mowat-centre-head-appointed-deputy-secretary-to-cabinet.

8 Conrad Black, "Duffy Trial is Just the Latest Sign of Stagnation in the Harper Government," *National Post*, April 11, 2015, http://news.nationalpost.com/full-comment/conrad-black-duffy-trial-is-just-the-latest-sign-of-stagnation-in-the-harper-government.

9 Peter Aucoin, "Influencing Public Policy and Decision-Making: Power Shifts" (notes for presentation to the 2004 APEX Symposium, "Parliament, the People, and Public Service," Ottawa, October 6–7, 2004), 4.

10 S. A. Saunders made this very point in 1984 in *The Economic History of the Maritime Provinces* (Fredericton: Acadiensis Press, 1984), 10.

11 Ibid., 83.

12 Ibid., 2.

13 Brad Wall wrote this on May 24, 2013, on his Facebook account, www.facebook.com/PremierBrad Wall/posts/10161623726474267. See also Jennifer Graham, "Saskatchewan Repeals Elected Senate Law, Passes Motion Calling for Abolition," CTVNewsGo, November 6, 2013, www.ctvnews.ca/politics/saskatchewan-repeals-elected-senate-law-passes-motion-calling-for-abolition-1.1530432.

14 Canadian Press, "Montreal-Area Mayors' Energy East Criticisms 'Short Sighted': Notley Says," CTV News Atlantic, January 22, 2016, http://atlantic.ctvnews.ca/montreal-area-mayors-energy-east-criticisms-short-sighted-notley-says-1.2748041.

15 James Bagnall, "Back to the Beginning: The Conservatives Burst a Hiring Bubble of Their Own Making," *Ottawa Citizen*, July 31, 2015, http://ottawacitizen.com/news/politics/back-to-the-beginning-the-conservatives-burst-a-hiring-bubble-of-their-own-making.

16 This comment was made by Doug Love, former deputy minister of the

Department of Regional Economic Expansion, at a meeting I attended.

17 Flanagan, "The Political Union Debate in Canada's Maritime Provinces," 122.

18 Ibid.

19 See, among others, McNutt, *New Brunswick: A History 1784-1867*.

20 L. Rolt, *Isambard Kingdom Brunel* (London: Penguin, UK, 1990).

21 As one of the reviewers of the manuscript pointed out, the region continued to build fishing schooners well into the twentieth century.

22 Saunders, *The Economic History of the Maritime Provinces*, 24.

23 Ibid., 23.

24 Ibid., 19.

25 Ibid.

26 Ibid., 61.

27 Ibid., 34.

28 "Agriculture in Saskatchewan," http://www.saskatchewan.ca/business/agriculture-natural-resources-and-industry/agribusiness-farmers-and-ranchers.

29 Robert Cooney quoted in Jessie I. Lawson and Jean MacCallum Sweet, *Our New Brunswick Story* (Toronto: Canada Publishing Company, 1948), 259.

30 Ibid., 205.

31 Ibid., 217.

32 Ibid., 252–3.

33 Tom Wappel, Chair, *Northern Cod: A Failure of Canadian Fisheries Management* (Ottawa: Government of Canada, Fourth Report, November 2005), www.parl.gc.ca/HousePublications/Publication.aspx?DocId=2144982&Language=E&Mode=1&Parl=38&Ses=1.

34 See, for example, Saunders, *The Economic History of the Maritime Provinces*, 192.

35 Nova Scotia, *Report of the Royal Commission on the Nova Scotia Coal Industry* (Halifax: Government of Nova Scotia, 1926), 31.

36 Saunders, *The Economic History of the Maritime Provinces*, 68-69.

37 See, among others, W. L. Morton, *The Kingdom of Canada* (Toronto: McClelland and Stewart, 1963), 465.

38 Ibid., 83.

39 Ibid.

40 Ibid., 84–5.

41 Canada, *Economic Action Plan 2013*, Federal Economic Development Agency for Southern Ontario, www.actionplan.gc.ca/en/initiative.ca.

42 Enrico Moretti, *The New Geography of Jobs* (Boston: Mariner Books, 2012), 5.

43 Keith G. Banting and Jon Medow, eds., *Making EI Work* (Montreal and Kingston: McGill-Queen's University Press, 2013).

44 See, for example, Alan Frizzell and Jon H. Pammett, eds., *The Canadian General Election of 1997* (Toronto: Dundurn, 1997), 103.

Chapter 12

THINGS WE DON'T DO

We Maritimers have an attitude problem when it comes to economic development. Perhaps a case of *la vérité fâche*, former Canadian prime minister Stephen Harper upset many Maritimers when he observed there was a "defeatist attitude" in Atlantic Canada; however, they overlooked Harper's further explanation as to why the culture took root when he spoke about the many decisions struck in Ottawa for "decades following Confederation."[1]

Leaving aside Ottawa, there are many things the region could do—but is not doing—to promote economic development. Asking why the Maritime region has not developed to its potential is not sufficient. We also need to ask fundamental questions about how we can position the region to capture better emerging economic opportunities and meet the challenges of the new economy. The next three chapters seek to address this issue, exploring how economic circumstances have changed and what the region can do about it.

As I've made clear, I maintain that more than other regions, we are comfortable with the status quo. More than other regions, we do not see opportunities where opportunities exist. More than other regions, we are all too often negative about our region's economic potential. More than other regions, we are not prepared to give change a chance. More than other regions—and because of our relationship with the government of Canada and its policies—we accept too readily that government has a role in managing economic success rather than establishing the circumstances for economic success. More than other regions, we say no to development, thinking that somehow or some way we can nevertheless sustain present levels of public service.

IT'S ABOUT THE STATUS QUO

Nova Scotia's recent high-profile economic development report *Now or Never: An Urgent Call to Action for Nova Scotians* went to the heart of the issue with the observation, "Throughout our discussions with Nova Scotians, we heard a frequent message that our province and our people need a 'new attitude' and a greater sense of being citizens of Nova Scotia and not just of their local area. There is an abundance of community spirit, but some negativity as well, stigmatizing success and resisting change. There is a clear need for Nova Scotians to come together and consider not only who gets what from our collective pie, but how we can make it bigger for all to share."[2] My sense is that the observation applies no less to New Brunswick and Prince Edward Island.

Don Mills, the region's leading pollster, has a sobering message for Maritimers and Atlantic Canadians. Mills built his message from extensive public opinion surveys of Atlantic Canadians based on more than thirteen thousand telephone interviews in recent years combined with a comprehensive knowledge of the region.[3] His surveys cover both the Alberta and Maritime regions, and I draw from both.[4]

The Mills surveys make it clear that the majority of Maritimers remain deeply concerned about their region's economic future. On a scale of 1 to 10, with ten "extremely concerned" and one "not at all concerned," Maritimers stand at 7.6 on the scale, suggesting a strong preoccupation about their region's economic future. Rural Maritimers are also somewhat more worried about their economic future at 7.7 on the scale, compared with 7.5 for their urban counterparts. Atlantic Canadians living in rural communities are reluctant to relocate to larger communities in search of employment opportunities. The scale (with 1 "completely disagree" and 10 "completely agree") tips at 3.8 for Atlantic Canada as a whole and ranges from 4.8 in Newfoundland and Labrador to 3.0 in Prince Edward Island. In the urban-rural split, the figure is 4.1 for urban areas and 3.4 for rural communities. This reveals that Atlantic Canadians have a particularly strong attachment to their home communities, notably their rural roots. Whether or not they are able to remain in their communities is a different question.

Atlantic Canadians also report little desire to commute in search of employment opportunities. On a 1 to 10 scale, with 10 "completely agree," the results vary from 5.5 in Prince Edward Island to 5.8 in Newfoundland and Labrador. With respect to the urban-rural split, the figure is 5.8 in urban areas compared with 5.5 for rural communities. I note, however, that many Maritimers commuted to Fort McMurray until late 2015.

Mills reported that a majority of Maritimers are reluctant to embrace further changes to the federal government's Employment Insurance policy. Some 55 per cent of them are opposed to the recent changes to the EI program, 40 per cent support the changes, and 4 per cent do not have an opinion. The urban-rural split is quite pronounced on this issue: 62 per cent of rural residents oppose the changes compared with 50 per cent in urban areas.

The Mills surveys also revealed that residents of rural communities in the three Maritime provinces are even more wedded to the status quo than urban residents when it comes to government policies and programs. Again, rural communities are also more dependent on government transfer payments than are urban communities. And, as noted, the Maritime region is more rural than the rest of Canada.

Mills is far from the only one to make the case that Maritimers support the status quo. Of course, Maritimers are not alone. Leading economists have written about the persuasive nature of the status quo and its negative impact for economic development.[5] For individuals and regions, change speaks to uncertainty while the status quo speaks to a known quantity; whether or not it can be sustained is another matter.

An important theme of the 2014 Nova Scotia economic development report was, "The challenge is to convince Nova Scotians that their province hovers now on the brink of an extended period of decline. Two interdependent factors—an aging and shrinking population and very low rates of economic growth—mean that our economy today is barely able to support our current standards of living and public services, and will be much less so going forward unless we can reverse current trends."[6] Richard Saillant painted a strikingly similar portrait for New Brunswick.[7] The Nova Scotia report identified several reasons for this state of affairs. It discussed a "loss of confidence," "a division between rural and urban perspectives," and "a lack of public confidence in private sector leadership of the economy."[8]

The Ivany Commission also addressed the need for "a strong entrepreneurial spirit," but added, "It would be optimistic to see it as a dominant trait of our provincial culture."[9] The commission did not work in isolation. It consulted widely by holding 35 public meetings across the province; 1,730 citizens contributed to group discussions; and 102 written submissions were received.[10] The consultations spoke to both the challenges and recommendations to strengthen the economy. The commission and many Nova Scotians it consulted underlined, time and again, the importance of "attitudinal" change. It identified a need for a more positive attitude toward entrepreneurs, immigrants, and visible minorities, and embracing a culture that values business sector contributions.[11] The recommendations centred around the call for higher rates of attraction and retention of interprovincial and international immigration; improved performance in productivity, trade, innovation, and value-added production; promotion of entrepreneurship; and pursuit of new opportunities in several key sectors, notably energy, tourism, fisheries, and agriculture.[12]

The Ivany Commission was well received in the media, with only a few dissident voices heard when the report was first made public. Columnists with the *Chronicle-Herald* and the *Cape Breton Post* voiced their strong support for the commission findings.[13] Some, however, did find fault in the commission. One argued the report "deploys a concept of entrepreneurship so broad as to be meaningless." Former Finance minister Graham Steele insisted the report would generate a "lot of chatter," but it would go "nowhere because the thoughts are too big and the solutions stop at the point where the questions get difficult." He highlighted the province's strong penchant for the status quo and asked, "Why are things frozen in an unsatisfactory status quo? Silence." Steele provided an answer: "There are powerful forces—social, psychological, historical, cultural, legal, economic—that have constructed our politics and that favour things continuing more or less as they are."[14] Again, Steele's observations apply no less to New Brunswick and Prince Edward Island.

The government of Nova Scotia reacted like Maritime governments usually do to commissioned reports on economic development: give the appearance of progress while standing still. The report was commissioned by the Dexter government but submitted to the McNeil government for consideration and implementation. The McNeil government's reaction confirmed Graham Steele's opinion that politics often gets in the way of change. Governments of one political persuasion are usually in no mood to implement a report of the previous government, especially one led by a different party.

McNeil responded in the manner governments do when they want to put a report on hold: appoint a panel to review the report. The panel's mandate was, "Finding ways to turn around the province's economy."[15] The fifteen-member panel brought together representatives of the private sector, labour, community groups, and the academic community.

It is not at all clear what the panel has been able to accomplish since it was established in June 2014. Inexplicably, the government commissioned yet another study in 2015 to understand the perceptions Nova Scotians have of their province's economic future.[16] The government conveniently overlooked the fact that the Ivany Commission had criss-crossed the province and put in place various measures to secure the views of Nova Scotians on the province's economic future. The government never explained why it felt the need to go over the same territory within less than two years.

The 2015 study confirmed, for the most part, much of Ivany's findings. It reported that many Nova Scotians (88 per cent) believe the province can grow its economy without losing "what makes it special," and, "Too often Nova Scotians look to others to solve their problems" (68 per cent).[17] The majority of Nova Scotians believe associations that work with all sectors are best positioned to lead "change" (67 per cent), followed by the private sector at only 9 per cent, universities at 5 per cent, government departments at 4 per cent, elected officials at 3 per cent, trade unions at 2 per cent and the media at 0 per cent.[18]

Nova Scotians were asked to identify five specific measures to promote the provincial economy. Their answers are revealing: 26 per cent suggest attracting more businesses, 16 per cent promoting entrepreneurship, 15 per cent addressing attitudes of distrust and discouragement and 8 per cent attracting new Canadians.[19] Yet, on immigration, Nova Scotians are divided on whether the province is better served by having more or less immigration. More Nova Scotians (38 per cent) favour the same number of immigrants as in previous years, while 35 per cent favour more immigrants and 21 per cent favour fewer.[20]

We do not have comparable economic development reports for New Brunswick and Prince Edward Island. However, anecdotal evidence suggests the findings from the Nova Scotia reports also apply to the other two Maritime provinces. Eddy Campbell, the president of University of New Brunswick, for example, maintained that all too often the province falls back on the status quo when it comes to economic development, relying on its declining sectors.[21] Recall that Frank McKenna decided, shortly after being elected premier of New Brunswick, one of the most promising ways to promote economic development was to change the attitudes of New Brunswickers.[22]

ONE STORY SPEAKS VOLUMES ABOUT ATTITUDE

Ben Cowan-Dewar went to Inverness, Cape Breton, as a twenty-five-year-old and saw a potential unnoticed by many Maritimers. Inverness is an old mining town, first settled by Highlands Scots who came to farm and fish in the early 1800s. Coal was discovered in 1863 and attracted investors from away. The community grew as the coal mines employed close to five hundred miners at their peak in the early 1900s. But there were problems. Inverness coal had a high sulfur and ash content, which made it more suited for power generation than steelmaking. Inverness lost its competitive edge when power generation shifted away from coal; the mines shut down in 1966.[23] The community fell in disrepair and people migrated. After coal, Inverness relied on fishing and farming for economic survival.

There was little energy, few businesses or new houses being built when Ben Cowan-Dewar visited the community in 2004. Yet, he saw in the landscape a world-class "links" golf course. Five years earlier, the entrepreneur had established a niche travel agency aimed at business executives wishing to go on golf trips. He had organized trips to some of the world's most beautiful golf courses, so that by 2004 he had an appreciation of what makes a great golf course.

When he first came to Inverness and discovered the potential awaiting, he set out to find financial partners and golf course designers. As is well-known, golf was born on links courses in Scotland, and some golfers go to great expense to play links golf. The courses differ from traditional golf courses found in North America; true links golf courses are built on a stretch of land linking good arable land to the ocean, hence the word *links*. In the eighteenth and nineteenth centuries, the links land served no economic purpose, making it ideal for golf.

There are precious few opportunities to build a links course in North America, but to Cowan-Dewar, Inverness had it all. He saw the Atlantic

Ocean washing up to the abandoned land where the coal mines were once located, adjacent to Inverness. He was able to secure the participation of Mike Keiser, the developer of Bandon Dunes, as a key financial partner and Rod Whitman as the architect and golf course designer. Cowan-Dewar also decided to move his family from Toronto to Inverness, where he built a home.

"THAT WON'T WORK"

Cowan-Dewar reveals that it was not easy pursuing his business dream in Inverness, particularly in the early days. He reports that some people in Inverness were uncertain about the initiative and he had to deal with ample negative comments at the local coffee shop and grocery store. He told a conference on community economic development that all too often, "People are for progress but are opposed to change." He added the "hardest part of his job was meeting the community expectation or rather lack of expectation." Some people told him the community would not support him, that people from away would not come to Cape Breton to play golf, and, in any event, there were already too many golf courses on the island. In essence, the verdict from many in the community was that his golf course was bound to fail, best for him not to try.[24] More often than not, he heard the observation, "That won't work." He persisted nevertheless, and today Inverness is home to an economic success story and two of the world's highest ranking golf courses.

The key lesson Cowan-Dewar learned about economic development in the Maritime provinces was, "You need grit to take an idea to completion. You need to face an unbelievable array of people saying that you cannot do it." He stressed, time and again in interviews, the importance of attitude in building communities and especially a new business in a rural setting. He reports, however, he had the support of a small core group of volunteers in Inverness who were strongly committed to the project and who had talked about the possibility even before he came to Inverness.

Cowan-Dewar and his partner subsequently decided to build a new golf course within sight of the existing one, Cabot Cliffs.[25] Both courses are enjoying rave reviews in golf communities in Canada and abroad. *Golf Digest* has ranked Cabot Links forty-two among the top one hundred courses in the world, and it is widely believed that Cabot Cliffs will crack the top ten. The *New York Times* gave Cabot Links front-page coverage on its sports page and described it as "a resort-quality high-end layout designed to be a true links golf course, a boutique category of Oceanside golf architecture exceedingly rare outside of the British Isles."[26] TSN labelled Cabot Cliffs "a masterpiece," with "18 holes of jaw-dropping beauty."[27] The *Golf Channel, Golf Digest, Canadian Golfer, Golf Magazine,* the *Wall Street Journal,* the *Globe and Mail,* and the *Toronto Star* have all sung the praise of Cabot Links and Cabot Cliffs. Matt Kuchar, a high-profile professional golfer who has won seven times on the United States PGA tour, had this to say about Cabot Cliffs: "I never thought I'd see something that makes Cypress Point (ranked number 2 of the world's greatest golf courses by *Golf Digest*) look small."[28]

Things have also improved considerably on the business front in Inverness, and the community now sees a great deal of merit in the golf courses. Jobs have been created and there are more students entering the local school than are leaving, with the school recently needing to split the grade 1 class into two. There is now, at least in the summer months, a traffic problem in the community, which residents boast about.

YOU ARE STILL HERE

The economic impact on Inverness and surrounding communities is obvious to any visitor. The community's population has grown in recent years, and youth unemployment in Inverness has fallen from 80 per cent to zero. The two golf courses now employ close to four hundred people. The community boasts a new restaurant, two new coffee shops, and new construction. Houses are being painted and there is a renewed sense of pride in the community.

The two courses are welcoming golfers from around the world. I visited the golf courses in the summer of 2015, and I met twice with Ben Cowan-Dewar, several employees, and some clients. I saw licence plates from New York, Georgia, Pennsylvania, Massachusetts, Vermont, New Hampshire, the Carolinas, and Ontario. I know private jets land at a nearby airport, bringing golfers from all parts of the United States and Europe.

I met a young woman who had left a stable job in Vancouver to return home to Cape Breton to work at the golf courses. While working there, she decided to launch a new business, making furniture from wood. Just Bored. The business is now exceeding her expectations. I met another woman, born and raised in Alberta, who decided to move to Inverness where her parents were born. She and her partner bought a house in the community and decided to raise a family there. I met a long-time resident of the community who reported how vastly different things are now. She explained, "Our youth would go to British Columbia to plant trees, spent much of the money they earned to get there and back. No more. Now, our young people stay here, earn enough money to go to university."[29]

Cowan-Dewar reported the community is now broadly supportive of the project; I definitely had the same sense talking to community representatives. Certainly, he worked hard getting the community on side. He agreed to have the buildings, from the club house and the hotel to the condos, offer a low profile to blend with the landscape and not obstruct the ocean view from the community. He also built a boardwalk to give everyone, not just golfers and his clients, access to the beach.[30] I asked him what those who once said, "That won't work," were now saying. He replied, "About half are now saying, 'you're still here,' and the other half, 'I knew all along that it would work!'"[31]

Cowan-Dewar dealt with the unexpected resistance and negative attitudes by tenaciously addressing local concerns. I also asked him if he felt Maritimers were more resistant to change than other Canadians. He does not see resistance to change strictly as a "Maritimes" problem. Rather, he ascribes it to a rural culture or an attitudinal challenge found in many rural areas across Canada. He reported that he grew up in rural Ontario, where he saw the same kind of resistance to change.[32] As I have noted on many occasions, the Maritime provinces remain substantially more rural than other Canadian regions.

What about the level of government assistance to the project? The Atlantic Canada Opportunities Agency provided a $2.5 million fully repayable loan in 2008 to build the first golf course, $750,000 in 2012 to build a hotel, and another $2.75 million in 2014 to build the second course. The government of Nova Scotia provided an $8.25 million interest-bearing fully repayable loan.[33] Cowan-Dewar reported the golf courses are profitable and the business is on schedule in repaying the loans.

SAYING NO TO DEVELOPMENT

Over the years, the Maritime region has relied on natural resources to grow its economy. We saw earlier the contributions of the fishery, forestry, agriculture, and mining sectors to the region's early economic development. More recently, natural resources underpinned the bulk of DREE, ACOA, and federal-provincial agreements in support of economic development in the three Maritime provinces. All three provincial governments rank "job creation" at the top of their priority list. If job creation is a priority and if history is a guide, then they need to look to natural resources as an important source of new jobs. The traditional sectors are mature with limited opportunities for strong growth, but in economic development, one works with what one has.

Between 2005 and 2008 mining companies tripled the number of claims for uranium in New Brunswick. Indeed, New Brunswick and Nova Scotia have attracted several mining firms looking for uranium in recent years. One of the world's largest mining companies, CVRD Inco, for example, spent about $4 million to buy uranium prospecting rights in New Brunswick. A senior CVRD Inco official told the media his company has "a 100-year history of mining and mining responsibly" and the firm would bring the culture to New Brunswick. He added the company did not "put the uranium" in New Brunswick.[34]

Then New Brunswick premier Shawn Graham initially voiced his support for the uranium and nuclear industry. The same can be said for the Nova Scotia government. Former Environment and Labour minister Mark Parent told the Nova Scotia legislature the government had "an open mind" on future uranium prospecting.[35] He was replaced in early 2009 by David Morse in the Environment portfolio, who often pointed to a "1994 report by staff at the departments of Natural Resources, Health and Environment that unanimously concluded that uranium can be mined safely under federal regulations."[36] That two successive ministers of the Environment voiced support for the industry did not stop many Nova Scotians from opposing uranium mining. The opposition bore fruit: Nova Scotia had enacted a moratorium on uranium exploration in 1984, which was set to expire on January 1, 1995. However, in the face of strong vocal opponents to the industry, the government decided on October 14, 2009, to convert the moratorium into law.[37]

In May 2008 the New Brunswick government announced it would introduce guidelines for firms wishing to explore for uranium in the province. The guidelines were based on those established for Saskatchewan, a province that has a well-established uranium mining sector.[38] The minister responsible explained, "The mining sector is a sector that's going to be a major economic sector for our province for the future."[39] The regulations prohibited exploration on municipal land and watersheds and fields with private wells. In addition, staked claims would not be permitted within 300 metres of private homes.[40] Private sector firms agreed with the proposed regulations and insisted there was "no scientific basis for the public fear of uranium exploration."[41] The government did not challenge this view and pointed to demanding regulations that would guide development, making the point that if strict regulations could work in Saskatchewan, why not in New Brunswick? The government also cited the sector's potential for the province's economic development and argued that development could take place while imposing robust environmental regulations.

The proposed regulations, however, were not enough. Communities, including Moncton and Sackville, lined up, calling for a ban on uranium mining. They were responding to reports that a uranium mining company had found enough uranium north of Moncton to move to the next stage of exploration. They wanted to put an end to uranium mining before it could get off the ground.

More than seven hundred people attended a public meeting held in Moncton, where public servants and environmental and nuclear energy experts were invited to explain how uranium exploration works and what safety measures could be introduced. The CBC reported the meeting did not go well and the experts were "overshadowed by agitated attendees."[42] The same fate awaited a public meeting held later in Fredericton. The government of New Brunswick insisted "a silent majority" in the province were in favour of exploration and understood the economic benefits the sector could bring to the province.[43] However, opposition only intensified at public meetings and the government lost the will to stick with what it labelled the "silent majority."

In Canada, mining is governed by the provinces, while uranium production falls under federal jurisdiction. Canada is rich in uranium resources, ranking fourth in the world after Kazakhstan, Australia, and Russia.[44] All of Canada's uranium production now comes from northern Saskatchewan mines.

Notwithstanding its economic potential, uranium mining remains controversial. Canadian provinces, including Nova Scotia and New Brunswick, took turns in declaring a moratorium or an outright ban on uranium mining. In the early 1990s, even the Saskatchewan government pondered phasing out uranium mining in the province because of its environmental impact. However, a joint federal-provincial panel carried out a thorough review of the challenges associated with health, safety, and the environment. The study concluded that replacing lost jobs would be difficult and the environmental impact of uranium mining could be managed and minimized.[45] Uranium mining continues in Saskatchewan.

The government of New Brunswick tried as best it could to have experts and public servants explain the risks and safety measures related to uranium mining and the nuclear industry. It also sought to explain how Saskatchewan is able to mine uranium with processes in place to protect the environment and deal with any potential health issue. After all, New Brunswick is home to a nuclear power generating plant and thus consumes uranium. The government, however, met with no success, and New Brunswick joined Nova Scotia in banning uranium mining.

In the Maritime provinces, opposition to uranium mining comes largely from rural areas. The town of Sackville, New Brunswick, for example, passed a resolution asking the New Brunswick government to ban both uranium exploration and mining in the province for the following reasons: "Whereas airborne and waterborne radioactive, chemically toxic wastes from uranium mining can permanently harm the health of soil, plants, wild game, pets and humans," and added, "whereas the exploration and mining companies would leave with the short-term profits while the present and future generations of New Brunswickers would be left with the radioactive toxic wastes and their continuing health, environmental, and economic burden."[46] Ted Wiggans, speaking for owners of small farms, insisted uranium mining would hurt their livelihood. He told the media, "I don't want to be living next to a potential uranium mine....I think people are going to have to be politically active, and actually make it very clear to the government that we don't want uranium mining in this province."[47]

Meanwhile, Brad Wall has been busy promoting Saskatchewan's uranium sector. He pointed to a potential sale of uranium to India that would yield "hundreds of millions in revenue and supporting jobs in the mining sector." He added the sale would be "huge in terms of job creation, job retention," particularly for Aboriginal workers.[48] Nova Scotia and New Brunswick have chosen a different path. Cowan-Dewar had a point when he claimed that Maritimers are in favour of economic development but opposed to change.

The anti-uranium mining movement was a precursor to the region's position on shale gas development. It also speaks to the apparent inability of governments to define and pursue the public interest. This, ironically, in a region that continues to rely heavily on government intervention to create jobs and ensure a high level of public service.

SAYING NO, OR MAYBE, TO SHALE GAS

Southwestern Energy Company (SWN), an American firm, came to New Brunswick in 2010 to explore for shale gas and oil. The government of New Brunswick rolled out the welcome mat and granted SWN permission to carry out seismic tests. SWN is a Texas-based energy firm with operations in Texas, Arkansas, Louisiana, West Virginia, and Pennsylvania and is listed on the New York Stock Exchange.

Seismic testing is harmless to the environment; it is in fact often carried out for a variety of reasons, including the construction of new roads. Fracking is a different matter. It is a controversial process in which water is mixed with chemicals and injected into a wellbore to create fractures so that gas or oil can migrate to the well. SWN could hardly undertake fracking until it knew if there were any deposits worth exploring.

Some members of local communities where seismic testing was taking place began to mobilize against SWN. Its workers and security personnel were harassed, and equipment, including two trucks, was burned. The police made a number of arrests. A leader of the movement explained the government was not listening to them, so they had to take matters into their own hands.[49]

A few weeks later, Canada's public broadcaster, CBC, held an open-line phone-in program in my region to debate the issue. Though I would not suggest for a moment the callers were necessarily representative of the region, well over 90 per cent were strongly supportive of the demonstrators. One called to say, "Democracy has broken out in the province," and several others followed to equate the movement with democracy. No matter that what SWN was doing was legal and had the support of a legitimately elected government, while some of the demonstrators had committed illegal acts. Democracy now means different things to different people, and some no longer believe that government can be fully trusted to define the common good or the public interest. Some believe they must mobilize like-minded citizens to define and drive the public interest, as they see it, independent of government.

The New Brunswick Anti-Shale Gas Alliance and three citizens decided in June 2014 to pursue the matter in court. The Alliance made it clear that it felt better suited to represent the province's public interest than the government. It called for a moratorium on the development of unconventional oil and gas exploration and argued that New Brunswick "should divert the social, political and economic resources currently at its disposal for unconventional oil and gas development into an energy supply system that is based upon renewable energy sources instead." It was, however, less forthcoming on how to proceed and what renewable energy sources the province should pursue. It also had little to say about the economic viability of such sources and who would come up with the necessary investments. Nevertheless, the Alliance alleged the government's support for shale gas exploration violated the Charter of Rights and Freedoms.[50] SWN, meanwhile, committed to spend $50 million in New Brunswick in exchange for a licence to explore 1 million hectares for oil and gas deposits. SWN laid out its plan of four major components: airborne gravity and magnetic surveys, surface geochemistry, 2D seismic imaging, and exploratory wells.[51]

Opposition to SWN surfaced shortly after it set up operations in the province. People from rural communities such as Penniac, Taymouth, Stanley, and Rogersville and several First Nations communities put up a roadblock around Stanley, effectively stopping SWN from carrying out its work. Protesters set up another blockade on Route 134 near a Mi'kmaw community, again stopping SWN from carrying out exploratory work. SWN successfully secured an injunction meant to stop protesters from playing havoc with its activities; however, protesters ignored the injunction and continued to block the highway, where they also set several police cars on fire. Some forty protesters were arrested for offences varying from uttering threats, mischief, firearms, and failure to comply with a court order.[52]

The provincial government stood firm in support of SWN. Then premier Alward explained,

> I want to be crystal clear, that we are supportive of shale gas, and its potential as an industry to help us achieve our goals. To not take advantage of this opportunity would be one of the most

> irresponsible things a government could do. I've had many people ask me why we are doing all these things, slow down, take the easy way out. That may be the most politically prudent approach, but I didn't sign up for this job to stand still and press pause.... We will not let the personal agendas of the minority be a roadblock to developing our province's bright future.[53]

Opposition to shale gas development did not die down. Opponents of shale gas became increasingly vocal and pressed political parties to take a stand on the issue, preferably one that opposed the government of the day. The leader of the Opposition declared that, if elected, his government would immediately call a moratorium on shale gas development. Some three months after winning a slim majority, New Brunswick premier Brian Gallant unveiled a moratorium on shale gas and oil development. He explained the moratorium applied to "hydraulic fracturing through any means." He added the moratorium would only be lifted after five conditions were met:

- a "social licence" is established through consultations to lift the moratorium;
- clear and credible information on the impacts on air, health, and water to develop a regulatory regime;
- a plan is established to mitigate impacts on public infrastructure and address issues such as waste water disposal;
- a process is in place to fulfill the province's obligation to consult with First Nations communities; and
- a "proper royalty structure" is established to ensure benefits are maximized for New Brunswickers.[54]

He appointed a commission to study hydraulic fracturing and asked it to report back within the year on whether the above conditions could be met.[55] He never explained what he meant by "social licence," a catch phrase that means different things to different people at different times.

The commission delivered its final report in January 2016. It essentially avoided taking sides on the issue, making the point that the decision to lift the moratorium belonged to elected officials. The commission did offer advice, should the government decide to lift the moratorium: appoint a single, independent regulator; develop a new strategy designed to shift the province to a knowledge economy and away from carbon energy; promote a new relationship with First Nations peoples; develop a plan to deal with fracking waste water; and come up with a royalty structure that does not fluctuate to accommodate changes in volatile world gas prices. It was, however, less forthcoming on how to implement the proposals.[56]

Nova Scotia premier Stephen McNeil, a fellow Liberal, declared a ban on shale gas development on September 3, 2014, on the eve of New Brunswick's election. The government announced, "Nova Scotians have overwhelmingly expressed concern about allowing high-volume hydraulic fracturing to be a part of onshore shale development in this province at this time.... This is neither a permanent nor a time-limited ban.... Instead, our government recognizes that the availability and understanding of the science of hydraulic fracturing in shale will evolve one way or the other. Our decision will allow the Nova Scotia legislature to have an opportunity for debate and comment should a decision to allow hydraulic fracturing in shale formations be allowed in our province at some future date."[57]

The Nova Scotia government introduced the moratorium after an independent panel released a report on the prospects of hydraulic fracturing in the province. In carrying out its mandate, the panel launched a series of public consultation exercises. Andrew Younger, the minister responsible for Energy, expressed concern that "people outspokenly opposed to fracking are hijacking the public sessions." The comprehensive 387-page report argued that shale gas development through fracking may be appropriate in the future, but the province did not have sufficient knowledge of the industry and the required regulations in place to proceed in 2014.[58] It essentially recommended a go slow approach.

The above makes the point that both New Brunswick and Nova Scotia have instituted a moratorium on shale gas development before getting to the exploratory wells stage. Prince Edward Island has not taken a position on the issue; few private sector firms have expressed an interest in pursuing shale gas exploration on the Island.

I note that I have been an active participant in the shale gas debate in my province. I put a question to opponents of shale gas in New Brunswick within days of SWN's arrival in my province: "How can we, on both economic and moral grounds, accept transfer payments from other regions that are generated largely by shale gas and oil development and at the same time say no to shale at home?" I have yet to receive an answer.

The potential of shale gas development has been hotly debated in the region, particularly in New Brunswick. Public opinion surveys reveal New Brunswickers are about evenly split on the issue. Some 67 per cent of New Brunswickers surveyed "completely or mostly agree" the shale gas industry would lead to long-term economic benefits for the province. Still, some 54 per cent "completely or mostly agree" the exploration and production of shale gas would have negative environmental impacts that will outweigh the economic benefits.[59]

David Campbell, an economic development consultant from New Brunswick and more recently a senior New Brunswick government official, wrote he has "never seen such a passionate outcry against any form of industrial development in my nearly 25 years studying economic development. Environmental groups, opposition provincial political parties and even most local politicians appear to be nervous about what shale gas might do to the environment. One company doing exploration in New Brunswick has reported vandalism and has hired security guards to protect its workers from angry protestors." And yet, he added, "Across North America, the shale gas industry will be an important economic growth engine. The Obama administration has called shale gas a vital part of the U.S. energy strategy and former President Bill Clinton says shale gas will be one of the economic drivers that will revive the moribund U.S. economy."[60]

Nonetheless, a number of independent studies on shale gas have essentially recommended a "not yet," "not now," or "go-slow" approach. The industry involves a number of controversial issues: from environmental risks, impacts on farms and farming communities, the need to consult Aboriginal communities, health and safety concerns, and who benefits.

In a major independent study on shale gas, the Council of Canadian Academies (CCA) concluded shale gas is having a "profound economic, environmental and social impact across much of North America." It had a list of concerns, ranging from a disruptive impact on land, the degradation of groundwater and surface water, and adverse effects on human health. It recommended a "go-slow approach," making the case that there have been a number of improvements over the past twenty years in the sector, but further investment in research and monitoring is needed.[61]

More recently, a report from the United States Environmental Protection Agency (EPA) pointed out that fracking for either shale gas or oil has not led to widespread pollution of drinking or surface water. The five-year study reported it had found some isolated cases of water contamination, but "the number of identified cases was small compared to the number of hydraulically fractured wells."[62] It set a positive tone for shale gas and oil exploration.

A team of New Brunswick academics came together in 2014 to gain a better understanding of a potential shale gas sector in the province and explore the pitfalls. They argued shale gas was "an important New Brunswick natural resource" and urged new forms of partnerships to pursue opportunities. They also called for a new research agenda that would generate "evidence-based research and analysis of the environmental and various other risks and consequences of the development of a shale gas industry in the province."[63]

Why would the Maritime provinces be reluctant to embrace shale gas- and oil-related development while the wealthier provinces are not? It is ironic, given the roots of the industry can be traced back to the region, to a Maritimer born in Nova Scotia from Loyalist parents, who worked in New Brunswick as its first geologist and who also gave the first public demonstration in history on the development of bitumen as a lamp fuel in Prince Edward Island. Abraham Gesner is known as the father of the hydrocarbon lamp fuel. The lamp, in turn, signalled the "birth of the petroleum refinery." It was Gesner who labelled the new product "kerosene" in 1850. He was later able to secure United States patents for "improvement in kerosene burning fluids."[64] The rest is history, but much of that history happened and is still happening elsewhere in the world.

Maritime political leaders responding to the real or perceived wishes of their electorates have said no, or maybe, to both uranium mining and shale gas exploration and production. The Maritimes are also slow to accept change in other sectors. For example, Saint John, New Brunswick, home to Canada's largest refinery, was the last jurisdiction to accept self-service at gas pumps. Those opposed to the shift away from full-service to self-service based their arguments on safety issues and job loss.

The region has also been reluctant to consider suggestions that we should reform existing government programs to promote development. It has consistently opposed all attempts to overhaul Ottawa's Employment

Insurance program from the Forget Commission, the Chrétien reforms of the mid-1990s, to the more recent Harper reform measures. In all cases, the measures were fairly modest, and political and community leaders from the region had little to offer other than defend the status quo.[65] The political careers of senior politicians from the region were cut short after the government, of which they were a part, introduced the reforms (as noted, Doug Young and David Dingwall from the Chrétien government, and later Bernard Valcourt from the Harper government).

I suggested in the 1980s that the federal government should review its own remuneration policy, which offers the same salary levels in all regions regardless of whether it is needed to secure qualified staff. My point was the federal government should be able to attract similar qualified people at less salary in, say, Saint John, New Brunswick, than in Toronto. I argued there is no reason why the federal government should pay more than local private sector firms to attract qualified personnel. This would enable the federal government to locate more of its units and staff in the regions, enable the local private sector to compete for qualified staff at a lesser cost than their competitors in other regions, enable the federal government to capture the savings, and if it chooses, to invest in economic development measures in the Maritime provinces.[66] The reaction to my suggestion was highly negative in the region.[67] I return to this point in the concluding chapter.

LOOKING BACK

Are there things peculiar to the Maritime region that motivate its citizens to favour the status quo? Why do many in the region believe the status quo can be maintained when emerging economic circumstances suggest that change cannot be avoided or that change and economic development go hand in hand? Past failures to deliver what new approaches to regional development promised may well explain why many Maritimers are unwilling to abandon the status quo in other government programs.[68]

Federal transfers in the form of Employment Insurance and Equalization payments work well, at least from their perspective, and so why not leave well enough alone? They are a known economic quantity, change is not. Having a federal public servant working in their region paid the same as a public servant working in Toronto holds merit not only for those working in the federal public service, but also for those in the region selling goods and services. It makes less sense, however, to the unemployed in the region who would benefit from a more dynamic economy, to businesses trying to attract qualified staff and remain competitive, or to the Maritimer who has to relocate elsewhere because the region is unable to generate new economic activities.

There are other factors favouring the status quo. The region attracts few new Canadians and, as we saw earlier, immigrants are rightly viewed as assets for society building.[69] The Maritime population remains predominantly rural, when compared with other Canadian regions, and of old stock: Aboriginal peoples, Acadians, Loyalists, Irish, and Scots. With the exception of Newfoundland and Labrador, the region is also home to an older and faster-aging population compared with other regions. Leaving aside mid-size Halifax, Maritimers live one thousand kilometres away from a large urban centre—Boston. As we saw earlier, young university graduates are particularly attracted to those large urban centres, and they are the ones usually more willing to challenge the status quo.

NOTES

1 "Harper Plans to Battle 'Culture of Defeatism' in Atlantic Canada," CBC News Canada, May 30, 2012, www.cbc.ca/news/canada/harper-plans-to-battle-culture-of-defeatism-in-atlantic-canada-1.306785.

2 Nova Scotia Commission on Building Our New Economy, *Now or Never: An Urgent Call to Action for Nova Scotians* (Halifax: Government of Nova Scotia, February 2014), 6. Also known as the Ivany Report.

3 Information drawn from a paper by Don Mills for the Georgetown Conference held in Georgetown, Prince Edward Island, June 2013.

4 I recognize, as one of the manuscript reviewers pointed out, that there are limits in relying on the unpublished work of a single pollster.

5 See, among many others, Daniel Kahneman, Jack L. Knetsch, and Richard H. Thaler, "Anomalies: The Endowment Effect, Loss Aversion and Status Quo Bias," *The Journal of Economic Perspectives* 5, no. 1 (Winter 1991): 193–206.

6 *Now or Never: An Urgent Call to Action for Nova Scotians.*

7 Saillant, *Over the Cliff.*

8 *Now or Never: An Urgent Call to Action for Nova Scotians.*

9 Ibid.

10 Ibid., 2.

11 Ibid., 25–28.

12 Ibid., section E.

13 See, among others, Pat Bates, "Ivany Report is a Sound Outline for all of Atlantic Canada," *Cape Breton Post*, March 10, 2014; and Roger Taylor, "N.S. Must Act on Ivany Report," *Chronicle-Herald*, February 14, 2014.

14 Don Nerbas, "Ivany Report Put Fresh Coat of Pain on Decades-Old Mantra," *Chronicle-Herald*, May 27, 2015; and Graham Steele, "Ivany Report Means Whatever You Want it to Mean," CBC News Canada, February 13, 2014, www.cbc.ca/news/canada/nova-scotia/graham-steele-ivany-report-means-whatever-you-want-it-to-mean-1.2535953.

15 "Ivany Report Panel Named by Stephen McNeil," CBC News Canada, June 2, 2014, www.cbc/news/canada/nova-scotia/ivany-report-panel.-named-by-stephen-mcneil-1.2662484

16 Engage Nova Scotia, a not-for-profit group, in turn commissioned Corporate Research Associates (CRA) to carry out a survey of Nova Scotians. See *Cultural Levers for Change: Research Study*, June 2015, www.engagenovascotia.ca.

17 Ibid., 27.

18 Ibid., 28.

19 Ibid., 29.

20 Ibid., 34.

21 Eddy Campbell, "A Better New Brunswick," UNB Newsroom, September 23, 2014, http://blogs.unb.ca/newsroom/2014/09/23/a-better-new-brunswick-eddy-campbell-commentary/.

22 Savoie, *Pulling Against Gravity*.

23 J. H. Calder, K. S. Gillis, D. J. MacNeil., R. D. Naylor, and N. Watkins Campbell, *One of the Greatest Treasures: The Geology and History of Coal in Nova Scotia* (Halifax: Nova Scotia Department of Natural Resources, Information Circular no. 25, 1993), 18.

24 Donald J. Savoie, *Rural Development: It's All About Attitude, Up to a Point* (Georgetown, PE: The Georgetown Conference, 2013), 13.

25 Ibid.

26 Charles McGrath, "In Cape Breton, a Rugged Golf Getaway," *New York Times*, June 7, 2013, www.nytimes.com/2013/06/09/travel/in-cape-breton-rugged-golf-getaway.html

27 Bob Weeks, "Cabot Cliffs Is a Masterpiece," TSN Golf, July 2, 2015, www.tsn.ca/cabot-cliffs-is-a-masterpiece-1.324321.

28 Matt Kuchar quoted in Josh Sens, "Meet Cabot Cliffs, the Most Anticipated New Course of 2015," *Golf* 57, no. 8 (November 20, 2014): 91.

29 Consultations with the owner of the Bear Paw gift shop, Inverness, Cape Breton, August 6, 2015.

30 Consultations with Ben Cowan-Dewar, Inverness, Cape Breton, August 5–6, 2015.

31 Ibid.

32 Ibid.

33 Ian Fairclough and Patricica Brooks Arenburg, "N.S. Announces $8.25 Million Loan for Cabot Links Golf Course," *Chronicle-Herald* (Halifax), August 11, 2013, http://thechronicleherald.ca/novascotia/1147236-ns-announces-825-million-loan-for-cabot-links-golf-course.

34 Quoted in Chris Arsenault, "Uranium Rising," *The Dominion*, July 6, 2007, www.dominionpaper.ca/articles/1270.

35 Quoted in EHANS, "Leave Uranium in the Ground: Citizens Want Complete Ban," Fall 2008, accessed July 24, 2015, www.environmentalhealth.ca/fall08uraniumnews.html.

36 Chris Benjamin, "Morse's Environmental Shakeup," *The Coast*, January 23, 2009, www.thecoast.ca/halifax/enviro-shakeup/Content?oid=1070548.

37 "Uranium in Canada," World Nuclear Association, accessed July 27, 2015, www.world-nuclear.org/information-library/country-profiles/countries-a-f/canada-uranium.aspx.

38 "N.B. Establishes Uranium Exploration Guidelines," CBC News New Brunswick, May 27, 2008, www.cbc.ca/news/canada/new-brunswick/n-b-establishes-uranium-exploration-guidelines-1.698152.

39 "N.B. Establishes Strict Uranium Exploration Rules," CBC News New Brunswick, July 4, 2008, www.cbc.ca/news/canada/new-brunswick/n-b-establishes-strict-uranium-exploration-rules-1.694905.

40 Ibid.

41 Ibid.

42 "700 Opposed to Uranium Mining Show Up at N.B. Meeting," CBC News New Brunswick, June 6, 2008, www.cbc.ca/news/canada/new-brunswick/700-opposed-to-uranium-mining-show-up-at-n-b-meeting-1.694906.

43 Ibid.

44 Canada, Natural Resources Canada, www.nrcan.gc.ca/energy/uranium-nuclear (site discontinued).

45 "Uranium in Canada."

46 Sackville, "Martin to Ban Uranium Exploration and Mining in New Brunswick," undated, mimeo.

47 Quoted in "Many New Brunswickers Concerned about Uranium Exploration," CBC News New Brunswick, April 10, 2008, www.cbc.ca/news/canada/new-brunswick/many-new-brunswickers-concerned-about-uranium-exploration-1.708077.

48 Josh Wingrove, "Looming India Uranium Deal Huge for Saskatchewan, Premier Says," Bloomberg.com, April 10, 2015, www.bloomberg.com/news/articles/2015-04-10/looming-india-uranium-deal-huge-for-saskatchewan-premier-says.

49 "Situation in Kent County Getting Dangerous, Warn RCMP," CBC News New Brunswick, June 29, 2013, www.cbc.ca/news/canada/new-brunswick/situation-in-kent-county-getting-dangerous-warns-rcmp-1.1360667.

50 "Anti-shale Gas Group Suing New Brunswick Government," CBC News New Brunswick, June 23, 2014, www.cbc.ca/news/canada/new-brunswick/anti-shale-gas-group-suing-new-brunswick-government-1.2684758.

51 "Exploration Program in New Brunswick," SWN Resources Canada, n.d., http://web.archive.org/web/20131020100529/http://www.swnnb.ca/exploration.html#exploration-fact-sheet.

52 See, among others, "RCMP, Protesters Withdraw After Shale Gas Clash in Rexton," CBC News New Brunswick, October 17, 2013, www.cbc.ca/news/canada/new-brunswick/rcmp-protesters-withdraw-after-shale-gas-clash-in-rexton-1.2100703.

53 Hon. David Alward, "Celebrating the Past: Energizing the Future" (speech, State of the Province, Fredericton, New Brunswick, January 29, 2014), 4 and 10.

54 "Shale Gas Moratorium Details Unveiled by Brian Gallant," CBC News New Brunswick, December 18, 2014, www.cbc.ca/news/canada/new-brunswick/shale-gas-moratorium-details-unveiled-by-brian-gallant-1.2877440.

55 "Fracking Commission Appointed to Study Shale Gas Conditions," CBC News New Brunswick, March 24, 2015, www.cbc.ca/news/canada/new-brunswick/fracking-commission-appointed-to-study-shale-gas-conditions-1.3006938.

56 "Shale Gas Commission Calls for Independent Regulator if Moratorium Lifted," CBC News New Brunswick, February 26, 2016, www.cbc.ca/news/canada/new-brunswick/shale-gas-fracturing-fracking-moratorium-1.3464936.

57 "Government to Prohibit Hydraulic Fracturing," September 3, 2014, https://haligonia.ca/government-to-prohibit-hydraulic-fracturing-97309/; and Bruce Erskine, "Nova Scotia to Ban Fracking," *Chronicle-Herald* (Halifax), September 3, 2014, http://thechronicleherald.ca/business/1233818-nova-scotia-to-ban-fracking.

58 Frank Atherton et al., *Report of the Nova Scotia Independent Review Panel on Hydraulic Fracturing* (Sydney, NS: Cape Breton University, 2014).

59 "Shale Gas Development Divides Voters, CBC Poll Finds," CBC News Canada, September 7, 2014, www.cbc.ca/news/canada/new-brunswick/new-brunswick-votes-2014/shale-gas-development-divides-voters-cbc-poll-finds-1.2758482.

60 David Campbell, "Why Shale Gas Could be a Game-Changer for the Maritimes," op-ed., *Globe and Mail*, November 29, 2011, A7.

61 Expert Panel on Harnessing Science and Technology to Understand the Environmental Impacts of Shale Gas Extraction, *Environmental Impacts on Shale Gas Extraction in Canada* (Ottawa: Council of Canadian Academies, 2014).

62 *Assessment of the Potential Impact of Hydraulic Fracking for Oil and Gas on Drinking Water Resources: Executive Summary* (Washington, DC: Office of Research and Development—Environmental Protection Agency, June 2015), ES-6.

63 Richard Saillant and David Campbell, eds., *Shale Gas in New Brunswick: Towards a Better Understanding* (Moncton: Canadian Institute for Research on Public Policy and Public Administration, 2014), 286.

64 Loris S. Russell, "Gesner, Abraham," in *Dictionary of Canadian Biography*, vol. 9, University of Toronto/Université Laval, 2003–, http://www.biographi.ca/en/bio/gesner_abraham_9E.html.

65 See, among others, Canada, *Unemployment Insurance in the 1980s* (Ottawa: Employment and Immigration, July 1981); and Canada, *Commission of Inquiry on Unemployment Insurance: Report* (Ottawa: Minister of Supply and Services, 1986).

66 Savoie, *Regional Economic Development*, chapter 14.

67 Based on correspondence, telephone calls, and discussions with Maritimers in the months following the publication of *Regional Economic Development: Canada's Search for Solutions*.

68 David Johnson, Susan Hodgett, and Stephen A. Boyle, "Regional Development and the Development of Theory," in *Doing Development Differently: Regional Development on the Atlantic Periphery*, ed. Susan Hodgett, David Johnson, and Stephen A. Royle (Sydney: Cape Breton University Press, 2007), 18.

69 Katja Sarkowsky, Rainer-Olaf Schultze, and Sabine Schwarze, eds., *Migration, Regionalization, Citizenship: Comparing Canada and Europe* (Wiesbaden and Heidelberg: Springer, 2015), 32.

Part 5

NO LONGER A MARKET FOR THE BLAME GAME

Chapter 13

IT IS A DIFFERENT WORLD

David Held, a leading political scientist, maintained "Globalization is fundamentally a spatial phenomenon....It is about the stretching of connections, relations and networks between human communities, an increase in the intensity of these and a general speeding up of all these phenomena."[1] Trade between countries has never been as open as it is today nor has the competition for economic activities and jobs been as intense. We have reached the point where transnational corporations are unstoppable and investment is no longer constrained by geography. A borderless economy is redefining the role of government with wide implications for all Canadian regions, not the least for the Maritime provinces.[2] More to the point, government cannot be the key economic driving force it once was.

The new economic and political order, the new media, the shift of attitudes from collectivist to individualist, and the arrival of new Canadians from non-European countries continue to have a profound impact on Canada's body politic. The consensus—or the bargain between Ottawa and the regions that emerged from several Royal Commissions, from Rowell-Sirois to the Gordon Commission—that led to a number of federal transfer schemes to the provinces and individuals, is not as strong as it once was. Time will tell if it can be sustained.

The bargain emerged from the view that those regions impoverished by the National Policy, which was pursued in Canada's "general interest," should be compensated with "public expenditures." As noted, Janine Brodie summed up the bargain well when she wrote that federal government transfers "would simply help to underwrite some of the social costs of uneven development within certain political jurisdictions, for example, New Brunswick, while the economic relationships that promoted uneven development remained unchallenged."[3] The Canada-Unites States Auto Pact of the 1960s and its direct economic benefits to Canada's industrial heartland speaks directly to this point.

As chapter 9 makes clear, Canada still has uneven development. National Policy remains in part responsible, at least from a historical perspective. Again, history matters in all things, and economic development is no exception. Ottawa's ability to pursue a national policy of the kind it introduced in 1878, however, is now seriously compromised. No one knows this better than the regions that have benefitted from the policies that "promoted uneven development." To the extent that the federal government can now pursue a national economic development policy, it takes the form of investments in infrastructure, in R&D, deregulation of the economy, the location of federal public service jobs, low taxes, and tax expenditure. In short, as before, putting in place circumstances for economic success is still the goal, but the instruments have changed. With some notable exceptions, these instruments do not favour Ontario to the extent that National Policy circa 1878 did. Ottawa can no longer grow the "national economy" through high tariffs, other protective policies, and direct cash subsidies to businesses. Globalization and regional free trade agreements have turned economic development upside down, and the regions outside of the Quebec-Windsor corridor are no longer captive markets for central Canadian producers. If they are no longer captive, the country's industrial heartland is asking why transfer payments should be maintained.

Officials in the economic development field have transitioned, in one generation, from thinking of the competition as neighbouring provinces, states, or regions to thinking of countries halfway around the world. There was a time when DREE sought, through financial incentives and other means, to shift jobs from one region of Canada to another to promote balance in the national economy. Back then, it was important for DREE officials to assist the country's political leadership in managing a political space, given tensions that could, and did indeed, surface among provinces over a shift in employment between regions. Today, the head of

Nova Scotia's economic development agency explains that he "competes with India, China, the Philippines, Eastern bloc countries and now South America and less with other Canadian regions and provinces."[4] This is no less true for the have provinces.

The Maritime provinces in Canada could, at least in the past, demonstrate that they had lost manufacturing jobs to Ontario and Quebec because of National Policy and the federal government's deliberate economic development efforts in Central Canada. It is much more difficult for them to point the finger at China and its low-wage economy and abundant workers, for example, to explain their own economic difficulties. Every Canadian region can make the same point, even more so in the case of Canada's industrial heartland. The first is a result of geography, political decisions, and the impact of public policies in the national context; the second is the result of China's comparative advantages, market forces, and a low-wage economy. No political market in China is concerned with the economic woes of the Maritime provinces, and now less and less in other Canadian regions.

Globalization and the proliferation of free trade agreements are redefining the relationship between have and have-less regions, particularly between Canada's industrial heartland and other regions. With global firms extending their reach into the Maritime provinces, economic opportunities and profits are more and more flowing to them rather than to firms in Central Canada. The industrial heartland and the energy-producing provinces are increasingly seeing federal transfers as a financial drain because the transfers fail to return to their regions to purchase goods and services.

Globalization has also had a profound impact on businesses that have decided to stay home. The competitiveness of the global economy reaches down to small firms in small communities in remote regions as well as to large firms in large urban areas. Firms may decide to stay home, but the competitive nature of the global economy will know where to find them. Michigan and Ontario, for example, have fewer and fewer reasons to be concerned with the economies of, say, Vermont or Nova Scotia. The traditional east-west trade within Canada and the United States respectively is giving way to a north-south and increasingly a global pattern. For this reason, it is becoming more and more difficult for national governments to define a national economic interest that speaks to all their regions.

Former Ontario premier Dalton McGuinty spoke to this development when he said his government would consider introducing a surcharge on Hyundai and Kia vehicles unless Korea opened access to its domestic markets to Ontario manufacturers. McGuinty explained he had "a responsibility to find new and creative ways to protect our workers and our jobs."[5] Canada's auto manufacturing sector is concentrated in Ontario, and the premier, unlike the Canadian prime minister, does not need to balance the interests of that sector with those of the non-renewable energy sector, for example, which is largely concentrated in Western and Atlantic Canada. Thirty years ago, subnational regions were better integrated into national economies, and the Ontario premier had no good reason to muse about launching a trade war with a foreign country. He could see the economic interest of Ontario square nicely with Canada's economic interest. This is no longer the case.

Two points are worthy of underlining. First, most countries in the western world, and elsewhere, have liberalized their investment environment to attract foreign investment and to promote a more competitive economy. The business community has responded. Second, the international architecture in place to establish the rules of the game—the International Monetary Fund (IMF), the World Bank, the United Nations and its agencies, the General Agreement on Tariffs and Trade (GATT), now the World Trade Organization (WTO), and the Organisation for Economic Co-operation and Development (OECD)—has, in the opinion of a former Canadian director at the IMF, remained "largely unchanged," notwithstanding the "dramatic events of the last sixty years."[6] This has implications for nation states, and Canada is no exception.

Economic adjustments flowing out of a more integrated global economy were accelerated following the signing of the Canada-Unites States Free Trade Agreement and again with its successor, the North American Free Trade Agreement (NAFTA).[7] Nowhere is this more evident than in the automotive sector concentrated in Ontario, as it has been since Canada and the United States signed the Auto Pact in the 1960s. Andrew Stark wrote in his preface to Thomas Courchene and Colin Telmer's *From Heartland to North American Region State*, "Thirty years ago, Ontario was Canada's heartland. Whatever was in the interest of Ontario was in the interest of Canada. Whatever was in the interest of Canada was in the interest of Ontario. And both Ontarians and other Canadians believed this." Courchene and Telmer go on to argue, "Heartland Ontario is no more and the province is being transformed into a North American region state."[8]

Ontario now appears less certain about its place in the federation and in its relations with the federal government and the other provinces. One observer of Queen's Park remarked, "Historically, Ontario was always the province most comfortable with Canadian federalism. Ontarians saw the government in Ottawa as their government, acting for a nation they saw as their own.... Ottawa took care of Canada for Ontario...and it worked. Ontario is coming to the conclusion that Ottawa no longer works in its interest."[9] There are also increasing signs that Ontario may follow Quebec in adopting a policy of provincial economic activism. While it may have made economic sense to support transfer payments to slow-growth regions forty years ago, it is less clear this is the case today. The findings of the Ontario government's three-volume report entitled *Competing in the New Global Economy* provide an excellent example of this shift in thinking.[10] As we will see later, Ontario never hesitates to ask for its share of federal transfer payments nowadays. In this sense, Ontario is now no different than the other nine provinces.

As Ontario adjusts to NAFTA and other global economic forces, it is joining Alberta, British Columbia, and Saskatchewan in asking why programs designed to maintain Canada's east-west links—whether in the form of transfer payments to individuals or of federal regional development programs—should continue. This question bears out even if Ontario has recently been on the receiving end of Equalization payments, even if all ten provinces benefited from equalization at one time, and even if an economic argument can be made that equalization is of benefit to the have provinces if only because they receive highly skilled workers from, and paid for by, the have-less provinces. Still, measures to undercut Michigan's cost structure are more pressing for Ontario than securing east-west links. Global economic forces will also have a major impact on the evolution of the political economy of all of Canada's regions. As these regions become inserted differently into the global economy, their links with the outside world are becoming "more important than their economic linkages with Canadian regions."

IT'S ALL ABOUT CHANGE

All Canadian provinces are buffeted about by constant challenges to the status quo. We are told by several observers of public policy that change is key to understanding the new economy. Kevin Lynch, former clerk of the Privy Council and Canadian director of the IMF, recently wrote, "One key factor shaping policy making in the 21st century is the reality that change is now an unelecting constant." He explained further, "Disruptive innovations and globalization are at its core."[11]

The new economy is fast changing Canada's economic landscape. Private sector firms competing at national and international levels either adjust or die, and many are dying. There is no longer any place for these firms to hide behind the status quo. Even firms wishing to focus on their regional markets are not immune to the imperatives of globalization.

In 2003 one Moncton entrepreneur established a new plant to produce kitchen cabinets in China. When I asked him why, he responded, "The reason is very simple—I can ship a tree from Canada to China, produce a finished product from my plant there and ship the product back anywhere in Canada much more cheaply than if I were to take the same tree and process it at my plant in Moncton."[12] The entrepreneur decided to establish a plant in China to ensure his business would remain competitive at home, not to become competitive in China— his market, the Maritime provinces and northeastern United States. NAFTA has opened new markets for the entrepreneur, markets outside of Canada.

In 2004, OAO Technology Solutions, a large US firm, decided to transfer 140 jobs from Moncton to India, despite only a few years earlier having received provincial government assistance to establish operations in Moncton. The decision, OAO explained, was strictly business: it could save money for its shareholders if it ran its operations from India. In January 2008 another large American firm, AOL, announced that it was eliminating 100 jobs from its Moncton operations. In 2015 ExxonMobil confirmed it would transfer 20 per cent of the jobs at its business-support centre in Moncton to India.[13] Moncton is far from alone in confronting both challenges and opportunities flowing from the global economy, and it can scarcely be described as one of the most global-oriented communities in the western world.

To appreciate what the rise of the global economy has meant for the location of economic activities and for Canadian businesses large and small, consider this: Thirty years ago, China held that foreign trade amounted to nothing more than treason, while today it is open for business to virtually anyone with investment dollars. It has become an economic powerhouse, made possible in no small measure by foreign investment. Forty years ago, Canada had an agency with a mandate to control the flow of investment dollars coming into the country. Today, it has an agency with a mandate to do the exact opposite—attract foreign investment. Thirty years ago, Canada sent aid to India. Today, many Canadian businesses hire firms or workers from India to build their websites and service their customers.[14] Thirty years ago, US automakers dominated the North American market. Today, American manufacturers are struggling, while some Japanese and European firms are doing well. In late 2008 the Big Three automakers went to Washington and Ottawa, cap in hand, "pleading" for public funds in order to survive, making the point that although we live in a global economy, it is still national governments that are asked to pick up the pieces when things go wrong.[15] Thirty years ago, the Soviet Union dominated Eastern Europe, where private property was not permitted. Today, some of the world's wealthiest individuals are Russian, and capital flows easily in and out of Eastern Europe.

EVOLUTION OF CANADA'S MANUFACTURING SECTOR

Bill Hammond, appearing on CBC's *The National*, explained the shift of manufacturing jobs from Canada's industrial heartland to Mexico: "The manufacturing sector as we know it in Canada will not be around."[16] Hammond runs a family business that manufactures transformers. The firm set up its first manufacturing plant in Guelph, Ontario, in 1917. However, like many other firms in the Montreal-Windsor corridor, it got its big break in the 1940s through the war effort, when it began to build specialized transformers and reactors for the military. The firm grew, during the war years, from less than fifty employees to over three hundred "almost overnight."[17]

A few years ago, Hammond decided to set up shop in Monterrey, Mexico, where he now operates two plants. He did so because labour cost in Mexico is ten times less than in Canada. He remarked, "There was a time when Mexico had a reputation of building shoddy product.... We're finding now that global manufacturers are more than willing to accept products coming out of Mexico because the quality levels are as good as they are out of the United States or Canada."[18] Hammond is hardly the only manufacturer moving to Mexico. Canadian manufacturers, from the makers of luxury kitchen and bathroom faucets to domestic appliances, have chosen to build new plants in Mexico rather than at home.[19]

Nowhere is the shift to Mexico more evident than in the automobile sector. Auto manufacturers invested some $7 billion (US) in Mexico in 2014, but only $750 million in Canada. Mexico now accounts for nearly 20 per cent of North American vehicle output, and the number is growing. Canada's share, meanwhile, has fallen to 14 per cent, its lowest level since 1987.[20] Not only is labour cost considerably lower in Mexico, but also the Mexican government offers generous incentive to manufacturers to locate in designated areas much like IT&C, DRIE, DREE, and ACOA did before the 1994–97 program review.[21]

It is critical to emphasize the importance of the automobile sector to Ontario, at least until the arrival of trade agreements and a more integrated global economy. Before the turn of the century, the automobile and automotive parts industry constituted more than 20 per cent of Ontario's manufacturing GDP and amounted to nearly 50 per cent of Ontario's merchandise exports to the United States. The North American auto industry was then structured along continental lines.[22] It is now global, and Canada—more particularly Ontario—is feeling the impact.

Magna, one of Canada's success stories in the auto parts industry, has also decided to shift more and more of its manufacturing capacity to Mexico. The global firm now operates twenty-nine plants and employs 24,000 people in Mexico—more than in any other country where Magna operates. The firm is doing what many auto makers are doing: shifting operations to Mexico where assembly plant workers earn about $2.90 (US) an hour, about 10 per cent of what a full seniority worker makes in Canada.[23]

Data from Statistics Canada confirm that the shift of the automobile sector away from Ontario continues. In 1991 Canada—again, essentially Ontario—employed 53,298 people; by 2012, the figure had dropped to 37,155. Canada's auto sector is even losing ground to neighbouring regions south of the border. In 2011 Ontario produced 2,125,000 automobiles and 2,369,961 in 2013. Michigan's production jumped from 1,924,000 to 2,457,000 during the same period, while Kentucky went from 639,000 to 1,251,000.[24]

THE BARGAIN COMES UNGLUED

It was only a matter of time before regional trade agreements and a more integrated global economy would start to unravel the Canadian economic bargain. As noted above, the bargain, going back to the 1880s, was straightforward. Give Ottawa a free hand to shape a national policy and establish the conditions for economic success in Ontario and Quebec, but then put in place measures to ensure some of the benefits from that success could be shared with other Canadians through various federal government programs.

If the manufacturing sector as we know it in Canada will not be around, and if Canada's industrial heartland has to deal with unrelenting economic challenges and change, Canada's ability to sustain its political commitment in wealthier regions to interregional redistribution will be difficult. Much like the Maritimes were forced to look inland rather than to the seas when the region joined the Canadian federation, all Canadian regions now have to look to the global economy for economic opportunities.

Richard Simeon saw this trend emerging some twenty-five years ago, when he echoed former Saskatchewan premier Allan Blakeney and wrote that Canada would become less able to act as a giant "mutual insurance company."[25] His point was that focusing on how to compete with Michigan, California, Mexico, or China forces the hands of Canadian regions to look after their own immediate economic self-interest. Put differently, it is less in Ontario's or for that matter other regions' economic interest today than it was thirty years ago to see Canada's giant mutual insurance company continue to operate. But that is not all. Regional trade agreements and global pressures are also increasingly constraining federal policy instruments such as fiscal, trade, and regional development incentives, and redistributive policies. It is provincial government instruments, from education to infrastructure spending, that become the more important instruments to promote economic development. This favours provinces that have the fiscal capacity to spend and to innovate in delivering public services.

All provinces have little choice but to look to their own immediate economic interests and focus on what their public sector requires to establish the circumstances for economic development. Assuming they have the fiscal resources, they also have little choice but to implement measures to encourage their private sector to pursue new economic opportunities abroad in order to build a competitive economy at home. Those provinces with a stronger balance sheet stand a better chance of putting in place the circumstances for economic success than the fiscally weak ones.

That said, not all have provinces are out to abolish Ottawa's Equalization program or its regional development agencies. Rather, the have provinces now want their share of Ottawa's spending. The political conditions that encouraged the federal government to introduce the Equalization program no longer exist. All regions now see themselves on the same economic footing, which explains why some premiers of have provinces do not hesitate to call on Ottawa to redirect its spending to favour their provinces.

Moreover, some premiers of have provinces are questioning why the Equalization program is flowing as much funding as it does to the have-less provinces. Turn down the equalization tap, they argue, and turn it up on more productive sectors to ensure their region is more competitive in a global setting. The Ontario government has made this point, time and again, as has one of the research institutes it finances, the Mowat Centre.[26] Saskatchewan premier Brad Wall has also called for a review of Ottawa's Equalization program and written to leaders of national political parties, asking them to explain their positions on the issue.[27] For Wall, Ottawa's Equalization "is a lot of money to go out in a way that seems to be dated and not always efficient, and infrastructure and tax relief might be an option instead."[28] The recent collapse of oil prices has only intensified the call from resource-rich provinces to revise the Equalization program.

In part because Canada is increasingly urban, in part because of the competitive nature of the global economy, in part because the Maritime provinces are fast losing political clout in deciding who wins power in Ottawa, and in part because we have branded some form of federal transfer payments as a recipe for creating an economic dependency (or labelling it the "help that hurts"), the federal government's commitment to equity continues to wane. As a result, Ottawa is slowly but surely slowing down its transfer payment tap to slow-growth provinces and shifting more of its spending to the have provinces. Ottawa's decision to calculate federal transfers for health and social services on a per capita basis speaks directly to this development and is part of the federal government's agenda to reduce what it labels "backdoor equalization" since the mid-1990s.[29] Ontario, Quebec, Alberta, British Columbia, and more recently, Saskatchewan, have been leading the charge for "fair share federalism." *Fair share federalism* is code to say that have-less provinces are receiving too much in federal transfers, while the have provinces are not receiving enough.

Ottawa introduced changes to its Equalization program in 2004 to address the concerns of the have provinces. Ontario's then premier Dalton McGuinty told Ottawa, "If there is more money available from the federal government, we'd rather that it be distributed in such a way that…[i]t benefits all of us, including supporting, for example, postsecondary education in the province of Ontario."[30] He later expressed his support for Ottawa's changes to the program because Ottawa acted on some of his concerns, to Ontario's benefit.

The 2004 revisions to Equalization shifted half of the program's funding to a per capita basis. Quebec pushed Ottawa to adopt the per capita formula because it stood to gain far more than the other receiving provinces. Ottawa chose to support Quebec's position since Quebec had seventy-five MPs in the House of Commons (seventy-eight since 2015). Then Nova Scotia premier John Hamm argued, "That's absolutely the wrong way to go. I didn't agree with that. The one program that must never go to per capita funding is equalization."[31] Then New Brunswick premier Bernard Lord also maintained, "Per capita goes against the fundamental principle of equalization."[32]

Journalist Jim Travers provided an enlightening explanation for Ottawa's position on the debate: "Martin's federal Liberals share with Jean Charest's provincial Liberals a pressing interest in securing for Quebec the best possible arrangement. After effectively losing a majority to the Bloc Québécois in the last election, Martin is determined to do everything possible to recover it and throwing money at Quebec never hurts."[33] The federal government never explained how the per capita criteria relates to equalization or answered Andrew Coyne's charge that per capita "by a happy coincidence raises Quebec's share of the total (i.e., paid under the program), but obviously has nothing to do with equalization."[34] No matter, Quebec had, and still has, nearly three times more seats than the Maritime provinces combined. In 2009 Equalization payments were capped to nominal GDP growth. Over the years, the Senate meanwhile had little to say and no influence on revisions to the Equalization program.

Ontario has joined the other have provinces in having "profound regional grievances," and it turns to federal transfer payments and total federal government spending in all regions to make the point. Globalization is promoting a growing sense of regionalism in all regions, and all regions view the federal government as impeding their way as they try to compete in a global setting.[35] However, all regions are conveniently overlooking several considerations in making their point. In the case of the have provinces, total government spending does not tell the whole story. The nature of the spending matters (i.e., a dollar in R&D is worth more than a dollar spent under the Employment Insurance program). The federal government's tax expenditures favour, by an extremely wide margin, the have provinces, but they never take this into account when they make a pitch for fair share federalism. The have-less provinces, meanwhile, are asking for more federal transfers without making much of an effort to make their delivery of public service in health care and education more efficient.

It is difficult to imagine that federal transfers to the Maritime provinces will be much more generous in the future. Ontario will continue to push its considerable political weight on Ottawa to slow the transfer payment tap because of its own difficult fiscal position, while Alberta will be dealing with difficult challenges in its oil and gas sector for some time.[36] My point, once more, is that the Maritime region will not be able to rely on federal transfer payments as much as it has in the past.

The federal government decided to overhaul its transfers to the provinces for health care and education in 1977. The reforms reshaped the transfers into tax points and cash. A tax point transfer is an agreement whereby the federal government agrees to lower its tax rate so the provinces can raise their own.[37] The federal government of the day recognized that a tax point is worth less to the have-less provinces than to the have provinces, so it decided to provide a higher cash transfer to the have-less provinces to ensure the transfers were essentially the same for all provinces, hence, the term *backdoor equalization*.

As part of its program review exercise, Ottawa merged two existing programs to create the Canada Health and Social Transfer (CHST) program, which included both a transfer of cash and tax points, and the initial transfers were below levels established in earlier programs. In addition, Established Programs Financing and Canada Assistance Plan had an equalization component that provided additional cash to have-less provinces. The new program, which once again divided funding between health and social transfers, moved more of the funding to a per capita payment, which favoured provinces with expanding populations, notably Alberta and Ontario. New funding adjustments were subsequently made.[38] In addition, as we saw earlier, a high-profile First Ministers' Conference on health care, held in September 2004, added $41 billion of new money over a ten-year period under CHST.[39]

The First Ministers' Accord on Health Care Renewal in February 2003 led to the restructuring of the CHST to create two new transfers: the

Canada Health Transfer (CHT) and the Canada Social Transfer (CST). They also agreed to allocate 62 per cent of the funding to health care and 38 per cent to education programs for children and social programs.[40] It is important to stress the 2007 federal budget restructured the CST or social transfers to provide funding on an equal per capita basis. By 2014-15 Ottawa decided to put CHT on an equal per capita basis, which brought backdoor equalization to an end for all federal transfers.[41] This works to the benefit of the have and growing provinces.

Given the Maritime region's fast-aging population in relation to the rest of Canada, the need for backdoor equalization on federal transfers is even more apparent today than it was in the 1970s; however, the appetite for redistributive politics is not apparent. Keith Banting and John Myles summed it up well when they wrote, "The redistributive state is fading in Canada," and, "changed politics generate changed policies."[42] They point out changed politics is due in large part to Canada's particular vulnerability to "globalization and neoliberalism." In short, all regions and all provinces, including the have provinces, now feel vulnerable to international competition.

It was a great deal easier forty years ago than it is today for Canadians to conclude that it was important for Canada to ensure a relatively same level of public service across Canada without some provinces having to impose an unbearable level of taxation. The highly competitive nature of globalization and changes to Canada's body politic explain why it is now much less the case.

POLITICS IS ALSO DIFFERENT

More than other countries, Canadian politics equates to territorial politics.[43] That much remains a constant. How Canadian politics is conducted, how policies are struck, and how territorial politics is managed have remained far from constant. Three things continue to define Canada's territorial politics: rep by pop decides who holds political power in Canada at the national level; population is shifting to Ontario and Western Canada; and the prime minister and his closest advisors dominate more and more the policy-making, the decision-making, and the appointment processes in Ottawa. It bears repeating once more that Canada, unlike other federations, does not have an effective upper house to balance the power of rep by pop in shaping policies. Given Canada's geography, its regional and linguistic diversity, the population difference between the biggest and smallest provinces, and distinct regional economic circumstances, the country cries out for an effective upper house. The cry has not been heard where it matters: in Ottawa, and in some of the provincial capitals. Many Maritimers have left the region in search of opportunities, while most new Canadians go where other new Canadians are, in large urban settings such as Toronto, Vancouver, and Calgary. Nothing much new here.

What is relatively new, however, is how policies are struck in Ottawa. The prime minister has come to dominate both the Ottawa policy-making and decision-making processes to the point where all major, and even minor, administrative decisions come to his office for resolution if he decides he wants them on his desk. The degree of centralization within the federal government is without parallel in other jurisdictions, and the shift from Cabinet government to governing from the centre in Canada is now complete. B. Guy Peters, a leading scholar of US politics, dismissed the suggestion that we are witnessing the "presidentialization of the prime minister in Canada," and insisted, "the United States president does not have anywhere near the power that our prime minister has."[44] A comparative study of heads of government reveals the Canadian prime minister leads the pack in governing from the centre and in the ability to control the levers of power.[45]

Consider the following: two key decisions on Canada's deployment in Afghanistan, one by a Liberal government and the other by a Conservative government, were made by prime ministers and their courtiers when the relevant ministers (National Defence and Foreign Affairs) were not even in the room.[46] It is one thing to strike major political decisions without consulting Cabinet. It is quite another to not even involve the responsible ministers. Cabinet government, it seems, now belongs to the history books. But that is not all. All program review decisions, however small, in both the Chrétien and Harper exercises were brought to the prime minister for final approval. There are many other examples, making the case that governing from the centre—or from the prime minister, his office, and other central agencies—is now firmly entrenched in Ottawa. The prime minister does not have to look very far to see where he can win power: he only needs to look first to Ontario, then to Quebec, and more recently, to one or two of the western provinces.

The 2015 election campaign spoke volumes about where the prime minister and aspiring prime ministers will wish to focus their efforts. John

Ibbitson, with the *Globe and Mail,* wrote the GTA (Greater Toronto Area) "elects the government," and Richard Warnica made the same point in the *National Post.*[47] Alex Boutilier, of the *Toronto Star,* wrote, "Pity Atlantic Canada, left out of the steady stream of political rallies, stump speeches and photo ops in the lead-up to Canada's 42nd federal election.... A *Star* analysis of the four main federal party leaders' travels between Jan. 1 and Aug. 1, 2015, shows the Atlantic region has been largely left off the itinerary." He added, "'Toronto, British Columbia's Lower Mainland and Quebec have had plenty of attention."[48] Indeed, they have because they decide who holds political power in Ottawa.

There was a time when regional ministers had clout in Ottawa, even regional ministers from Atlantic Canada such as Allan J. MacEachen, Roméo LeBlanc, and Don Jamieson. One is now even hard-pressed to identify who are the regional ministers. Without putting too fine a point on it, regional ministers have lost their place to polling data and analytic measures with a partisan political bent. They have also been replaced by courtiers in the Prime Minister's Office and the Privy Council Office, by carefully selected lobbyists, and by the prime minister's favourite pollsters. As already noted, Justin Trudeau decided to do away with regional ministers.[49]

The loss of regional ministers and their influence has important implications for the Maritime provinces and for regional economic development. Regional ministers had a direct line to the prime minister and could, occasionally at least, sell to the government an initiative for their regions. As noted earlier, Gordon Osbaldeston, a former federal deputy minister of Industry and clerk of the Privy Council, once observed that economic development in the Maritime provinces is relegated to the "odd penalty shot" or "breakaway."[50] His point was that the region could occasionally break out of its reliance on natural resources to secure a major economic development initiative led by a regional minister in the new economy. Osbaldeston had the Mitel project destined for Bouctouche, New Brunswick, and the work of a powerful reginal minister in mind.

With much fanfare, DREE announced that Mitel, a Canadian high-tech company that had enjoyed tremendous growth during the 1970s, would locate two new manufacturing plants in Bouctouche, New Brunswick. The plants were expected to create about one thousand new jobs. DREE would contribute a $15.7 million incentive grant to the Mitel project, which involved a total capital investment of $48 million.[51] The project was strictly a federal initiative; the provincial government first learned of the project through the news media, as did the residents of the province. What's more, the federal Department of Industry also learned of it only as a *fait accompli*. Yet, the Department of Industry considered the high-tech sector its own, not to be shared with DREE. It was busy promoting the sector in such areas as Kanata, Montreal, Toronto, and Waterloo, and it saw no reason why DREE should elbow its way in to bring new investment to areas, which, it concluded, were not particularly suited to the high-tech sector, areas such as Bouctouche, a small Acadian village some fifty kilometres north of Moncton. DREE was disbanded shortly after the Mitel announcement. With the fall of regional ministers, even the odd penalty shot has now become a thing of the past.

A spokesperson for Prime Minister Justin Trudeau explained there is no need for regional ministers because all Cabinet ministers are now expected to "work collaboratively with provinces, territories and communities."[52] The role of regional ministers was hardly limited to working with provinces and communities.[53] The Trudeau government is shaping up to be the most Ontario-centric government in Canadian history—even Sir John A. Macdonald had regional ministers.

Consider that Ontario ministers occupy all key economic portfolios; all regional agencies, including ACOA, no longer report directly to a minister from their regions, except the agency for Southern Ontario. Trudeau's transition team members all had ties to Ontario. The same is also true for senior members of the Prime Minister's Office. Mandate letters that Trudeau sent to all his ministers make no, or very little, reference to Canada's regional circumstances and chiefs of staff appointed by the PMO, rather than by ministers, have a decidedly Ontario bias. One would have expected the minister responsible for Innovation, Science and Economic Development would have been assigned a chief of staff from outside Central Canada, given that he is from Mississauga–Malton, his parliamentary secretary is from Quebec, and that he has responsibility for all the regional agencies, including ACOA. The chief of staff is a senior Bay Street lawyer. This, after the three Maritime provinces, for the first time in history, only sent Members of Parliament on the government side.

It is often said, "Canada is a country of regions."[54] The above further substantiates the case that our national political and administrative institutions were not designed, and have never been adjusted, to reflect Canada's regional character. All eyes are on the House of Commons, not for its ability to hold the government to account, but rather to decide who will hold power or who will be able to govern from the centre for four years.

The West wanted in and pressed for a Triple-E Senate, until Stephen Harper held the reins of power and pushed the Ottawa system to look to Western Canada. Justin Trudeau is now tilting things back to the Ontario and Quebec economic agenda. The "Ottawa system" and the national media have not raised any concerns with the new order. The voices of the three Maritime provinces have not carried much weight in the past, as earlier chapters make clear. The region's voice has less and less influence in shaping national policies and in bringing forward an economic development agenda that will resonate where it matters, in Ottawa.

LOOKING BACK

Canada's economic landscape has changed. The east-west trade patterns that have long favoured the country's industrial heartland have been redefined by a more integrated global economy. Canada's political landscape has also changed. The political power of rep by pop has, if anything, been strengthened in recent years, as powerful regional ministers of the past have become relics of Canadian politics. There is now little in the way to inhibit a prime minister from focusing efforts on regions that can help him win and maintain power.

Canada's public policy landscape has changed in tandem. Canada is slowly moving away from redistributive policies, particularly when it comes to transfers to provincial governments. The Maritime provinces, notably their premiers, have been left on the sideline, still calling for more of the same, for the status quo, at least when it comes to federal transfer payments. Their voices, however, are not as well heard as they once were.

Given the loss of political clout, the requirements of a highly competitive global economy, and changes to Canada's body politic, it is unlikely the status quo in federal government programs can be maintained, including in the Maritime provinces. The region is losing even the slight political clout that it once had in Ottawa. For this and other reasons, the status quo in public policy, particularly when it comes to federal government transfers to slow-growth regions, is now unravelling. There is little support outside of the Maritime region to sustain it. In addition, federal regional development policy has lost its way. As we have seen, the policy is now present in all regions and is trying to be all things to all regions, capable of accommodating not only all political ideologies, but also political requirements on the ground. Globalization is here to stay, notwithstanding nationalist noises coming from the Trump administration in the US.

What to do? What now for the region? What should provincial governments do? What can we expect from the federal government? How can we grow the regional economy? The concluding chapter seeks to answer these important questions.

NOTES

1 David Held et al., quoted in *Global Transformations* (Redwood City, CA: Stanford University Press, 1999).

2 See, among others, Kenichi Ohmae, *The End of the Nation State: The Rise of Regional Economies* (New York: Simon and Schuster, 1995).

3 Brodie, *The Political Economy of Canadian Regionalism*, 145.

4 "Development Agency Seen as Model for this Province," *Saint John Telegraph-Journal*, January 11, 2008, B1.

5 "Ontario's Premier Threatens Surcharge on Korean Cars," *Globe and Mail*, January 23, 2009, A4.

6 Kevin Lynch, clerk of the Privy Council and secretary to the Cabinet in the government of Canada, made this point in his "Succeeding in a Globalized World: Canada's Challenge and Opportunity" (remarks delivered to the Ivey Business School, University of Western Ontario, London, ON, November 15, 2007), 1.

7 See, among others, David A. Wolfe and Meric S. Gertler, "Globalization and Economic Restructuring in Ontario: From Industrial Heartland to Learning Region?" (paper prepared for the NECSTS/RICTES-99 Conference on Regional Innovation Systems in Europe, Donostia-San Sebastian, Spain, September 30-October 2, 1999), mimeo, 3.

8 Andrew Stark, "Preface," in Thomas J. Courchene with Colin R. Telmer, *From Heartland to North American Region State* (Toronto: Monograph Series on Public Policy, Centre for Public Management, 1998), iv and 86.

9 Thomas Walkom, "The Year Ottawa Elected Its Own PM," *Toronto Star*, December 29, 1990, D4.

10 *Competing in the New Global Economy*, 3 vols. (Toronto: Government of Ontario, 1988-89).

11 Kevin Lynch, "Canada's Public Service and the New Global Normal of Change," *Policy* (July/August 2015): 4.

12 Quoted in Donald J. Savoie, *Power: Where Is It?* (Montreal and Kingston: McGill-Queen's University Press, 2010), 19.

13 "Moncton Exxon Mobil Jobs at Risk," *Saint John Telegraph-Journal*, July 30, 2015, https://www.telegraphjournal.com/times-transcript/story/43346775/moncton-exxonmobil-jobs-at.

14 See, among many others, "Janis Grantham on How to Grow a Business," *Globe and Mail*, December 21, 2007, B2.

15 "Industry Pleads for Help to Ease Crisis," *Globe and Mail*, November 4, 2008, B1.

16 Bill Hammond, interview by Peter Mansbridge, *The National*, CBC, August 10, 2015.

17 "Our History," Hammond Power Solutions, accessed on August 17, 2015, www.hammondpowersolutions.com/about-us/our-history.

18 Pete Evans, "Carmakers Say Adios to Canada as Mexico Shifts into Higher Gear," CBC News Business, June 15, 2015, www.cbc.ca/news/business/carmakers-say-adios-to-canada-as-mexico-shifts-into-higher-gear-1.3108148.

19 See, for example, "Manufacturing: Why Mexico is Eating Canada's Lunch," BlazingCatFur, April 17, 2015, www.blazingcatfur.ca/2015/04/25/manufacturing-why-mexico-is-eating-canadas-lunch/.

20 See, for example, Greg Keenan, "Mexico Races Ahead in Auto Industry as Canada Stalls," *Globe and Mail*, February 9, 2015, www.theglobeandmail.com/report-on-business/international-business/latin-american-business/mexico-races-ahead-in-auto-industry-as-canada-stalls/article22885336/.

21 Ibid.

22 Wolfe and Gertler, "Globalization and Economic Restructuring in Ontario" 15-16.

23 See Greg Keenan, "Made in Mexico: An Emerging Auto Giant Powers Past Canada," *Globe and Mail*, February 13, 2015, www.theglobeandmail.com/report-on-business/international-business/latin-american-business/mexico-feature/article22987307/; and Greg Keenan, "Toyota Moves Corolla to Mexico, Highlighting High Costs in Canada," *Globe and Mail*, April 14, 2015, www.theglobeandmail.com/report-on-business/international-business/toyota-moves-corolla-to-mexico-highlighting-high-costs-in-canada/article23963034/.

24 Canada, Statistics Canada, CANSIM, table 281-0024.

25 Richard Simeon, "Thinking about Constitutional Futures: A Framework" (paper prepared for the C. D. Howe Institute, December 1990), mimeo, 12.

26 Please consult Mowat Centre's website for several studies on the issue, www.mowatcentre.ca.

27 "Western Premiers Say Scales Tipped Against Rich Provinces," *Times and Transcript* (Moncton), August 27, 2015, 1 and 6.

28 Quoted in Steve Lambert, "Have-not Provinces Getting too much Equalization Money, Brad Wall Says," *National Post*, August 6, 2015, http://news.

nationalpost.com/news/canada/have-not-provinces-getting-too-much-equalization-money-brad-wall-says.

29 See, for example, Starr, *Equal As Citizens*.

30 Quoted in John Ibbitson, "The More Things Stay the Same," *Globe and Mail*, October 27, 2004, www.theglobeandmail.com/news/world/the-more-things-stay-the-same/article746662/.

31 Quoted in "Deal Worth $28 Billion," *Chronicle-Herald* (Halifax), October 27, 2004, 1.

32 Quoted in "Atlantic Premiers Protest," *Toronto Star*, September 29, 2004, A7.

33 Jim Travers, "Kings and Barons Divvy up Pie," *Toronto Star*, October 26, 2004, A7.

34 Andrew Coyne, "Equalization, without the Equalization," *National Post*, October 30, 2004, A16.

35 See, for example, Murray Campbell, "Ontario Struggles to Decide whether or not It Exists," *Globe and Mail*, August 2, 2008, A13.

36 Don Drummond made this point in his report *Commission on the Reform of Ontario's Public Services* (Toronto: Queen's Printer for Ontario, 2012), chapter 20.

37 Saillant, *A Tale of Two Countries*.

38 Canada, "Address by Prime Minister Paul Martin at First Ministers' Meeting," (Office of the Prime Minister, September 13, 2004), 5–7.

39 "New Federal Investments on Health Commitments on 10-year Action Plan on Health" (Health Canada news release, September 16, 2004). It should be noted that, combined with CHST tax points, the total transfer stood at $30.6 billion in 2005–06.

40 Canada, *History of Health and Social Transfers* (Ottawa: Department of Finance, n.d.).

41 Ibid.

42 Keith Banting and John Myles, eds., *Inequality and the Fading of Redistributive Politics* (Vancouver: UBC Press, 2013), 1.

43 Jane Jensen, "Historical Transformation of Canada's Social Architecture: Institutions, Instruments and Ideas," in ibid., 48.

44 Senator Lowell Murray, quoting from B. Guy Peters, made this observation in Bouctouche, NB, June 8, 2011.

45 Carl Dahlstrom, B. Guy Peters, and Jon Pierre, eds., *Steering from the Centre: Strengthening Political Control in Western Democracies* (Toronto: University of Toronto Press, 2011).

46 Lowell Murray, "Power, Responsibility, and Agency in Canadian Government," in *Governing: Essays in Honour of Donald J. Savoie*, ed. James Bickerton and B. Guy Peters (Montreal and Kingston: McGill-Queen's University Press, 2013), 27.

47 Richard Warnika, "Toronto the Kingmaker: A Handful of GTA Ridings Will Likely Decide the Election," *National Post*, August 17, 2015, http://news.nationalpost.com/news/canada/toronto-the-kingmaker-a-handful-of-gta-ridings-will-likely-decide-the-election; and "Battleground: Mississauga Centre," *Globe and Mail*, accessed August 22, 2015. www.theglobeandmail.com.

48 Alex Boutilier, "Following the Leaders: Parties Sharpen Focus on Battleground Provinces," Star.com, August 22, 2015, www.thestar.com/news/canada/2015/08/22/following-the-leaders-parties-sharpen-focus-on-battleground-provinces.html.

49 Mia Rabson, "Trudeau Doing Away with Regional Cabinet Ministers," *Winnipeg Free Press*, November 18, 2015, www.winnipegfreepress.com/canada/Trudeau-doing-away-with-regional-cabinet-ministers-351527191.html.

50 Gordon Osbaldeston made the observation at a meeting I attended in Ottawa in 1982.

51 "La venue de 2 usines à Bouctouche créera 1,000 emplois dans Kent," *L'Évangéline* (Moncton), July 17, 1981, 3.

52 Rabson, "Trudeau Doing Away with Regional Cabinet Ministers."

53 See, for example, Herman Bakvis, *Regional Ministers: Power and Influence in the Canadian Cabinet* (Toronto: University of Toronto Press, 1991).

54 Ailsa Henderson, "Regional Political Culture in Canada," *Canadian Journal of Political Science* 37, no. 4 (2004): 595–615.

Chapter 14

WHAT NOW?

The Maritime region has been pulling against gravity to promote economic development virtually since Canada was born. We can once again return to John K. Galbraith's question, posed in the Introduction, to offer an inventory of contributing factors: geography; the shift to a continental economy; the arrival of the railway; National Policy, which forced the region to look inland rather than to the seas; the rep by pop bias of national political institutions; the old dictum in economic development that success breeds success and failure breeds failure; and the region's resistance to change all contribute to the answer. I can only repeat that when it comes to economic development, the more important factor is geography. which explains two-thirds of everything. How then can the region plan its economic future? This is the more important question, given changing economic circumstances and the changes to Canada's body politic at play.

DRAWING FROM THE THEORIES

As we saw earlier, we now have many theories to explain the location and pace of economic development. Yet, we have only made modest progress since the Economic Council of Canada concluded—after an exhaustive review of regional development efforts—that we had yet to find a "penicillin" to deal with Canada's regional development problem.[1] The Economic

Council tried hard to make the regional disparity problem go away by looking at various economic indicators to make the point that things were not so bad. However, it knew politicians were not likely to throw in the towel, and it had this unhelpful advice for them: go and try "this and that."

Many economists would like to see government simply give up on regional development. Albert Breton astutely asked why governments everywhere in the world are pursuing regional development policies when economists say they should not and that they should be encouraging the mobility of people instead.[2] However, politicians from slow-growth regions in particular have never given up and are unlikely to do so in the future. They will continue to try "this and that" because there is not much else available.

Certainly, the theories discussed in chapter 3 resonate with students and with some practitioners of regional development. Maritimers, for example, can actually see both sides of the dependency debate. Perroux's work was valid, as a theory, if misapplied. Entrepreneurship is key to economic development no matter the region, comparative advantages explain a great deal about the location of economic activities. And Moretti's new geography does shed light on patterns and location of regional economic activities. These theories all hold a kernel of truth but not the complete answer. They apply, some of the time, to some regions but not all the time and to all regions. Some of the theories may well explain the behaviour of regions and their residents but are of limited immediate political value to policy-makers. This has left politicians to argue that when it comes to regional development, "it depends" and to make outlandish claims when introducing a new approach to regional development.

Perhaps in time, we may have to admit defeat, but for now it is not possible to define a general theory of regional development. There are several important roadblocks. Such a theory would have to draw from a number of disciplines and deal with an increasingly complex and interwoven global economy. Regional development is about economics, the working of political institutions, bureaucracy, the urban-rural structure, the people factor, and attitudes, and still more factors.

My own contribution is limited to making the case that the institutional setting found in the Maritimes at national, provincial, and community levels has a great deal to answer for, which speaks to the central theme of this book. Leaving aside geography, the pace of the region's economic development is tied to the ability of governments to establish the circumstances for economic success. In the case of the Maritime provinces, governments at all levels, but mainly the national government, have focused their regional development efforts on managing political expectations and a political agenda. We saw earlier, for example, that the federal government, no matter the party in power, has been particularly adroit at unveiling a major reform effort in regional development or ambitious new measures when a national general election is looming. The institutional setting has not only failed to establish the circumstances for economic success in the Maritime region, it has also given rise to resistance to change and an ingrown conservatism of thought and action.[3]

Of course, Canada is not alone among western countries to have been trying this and that in regional development since the 1960s. Accordingly, we can draw from lessons learned to plan the way ahead for the Maritime provinces. Answering John K. Galbraith's question was, in many ways, the easy part. Introducing suggestions in complex and uncertain sociopolitical and economic environments is full of pitfalls. If there is one constant in this economic environment, it is change. New economic opportunities can emerge just as quickly as traditional sectors can hit a wall.

The best we can do is learn from experience and set a reform agenda that speaks to all economic actors. The region will need to look at itself, above all, but also to the community institutions, the private sector, the three provincial governments, and the federal government to set an economic development agenda to compete better in the global economy.

The one theory discussed in chapter 3 that holds some promise for the region is the literature on new regionalism. It looks at a global setting rather than a national perspective, recognizes the limits of top-down stewardship, seeks to develop clusters, encourages adaptation, stresses the importance of local institutions, looks to rural as well as urban development, attaches importance to the effective management of natural resources in a sustainable manner, and pursues niche markets.[4] New regionalism does not only look at formal institutions, but also at non-state coalitions and informal sectors to promote economic development. The challenge is how to make all of this work in three small jurisdictions that continue to lose population, are highly rural, and are home to a fast-aging population.

As this book makes clear, formal institutions, from national, political, and administrative institutions to the three small provincial governments jealously guarding their jurisdictions, have not always served the region's economic interests. Maritimers will have to be much more aggressive in pursuing economic development in the future, and formal institutions can never constitute the full answer.

SETTING THE AGENDA

Maritimers should recognize that having a strong central government has never been in their interest from an economic development perspective. The benefits flowing out of the Rowell-Sirois bargain did not lead to self-sustaining economic development (see the dependency debate in chapter 3), and in any event, the bargain is now on shaky ground. Over the years, Ottawa has employed its economic development instruments (from investments in R&D, the location of public servants, to tariffs and trade policies) to the benefit of the country's heartland—by happy coincidence the region that also decides who holds political power. We also saw in earlier chapters that political considerations, more than economic ones, fuelled all of Ottawa's new approaches to regional economic development.

This is not to suggest that the federal government should be let off the hook in setting an economic development agenda for the Maritimes. One thing it cannot do is sit back and tell the Maritime region to pick itself up by its own bootstraps. It has never asked that of Ontario, Quebec, or Western Canada, and it should not ask that of the Maritimes. The federal government needs to play an active role and revisit not only *what* it is currently doing in the region but also *how*. That said, the agenda extends far beyond the federal government, which is not the most important actor. It can provide support, adjust what it is doing to help, but it cannot lead for a variety of reasons, including the reality that the region does not command the necessary political clout to influence, in any appreciable manner, the country's economic development agenda.

The choice for the Maritime region is clear. It could encourage still more out-migration and see the population shrink to the 500,000 or so people who perhaps could be supported comfortably, though not luxuriously, through a natural-resource-based pattern of development—the ports, the beautiful coastline, the lakes and rivers, the small farms, tourism, and what remains of the fishery and forestry.[5] But even this is doubtful. It is not clear that the rest of Canada could successfully accommodate this level of in-migration, at least in the short or medium term. The region is also dependent on the government of Canada's willingness to continue to flow current or even higher levels of transfers to the regions. As noted, the Maritime provinces are confronting a serious demographic challenge in the years ahead, which will tax further the ability of the three provincial governments to deliver public services. The fiscal difficulties confronting all three provincial governments have been well documented.[6]

The region could do better, much better, on the economic development front. I do not accept that our region is devoid of ideas and potential for economic development. We can halt the slide, but we need to do so with a sense of urgency. Though I recognize there is some boosterism to the call, Nova Scotia's report *Now or Never: An Urgent Call to Action for Nova Scotians* had a point when it concluded that building the region is not only dependent on "federal government policies or the state of the world economy. It is about us—our courage, our imagination and our determination to do better."[7]

We also need to be realistic. The Economic Council of Canada had a point when it tried, in its most ambitious study of regional disparities, to make regional disparities disappear.[8] The Maritime region should accept that the goal of alleviating regional disparities now belongs to the history books, because that goal was born when confidence was high in the government's ability to pursue ambitious goals, when governments had healthy balance sheets, and when the baby boomers were coming of age to join the labour force.

Things on all fronts are vastly different today. As we saw earlier, regional economic disparities narrowed, particularly in per capita income, when Ottawa opened the transfer tap to both individuals and provincial governments. That too now belongs to the history books, unless someone arrives in Ottawa prepared to re-open the transfer payment tap to slow-growth regions. That, however, is unlikely. It appears the best the Maritimes can hope for, when it comes to federal transfers, is the status quo, especially at a time when the cost of delivering public services—particularly health care—will balloon because of the region's aging population. However, recent decisions to tie federal transfers to a per capita criteria suggest the status quo in delivering a nationally recognized level of services will not hold over the medium and long terms.

The region's economic development goal should be tied to making its private sector more competitive, creating jobs, attracting new residents, generating enough economic activities and revenues to sustain a solid level of public service, making our publicly sponsored institutions more competitive, and increasing the region's capacity for self-reliance. This requires a sharp wrench of the economic development wheel and the full participation of all economic actors in the region, including some that have never before considered themselves economic actors. This is why an economic development agenda for the region needs to begin with the people factor.

THE PEOPLE FACTOR

Wade MacLauchlan spoke on community development at the October 2013, Georgetown Conference, held in Prince Edward Island, and urged participants to push the "reset" button when it came to "attitude." He called on Atlantic Canadians to focus on new "creative ideas" that can transform communities and put them on the road to economic development. He made the point that a negative attitude, which is all too often seen in our region, leads nowhere. Less than two years later, MacLauchlan became premier of his province, and he still stresses the importance of attitude in economic development.[9] He is not alone.

In my report on the establishment of ACOA, I wrote that we must pay much more attention than we have traditionally to institutions, culture, historical processes, and the population factor. The latter two elements encompass attitudes, education, and all the other factors that affect the capacity of a people to contribute to its region's economic development. Current approaches to regional development only slight the population factor by dealing with people as a generic entity, ignoring intrinsic dynamics.[10] I wrote this twenty years ago, and if anything, the point is even more valid today.

I hasten to add that others have made the same point. It became a central theme of both the high-profile Ivany Report in Nova Scotia and New Brunswick's four-year economic development plan, tabled in 2012.[11] Don Mills, the region's leading pollster, had this to say: "On a wide variety of social, economic and political issues…[o]ne consistent theme has been the continuing resistance to change and the strong affinity for the status quo, which is evident across Atlantic Canada."[12]

The attitude problem in the Maritimes is pervasive. It speaks to a belief that somehow the region can cling to the status quo, to a notion that it can say no to emerging opportunities in some of the natural resources and mining sectors, expecting government will always intervene to make things right. Some in the region also hold the view that people and opportunities are better elsewhere. Charlotte LeBlanc's painful account of her son's battle with schizophrenia speaks to the latter point. In her book, she tells her son to get help in Toronto because "doctors in Toronto are probably smarter than the ones in Moncton."[13]

Why is the attitude problem more evident, or at least more discussed, in the Maritime region than in other regions? It is considerably easier to move away from a culture of defeatism if you are sitting in Alberta, where geography has handed you one of the world's largest reservoirs of oil and gas; or in Toronto, where the fast-growing Canadian financial sector is concentrated; or in Ottawa, where bootstraps are tied to thousands and thousands of well-paying federal public jobs and numerous consultant contracts and where more and more federal government jobs from the regions are transferred; or in Montreal and Ontario, where federal government investments in the automobile, aerospace, pharmaceutical, and high-tech sectors have created thousands of jobs and enabled entrepreneurs to launch new businesses.

Our region's attitude problem is rooted in the institutional setting and in our demography, not solely in individual Maritimers. The young Maritimer from Bouctouche who commuted to Fort McMurray between 2011 and 2015 does not have a culture of defeatism. The young Maritimer who picked up and moved to Ottawa because that is where the jobs are if one wants to work with the federal government does not arrive in the city sporting a culture of defeatism. In short, to the extent that a culture of defeatism and a deep attachment to the status quo exist more in the Maritimes than elsewhere, it is because of its institutions, the region's rural-urban split, its demography, and a lack of economic opportunities due to geography, policies, and decisions flowing out of our national politics—and just plain bad luck.

Apart from its aging population, the region's culture and attitude are also shaped by an economy of scarcity. A higher reliance on transfer payments, both at the provincial government and individual levels, reinforces caution and the status quo. The region also has a strong reliance on traditional occupations, which reinforces a respect for hierarchy, and is prone to favouring the status quo: the military, governments and their reliance on bureaucracy, health, education, and a concentration of ownership in the private sector. The latter has led many Maritimers to view the local private sector not as a dynamic engine for economic growth and job creation, but rather as a threat to the environment and the genesis of inequalities of income and wealth. When I ask them to provide an alternative, however, I am usually met by silence.

Economists may disagree on whether a culture of defeatism actually exists or what its root causes are. They do agree, however, that an important challenge for both the new and the old economy is dealing with the mismatch between the skills and competencies the workforce is offering and the ones employers actually need. Economists recognize countries such as Germany that have been able to establish a close relationship between education and work also have lower unemployment, particularly youth unemployment.[14] In short, skills and qualified people matter to the knowledge economy, the service economy, the cultural economy, the traditional economy, and no less to regional economies.[15] The emphasis in the Maritime region when pursuing the people factor should be on attitudes and skills development, writ large. The region needs a "vaccine" against quick fixes in human resources development, particularly the notion that we ought to focus our effort on growing entrepreneurs.[16]

I have no answer to the age-old question: are entrepreneurs born or formed? I suspect no one has. I undertook an ambitious research project on one of New Brunswick's best known entrepreneurs, Harrison McCain, in part to answer the question.[17] Even though I had full access to all his personal and business papers, to members of his family, and to his business associates, I could not provide an answer. I studied the life and work of K. C. Irving, arguably Canada's leading entrepreneur of the last century. I also had numerous discussions with leading entrepreneurs from my region, including John Bragg, Arthur Irving, and Jean-Claude Savoie. Still, I did not find the answer. Although I can detect similar characteristics among these entrepreneurs—for example, in all four cases, their fathers were themselves entrepreneurs—still it does not answer the question.

But other leading entrepreneurs from my region, such as Normand Caissie, the founder of Imperial Manufacturing Group in Richibucto, learned by doing, not from their fathers. Charles Khoury started with nothing and built a highly successful real estate firm. I asked him what his motivating force was, his role model in business—it was not his father. He told me he had no hope of getting "a good government job," the preferred option his parents had for him, so he decided to start a real estate business. He took no courses in entrepreneurship but learned by doing and pursued business success with single-minded purpose. He reports that the key to business success is to "stay focused." Indeed, if there is a common characteristic that stands out among all successful entrepreneurs with whom I have met, it is the ability and willingness to pursue business success with single-minded purpose. One doubts whether a government-sponsored program can teach single-mindedness.

The challenge with regard to the people factor in the Maritime region is to define an approach to human resources that speaks to a small region, with relatively small urban centres, and which remains dependent on natural resources (forestry, fisheries, mining, agriculture, aquaculture, transportation, and tourism). The approach also has to square with the region's aging population, out-migration of educated youth, and an inability to attract skilled workers from away. The challenge is formidable.

There is no shortage of universities (one in Prince Edward Island, four in New Brunswick, and six in Nova Scotia) and community colleges. The region has more post-secondary institutions per capita than anywhere else in Canada. More to the point, there is no need to throw more money at the region's human resources challenge. Money and institutions are not the issue, matching skills to jobs and generating a more positive attitude are.

Quality of education also does not seem to be the problem. Some 50 per cent of the students at Dalhousie University are from out of the province.[18] And yet higher education in the Maritimes is all too often seen as a ticket out of town. Investments in higher education in the Maritime region may well be contributing to the increased competitiveness of other Canadian regions.[19] The ticket out of town is tied to university graduates having the skills to secure higher paying employment outside the region and a lack of large urban areas at home. The most educated are the most mobile.[20] Ray Ivany, chair of the Ivany Commission and president of Acadia University, had a point when he remarked that the region's post-secondary educational institutions should stop training graduates to become bureaucrats in Ottawa.[21]

When it comes to human resources, all sectors in the Maritime provinces cry out for closer co-operation between governments, the private sector, and the para-public sector. And bureaucratic silos within these governments also need to be broken down. In turn, the private sector needs to be brought in more closely to assist in matching skills to jobs. These measures may not generate the kind of whiz-bang ideas or the kind of visibility politicians look for, but they do hold promise. The challenge is to deal with a problem common to many Maritime communities: people without jobs co-existing with jobs without people.

There are a number of entrenched problems we need to address. As discussed in chapter 9, the education and skills of the region's unemployed are low, when compared with other regions. We have jobs available in our region, but we do not have people with the right skills to fill them. Officials with the Halifax Shipyard were criss-crossing Canada in the fall of 2015, looking for qualified workers—from database administrators and electricians to production controllers (among many others)—to work on ships in support of the national shipbuilding procurement strategy. Armour Transportation Systems in Moncton, New Brunswick, was looking for sixty qualified truckers at a $60,000 salary in the summer of 2015.[22]

In recent years, I met with a number of local business owners who rank the lack of qualified staff as their number one challenge. This is particularly the case with the region's manufacturers and processors in the fishery and wood product sectors. One employer of four hundred skilled and low-skilled workers in the forestry sector in northern New Brunswick, an area plagued with economic difficulties including a constant loss of population, wrote to say, "The business is going great, only one problem—a lack of workers to do all the things that we could do."[23] An entrepreneur in the fish processing sector from southeastern New Brunswick told me the same thing.[24]

This calls for closer co-operation between employers and educational and training institutions. This challenge, in turn, calls for an approach that squares with the region's distinct economic circumstances and private sector. The region's private sector consists largely of small firms without an immediate capacity or the necessary resources to assist governments and community institutions in shaping a new approach to human resources development. Government officials and educational facilities have to reach out to small businesses, not the other way around.

I stress once again that the people factor extends beyond skills training. It also speaks to attitude and to a sense of community. I have had numerous discussions with business leaders from the region since the federal government published my report on the establishment of ACOA.

Without suggesting for a moment these discussions amount to a representative survey, I have heard time and again from local business leaders that Maritimers are too negative, hold a poor image of the region, and are overly parochial. Recall the discussion, in chapter 12, of the response Ben Cowan-Dewar received when he first decided to build world-class golf courses in Cape Breton.

On attitude, the best one can do is take today's political and business leaders back to Frank McKenna's agenda. As we well know, one of McKenna's most important contributions to economic development in New Brunswick was to instill in New Brunswickers a sense of pride and a can-do attitude. He decided to tackle the problem in many different ways. McKenna himself accepted numerous speaking engagements outside the province to sell the assets of New Brunswick and to report on "the diversity and strength of its people and its successes."[25] He went to major economic centres in Canada and abroad to promote the province and to "aggressively market New Brunswick to the world."[26]

At home, McKenna took a comprehensive approach to improve the image New Brunswickers had of their province and of themselves. For example, he turned to local firms to handle tourism promotion and other public relations work for the provincial government rather than using Toronto-based companies, as had been done in the past. The thinking here was that, given a chance, New Brunswickers would, in the great majority of circumstances, be as creative and productive as any out-of-province firm. He was proved right, and today New Brunswick is home to several highly successful public relations and communications firms. Many of these have gone on to secure contracts in other parts of Canada and abroad and to secure high-profile work contracts with leading New Brunswick firms, such as McCain and Irving.[27]

I have no data to compare the sense of regional community among Maritimers to other regions; however, I believe this issue needs attention. I wrote a report in 2010 for the government of Nova Scotia, *Invest More, Innovate More, Trade More, Learn More: The Way Ahead for Nova Scotia*, that speaks to this issue. On the very first page, I made the point that Halifax had "become the powerful economic engine not only for Nova Scotia but also for the other two Maritime provinces."[28] Leaving aside Halifax-based government officials, the reaction to this suggestion was anything but positive. I received comments from Cape Breton, Moncton, and Prince Edward

Island, essentially suggesting that Halifax did not need a boost from anyone since it already had more than its share of economic growth. Their suggestion was that instead economic development can somehow be easily directed away from the region's most important urban centre. We saw earlier observations from Cape Bretoners suggesting the region should not encourage growth in Halifax, which speaks to the politics of scarcity and to managing political expectations rather than establishing circumstances for economic success.

If the growth pole concept, however modestly conceived, is to have any continued relevance, one must conclude Halifax is now, even more than it was in 2010, the region's economic engine that can benefit all of the Maritimes. It is by far the region's largest urban centre, home to a marvellous port, a top-ranked university, an important naval establishment, a relatively large federal presence, a provincial government, and a draw for young educated Maritimers.

The role of Halifax extends well beyond its municipal boundaries. As an economic centre, it is home to the third largest container traffic port in Canada and draws migrants from other Canadian regions. Halifax is also home to a $26 billion shipbuilding contract that holds untold opportunities for businesses in the three Maritime provinces. The challenge for the region and its private sector is to identify and pursue the numerous opportunities flowing out of the contract and other developments in Halifax.

COMMUNITY INSTITUTIONS

The region's community organizations are also tied to the people factor. By community organizations, I am referring to the region's relatively large public and not-for-profit institutions, notably universities, hospitals, schools, and municipal governments. They are among the largest employers and purchasers of goods and services in the region.[29] They also possess specialized knowledge and presumably a deep commitment to their communities. A call centre may well decide to move its operations from Moncton to India to take advantage of lower wages, and with it, jobs away from the community. The two local hospitals and the local university are not going to pick up and leave. In that sense they are our anchor institutions.[30]

The Maritime region is late to the party of turning to community institutions to promote economic development. An increasing number of American communities have looked to their universities and hospitals as engines of economic growth. There is also mounting evidence that this approach is having an impact, particularly in the inner cities.[31] This is not to suggest Maritime community institutions have only had a modest impact on the region's economy. My own university, for example, has had a profound impact on its community and on the broader Acadian community. The university's budget is over $115 million annually, and it employs nearly one thousand people when we include both full- and part-time employees.[32] The university has also spawned an Acadian renaissance and given members of the Acadian community the confidence to launch numerous new businesses since its establishment.[33] I know many non-Canadian students who have decided to remain in the region after graduation and are productive members of society.

Dalhousie University's economic impact has also been well documented. It generates a direct and indirect employment impact of over ten thousand Full-Time Equivalents (FTEs), adds $1 billion to the province's GDP, and generates $243 million in personal and indirect taxes. The university also generates some $130 million in research funding.[34] It also attracts about 50 per cent of its students from the outside the province. Where Dalhousie and other Maritime universities fall short is in generating a "dynamic" economic impact.

Richard Florizone, Dalhousie's president, has admitted as much. He argued the university could do much more to provide students with "the skills to build companies" and to tie research more effectively to the needs of local firms.[35] The Ivany Commission, chaired by Acadia University president Ray Ivany, also asked the province's post-secondary institutions to do more in developing the province's economy.[36]

Community institutions give their communities job security and stability in the eyes of local businesses. What more could they do? The first step is for community institutions to accept they have a role to play in promoting economic development in their communities and regions that extends beyond their traditional functions. If they are committed to the economic health of their regions, they will need to go beyond teaching and carrying out research, looking after patients, collecting property taxes, and delivering municipal services. The challenge is to turn community institutions into something more than what they are. As Nevena Dragicevic explained, the test is to see them act as engines of economic development and for their leaders to take on a "new identity and [accept] the role and related responsibilities."[37]

Community institutions can simplify procurement processes, an important point in the Maritime region given that small businesses make up the bulk of the region's business community. They, or their administrative arms, as well as the in-house capacity found in the various faculties of management, could help small local businesses to develop proposals and submit tenders for procurement contracts. This is done in other regions.[38] More could also be done to assist small firms to tap into what community institutions, particularly the universities, have to offer in terms of expertise in fields from marketing to engineering. University faculties are still too prone to looking inward, and small firms do not have the capacity or resources to roam the halls of academia to see who or what may help their firms to grow and become more competitive. The challenge for public bureaucracies is to reach out to their community's business leaders rather than sit back and wait for the business leaders to knock on their doors. This applies particularly to provincial and federal bureaucracies in the economic development field.

THE PRIVATE SECTOR

Economic theory often has it right: higher productivity can translate into economic growth, lower costs translate into more employment, and market forces and the private sector can create thriving regional economies. Though both the private and public sectors have important roles to play, it is the private sector that is the driving force behind wealth creation and the pursuit of new economic opportunities. In addition, regional trade agreements are seeing nations, regions, and governments rely more and more on the business sector to generate economic activities and jobs.[39]

The Maritime region's private sector differs from that in other Canadian regions. As noted, it is made up of a handful of locally owned large firms, a number of large firms from away, many local businesses operating franchises (from auto dealerships to fast-food restaurants), as well as small manufacturers and processors in the food and forestry sectors. Maritimers can count on two hands the number of firms listed on the Toronto Stock Exchange.

Publicly traded companies have an obligation to make information about their financial situation publicly available and to answer to shareholders. Privately held firms have no such obligations. The reporting burden on publicly traded firms has become much heavier with the Sarbanes-Oxley

Act and its sister Canadian legislation, and even more demanding in the aftermath of the 2008 financial crisis.[40] The shift to greater transparency, however, has had little impact on the private sector in the Maritimes because we have so few publicly traded companies. This, too, contributes to the status quo, making it difficult for anyone outside the firms, large or small, to challenge what is being done and how it is being done.

The region also has precious few medium- and large-firm head offices. Large firms from away typically have their head offices in large urban centres in Ontario, Quebec, the United States, or Europe. Large privately held family firms are also moving their head offices out of the regions. McCain Foods is a case in point. While Harrison McCain, co-founder of the firm, was CEO, he resisted all attempts to move the head office to Toronto. Indeed, he continued to pile "everything he could into New Brunswick."[41]

Things began to change when a non-family member became CEO. Harrison McCain agreed, with some reservations, to move a few activities out of New Brunswick when then newly appointed CEO Howard Mann decided to establish his own office in Toronto. Mann explained he had no intention of sitting on his backside, indeed, more often than not, he would be on the road given that McCain Foods was now a global firm. Toronto, he pointed out, was far more accessible to Europe, Australia, and the United States than was Florenceville. He argued that most of the head office functions would remain in Florenceville; however, gradually more and more head office activities made their way to Toronto. Things that matter to the head office of McCain Foods are now located in Toronto; Florenceville remains the head office of McCain Foods essentially in name only. Florenceville is no match for Toronto, but much less so today than when Harrison McCain launched the business with his brother Wallace in the 1950s.

Global firms have their own requirements, even if they are family-owned and privately held. Senior managers will make the case that their firms need to attract top-flight talent in marketing, financial, and human resources management and have easy access to global transportation and information infrastructure. For instance, Imvescor Restaurant Group, founded by a Université de Moncton graduate, operates restaurants such as Baton Rouge, Mikes, and Pizza Delight. It decided in early 2015 to move much of its head office from Moncton to Montreal. The founder lost control of the firm when it went public, and management convinced the board of directors that Montreal was better suited than Moncton to attract talent and to connect with peers.[42]

In the spring of 2015, rumours began circulating in the region that Nova Scotia-based grocery giant Sobeys, located in Stellarton, was slowly moving head office functions out of the region. Sobeys business had shifted west when it bought Canada Safeway from California-based Safeway in 2013 for $5.8 billion. In May 2015 Sobeys announced it would move some head office functions to Calgary to look after western business operations. The thinking is that, in time, Sobey's will locate a central head office in Toronto with regional operations in Western Canada and Atlantic Canada. I note that a non-family member is now CEO at Sobeys.[43]

The head office of Co-op Atlantic was substantially slimmed down in 2015 after it shut down its food and gas retail businesses. The decision led to four hundred employees losing their jobs, with the bulk of the loss affecting the head office and its warehouse, both located in Moncton.[44]

One exception to this series of examples is the Irving business empire. It has steadfastly decided to locate all of its head office functions in the region. The various Irving businesses remain privately held, and members of the family continue to run all key operations. They employ leading experts in marketing and financial management and continue to lead several large organizations from Saint John, New Brunswick.

Does it matter? Yes, and for many reasons. Head offices employ highly skilled and well paid professionals. They also turn to highly qualified professional consultant services in virtually every facet of management. Key strategic decisions about investments and operations are struck in head offices. The head offices decide which lawyers, financial services, auditors, and IT specialists to retain. Key head office staff are not only well educated, but they are also high-energy and high-achieving individuals who are often willing to help their communities.[45] Head offices will invariably look to local charities when making philanthropic contributions. There are also head office biases. It is head office, for example, that decides where to locate the firm's R&D efforts, which, much more often than not, will be located in the same city.[46] It is also important to note regional operations tend to favour the status quo, with head offices often the only ones to drive meaningful change. Indeed, generally, only senior head office personnel have the mandate to define and pursue change.

Head offices tend to locate where other head offices are. They favour larger urban areas to attract highly qualified personnel. In addition, all regions and all communities, particularly urban areas, will make every effort to attract head offices. Recall that Ottawa became concerned over Canada's loss of head offices in the aftermath of the 2005-07 wave of foreign acquisitions and mergers.[47] Although its concern was limited to the narrow corridor between Montreal and Toronto.

The three Maritime provinces have all sought to attract head offices, but with little success. The Greater Halifax Partnership has led the charge in promoting the city as a place to locate head offices. It speaks to Halifax's strategic location for international business travel, lower costs, and access to a talented workforce. It redefined *head office* into *head and regional offices* to claim a leading position in eastern Canada.[48] Data from Statistics Canada suggest a different story. There are 2,756 head offices in Canada, employing 227,684 people. There are only 143 head offices in the Maritime provinces, employing 6,953 people.[49]

Some 95 per cent of private firms in the Maritime region employ less than a hundred people. Notwithstanding, the percentage of self-employed individuals as a percentage of the total labour force is lower in the Maritime provinces (13 per cent) than the national average (16 per cent). On the other hand, the Maritime region has been leading the national average in entry rates in launching businesses. Prince Edward Island had an entry rate of 13.7 per cent, Nova Scotia was at 13.2 per cent, and New Brunswick at 13.4 per cent, compared to 12.7 per cent at the national level. Conversely, the region also leads the national average when it comes to business exit rates: Prince Edward Island at 20.9 per cent, Nova Scotia at 17.3 per cent, and New Brunswick also at 17.3, compared to 12.9 for the national average.[50]

The point is that small businesses and regional operations of national and global firms make up much of the private sector in the Maritime region. This comes with its own set of challenges. Small firms often do not have either the resources or the inclination to invest in searching out new markets, promoting new thinking in marketing their products or services, and investing in R&D. This is where community institutions and governments can help. They can perform head office–type functions to assist small firms. If we are to grow the Maritime economy in this highly competitive and fast-changing global economy, community institutions have a particular responsibility to promote economic development by helping our business community.

We saw earlier the Maritime region has been successful in pursuing new markets after a wave of regional trade agreements were signed. Trade agreements, from NAFTA to TPP, offer growth potential for Maritime businesses; a return to pre–National Policy days as there is evidence that Canada's east-west trade patterns are not as strong as they once were; and make way for emerging global and regional trade patterns. The region is once again free to look to the seas, rather than inland, to identify and pursue new economic opportunities. Government and community organizations can play a role in applying the new regionalism approach to the Maritimes. Because of the size of its private firms, the region's private sector needs a helping hand to identify and pursue new markets flowing out of the TPP and European Union trade agreements.

The region's private sector lags behind in applying advanced technology in their work. We know that 48.7 per cent of large enterprises employ at least one advanced technology in their work compared with 34.7 per cent for small businesses. This may well explain why businesses in the Maritime region trail badly behind other regions in applying at least one advanced technology in their work: 15 per cent of the businesses in the region compared to over 40 per cent in the case of Ontario and Quebec.[51] Head offices play a lead role in both pursuing new markets abroad and promoting the application of advanced technologies. This is also where community organizations and government bureaucracies can help by playing a proactive role. This, in turn, makes the case that the region's innovation strategy should focus on being there rather than being first, and more is said about this below.

I have often heard representatives of the region's business community stressing the importance of greater co-operation between the three provincial governments. A number have told me that they favour Maritime political union and there are things that they could do to promote a Maritime perspective. The three provinces hold an annual "provincial" business hall of fame dinner to honour three business leaders. The business community would send a powerful message to the three provincial governments, and to Maritimers, if instead they were to hold one "Maritime" business hall of fame dinner to honour three business leaders. The business community, not just governments, has a responsibility for turning the region into something more than a region of the mind.

PROVINCIAL GOVERNMENTS

The global, national, and regional economies are shaped by powerful market forces and provincial governments have less influence in shaping the location and pace of economic activities within their jurisdictions than is generally assumed or that provincial politicians maintain—particularly during election campaigns. The three provincial governments in the Maritime region operate at the margin and are subject to major economic forces over which they have little control: monetary policy, the value of the American dollar, Ottawa's fiscal policy, and trade flows between major economic powers.

Provincial governments need to select very carefully where they want to focus their energies and resources, and this is particularly important for the three Maritime provinces given their difficult fiscal situation. Provincial governments also need to assess carefully where their efforts can have the most beneficial impact and guard against overloading their political and policy agendas as well as their fiscal capacity. Successful modern governments have been able to focus on three or four major policy issues, while those that sought to pursue numerous priorities, in the end, failed to have much of an impact.[52]

The region's public policy agenda, over the short and medium terms, will be dominated by an aging population and a particularly difficult fiscal challenge. This is a powerful brew that requires a determined and focused political will. Richard Saillant has documented the challenge well in his recent book *A Tale of Two Countries*, and there is no need to review the same territory here.[53] Suffice to note that if the challenge is not met, the consequences will reverberate in all sectors and in all communities.

The challenge requires the three provincial governments to do what they have failed to do in the past—break down political and bureaucratic silos. More to the point, the region will not be able to meet the challenge, continue to deliver quality public services, attract or even retain skilled workers, and provide the circumstances for the private sector to compete and grow, unless it deals with the economic and fiscal issues from a regional perspective. I cannot overstate the magnitude of the challenge. Governments will need to educate Maritimers on how we can reconcile the region's aging population with its deteriorating fiscal problem. Hardly a week goes by in my province without some association or some group calling for new spending in health care, in infrastructure (including roads), in education—even though our population is declining—and the list goes on.

In a span of a few weeks, the president of the New Brunswick Teachers' Association called for more government spending, insisting the province's "poor education scores show more resources are needed." He had, however, nothing to say on how to make up for lost days because of snow storms—sixteen days in 2015.[54] The province's medical society issued a prescription for better health care in the province: spend more, have more doctors, better access to primary care, and an "infusion of cash to pay for new nursing homes."[55] The two associations never made any suggestion as to where spending cuts could be made in their own or other sectors, which new taxes should be introduced, or which existing ones increased. Both groups are acting like a union rather than a professional association. The problem is that they do not have to deal with markets to test how much they can demand in new funding or salaries. Politicians are left to deal with the problem, a burden they cannot carry on their own.

The region also needs a mechanism that enables it to view health care, social services, and education from a Maritime perspective rather than a provincial one and make all key decisions accordingly. This may require the three legislative assemblies to meet once a year to debate on how to proceed, call for the three premiers and their Cabinets to meet periodically as a policy-making body, and involve new accountability mechanisms to ensure what is promised is delivered.

At the top of the to-do list for all three Maritime governments is the need to control cost in delivering public services, particularly in health care. If they cannot do this, then there is little hope they can do much else, and the region will pay a heavy price. Thinking the region can rely solely on Ottawa to deal with the increasing cost related to an aging population is not in the cards, unless the region demonstrates it is willing to restructure its own service delivery capacity. It cannot be a one-way street.

The three provincial governments also need to manage their programs and program spending more efficiently. At the moment, Prince Edward Island spends 25.8 per cent of GDP on government programs, New Brunswick 23 per cent, and Nova Scotia 19.1 per cent, which compares with 19.4 per cent for the Canadian average.[56] Given the Maritime region's fast-aging population, the pressure to spend more on health care and social services will only intensify at a time when all three provincial governments are confronting difficult fiscal challenges,and as Ottawa reorients its transfer payments to a per capita basis. The best chance the region has in better controlling program costs and delivering an acceptable level of service is to clear the way for close co-operation and explore new regional models for delivering public services.

The same applies to economic development. The region has committed too many resources in the name of economic development over the past fifty years. It made little sense to have three provincial governments competing to attract economic activities, even when their balance sheets were healthier than they are today and when the Canadian economy was relatively isolated from the global economy. It makes no sense today. The three provincial governments need to simplify their approach, coordinate their efforts, and focus on things that matter at a minimum cost to their treasuries. More than ever, economic development and getting the three governments' fiscal houses in order flow into one another.

The Maritime provinces should coordinate their efforts so that the region becomes more than a region of the mind. The constitution created provincial communities, not regional ones.[57] Regions of the mind have little in the way of policy instruments to promote economic development. The constitutional framework establishes clear political boundaries and empowers provincial governments to establish policies and programs, which inhibits a multi-province or regional perspective. There is a built-in inertia at the political, institutional, and bureaucratic levels that makes regional planning and integration extremely difficult. It is worth reiterating that individual Maritime provinces have shown little enthusiasm to coordinate their efforts to promote regional economic development. This approach hindered economic development in the past and holds even less promise for the future.

The three provincial governments should announce to the world that the region is open for business—and mean it. They should consistently prioritize the goal of making the Maritimes the most business friendly jurisdiction in North America. Implement demanding regulations and invite firms to explore for resources, including shale gas, and review corporate and income taxes with the objective to make them competitive. If the region wishes to attract and house head offices, provincial governments need to accept that "taxes (particularly high income tax levels) can also have a powerful influence on headquarters location."[58] High income tax levels are in reality a tax on head offices.

There is no reason, other than political and bureaucratic will, to stop the three provincial governments from declaring the region will be a free trade zone within three years, pursue with enthusiasm free trade protocols for all sectors, and put in place regional standards, not provincial ones. There is no reason to stop the three provincial governments from embracing a common tourism strategy, a common energy grid, a common liquor control commission rather than three small ones; common standards for skilled trades and professional licensing, transportation codes and vehicle legislation; common environmental protection, corporate, and securities regulations; and procurement policies.[59] If some of the changes should favour one community such as Halifax, then so be it.

The call for innovation and more R&D investments, for example, should be carefully adjusted to meet the economic circumstances of the Maritime provinces. Answering the innovation call in the same manner as other regions, from Southern Ontario to California, is not necessarily the solution. Pursuing innovation and R&D in a big bang fashion may often best be left to others.[60] It is likely the Maritime region might benefit more from innovation and R&D investments by strengthening the ability of local firms to adapt innovation to the operations rather than sponsor innovations. The best R&D investments for the Maritimes are often born out of the necessity for local firms to become more productive and competitive. I am thinking of Oxford Foods and the need to invent a machine to harvest blueberries. That machine had a substantial impact on productivity. It was developed by local workers, and it is now sold around the world.[61]

Scales, availability of human capital, and access to venture capital all matter in designing an innovation strategy. The Maritime provinces are lacking on all three levels. This explains why the region performs poorly on the innovation scorecard when ranking it against other Canadian provinces. The Conference Board of Canada looked at three indicators—capacity, activity, and results—to measure performance. It gave the three provinces D and D- grades, ranking all of them at the bottom. It concluded the three provinces perform poorly in business enterprise, R&D, and researchers engaged in R&D, including researchers employed in business, higher education, and government.[62] Given this assessment and the weak fiscal position of all three provincial governments, the region should help local firms adapt and adopt innovation rather than sponsor an ambitious and costly innovation strategy simply because it is now in vogue in the economic development field.

In short, the agenda for the three provincial governments is to put in place the circumstances for economic success in a highly competitive global economy. The global economy is here to stay, and Maritimers who want to stop it have as much of a chance of success as King Canute had in stopping the waves from washing on the shores of England.

LOOKING AHEAD: A FEDERAL AGENDA FOR THE MARITIMES

For well over a century, the federal government has failed to accommodate regional economic circumstances in shaping national policies simply because Canada's political institutions were not designed to accommodate regional circumstances. That the nation's capital is located in Ottawa and more and more federal government officials are located in the NCR in recent years have not helped matters.

It is unlikely we will see an overhaul of Canada's political institutions, at least in the short term. There are too many vested interests in the heavily populated regions to permit it. It is not asking too much from the federal government, however, to define an economic development agenda for the three Maritime provinces. For one thing, the time is long overdue for the federal government to update its approach to economic development at the regional level. For another, there are sectors that belong to the federal government that have a profound impact on the Maritime economy. The federal government has direct responsibility for the fishery, international trade, and immigration sectors—among others—which have come under heavy criticism from the Maritime provinces. A periodic policy and program review in these sectors can push relevant actors in federal government departments, provincial governments, and the private sector to update their approach and to improve or do more. Key decision-makers in federal government departments all work in head offices in Ottawa and are too often prone to "leave well enough alone" unless from time to time they are told to take stock and launch a comprehensive review of what they do and how they do it.[63]

The federal government should play a much stronger leadership role in making the Maritime region more than a region of the mind. It can do this simply by looking at its own organizations, starting with the agency mandated to promote "regional" development. The focus of ACOA is closely tied to its four provincial offices. This organizational model dates back to the early 1970s, when DREE introduced the General Development Agreements approach, which essentially repositioned federal efforts along federal-provincial programs. This serves to reinforce a provincial perspective. Rather than push for regional integration, federal regional development efforts continue to push in the opposite direction. ACOA should have a "Maritime" office, thus a Maritime perspective, and a Newfoundland and Labrador office. There is also a need to update ACOA's approach to economic development—it dates back to 1987, and to the program review exercise of the mid-1990s. Other federal government departments, agencies, and Crown corporations should also review their organizations to promote greater regional integration. The federal government should look to new regionalism, to regional trade agreements, and to a much greater co-operation among the three Maritime provinces to update its approach.

As noted, the Canadian Broadcasting Corporation (CBC) operates three large operations in the three Maritime provincial capitals. Rather than promote regional integration, CBC actually promotes both provincialism and parochialism. Its evening newscasts, for the most part, have a provincial perspective, if only because they are pursuing their mandates, which are provincial in scope. Morning radio news shows are divided along community lines, at least in New Brunswick, with one show for Moncton, another for Saint John, and yet another for Fredericton. This is by no means a way to make the Maritimes something more than a region of the mind.

The federal government should come to the three provincial governments with a proposal to restructure its machinery of government in the region. Savings from the restructuring could be repackaged in an economic development fund. In doing so, Ottawa should put everything on the table. It could go as far as restructuring the courts over which it holds jurisdiction. The three Maritime provinces have three Courts of Appeal, and there is strong evidence that not all have enough on their plates to be kept busy. One only has to look at the cases before the Court of Appeal of Prince Edward Island to see evidence of this.[64]

The region is confronting a daunting demographic challenge, which will be felt in all sectors, particularly in health care. The region cannot address the challenge by itself, and it should ask Ottawa to jointly sponsor a pilot project to cut cost while delivering an acceptable level of public services. The Maritime region will be the first to deal with an aging population, but other regions will follow, starting in Quebec and then working west from Ontario to Alberta.

That is not all. I borrow from my earlier work to, once again, make the case that incorporating regional economic circumstances into National Policy should not be a one-way street. The region itself must recognize it needs to adjust its expectations with regard to federal salaries and wages. These should not be determined by national pay scales applicable equally across Canada.[65] A national salary scale is incompatible with the fact that the Maritimes' economy is different from, say, Ontario's.

Regionally tailored policies are required on many fronts. A national public service pay scale is not compatible with private-sector practices in the regional economy: 40 per cent of Canadian manufacturers plan their pay based on regional differentials, an approach that is also widely employed in the United States. For example, the pay for employees in manufacturing is far higher in Alberta than in the Maritimes, with a gap as wide as 25 per cent.[66] There is every economic reason for the public sector to do the same. There is also a precedent in the federal government, which has two pay grids for its lawyers: one for Toronto-based lawyers and another for lawyers outside of Toronto.[67]

Of course, it is understandable that federal public servants in the Maritimes would prefer having their salaries tied to national standards. But this preference must be weighed against the fact that no salaries are going to the unemployed. Paying national salary levels makes sense if it is required to attract highly qualified people, but, if not, it can create unemployment. The central point here is the federal government should follow the private sector, not lead it. That is, if the private sector decides it needs to pay national salary levels to attract certain skills, then the federal government should do the same. But the obverse also applies. Currently, the federal government inhibits economic development and job creation in the Maritimes by paying higher salaries and wages than the private sector. If these were lower than the national standards, the region would be more competitive in the public sector itself, and the case to locate more federal government units in the region would strengthen. High salary levels can create an upward trend in salaries and wages and, by ricochet, reduce the demand for labour and make a region less competitive. ACOA recently announced a competition for a policy analyst, which calls for a university degree in economics and some experience in preparing reports, research papers, and the like. It pays between $87,128 and $97,678, plus very generous fringe benefits.[68] I know of no private-sector position in the Maritime provinces that would pay anywhere near this salary for similar responsibilities and comparable knowledge and skills.

The same principle should apply to other public-sector jobs in the region, including those in health and education. Equalization payments are responsible for 20 per cent of the salaries of all provincial public servants. If the goal is for the regional economy to generate sufficient resources to pay for public services consumed in the region, adjustments have to be made to enable the private sector to generate economic activities. Equalization payments can serve to prop up the salaries of provincial public servants in the Maritime provinces, but at the same time distort private-sector salaries. Potential employees, for their part, will have to weigh lower salaries against the superior lifestyle and other advantages, including much lower housing costs.

Costs, including salaries, wages, and qualified workers, matter to existing businesses and aspiring entrepreneurs. Why else would an American firm transfer 150 computer-programming jobs from Moncton to India? Employers will move activities from large urban centres to the Maritime provinces only if it makes business sense to do so, and the cost of doing business is often the determining factor. More to the point, it is an important factor in establishing the circumstances for economic success. Asking the federal government to better accommodate regional economic circumstances is not a one-way street. Maritimers should also call on the federal government to adjust the pay and benefits of its employees to reflect regional circumstances.

A federal government economic development agenda for the Maritime region can never be complete without enhancing opportunities for First Nations communities. The region continues to rely on natural resources to grow the economy and create employment, and exploiting natural resources matters to all Maritimers, especially to Aboriginal communities, given their association with these resources. The challenges confronting Maritime Aboriginal communities are not much different than for Aboriginal communities in other regions: fewer employment opportunities and lower earned incomes. Though some progress has been made, a number of issues, including land claims and participation in opportunities offered by natural resources, remain unresolved. Only Ottawa can take the lead in resolving them with the courts, having established an agenda for addressing First Nations communities' concerns.

As noted on many occasions here and elsewhere, the region remains highly rural when compared with other Canadian regions. Rural economies are confronting their own sets of challenges: the inability to attract new Canadians, the agricultural sector increasingly dominated by large firms, and an economic future linked to natural resources. It is far more difficult today for an entrepreneur to start a business in a rural setting than in an urban one. Access to capital, environmental regulations geared to the exploitation of natural resources, the need to encourage Aboriginal communities to become economic partners, and access to expertise and government decision-makers are factors, among others, that make the process much more demanding in rural communities. An entrepreneur can start an IT business in downtown Moncton or Halifax without spending much time dealing with governments and their regulatory demands; however, things are vastly different for a rural entrepreneur wishing to start a business in the natural resources sector. Governments have a responsibility to review their regulations and policies to deal with some of these challenges confronting rural entrepreneurs and their businesses if economic development is truly a priority.

The Martime regions' future is full of uncertainty. The hope is that the federal government can learn to accommodate both national and regional perspectives and adjust national policies to reflect regional circumstances rather than, as it has in the past, fall back on transfer payments or send guilt money our way. The hope is also that Maritimers can cast aside provincial or parochial thinking and give their regional economy a powerful wrench of the wheel to lay the groundwork for self-sustaining economic development. Finally, the hope is that Maritimers working in community institutions will look beyond their core responsibilities and explore how they can contribute to economic development for their communities and region.

NOTES

1 Canada, *Living Together: A Study of Regional Disparities* (Ottawa: Economic Council of Canada, 1977), 215–6.

2 Albert Breton, "The Status and Efficiency of Regional Development Policies," in *Equity and Efficiency in Economic Development: Essays in Honour of Benjamin Higgins*, ed. Donald J. Savoie and Irving Brecher (Montreal and Kingston: McGill-Queen's University Press, 1992), 161.

3 Clarence E. Ayres has made a similar point in his study of economic development at the international level in his *The Theory of Economic Progress* (Durham: University of North Carolina Press, 1944).

4 See, among many others, A. Amin, "An Institutionalist Perspective on Regional Economic Development," *International Journal of Urban and Regional Research* 23, no.2 (1999): 365–78; and Michael Kitson, Ron Martin, and Peter Tyler, "Regional Competitiveness: An Elusive yet Key Concept?," *Regional Studies* 38, no. 9 (2004): 991–9.

5 I made this same observation in my report on the establishment of ACOA. See Donald J. Savoie, *Establishing the Atlantic Canada Opportunities Agency* (report prepared for the Prime Minister of Canada, 1987), 5.

6 See, among others, Richard Saillant, *Over the Cliff?*.

7 The Nova Scotia Commission on Building Our New Economy makes the same point in *Now or Never: An Urgent Call to Action for Nova Scotians* February 2014, viii, http://onens.ca/wp-content/uploads/Now_or_never_short.pdf.

8 Canada, *Living Together*.

9 See "It's All About Attitude," in Savoie, *Rural Development: It's All About Attitude, Up to a Point*, 8–10.

10 Savoie, *Establishing the Atlantic Canada Opportunities Agency*, 2.

11 *Rebuilding New Brunswick: Economic Development Action Plan, 2012–2016* (Fredericton: Government of New Brunswick, 2001); and *Now or Never: An Urgent Call to Action for Nova Scotians*.

12 "Don Mills: Refashion Rural Nova Scotia Economy with 8 Urban Building Blocks," *Chronicle-Herald* (Halifax), May 22, 2015, http://thechronicleherald.ca/opinion/1288409-don-mills-refashion-rural-nova-scotia-economy-with-8-urban-building-blocks?from=slidebox.

13 Charlotte LeBlanc, *Sidetracked by Schizophrenia: A Mother and Son's Struggles and Victories* (Victoria: Friesen Press, 2011), 27.

14 See, for example, "Generation Jobless: Where Are the Skilled Ones," *The Economist*, April 2013, 59.

15 See Allen J. Scott, "A World in Emergence: Notes toward a Re-synthesis of Urban-Economic Geography for the Twenty-First Century," in Philip Cooke, *Re-framing Regional Development: Evaluation, Innovation and Transition* (Abingdon, Oxon: Routledge, 2013), 29–53.

16 I owe this observation to my colleague Richard Saillant in conversation with the author, August 2015, Moncton.

17 Donald J. Savoie, *Harrison McCain: Single-Minded Purpose* (Montreal and Kingston: McGill-Queen's University Press, 2013).

18 Consultations with the president of Dalhousie University, Richard Florizone, various dates.

19 Steve Garlick et al., *Supporting the Contribution of Higher Education Institutions to Regional Development: Peer Review Report: Atlantic Canada* (Paris: OECD Directorate for Education, 2008), 14.

20 Ibid., 25.

21 Consultations with Ray Ivany, various dates.

22 See, among others, Brent Jang, "Oil Slump Hits Fort McMurray's Housing Market," *Globe and Mail*, August 2, 2015, www.theglobeandmail.com/report-on-business/economy/housing/oil-slump-hits-fort-mcmurrays-housing-market/article25814458/; and discussions with representatives of the New Brunswick Business Council, August 27, 2015.

23 Jean-Claude Savoie, owner of Groupe Savoie in an email to the author, September 2, 2015.

24 Normand LeBlanc, owner of Captain Dan's, in conversation with the author, Moncton, New Brunswick, June 24, 2015.

25 See, among others, Claire Morris, "The New Brunswick Experience" (remarks before the Ontario Management Forum, June 1995), 11–12.

26 Quoted in "Looking Back and Looking Ahead," *New Brunswick Business Journal* 8, no. 1 (1991): 1.

27 Examples include Hawk Communications and Group M5, both located in Moncton and employing over fifty people.

28 Donald J. Savoie, *Invest More, Innovate More, Trade More, Learn More: The Way Ahead for Nova Scotia* (Halifax: Government of Nova Scotia, 2010), 1.

29 See Nevena Dragicevic, *Anchor Institutions* (Toronto: Mowat Centre, August 2015), 5.

30 See, among others, Eugenie Birch, David C. Perry, and Henry Louis Taylor, "Universities as Anchor Institutions," *Journal of Higher Education Outreach and Engagement* 17, no. 3 (2013): 7–15.

31 Initiative for a Competitive Inner City, "Anchor Institutions and Urban Economic Development: From Community Benefit to Shared Value," *Inner City Insights* 1, no. 2 (June 2011): 1–9.

32 Benjamin Higgins and Maurice Beaudin, *Impact of the Université de Moncton on the Regions of Moncton, Edmundston and Shippagan* (Moncton: Canadian Institute for Research on Regional Development, 1988).

33 See, among others, Savoie, *I'm from Bouctouche, Me.*

34 Gardner Pinfold, *Economic Impact Analysis: Dalhousie University* (Halifax: Gardner Pinfold Consulting Economists, March 2011).

35 See, among others, Stephanie Rogers, "Potential Unlocked: President Florizone Shares Dal's Economic Impact Strategy with Truro and Colchester Chamber of Commerce," *Dal News* (Halifax: Dalhousie University, March 27, 2015).

36 *Now or Never: An Urgent Call to Action for Nova Scotians*, 37–41.

37 Dragicevic, *Anchor Institutions*, 17.

38 Ibid., 24.

39 See, among others, Mario Polèse and Richard Shearmur, *The Periphery in the Knowledge Economy: The Spatial Dynamics of the Canadian Economy and the Future of Non-metropolitan Regions in Quebec and the Atlantic Provinces* (Montreal and Moncton: Institut national de la recherche scientifique/INRS-Urbanisation, Culture et Société and the Canadian Institute for Research on Regional Development, 2002).

40 Ehud Kamar, Pinar Karaca-Mandic, and Eric Talley, "Going-Private Decisions and the Sarbanes-Oxley Act of 2002: A Cross-Country Analysis" (working paper, Santa Monica, CA: RAND Corporation, April 2008).

41 Drawn from documents in Harrison McCain's papers, Florenceville, New Brunswick.

42 See, for example, Robert Gibbens, "Restaurant Owner Imvescor Consolidates HQ in Montreal," *Montreal Gazette*, January 20, 2015, http://montrealgazette.com/business/imvescor-consolidates-in-montreal.

43 Chris, Powell, "Sobeys Reorganizes its Western Business," CanadianGrocer.com, May 6, 2015, www.canadiangrocer.com/top-stories/sobeys-reorganizes-its-western-business-53017.

44 Canadian Press, "Co-Op Atlantic to Lay Off 400 Employees and Close Four Food Stores," CTV News Atlantic, June 25, 2015, http://atlantic.ctvnews.ca/co-op-atlantic-to-lay-off-400-employees-and-close-four-food-stores-1.2440699.

45 See, for example, Michael Bloom and Michael Grant, "Valuing Headquarters (HQs): Analysis of the Role, Value and Benefit of HQs in Global Value Chains" (Ottawa: Conference Board of Canada, 2011).

46 Ibid., 219.

47 See, for example, Roger Martin and Gordon Nixon, "A Prescription for Canada: Rethink our Tax Policy," *Globe and Mail*, July 1, 2007, www.theglobeandmail.com/report-on-business/a-prescription-for-canada-rethink-our-tax-policy/article1077791/?page=all.

48 *Head at Regional Offices* (Halifax: Greater Halifax Partnership, n.d.).

49 Statistics Canada, CANSIM, table 528-0002, accessed June 2, 2016, www5.statcan.gc.ca/cansim/a26?lang=eng&id=5280002.

50 I obtained the information from the Atlantic Canada Opportunities Agency and its work on *The State of Small Business and Entrepreneurship: Atlantic Canada* (Moncton: ACOA, various dates).

51 Canada, *Survey of Innovation and Business Strategy* (Ottawa: Statistics Canada, undated).

52 See, among others, Savoie, *What is Government Good At?*.

53 Saillant, *A Tale of Two Countries*.

54 *School Closure Due to Inclement Weather* (Fredericton: Government of New Brunswick, October 2015), 4; and "NBTA President says Province's Poor Education Scores Show More Resources Needed," *Saint John Telegraph-Journal*, accessed on October 9, 2014, www.telegraphjournal.com.

55 "More Doctors, Nursing Homes Needed to Improve Health System," August 29, 2014, http://www.cbc.ca/news/canada/new-brunswick/more-doctors-nursing-homes-needed-to-improve-health-system-1.2750198.

56 Statistics Canada, CANSIM, Fiscal Reference tables 051-0001 and 384-0038.

57 See D. E. Smith, "The Prairie Provinces," in *The Provincial Political Systems: Comparative Essays*, ed. D. J. Bellamy, J. H. Pammett, and D. C. Rowat (Toronto: Methuen, 1976), 274.

58 Ibid., 219.

59 Consultations with George Cooper by the author, Halifax, Nova Scotia, December 14, 2015.

60 See G. Hodgson, *Economics and Evolution: Bringing Life Back into Economics* (Cambridge: Polity Press, 1993).

61 Based on various conversations between John Bragg, owner of Oxford Food, and the author.

62 Conference Board of Canada, "How Canada Performs: Provincial and Territorial Ranking: Innovation," data current as of September 2015.

63 Savoie, *What Is Government Good At?*

64 See www.courts.pei.ca.

65 "Regional Pay Differences Become Common Study," *Globe and Mail*, November 16, 2004, B15.

66 Statistics Canada, Annual Estimate of Employment, Earnings and Hours 1991-2004, based on the North American Industrial Classification System (NAICS)-2002.

67 Jennifer Brown, "Fellow Lawyers just Catching Up to Provincial Salary Levels," Legal Feeds Blog, February 14, 2014, www.canadianlawyermag.com/legalfeeds/1884/federal-lawyers-just-catching-up-to-provincial-salary-levels.html.

68 Salary Scales for an EC-07 as of June 22, 2013.

INDEX

A

B

C

E

F

G

I

J

K

L

M

N

O

Q

R

T

U

V

W

Y